CHINA TODAY

China is increasingly influenced by international affairs, especially since its entry into the World Trade Organization in December 2002. Despite this, domestic reforms remain a priority, and as China adapts its economic structure to these ongoing domestic reforms, there are significant social and political consequences.

These issues are thoroughly analysed in this volume, which includes chapters by both Eastern and Western specialists, thereby providing an interdisciplinary vision of contemporary China. Particular attention is devoted to questions such as the social compact in urban China, emerging social conflicts, nation building dynamics, and the redefinition of collective identities amidst the current dialectics between control and cohesion. The enduring theme of the book is the complexity of current developments in today's China.

Taciana Fisac is Titular Professor of Chinese Language and Culture, and Director of the Centre for East Asian Studies at the Universidad Autónoma de Madrid, Spain. She has published several books and many articles on contemporary Chinese society and culture, focusing mainly on literature, intellectuals and gender issues. **Leila Fernández-Stembridge** is Associate Professor of Chinese Economy and History at the Universidad Autónoma de Madrid, Spain. She is also Visiting Professor at the China–Europe International Business School in Shanghai. She has published extensively on China's labour market, rural–urban migration and macroeconomic development.

CHINA TODAY

Economic reforms, social cohesion and collective identities

Edited by Taciana Fisac and Leila Fernández-Stembridge

RoutledgeCurzon
Taylor & Francis Group
LONDON AND NEW YORK

First published 2003
by RoutledgeCurzon
11 New Fetter Lane, London EC4P 4EE

Simultaneously published in the USA and Canada
by RoutledgeCurzon
29 West 35th Street, New York, NY 10001

RoutledgeCurzon is an imprint of the Taylor & Francis Group

Typeset in Times by Exe Valley Dataset Ltd, Exeter
Printed and bound by Gutenberg Press Ltd, Malta

British Library Cataloguing in Publication Data
A catalogue record for this book is available from the British Library

Library of Congress Cataloging in Publication Data
China today: economic reforms, social cohesion, and collective identities / edited by Taciana Fisac and Leila Fernández-Stembridge.
p. cm.
Includes bibliographical references and index.
1. China–Social conditions–1976– 2. China–Economic conditions–1976– 3. Chinese–Ethnic identity. 4. Nationalism–China. I. Title: Economic reforms, social cohesion, and collective identities. II. Fisac Badell, Taciana. III. Fernández-Stembridge, Leila, 1972–

HN733.5.C437 2003
306′.0951–dc21 2003041581

ISBN 0–415–31267–1

CONTENTS

ILLUSTRATIONS

Figures

Tables

CONTRIBUTORS

Børge Bakken is Fellow at the Research School of Pacific and Asian Studies, the Australian National University. His most current book is *The Exemplary Society: Human Improvement, Social Control, and the Dangers of Modernity in China* (2000).

Yun-han Chu is Professor of Political Science at the National Taiwan University and serves concurrently as Vice-President of the Chiang Ching-kuo Foundation for International Scholarly Exchange. His most recent publications include *China Under Jiang Zemin* (2000) and *Consolidating Third-Wave Democracies* (1997).

Fan Gang is Professor of Economics at the Graduate School of the Chinese Academy of Social Sciences and Director of the National Economic Research Institute, China Reform Foundation, Beijing. His recent publications include *Mianxiang xinshiji de Zhongguo hongguan jingji zhengce* (China's Macroeconomic Policies Towards the New Century) (co-authored with Zhang Xiaojing) (1999) and *Jianjin gaige de zhengzhi jingji xue* (Political Economy of Incremental Transition) (1996).

Leila Fernández-Stembridge is Associate Professor of Chinese Economy at the Universidad Autónoma de Madrid. She has published extensively on migration and labour issues in Chinese, English and Spanish and is currently preparing a book on China's contemporary economic history.

Taciana Fisac is Titular Professor of Chinese Language and Culture and Director of the Centre for East Asian Studies at the Universidad Autónoma de Madrid, where, since 1998, she has also been Vice-Rector for International Relations. Her most recent publication is *China en transición: sociedad, cultura, política y economía* (China in Transition: Society, Culture, Politics and Economics) (co-edited with Steve Tsang) (2000).

Brian Hook is currently Emeritus Leverhulme Fellow and Visiting Professor in the Business School at Middlesex University. Among his recent publications are *Hong Kong in Transition: The Handover Years* (co-edited with Ash, Ferdinand and Porter) (2000) and *Beijing and Tianjin: Towards a Millennial Megalopolis* (1998).

Chia-lung Lin received his PhD degree from Yale University and is currently Assistant Professor of Political Science at the National Chung Cheng University in Taiwan. He has edited several books, including *Nationalism and Cross-Strait Relations* (2000) and *Party–State Transformation and Democratic Reform in Taiwan and China* (1999). His new book *Paths to Democracy* is soon to be published by Oxford University Press.

Werner Meissner is currently Head of the Department of Government and International Studies, Hong Kong Baptist University. His main publications include *Die Deutsche Demokratische Republik und China, 1949–1990: Politik Wirtschaft und Kultur. Dokumente* (The German Democratic Republic and the People's Republic of China, 1949–1990: Politics, Economy and Culture. Documents) (1995) and *China zwischen nationalem Sonderweg und universaler Modernisierung: Zur Rezeption westlichen Denkens in China* (China Between National 'Special Way' and Universal Modernisation: On the Reception of Western Thought in China) (1994).

Barry Naughton is So Kwanlok Professor at the Graduate School of International Relations and Pacific Studies, the University of California, San Diego. He is currently researching provincial growth and national integration in China. His book on transition in China, *Growing Out of the Plan* (1995), won the Ohira Memorial Prize in 1996.

Gladys Nieto is Associate Professor of the Anthropology of China at the Universidad Autónoma de Madrid. She has published in national and international journals and is now preparing a book on overseas Chinese associations in Spain.

Jean-Louis Rocca is Research Fellow at the Centre d'Etudes et de Recherches Internationales, Fondation Nationale des Sciences Politiques, Paris. He is the author of articles published in major international journals. Two of his most well-known books are *La corruption* (1993) and *L'empire et son milieu: la criminalité en Chine Populaire* (1991).

Steve Tsang is the Louis Cha Fellow at St Antony's College, Oxford University, where he is also Director of its Asian Studies Centre. His most recent publications include *Democratization in Taiwan: Implications for China* (co-edited with Hung-mao Tien) (1999) and *Hong Kong: An Appointment with China* (1997).

PREFACE

In the last two decades of the twentieth century, China has longed for an important role on the international economic scene and has therefore tried to promote an image of modernization. Its interest in becoming a member of the World Trade Organization (WTO) and the efforts invested towards the selection of Beijing as the future host of the 2008 Olympic Games are two significant examples. After the events of 11 September 2001, the world order has undoubtedly changed, and China – just like the rest of the countries in the world – has been affected by the political and economic tensions emerging as a result of the savage terrorist attacks against the United States and the ensuing no less frightening reprisals. Paradoxically, and despite the risks of economic instability that these events have provoked, initially China has increased its efforts towards international integration, relaxing its tensions with the United States and placing itself on the same path as that followed by most Western countries. No doubt China's internal affairs are influenced by the international situation. Nevertheless, domestic reform continues to be the Middle Kingdom's biggest challenge. Up to now (2002), reforms have been particularly positive in macroeconomic terms, and a significant proportion of the population has benefited from increasing prosperity. But at the same time, new pressures have emerged.

When we refer to China's reforms, it is necessary to go back to their launching in 1978, as well as to the changes introduced since then by Deng Xiaoping and his successor Jiang Zemin. Although reforms have been evolving for more than twenty years, the country is still undergoing a period of transition. The three decades of Maoism have been such a heavy burden for China that the country still needs a few more years in order to overcome that legacy in the economic, social and political spheres. The prominence given by the Chinese Communist Party (CCP) to economic reform is unquestionable. Nevertheless, the complexity of the challenges China has to confront cannot be explained only in economic terms. There are many other social and political variables that have an effect on the Middle Kingdom today. The reshaping of the social compact in all those areas that are linked to the labour market, or in a wider sense to the emergence of all markets, is certainly a prominent process. However, as in the past, the spirit of economic regulation continues to be intermingled with the rise of a discourse about collective identity, which prevails in the political sphere. The discourse on national construction has become a point of contestation among overseas Chinese communities, which are searching for their role within the framework of Greater China. This is why the economic changes, the search for a social compact in urban China, the identification of new social conflicts that coexist in the dialectics of control and cohesion, and the problem of nation-building and collective identities have become so important in today's China. All these aspects are thoroughly analysed in this volume.

From the economic perspective, Part I shows how China is currently undertaking a whole set of domestic reforms, while adapting its economic structure to international pressures. Barry Naughton shows how the restructuring of state enterprises has brought about changes in the relationship between enterprise and worker in urban China, implying the renegotiation – slow but progressive – of an entirely new urban social compact framed within China's macroeconomic tendencies. Fan Gang analyses some of these macroeconomic tendencies and explains how, in response to the Asian financial crisis, China's economy has been further opened under the pressure of globalization, readapting sectors such as trade, foreign investment, and services. Nonetheless, it still seems far from solving troublesome problems such as income disparities, corruption, or unemployment.

Part II focuses on the social compact and its new reshaping. Leila Fernández-Stembridge argues that the re-employment of laid-off workers has helped to alleviate unemployment and prevent social instability. However, there still needs to be further adjustments in terms of human capital, with a restructured industrial sector, a better balance between state-owned and non-state owned sectors, and the end of the rural–urban divide. Jean-Louis Rocca introduces the reader to the urban social struggle resulting from the emergence of a new working class claiming more protection from the state, while implicitly supporting the CCP's labour policy. In that sense, Brian Hook's article on the urban housing market provides an illustration of the 'rise of the social concerns' of the state. But while China's society integrates a whole new set of changes, conflicts inevitably emerge.

In Part III, Børge Bakken analyses how the police forces develop their own social norms through corrupt mechanisms, while Taciana Fisac uses Durkheim's concept of anomie as an explanation for such contemporary social problems as corruption and suicide and for the exacerbated nationalism that characterizes the contemporary political discourse of the CCP. In fact, nationalism has been used, in an alternative form, as a socially cohesive instrument beyond China's frontiers, installing itself in the diaspora communities, as illustrated by Gladys Nieto's case study in Spain.

Part IV addresses both nation-building and collective identities. Werner Meissner offers a broad historical and theoretical approach of European nationalism, referring to the German process in particular, as opposed to China's trends of nationalism. This general framework allows a better understanding of how competing identities have evolved in Hong Kong and Taiwan. Steve Tsang goes through Hong Kong's history and the creation of its own identity, describing the development of a local identity centred around Hong Kong's Chinese community, while Yun-han Chu and Chia-lung Lin refer to the relationship between Taiwan's democracy, state and nation-building, in the context of Cross-Straits relations.

China is complex and dynamic. Thus, it is practically impossible to address fully all the trends characterizing its current transitional process of reforms. In this volume, most relevant spheres of analysis are included, although tangentially on occasion. For instance, it is evident that banking and financial reforms are tightly dependent on the course of state-owned enterprise reforms, with regard to corporate governance and the dynamics of an independent monetary policy. China's recent accession to the WTO is certainly a hot issue now, with short-term and long-term changes in all those economic sectors that have traditionally been protected by the state (agriculture, telecommunications, automobile, insurance, banking, etc.), as they will be further exposed to the dynamics of market competition. Agriculture deserves in that sense special attention, as rural unemployment will dramatically increase, and rural–urban migration flows will again become a major factor in the Chinese political economy. While the rural sector will need to be readjusted and regional disparities threaten to widen, the urban economy and the coastal areas in particular are likely to benefit from an exponential increase in foreign direct investment. Economic dynamism is a double-edged sword, where opening and control are part of a similar logic. In this sense, the new leadership in the CCP emerging from the autumn of 2002 is expected to be a consequence of today's reforms, although it would be misleading to underestimate the surprise ingredient in China's state of social flux. In other words, China is a puzzle that cannot possibly be solved in one conference volume. However, we are confident that the reader will profit from the information condensed here.

This volume reflects the proceedings of the Second Annual Conference of the European Union–China Academic Network (ECAN), which took place in Madrid in January 1999. ECAN was created in 1997, thanks to the logistical and financial support provided by the European Union. Its primary purpose has been to bring together – both physically and intellectually – specialists on contemporary China, enhancing the cooperation of the academic community with those in charge of public affairs. During the Madrid Conference, not only reputable European specialists on Chinese issues were present, but also very prominent academics and government advisers were invited from Mainland China (Fan), Taiwan (Chu and Lin) and the United States (Naughton). The discussions initiated in 1999 have been updated in this publication. On occasion, the authors have different views on a common topic. For the sake of intellectual freedom and criticism, even if repetitions may emerge, we have decided to preserve the original version of each one of the chapters included.

We would like to thank Bob Ash, the ECAN Coordinator at the time, and members of the Centro de Estudios de Asia Oriental (Universidad Autónoma de Madrid, Spain), for all their help in making the meeting a success, and for revising part of the written work that followed. Professors Ramon Myers and Yves Chevrier have provided us with very useful suggestions. We would also like to thank the European Commission's China Unit (then, DGI), in particular Angelos Pangratis and Ana Gonzalo, for having participated in the above mentioned conference and for supporting the production of this volume. Finally, we thank RoutledgeCurzon for their positive response to the publication of, as we see it, this encouraging and interesting project.

Taciana Fisac and Leila Fernández-Stembridge
Universidad Autónoma de Madrid
June 2002

Part I

ECONOMIC PERSPECTIVES AND STATE-OWNED ENTERPRISE REFORMS

1

STATE ENTERPRISE RESTRUCTURING

Renegotiating the social compact in urban China

Barry Naughton

'Enterprise restructuring' is the most recent of a series of Chinese policies designed to improve the performance of state-owned enterprises. As such, it has sometimes been hard to distinguish from its predecessors, and opinions have been mixed as to whether it has succeeded, indeed even as to whether it has been systematically pursued.[1] In fact, as this chapter will make clear, the programme of enterprise restructuring that developed with increasing velocity during 1996 represents a major change in the relationship between enterprise and worker in urban China, and thus amounts to a fundamental renegotiation of the entire urban social contract. Whether or not enterprise restructuring results in dramatically improved economic performance, it has certainly changed the basis of social relations in urban China and its importance is guaranteed on this ground alone.

Enterprise restructuring reflects deeply rooted trends in the Chinese economy. Its impact depends partly on central government policy stance, but more fundamentally on the working out of these powerful economic and social trends. Central government policies have cleared the way for these forces to reshape urban social relations, by removing ideological blockades, by creating a (rickety) framework for social service delivery outside the enterprise, and by sanctioning the flow of resources into welfare-like job creation programmes. However, the key forces driving the process lie outside the scope of government policy. They include a more intensely competitive product marketplace, new opportunities for urban residents in higher-income occupations, increased job market competition for urban residents from rural migrants, and the elimination of constraints on enterprise hiring and (especially) firing. These forces will continue to drive enterprise restructuring forward, albeit at an uneven and inconsistent pace.

State enterprise restructuring has already affected the fundamental relationship between the government and the urban citizen. The nature of the urban social contract has been profoundly altered, and yet there is no clear consensus on the new social forms that are emerging. It is relatively easy to track the modifications in central government policy toward restructuring. We can get a good sense of the most important outcomes, including changes in employment and unemployment. Finally, we can clearly see that the actual outcomes of restructuring are predominantly the product of local government action, and we can trace the main forces operating on local government decision-makers. Thus, enterprise restructuring gives us significant insight into the political economy of Chinese decision-making and specifically the interplay between national and local forces. But enterprise restructuring also has profound implications that go beyond the immediate interplay of political and economic forces. Enterprise restructuring has been the means by which the fundamental urban social contract has been dissolved, and only partially reconstituted. Whether the new terms of urban citizenship in China turn out to be stable and viable cannot yet be determined.

The process of enterprise restructuring

Enterprise restructuring refers to a cluster of policies that have as their common objective clarifying ownership relations in public enterprises. At one end of the spectrum, restructuring can be as mild as so-called 'corporatization', converting a previously bureaucratically run state-owned enterprise (SOE) into a company with defined ownership shares and a board of directors to exercise control. Such corporatization is consistent with continued exercise of control by the same government agencies as before, simply requiring these agencies to establish institutions that give the enterprise more legal independence and create some possibility that an 'arm's length' form of governance could develop. At the other end of the spectrum, restructuring can include overt privatization, with a new set of private owners replacing the vaguely defined public interest. In between, a range of alternatives includes mergers, consolidations, and conversion to employee-owned joint stock companies. Typically, restructuring includes some real changes in the scale of the enterprise operation, and particularly a reduction in the workforce. In some cases, bankruptcy and plant closures are the main outcome. Diversity is a prime characteristic of the restructuring process.

Central government policy

Public ownership restructuring began with central government policy initiatives. The foundation that made a serious programme of enterprise restructuring possible was laid by central government policy-makers soon after Zhu Rongji assumed effective control over economic policy in mid-1993. Two fundamental policy shifts were of enormous importance in creating the conditions for enterprise restructuring. First, Zhu Rongji presided over a fundamental shift in macroeconomic policy toward a much more conservative policy stance. Macroeconomic austerity gradually brought inflation under control. As Figure 1.1 shows, the effects were not immediate, and inflation peaked during 1994. Gradually, however, inflation came down and dropped below 10 per cent in the first quarter of 1996. During 1996 and 1997, policy-makers congratulated themselves on having engineered a 'soft landing', controlling inflation without harming economic growth. After the beginning of 1998, though, the economy slipped gradually into deflation, and prices fell throughout 1998 and 1999. Tough macroeconomic policies had become deeply entrenched in the economy. The success in controlling inflation was important for the subsequent enterprise restructuring in numerous ways. The ability to control growth of the money supply and credit shows that Zhu Rongji had at least temporary success in his efforts to reduce enterprise dependence on the banking system for cheap credit. A more 'arm's length' relationship was created between state-owned banks and state-owned enterprises that made it much more difficult for failing enterprises to turn to the banking system for bail-outs. This was achieved partly just by throwing the weight of central government bargaining influence on the side of the banks, and partly by reorganizing the banking system in ways that made it less dependent on local government officials and local economic interests. Moreover, nominal interest rates – still administratively set by the government – were adjusted downward much more slowly

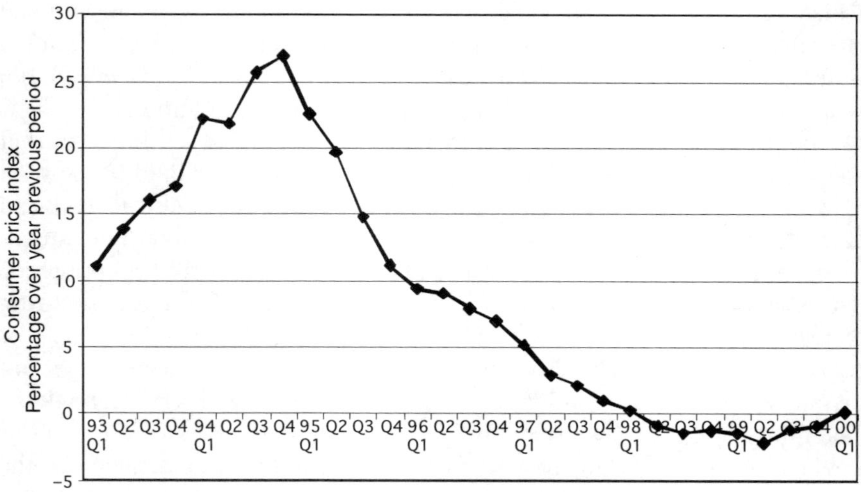

Figure 1.1 Consumer price inflation.

than the inflation rate dropped. As a result, real interest rates (nominal interest minus the actual inflation rate) turned positive at the beginning of 1996, and stayed significantly positive (over 5 per cent) after the beginning of 1997. Credit, in other words, became more difficult for state-owned firms to get, and much more expensive when it was available.

The secondary effects of macroeconomic austerity were, if anything, even more important. As growth slowed, competition became fierce. The falling price level after 1998 testifies to the intensity of competition and the abundance of supply. An enormous amount of industrial capacity had been created during 1992–96. Not only were domestic investment rates high, but a cumulative total of US$153 billion worth of foreign direct investment, mostly in manufacturing, flowed into China during those five years. As growth slowed, and much of this new industrial capacity came on stream, a fierce competitive environment developed. As numerous articles put it, China bid 'farewell to the shortage economy, and hello to the buyer's market'. Under these conditions, enterprises faced intensified competition on product markets, just at the time when their access to easy credit was being cut. Squeezed between two increasingly unforgiving forces, enterprises began to search intensively for solutions to their predicament.

The second overall central government policy initiative that made restructuring possible was a shift to a more rule-based approach to enterprise reform. The pace of economic legislation stepped up, but what was more significant was a government commitment to use 'rule by law' to impose a roughly equivalent set of economic obligations on most firms. Particularly during 1994–95, there were a number of important legislative milestones. First of the blocks was the tax reform implemented on 1 January 1994, which shifted government reliance to a broad-based value-added tax, and which also lowered and unified corporate profit tax rates. The tax reform had the effect of substantially (though not totally) equalizing tax rates among different businesses, and established the principle that different ownership systems should be subject to the same tax treatment. In addition to the new tax code, three important regulatory laws were passed in 1994–95 that shaped the environment for enterprise restructuring. The Banking System Law (1995) reinforced many of the *ad hoc* changes that Zhu Rongji had carried out in the previous years, strengthening the banking system's independence and its ability to withstand (especially local) political pressures. The Company Law, also in 1995, provided an ownership and accounting framework that enabled all public enterprises to begin the process of reorganization, with clearly defined capital contributions, ownership, and executive bodies that represented the interest of the owners (shareholders). The third regulatory law, passed in 1994, was the Labour Law.[2] The Labour Law had many important provisions, but the defining characteristic was the shift to compulsory universal labour contracts. The labour relationship henceforth was to be governed, in all cases, by a contract voluntarily signed by the employer and employee. By clear implication, the 'iron rice bowl' system of permanent employment was abolished, and an employment relationship of specified duration, which either side could dissolve at will, was created in its place.

The central government not only establishes the framework for economic policy, it also signals to local governments the scope for policy experimentation. In the case of enterprise restructuring the central government began to signal a permissive attitude as early as 1995. In April 1995, the State Council approved a report on 'Re-employment Projects' from the Ministry of Labour, creating a framework for local governments, enterprises and social welfare agencies to contribute resources to expanded training and job creation programmes.[3] With this addition, by the end of 1995, the central government had in place a rough regulatory framework and a rudimentary social safety network. The social safety net, although full of holes, at least provided a framework for those local governments which had resources to provide help to unemployed and impoverished urban residents. Under construction since the mid-1980s, the social safety net included unemployment compensation, retirement funds independent of individual enterprises and, now, training and job creation programmes. With these elements in place, a framework – albeit fragile and rickety – was in place that could support an accelerated programme of enterprise restructuring.

Through 1996 and 1997 the official media gave increasingly prominent, positive coverage to localities that had carried out thorough enterprise restructuring. Particularly thorough coverage was given to the case of Zhucheng in Shandong, discussed further below. During the course of 1997, it became increasingly clear that the central government was allowing local governments enormous leeway in the pursuit of SOE restructuring. Moreover, beginning in early 1997, public discussions increasingly stressed the need for the private sector to pick up some of the slack created by public sector downsizing, and the need for a rapid growth in the 'non-public' economy.

The XVth Communist Party Congress in September 1997 marked a new peak of central government enthusiasm for restructuring. In his main report to the Congress, Jiang Zemin carefully chose a formulation describing ownership under the socialist market economy which subtly but unmistakably increased the role and legitimacy accorded to private ownership. Zhu Rongji emerged as Premier-designate at the Congress, and promoted a series of active policies designed to shrink and restructure the state sector. The dominant policy at the Congress was that of 'grasping the large, and letting the small go' (*zhuada fangxiao*). Under this formulation, central government organs would intensify the pace of managed restructuring of large state firms, while allowing small state and collective firms to be restructured by market forces. This Party Congress thus marked a major increase in the impetus given to restructuring, both by relaxing ideological constraints and by actively advancing central government support for a wide array of restructuring initiatives.

This level of enthusiasm for restructuring lasted through the National People's Congress in March 1998. Zhu Rongji formally became Premier, and immediately announced a wide-ranging programme of accelerated change. Characteristically, he used the format of a nationally televised press conference, displaying his own authoritative position as well as his commitment to continued reforms, while keeping specifics to a minimum.[4] Yet even as Zhu spoke, the central government policy emphasis was beginning to shift. With the Chinese economy continuing to slow and the Asian Crisis showing few signs of abating, Chinese leaders were becoming increasingly concerned about rising unemployment. Some signs of increased concern emerged at the Congress, and were incorporated into official policy in subsequent months, notably in a May 1998 special State Council meeting on unemployment and lay-offs.[5]

From that time through to the end of 1998, we saw a classic case of Chinese policy reformulation. While the central government repeatedly reaffirmed the original pronouncements on state enterprise, the emphasis of new proclamations clearly shifted. Stress was placed on the need to arrange new employment for laid-off state workers. Moreover, local governments were warned that privatization was not the sole means for restructuring private firms, nor was it preferable to other means (!). Clearly the emphasis of central government intervention had shifted from giving additional impetus to local restructuring to urging caution and setting bounds. Yet despite this apparent shift, incidents of more and less successful local restructuring efforts continued to appear in the press. Moreover, subsequent data make clear that the pace of enterprise restructuring – as measured by the number of laid-off public sector workers – did not decelerate significantly or at all during 1998 or 1999. In fact, this is not surprising. Some degree of central support is clearly necessary to unleash a process like enterprise restructuring. However, once unleashed, such a process is not necessarily sensitive to fluctuating nuances in central government proclamations. That is particularly true when powerful external conditions strongly support the continuation of the process.

Central and local in the restructuring process

The policy of 'grasping the large, and letting the small go' clearly signals the dual nature of enterprise restructuring, and the extent to which policy was differentiated into central and local policies. Underlying this dualism are the dramatically different ways in which the central and local state industrial sectors have evolved over the reform era. After twenty years of reform, the central government's control of industry has become increasingly concentrated on energy, natural resources and a few sectors in which economies of scale provide significant barriers to entry.[6] In other words, the central government's industrial sector is composed primarily of regulated and protected national monopolies. By contrast, local governments continue to run factories in a large variety of industrial sectors. As a consequence, not only are local government-run factories much smaller on average than those of the central government, they are also much more exposed to competitive pressures. Local government industries are more like diversified businesses.

These differences are clearly reflected in data on profitability. Overall, profitability of industrial SOEs has declined steadily through the reform era, with gross profits dropping from 15 per cent of gross domestic product (GDP) in 1978 to under 2 per cent in 1997. In the last few years, though, an especially sharp difference has emerged in the profit performance of large and small enterprises, as Figure 1.2 shows. Large industrial SOEs – those predominantly managed by the central government – have maintained roughly unchanged profits of around 60 billion Rmb. By contrast, small and medium SOEs – predominantly managed by the local government – have seen net profits disappear. Still earning 20 billion Rmb in 1993, small SOE profits evaporated the following year, and the sector ran a net deficit of 20 billion Rmb in 1997.

As a result, the dynamics of restructuring are quite different at the central and local levels. At the centre, the government primarily controls profitable firms that are, moreover, frequently in sectors seen to be of 'strategic importance' to the economy. There is thus limited impetus for significant privatization. Instead, debate focuses on the intensely political (and patronage-

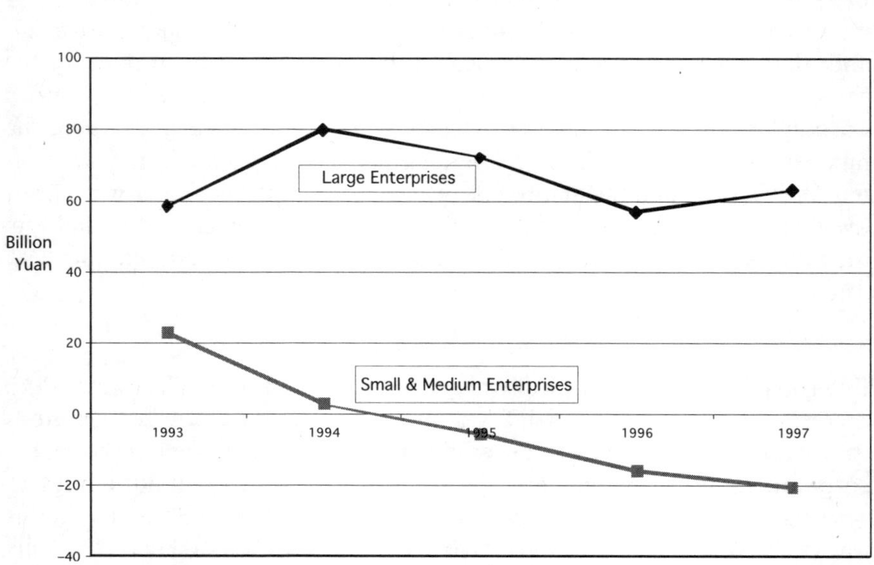

Figure 1.2 Industrial SOE profits: large vs. small and medium.

related) questions of whether these firms will be organized into diversified conglomerates, and on what basis such conglomerates would continue to receive state support. Different leaders have different views, and economic difficulties in Korea have naturally dampened enthusiasm for creating *chaebol*-like national champions.[7] Outside observers, discussing 'state enterprise reform', are often implicitly assessing the success or failure of these reorganizations of the large-scale, central government control sector, and they often note the limited efficacy of reform. The view of this author is that, whatever the outcome of these debates, the resultant policies are unlikely to reshape Chinese industry fundamentally.

By contrast, at local levels, restructuring comes in response to very intense economic pressures. The policies associated with Zhu Rongji since 1993 have greatly intensified those pressures. Tax reforms cut into enterprise profits, and created new rules that attenuated local government ties to their SOEs. Macroeconomic austerity, combined with a much stricter attitude toward the banking system, greatly reduced the access which local SOEs had previously enjoyed to easy credits from the banking system. These systemic changes compounded the pressures created by a slowing economy and, indirectly, by the effects of the Asian Crisis. In turn, these competitive pressures ensure that restructuring will proceed under the impetus of local decision-makers, notwithstanding fluctuations in central government commitment.

Perhaps surprisingly, Shanghai was a pioneer in some aspects of the restructuring process. In particular, Shanghai is richer and has a lower population growth rate than any other Chinese province (or province-level unit). As a result, Shanghai can afford to be bolder in dealing with unemployment than other provinces. There is less absolute pressure on employment, and more resources available to deal with the unemployed. In fact, in the early 1990s, Shanghai began systematically to place state workers into a furloughed, or laid-off category (*xiagang daigong*). As early as 1993, the number of laid-off workers in Shanghai surpassed 150,000, and was significantly larger than the number of registered unemployed.[8] This was one of the early experiments with a controlled downsizing that seemed to indicate the process could be managed, and it emboldened the leadership to proceed.

The restructuring process

Enterprise restructuring typically takes the following forms. The former SOE is converted into a limited liability joint stock corporation. A key feature is that workers and managers generally have some recognized stake in the corporatized firm. In some cases, shares are distributed without charge to workers and managers, with a cap of 20 per cent of shares distributed in this way (with some exceptions noted below). In other cases, workers receive only the right to purchase significant shares – sometimes all the shares – of the new corporation, typically at a significant discount. However, in addition, significant shares will frequently be sold or assumed by other corporate entities, and significant shares are often sold to the public. The process recognizes that existing workers and managers have a stake in the firm, and that privatization that attempted to ignore that stake would most likely not succeed. At the same time, the process does not generally involve worker ownership as such.

The process, and some of its limitations, can be exemplified by one of the earliest and most prominent local models, that of Zhucheng in the province of Shandong. By the mid-1990s, Zhucheng divested itself of 85 per cent of its publicly owned enterprises. Zhucheng converted 210 firms, including 32 SOEs, into 'joint stock cooperative enterprises' (*gufen hezuo zhi*). This complex term, like many complex formulations in the course of Chinese reform, represents an attempt to compromise between two qualitatively different types of ownership.[9] In a joint stock enterprise, ownership (that is, both control and income) of the firm is allocated to owners of capital, with one share having one 'vote' in firm decision-making. By contrast, in a cooperative enterprise, as that term has been understood in China over the past fifty years, ownership (again, both control and income) is allocated to workers, with each worker having one 'vote' in firm decision-making. The use of the term 'joint stock cooperative' appears to be an attempt either to avoid specifying the reality of the reform, or else to indicate a privatization in which existing workers and managers have taken the predominant, perhaps even exclusive role.

In the Zhucheng case, in which all the restructured firms were fairly small, the process ended with all ownership shares held by the original workers and managers. However, the process by which this was accomplished was quite interesting. First, rights to purchase shares in the restructured firm were allocated to existing workers and managers. This allocation was not, however, equal. Enterprise managers were generally entitled to four times the allocation of ordinary workers, though in some cases they received more. Second, workers and managers had to activate their allocations by actually purchasing the shares to which they had been allocated rights: a standard of 5,000 Rmb per share was established, a significant sum for most worker households, about equal to the annual wage. Third, payments for shares were to be made within two years, but in practice most workers and managers had access to fairly generous credit to finance their purchases. Fourth, in some firms, additional shares were made available for purchase by existing workers and managers, apparently on somewhat less favourable terms. By the end of the process, one manager had purchased 178,000 Rmb worth of shares in his firm, more than thirty times that of an average worker. This was the maximum degree of inequality in distribution. When all the shares had been sold, the firms were converted into joint stock companies. After a year, workers were permitted to sell their shares to other workers or managers. At the end of the process, the firms were joint stock companies, with ownership distributed strictly according to share ownership. In Zhucheng, there were no corporate or outside investors: thus, all share owners had been workers and managers in the firm.

Another important case of restructuring in progress is the computer firm Legend (Lianxiang). Created in the mid-1980s, Legend is one of China's success stories, having grown extremely rapidly, and currently assembling personal computers and producing an array of components, peripherals and software. Legend is also an SOE, 'owned' by the Chinese Academy of Sciences, which provided the technical and entrepreneurial skill for its creation. Legend is being corporatized, and all agree that the founders should receive substantial stakes. The managerial group initially proposed that they assume a 38 per cent stake, but this ran into an existing limit, set by the State Asset Management Bureau, that no more than 20 per cent of the ownership of an SOE was to be distributed to existing employees as part of corporatization (note that this would be a distribution, not an allocation of a right to purchase, as in Zhucheng). After intense negotiations, the Asset Management Bureau agreed to allow employees to purchase, on highly favourable terms, 30 per cent of the company. This enabled the Bureau to hold the line on the limit to distributed shares, and also meant the Academy of Sciences retained a majority ownership share. This outcome was probably disappointing to Legend's management team, despite the fact that they could probably count on the non-interference of the Academy's shareholders, particularly given the company's entrepreneurial success.[10] While Legend failed to become a flagship for privatization, it did lead the way for a further round of restructuring with an enhanced degree of private control. During 1999, the Chinese government announced a set of new policies designed to stimulate technological progress. Taking their cue from Silicon Valley and the vitality of the US high technology sector in the last few years, the emphasis of these policies was on the creation of a vigorous small-scale high technology sector. This policy direction has been crystallized by a late 1999 decision which puts for a set of practicable policies to foster domestic technology development.[11] In essence, the high technology initiative opens up another, more permissive avenue for enterprise restructuring. If it can plausibly be considered 'hi tech', the requirements for private control will be substantially reduced. If a planned 'second board' sees the light of day – that is, a small-cap, mostly high technology stock market like the NASDAQ in the US – such firms would also have expanded access to capital markets.

In other cases, enterprise restructuring has meant mergers and acquisitions. The Qingdao Beer company, under increasing pressure from foreign-invested beer companies, purchased controlling stakes in two local beer Companies during 1997 (one in Xi'an and one in Yangzhou). The Hai'er Consumer Appliance Company, one of China's most successful firms, created a new subsidiary in Guangdong's Shunde County (the largest consumer appliance production area) in a 60/40 joint venture with a Guangdong

Company. In at least three other cases during 1997, Hai'er assumed a controlling interest in firms in Shandong, Anhui and Zhejiang by contributing its own 'intangible capital' – brand name, production technology, and management skill – rather than cash.[12] In these cases, relatively successful firms were expanding rapidly through the takeover process. In many other cases, local governments were using merger and acquisition – or simple bankruptcy – to get rid of unsuccessful firms.

Finally, in many cases, enterprise restructuring means privatization. Restructuring can include privatization in many different forms. In joint stock cooperative enterprises, there are restrictions on re-sale of shares by employees, but such restrictions only last for a specified number of years, and are relatively easy to evade. State enterprises are sometimes directly auctioned off in the process of restructuring, or forced into bankruptcy and then sold off. Many examples and case studies point to the importance of these measures, but there are no aggregate data. Indeed, Chinese policy is to intentionally obfuscate the degree of privatization that is going on, by separating various privatization procedures into different kinds of restructuring, and not releasing aggregate data. One indication of the magnitude of privatization is that the 1997–98 annual survey of private enterprises (i.e. those with eight or more workers) found that 4.5 per cent of these had been established through the taking over of assets from state-owned enterprises, either bankrupt or still functioning.[13] While the percentage may seem low, recall that there were 1.2 million private firms in 1998, implying that 54,000 firms had been founded with privatized state assets. By comparison, there were about 100,000 state-owned industrial and 600,000 state-owned commercial enterprises when restructuring began. Relative to the state sector and to the restructuring process as a whole, privatization has been significant.

Outcomes: shrinking public sector employment

State restructuring should be considered in light of overall changes in public sector employment. Through the first fifteen years of reform, public sector employment continued to grow. Total state employees increased from 75 million in 1978 to 109 million in 1993, while urban collective employees increased from 10 million to 34 million in the same period. And even though state-owned industry shrank as a share of industrial output and employment, its workforce increased in absolute numbers from 31 million in 1978 to 45 million in 1992. These trends have been dramatically reversed since 1993, and the urban public enterprise sector has declined sharply.

The dramatic changes are summarized in Table 1.1. Between 1992 and 1998, total employment of the state enterprise sector shrank by 23 million workers, almost a third. Urban collective enterprise employment shrank by 16 million, proportionately an even greater reduction. Some portion of this reduction in employment might be accounted for merely by a change in

Table 1.1 Urban workers, by ownership (million workers, year-end)

	1992	*1998*	*Change*
State administration	32.0	37.0	+4.0
State enterprises	76.0	53.0	−23.0
Urban collectives	36.0	20.0	−16.0
Joint stock ltd. liability	0.0	11.0	+11.0
Private	7.0	32.0	+25.0
Foreign invested	1.0	6.0	+5.0
Registered unemployed	3.6	6.2	+2.4
Laid-off workers (without jobs)	0.0	6.0	+6.0

Sources: Statistical Abstract (1999: 33, 35); Statistical Yearbook (1993: 111).

Note:
The estimated number of laid-off workers without a job is quoted from Yang (1999).

categories. The joint stock, limited liability and other forms of enterprise – which scarcely existed in 1992 – employed 11 million in 1998. Some proportion of these 'new' enterprise forms, to be sure, are simply the same old public enterprises with new signboards to indicate their accordance with reform measures. But even if 100 per cent of the new enterprise forms were insignificantly different from old public enterprises, we would still face a situation in which public enterprises had reduced total employment by 28 million workers (39 million shed by state and urban collective firms, minus 11 million added by new corporate forms), which would still be a 25 per cent reduction from the 112 million employed by public enterprises in 1992. Moreover, as discussed below, we know that restructuring and laying off of public enterprise workers continued unabated during 1999 and 2000. The workers shed by public enterprises went either into the new private sector (including foreign-invested firms), which added 30 million workers, or into the unemployed and laid-off workers, which increased by 8.4 million. Clearly, the weight of the public sector has declined dramatically in the wake of enterprise restructuring.

Increasing unemployment

The reductions in public employment coincide with a major increase in unemployment. Official unemployment data are misleading if used without correction, but still yield important information about trends and levels of unemployment. The official unemployment rate captures only permanent urban residents who have registered with local employment offices. According to this measure, unemployment has increased slightly, from 2.6 per cent in 1993 to 3.1 per cent in 1998. However, the government also publishes numbers of laid-off (*xiagang*) enterprise workers, who have increased rapidly both in absolute terms and as a share of the urban workforce. Laid-off workers are those who cease actually to work for their former employers (usually SOEs), but who remain formally affiliated either to that enterprise or to the municipal re-employment centre, rather than becoming formally 'unemployed'.

The trends in the two series, initially so dissimilar, are in fact compatible. Registered unemployed consists of both young school-leavers entering the labour force for the first time, and previously employed workers searching for new jobs. As recently as 1993, the bulk of registered unemployed were young school-leavers, who accounted for 3 million out of 4 million unemployed. Since 1993, however, the number of unemployed school-leavers has declined to 2 million. This decline reflects demographic changes to some extent, but more important is the fact that school-leavers typically no longer register with the local labour bureau in order to find their first job. However, the number of unemployed who had been previously employed has increased sharply, from 1 million in 1993 to about 3.8 million in 1997. This trend is in fact quite similar to the trend in laid-off workers, the number of whom has also more than tripled in the same period.[14] Both measures show dramatic, rapid increases in unemployment of previously employed workers. While neither one by itself is a valid measure of the *level* of unemployment, each traces a similar picture of rapidly *increasing* unemployment.

Figures on laid-off (*xiagang*) workers are abundant, but extremely difficult to use. First, coverage is inconsistent: figures cited sometimes refer only to laid-off state enterprise workers, sometimes to workers laid off from all kinds of enterprises, and sometimes there are estimates of all laid-off workers (including government administrative employees and employees of non-profit institutions). According to one knowledgeable source, state-owned enterprise workers account for about two-thirds of all laid-off workers.[15] Second, the procedures for counting laid-off workers differ. Until 1997, the most frequently quoted figures were for the cumulative total laid-off workers (in practice, since 1993). Of course, this statistical convention would have led to the number of laid-off workers increasing indefinitely! Since 1998, there have been sporadic efforts to differentiate between the number of newly laid-off workers during the course of a calendar year, and the number of laid-off workers at year-end who have not found formal re-employment. (Of course, certain identities should link the two numbers: year-end laid-off workers equals laid-off workers from the previous year, plus newly laid-off workers during the year, minus laid-off workers who have found new gainful employment.) In practice, however, it is often unclear which definition is being cited by a given source, and many sources give numbers without understanding themselves the different definitions. Finally, the numbers refer to workers who have gone through a formal process of being laid off. They do not include workers who simply have no work because their factory has ceased operating (*tinggong bantinggong*), since such a factory in practice has no resources to put workers through the lay-off process!

Despite the difficulty in getting the diverse numbers to correspond exactly, they do tell an extremely consistent story. If we focus on SOE workers, who are most consistently documented, the following story emerges. In the period 1993–95, a cumulative total of about 3.6 million SOE workers were laid off. In 1996, the pace began to accelerate such that some 4 million SOE workers were laid off. Then from 1997, the data begin to specify more clearly that during 1997, 6 million SOE workers were *newly* laid off; this then decreased slightly to 5.6 million SOE workers in 1998, and an identical 5.6 million in 1999.[16] These numbers are only a little misleading: in fact, it became slightly more difficult to be listed as a laid-off worker during 1998, because of the insistence that all laid-off workers be registered with re-employment centres (in fact, 98 per cent were alleged to be so registered). The result was that some laid-off workers were excluded from the calculation. Nonetheless, these data tell us, with a fairly high degree of confidence, that a total of approximately 25 million SOE workers were laid off between 1993 and 1999, and that probably almost 40 million workers were laid off in urban China, if we include other ownership forms, and government and non-profit workers. Moreover, the pace of this process did not significantly slow down after 1997, but remained high through the entire 1997–99 period. These numbers are consistent with the shrinkage of the public enterprise labour force we documented in the previous section.[17]

Not all laid-off workers are without gainful employment. Our best data come from a survey conducted in December 1997 and January 1998, which found that 26 per cent of laid-off workers had found new employment. This number is consistent with an earlier survey that had found 60 per cent of laid-off workers still looking for permanent, full-time employment. Together these imply that another roughly 14 per cent of laid-off workers had withdrawn from the labour force, mostly through early retirement, though some may engage in part-time or informal labour 'off the books'. Applying these data to year-end 1997 numbers, Mo Rong[18] computes a total of 7.2 million unemployed laid-off workers, plus 5.7 million registered unemployed, for a total unemployed population of 12.9 million, about 7 per cent of the urban labour force. We can roughly duplicate Mo Rong's method on earlier years, and express the numbers of unemployed as a percentage of the permanent, registered urban labour force.[19] Such a procedure shows the total unemployment rate increasing from 3.7 per cent in 1993 to 7 per cent in 1997. This aggregate number conceals a near quadrupling of the rate of unemployment of the previously employed from 1.7 per cent to 6 per cent, masked by a decline in the ratio of unemployed school-leavers to the urban labour force from 2 per cent to 1 per cent. This count of total urban unemployment is a reasonably accurate lower bound estimate to unemployment: it understates the total by omitting some workers laid off from bankrupt or defunct enterprises, who have not registered as unemployed or laid-off; it probably misses a few school-leavers in the labour market for the first time; and of course it completely excludes rural migrants to the city.

Diverse local conditions

The available reports on enterprise restructuring indicate very substantial diversity among provinces in the speed and thoroughness with which restructuring has been implemented. Certain provinces, such as Shandong and Zhejiang, have consistently appeared as aggressive frontrunners, pioneering many techniques, including privatization. Conversely, many inland provinces have had clear difficulties proceeding with restructuring, largely because of the fear of unemployment.

Underlying these differences are the increasing differences in the degree to which provincial industrial economies have moved away from reliance on state ownership (see Table 1.2). By the late 1980s, very substantial differences had opened up between the ownership structure of southern coastal provinces and the rest of China. Even without significant privatization, the southern coast became much less dependent on state industry because of the rapid growth of private and foreign invested industry. In 1989, state industry had declined to less than half of industrial output in five coastal provinces (Zhejiang, Jiangsu, Guangdong, Shandong and Fujian).

Restructuring now seems to be further increasing the differences between rapidly growing coastal provinces and the rest of China. In those provinces where the non-state sector has grown rapidly, laid-off workers have more opportunities for re-employment, and local government officials are less constrained by fears of unemployment. Moreover, the nature of political incentives has changed more in those provinces: local governments are already dependent on tax revenues from a diversified ownership base, rather than on the profit stream from their client enterprises. Leaders there are likely to see their interests as congruent with a broad tax base, rather than with a large state-owned sector. Moreover, leaders in these provinces have forged political and economic alliances with newly emergent entrepreneurs. Restructuring provides them with opportunities to cement these alliances, and in some cases to enrich their friends or relatives.

The result is that restructuring seems to be proceeding more rapidly in areas where the economy is already more private. For example, the fifteen provinces least dominated by the state sector in 1989 had industrial output that was 45 per cent produced by non-state firms. By 1997, that had grown to 77 per cent, an increased of 32 percentage points. The fifteen provinces most dominated by the state sector increased their non-state share from 25 per cent to 46 per cent over the same period, an increase of 21 percentage points. The gap is increasing. In Zhejiang, only 9.4 per cent of industrial output in 1997 was produced by state firms; in Guangdong, it was only 12.7 per cent. But there were still ten inland provinces where SOEs produced more than 50 per cent of total output.

In the coastal provinces, growth has been more vibrant, so officials have more resources to facilitate restructuring, including investments in new

Table 1.2 Provincial economic conditions

Provinces	*Percentage of SOE workers laid off (1993–98)*	*Percentage of industrial output produced by SOEs, 1995*
Hunan	42.7	37.4
Heilongjiang	36.8	62.7
Jilin	36.6	60.2
Jiangxi	33.4	48.9
Hubei	29.7	32.7
Inner Mongolia	27.6	59.8
Henan	26.3	31.1
Jiangsu	25.6	20.7
Liaoning	25.5	41.0
Qinghai	24.6	81.8
National	24.3	31.5
Shanghai	24.3	37.2
Shaanxi	24.0	56.2
Guizhou	23.7	63.3
Anhui	23.0	28.5
Sichuan	22.8	36.4
Shanxi	22.7	43.0
Fujian	19.8	16.4
Guangxi	19.3	36.2
Guangdong	19.3	15.8
Zhejiang	18.6	12.7
Shandong	18.5	28.8
Tianjin	15.1	31.0
Hebei	14.4	33.5
Ningxia	14.2	65.9
Hainan	13.8	36.4
Yunnan	13.4	66.4
Gansu	13.3	63.7
Xinjiang	11.7	72.3
Beijing	9.9	50.6

Sources: State Statistical Bureau and Ministry of Labour of the PRC (1998: 433 and 1999: 448); 1995 Industrial Census.

facilities and in worker training. At the same time, finding new jobs for laid-off state workers is easier, because there are more opportunities in the private and foreign-invested sectors. And, politically and ideologically, leaders in those provinces see fewer problems in a strategy of tilting toward the private sector. Thus, restructuring feeds a further cycle of restructuring in rapidly growing coastal areas, while economic and political constraints hold back the pace of change in those inland areas that are growing more slowly. In Table 1.2, the coastal provinces stand out because they have *both* a relatively low share of industrial output accounted for by SOEs, and a relatively small percentage reduction in the SOE workforce (Jiangsu, the highest, is only slightly above the national average). More traditional, SOE dependent provinces fall into two groups. Towards the top of Table 1.2 are the three north-eastern provinces of Heilongjiang, Jilin and Liaoning. These provinces are the inverse of the south coast. They have *both* a high dependence on SOEs and a large shrinkage of the state labour force. In these provinces, the impact of restructuring on the entire economy has been severe, and the process has been extremely painful. Not surprisingly, most of the reports of urban unrest come from this region. There is also a third distinct group of inland provinces with high dependence on SOEs and relatively small shrinkage of the state labour force. These provinces continue to receive significant subsidies from the central government, which buffers their public enterprises from the full force of restructuring. Other provinces are scattered around these three clusters.

Similar local interests

Despite the diversity in local-level conditions, local officials in most of China appear to have basically similar interests: 'growth' and 'stability'. Local officials are charged with balancing and reconciling two interests that are fundamentally in tension. While consistent in the long run, growth and stability frequently present contradictory demands on local officials in the short run. First, local officials are concerned with creating (and defending) a competitive local industrial economy. Competition within China is intense, and many local officials believe that their regions must ultimately be competitive in the international marketplace as well. Second, local officials wish to ensure 'stability', in particular to defuse the discontent that comes with unemployment and changes in the status of urban workers.

The incentive for growth is multi-stranded. Most significantly, local officials recognize that a vibrant local economy increases their tax revenues, their command of other economic resources, and the opportunities for patronage and political alliances. Second, the incentive system within the Chinese bureaucracy strongly rewards economic growth, both by linking bonuses to economic performance, and because of the strong association between promotion and economic success.[20] In some cases, a growth imperative may feed into a corruption opportunity incentive, since privatization of assets obviously creates opportunities for personal gain. Generally speaking, local officials also recognize that creation of a competitive economy requires reducing enterprise workforces, laying off workers, and improving incentives for managers: competitiveness requires enterprise restructuring. As managers of local industrial systems, local officials also recognize that cost-cutting is made easier by hiring immigrant rural workers, who are generally recognized to work harder for a much lower total compensation package. If skill levels are not especially demanding, rural workers will be a cost-effective solution.

The incentive for stability is also multi-stranded. Here, the hierarchical incentives of the Chinese political system probably deserve first mention.

The central government has displayed extreme sensitivity to the possibility that unemployed, discouraged urban workers will coalesce into a political opposition group. That consistent sensitivity erupted into brutal suppression of modest organizing efforts in December 1998, abruptly reversing a year-old liberalizing trend. Local officials are evaluated annually on their performance in maintaining social stability. Moreover, since at least spring 1998, the central government has clearly signalled that local officials must at least be perceived to be making an effort to minimize unemployment and provide some re-employment for laid-off workers. Even aside from central government-mandated incentives, local officials undoubtedly respond to state workers as part of their core constituency. While there is no electoral democracy in China's cities, a successful local politician must be perceived to have benefited his or her core constituency. Rural immigrants, for example, are not part of an urban politician's constituency.

Local policy diversity

The similarity of local interests described in the previous section does not necessarily create similar policies. Not only do local conditions vary substantially, but local officials have to create strategies to balance conflicting objectives as best they can. Given the tensions among objectives, strategies will necessarily differ. Solinger, discussing local policies toward labour markets and rural migrants, describes the situation as follows: 'City administrations have been handed the daunting and probably impossible task of facilitating the formation of a unified labor market that can at once manage outside labor and yet guarantee locals' full employment'.[21] Solinger goes on to describe the different policies adopted in Shenyang, Wuhan and Guangzhou toward state worker re-employment. These range from a welfare-oriented employment strategy (in Shenyang) that Solinger labels 'Keynesian', to the private-sector reliant strategy (in Guangzhou) that seems more 'Thatcherite'.

Solinger's dichotomy is useful because it reminds us that besides deciding how actively to expedite restructuring, local officials also must decide how much transitional support to give to laid-off workers. The experience in Shanghai exemplifies what is probably the maximum feasible transitional support given to laid-off workers. Shanghai established a re-employment centre (REC) in July 1996, initially for laid-off workers from the textile and instrument sectors which were undergoing early consolidation. The REC was funded by the SOE, the SOE's managing corporation, and the municipal government in approximately equal parts. The REC then took over the laid-off workers employment affiliation, undertaking to provide social security benefits and a laid-off workers subsidy for up to two years. In this way, the bonds with the initial SOE could be crisply snapped, without subjecting the worker immediately to full unemployment, and with the financial burden to the SOE significantly reduced.[22] In practice, however, this outcome was achieved in Shanghai only at the price of transferring most of the financial burden to the REC. At least through the end of 1996, most workers either took early retirement (in which case they received a city pension until the end of their lives), or else retained their labour affiliation with the REC while accepting temporary work elsewhere, either in the informal sector or through temporary contracts with other enterprises. Less than 10 per cent of the laid-off workers found new formal employment within the first year of operation.

As a result, Shanghai's programme was extraordinarily expensive. In 1996, the REC set up for just the instruments and textiles sectors served 100,000 laid-off workers, at a cost in that year of 420 million Rmb, of which 140 million were municipal budget outlays. In 1997, seven industrial sectors set up nine RECs that served 250,000 workers, at a total cost of 1 billion Rmb, of which somewhat over 300 million was carried by municipal finances. Moreover, by encouraging early retirement as a major way of taking care of laid-off workers, the city accumulated ongoing liabilities, which according to one estimate increased municipal pension liability by 1.2 billion Rmb annually.[23] In essence, Shanghai, a growing and relatively wealthy jurisdiction, was able to provide massive subsidies to SOEs and laid-off workers, protecting their standard of living while easing their exit from the state sector.

An instructive contrast with Shanghai is provided by Heilongjiang, which, far from being able to provide an additional billion Rmb annually for early retirements to facilitate restructuring, is unable even to meet its existing pension obligations. As of September 1997, Heilongjiang was in arrears of its pension obligations by almost exactly a billion Rmb (1.011 billion Rmb), affecting nearly half a million SOE retirees. Total national pension arrears registered on that date were 3.2 billion Rmb, with the three north-eastern provinces of Heilongjiang, Jilin and Liaoning accounting for over half the total.[24] Heilongjiang would simply not be in a position to provide transitional support for laid-off workers on the scale of Shanghai – but then, neither would very many other Chinese provinces either.

Another example, more closely related to Heilongjiang than to Shanghai, is that of Mianyang, a medium-sized city in Sichuan province. Mianyang, a city with severe economic problems (but also an extremely successful consumer electronics firm, Changhong), was selected in 1996 as a key-point test city for industrial restructuring. In the subsequent two years, 62 state-owned enterprises were declared bankrupt, with over 21,000 workers (7 per cent of the municipal total) being laid off. But there were major demonstrations in Mianyang, caused not only by the lay-offs, but also by failures to pay wages and pensions at these and other firms. Demonstrations were apparently met with a brutal police response, which according to one report led to scores of deaths and hundreds of injuries.[25] Despite the remoteness of Mianyang, reports of these demonstrations made their way through China's dissident network to the West, where they were given significant play in human rights publications and newspapers. Undoubtedly the Mianyang experience provided a sharp warning to Chinese policy-makers.

Among provinces undergoing slower growth of the non-state sector, we would expect relatively wealthy provinces to try to protect and subsidize their firms, while being less activist in promoting restructuring (partly because of the relative difficulty of the process). This seems to describe the north-eastern provinces, particularly Liaoning, which has traditionally enjoyed abundant financing, but currently faces serious difficulties. Solinger cites scattered statistics on retraining and re-employment programmes in a variety of cities, indicating that Shenyang set aside 100 million Rmb for re-employment projects; while in Wuhan, a city of similar size, only 30 million Rmb was spent. But these provinces face the danger that as restructuring stalls and growth slows, the money will eventually prove to be inadequate to carry the ongoing expenses. Already, this seems to be the situation in Heilongjiang and Jilin. Finally, numerous poorer provinces are unable to provide substantial subsidization to the restructuring process from their own resources. Such provinces, many of them predominantly rural and located in inland China, either appeal to the central government for support, or else are forced to let the pace of public enterprise restructuring be dictated primarily by market forces.

The impact on the social compact

State sector restructuring reflects a historic turn in the political economy of China. For four decades – and throughout most of the reform era – urban workers were a privileged social and political class in China. Within urban areas, incomes and social benefits were quite evenly distributed. Membership in the privileged group of urbanites in and of itself produced higher incomes and benefits, with workers in SOEs having slightly more generous benefits than workers in other types of organizations. Lifetime membership in the work unit (*danwei*) was the specific institutional mechanism through which the urban dwellers' privileged position was realized.[26] For the first fifteen years of reform, the government guarantee of a job to all registered urban dwellers was not only unshaken, it was in many respects strengthened. At the end of the 1970s, China's cities absorbed millions of rusticated youth, sent to China's countryside during the Cultural Revolution. Jobs were provided for virtually all these individuals. As discussed above, public sector employment grew steadily through the reform era until 1993. Moreover, workers were almost never fired. Even through the first fifteen years of the reform process, this basic arrangement did not change. Reforms introduced some flexibility into the system, but lay-offs, resignations and dismissals from the state sector remained extremely small through 1992.

Detailed analysis of 1988 household surveys showed that distribution of income (including benefits) within the urban sector was highly equal (Gini coefficient equal to 0.23). Inequality within China was primarily due to the large urban–rural gap.[27] Returns to education were nil, and remaining differentiation among urbanites was due largely to political status. This scenario began to change dramatically during the 1990s. Already by 1995, household income surveys showed significant changes from 1988. The Gini coefficient for 1995 urban income jumped to 0.33, a remarkably quick increase in inequality. Meanwhile, the urban–rural gap, properly accounted for, actually shrank modestly (once a reduction in overt urban subsidies is accounted for).[28] It seems likely that these changes have accelerated in the years since 1995. Relative wages have fallen for unskilled production workers (such as miners), and increased for skilled workers, particularly those in finance, real estate and entertainment. Returns to education and skills training appear to be increasing rapidly. Most fundamentally, the workers' lifetime affiliation with the work unit has begun to dissolve. With the fraying of those bonds, employment security is also eroding. The 'iron rice bowl' is gone. On balance, public sector employment is shrinking, and turnover within the sector is increasing.

Clearly, these changes are disadvantaging millions of urban workers. Dissatisfied groups include the unemployed, the laid-off, pensioners seeing their benefits eroded or not getting paid at all, and production workers seeing their relative income standing fall, and perhaps their absolute real incomes as well. One particularly poignant example of a group losing ground is the demographic group which came of age during the Cultural Revolution. Born during the first part of the 1950s, this group had its education interrupted by the Cultural Revolution, and many members of the group were sent to the countryside between 1969 and 1975. According to one estimate, of the 15.3 million middle-school students affected by the Cultural Revolution, at least 13.7 million never got any advanced education.[29] In the early reform period, members of this group recovered their status somewhat as they returned to the cities and rebuilt their lives. Today, these workers are now in their forties, and relatively poorly educated and poorly skilled. They are typically among the first to be laid off when lay-offs occur. The bitter irony of their position has not escaped them.

Not all urbanites are suffering from the current changes: there will continue to be an urban elite, more privileged in relation to the rest of society than ever before. But that elite will be defined by wealth and skills, not by simple residence in an urban area. Urban workers without special skills or education, without wealth, or connections to the wealthy and powerful, increasingly find themselves slipping down the social and economic scale. Enterprise restructuring is simply one part of these vast and fundamental changes in the social and economic position of urban residents. Whatever else enterprise restructuring involves, it certainly implies the end of the work unit system as the predominant method for organizing urban dwellers in China.

The certainty with which we can make these statements contrasts sharply with our uncertainty about exactly how far this process has proceeded. Two specific areas are worth discussing separately. First, while the urban worker's ties to the work unit have frayed, for many workers they still remain important. This includes retired and laid-off workers. The basic institutional arrangement is precisely that laid-off workers maintain ties with their work unit, for this is what differentiates them from the 'unemployed'. Similarly, retirees maintain a link with their former work units despite the existence of socialized pension funds. In fact, pensions are still paid by work units, but those work units then 'settle up' accounts with the municipal or provincial pension funds, based on their net liabilities or balances payable. This is one of the main reasons why some retirees do not get their pensions, because some enterprises in financial difficulties do not pay their share to their retirees, or else get cut off by the pension funds because they have not paid their contributions to the funds. Conversely, the socialized pension funds sometimes run out of money themselves, so retirees from a wealthy unit are well-advised to maintain their connections there.[30] In addition, wealthy work units still provide supplemental benefits of various kinds to their retirees because of long-standing links and a feeling of obligation. Thus, despite the major changes under way, the *danwei* still plays an important role in the life of most urban dwellers.

A second area of uncertainty is the extent to which urban workers – and especially laid-off urban workers – are in competition with China's vast reservoir of rural workers. There is no doubt about the increased mobility of China's workers, which has brought rural residents into urban job markets in unprecedented numbers. But it is also clear from numerous studies that urban job markets remain substantially bifurcated, with rural migrants barred from some occupations, and discriminated against in others. Some labour market competition is nonetheless emerging around the margins. In part, this is because laid-off workers have a strong incentive to maintain their ties to work units or re-employment centres, but work in informal grey markets at the same time. When they go to the informal markets, they encounter rural immigrants offering similar labour services. In part, emergent competition is due to the fact that economic pressures on existing urban enterprises – including SOEs – is so intense that they have strong incentives to ignore regulations and hire rural migrants, who are much cheaper and have a reputation as harder workers.[31] What is also clear is that for many urban workers in this intermediate zone, competition is not 'fair'. Not only do urban administrations side with urban residents, in addition those urban residents often continue to receive various kinds of subsidies. Thus, although they may earn the same wages as rural migrants, their total incomes remain higher. But again, it is very difficult for us to judge how far this process has proceeded.

The specific uncertainties about remaining links to work units and the degree of competition with rural migrants provide an indication of our uncertainty about the ultimate form of the urban society – and urban social compact – that is emerging in China. It is clear that urban residents are losing security but gaining opportunity. For some, this trade-off leaves them clearly worse off. The Chinese government appears quite ready to override the preferences of this group, cracking down hard on individual manifestations of discontent, and especially hard on embryonic political organizations. The social safety net that protects urban residents is frayed and leaky, but still in place for a large majority of urbanites. But the new institutional framework governing the economic, social and political life of urban dwellers has been slow to emerge.

Notes

1 For example, Miller and Nathan (1998: 2) say: 'After much fanfare last year, China's drive to reform the state-owned firms has stopped, if not stalled, experts say. 'The reforms have faltered,' former U.S. official Chas Freeman [said] last month.'
2 For summary, analysis and text, see Lauffs (1995).
3 Ru (1998: 48).
4 O'Neill (1998a, 1998b).
5 Chan (1998).
6 For example, of central government investment in manufacturing in 1996, more than two-thirds was in three sectors: petroleum refining, chemicals, and steel. State Statistical Bureau (1998: 63–67). Local government manufacturing investment was about 70 per cent larger in total, and much more dispersed across industrial sectors.
7 Wo (1998).
8 Wu (1996: 28–30); Shanghai Statistical Office (2000: 47, 56).
9 The following discussion, and most of the material on Zhucheng, draws largely from Huang and Huang (1988).
10 For a recent story on Legend, see Wang (1999).
11 The account in the following pages is taken from the website of the State Council Development Research Centre (n.d.) or from VCChina.com (2000).
12 Shao (1998).
13 Zhang (1999). I am indebted to Kellee Tsai for this reference.
14 In theory, there should be no overlap between laid-off workers and registered unemployed. The status of 'laid-off worker' implies that one's employment search and welfare benefits are being handled by an existing enterprise or labour bureau re-employment project, not the office that handles the unemployed.
15 Mo (1998: 16). This is an essential source for disentangling the different figures and definitions.
16 These estimates are constructed from the data in Mo (1998), State Statistical Bureau and Ministry of Labour (1996: 409; 1997: 405; 1998: 431–433; 1999: 441–442); and State Council Development Research Centre (2000).
17 For more data on unemployed workers, refer also to Bakken, Fernández-Stembridge and Rocca in this volume.
18 Mo (1998: 28).
19 The official urban labour force data have been revised upward in recent years to reflect the large number of rural migrants working in the cities. The total urban

labour force at year-end 1997 was thus almost 208 million. However, since the unemployed do not include unemployed rural migrants, it seems more appropriate to express unemployed as a percentage of permanent urban residents in the labour force, about 184 million at year-end 1997.

20 Whiting (1998).
21 Solinger (1998).
22 Because only one-third of the cost was borne by the SOE, and the time of promised support was capped at two years. Beijing University Chinese Economics Research Centre, Urban Labour Market Research Group (1998: 102).
23 *Ibid.* (1998: 108).
24 Mou (1998: 56–57). The source notes that the worst offenders in Heilongjiang were state farms and lumber camps, rather than factories.
25 Mo (1998: 18).
26 See Lü and Perry (1997).
27 Khan et al. (1993).
28 Khan and Riskin (1998).
29 Chen (1999).
30 Mou (1998: 57–58).
31 These viewpoints are strongly argued in Beijing University Chinese Economics Research Centre, Urban Labour Market Research Group (1998).

References and further reading

Beijing University Chinese Economics Research Centre, Urban Labour Market Research Group (1998) 'Shanghai: Chengshi zhigong yu nongcun mingong de fenceng yu ronghe' (Shanghai: Stratification and Integration of Urban and Rural Workers). *Gaige*, no. 4, pp. 99–110.

Chan, Yee Hon (1998) 'Party Chiefs Stress Need to Create Jobs'. *South China Morning Post* [Internet], 14 March. http://www.scmp.com.hk.

Chen, Yixin (1999) 'Cong xiafang dao xiagang, 1968–1998' (From Being Sent Down to the Countryside, to Being Laid Off From Work, 1968–1998). *Ershiyi shiji*, December, pp. 122–135.

Huang, Sha'an and Huang, Lijun (1988) ' 'Zhucheng xianxiang'' zaixi' (A Further Analysis of the 'Zhucheng Phenomenon'). *Gaige*, no. 2, pp. 38–47.

Khan, Azizur, Griffin, Keith, Riskin, Carl and Zhao, Renwei (1993) 'Sources of Income Inequality in Post-Reform China'. *China Economic Review*, vol. 1, no. 4 (Spring), pp. 19–36.

Khan, Azizur and Riskin, Carl (1998) 'Income and Inequality in China: Composition, Distribution and Growth of Household Income, 1988 to 1995'. *China Quarterly*, no. 154 (June), pp. 221–253.

'Latest Development on Workers Demonstrations in Mianyang, Sichuan' (1997) *China News Digest*, 20 July, p. 1.

Lauffs, Andreas (1995) *China Update: The PRC Labour Law*. Hong Kong, Asia Law and Practice.

Lü, Xiaobo and Perry, Elizabeth J. (eds) (1997) *Danwei: The Changing Chinese Workplace in Historical and Comparative Perspective*. Armonk, M. E. Sharpe.

Miller, Rich and Nathan, Sara (1998) 'China's Balancing Act'. *USA Today*, 17 November, p. 2.

Mo, Rong (1998) *Jiuye: Zhongguo de zhiji nanti* (Employment: China's Problem of the Century). Beijing, Jingji kexue.

Mou, Daquan (1998) *Gongzhi anquan wang: Zhongguo shehui baoxian chaoshi* (A Collective Safety Net: Trends in China's Social Insurance). Beijing, Jingji kexue.

O'Neill, Mark (1998a) 'Premier Sets Out 'Five Years of Rapid Change'. *South China Morning Post*, 20 March. http://www.scmp.com.hk.

—— (1998b) 'Zhu's Press Conference: 'I will blaze my trail . . . I have no hesitations''. *South China Morning Post*, 20 March. http://www.scmp.com.hk.

Ru, Xin (1998) *1998–nian: Zhongguo shehui xingshi fenxi yu yuce* (1998: An Analysis and Projection of China's Social Condition). Beijing, Shehui kexue wenxian.

Shanghai Statistical Office (2000) *Shanghai tongji nianjian 1999* (Shanghai Statistical Yearbook). Shanghai, Shanghai tongchi.

Shao, Jun (1998) 'Shandong qiye jianbing huodong huigu' (A Glance Backward at Mergers and Acquisitions by Shandong Enterprises). *Zouxiang shijie*, no 1 (January), pp. 7–10.

Solinger, Dorothy J. (1998) 'The Impact of Openness on Integration and Control in China: Migrants, Layoffs, and Labor Market Formation'. Working Paper (December). Irvine, University of California.

State Council Development Research Centre of the PRC (n.d.) *Guowuyuan fazhan yianjiu zhongxin xinxiwang* (State Council Development Research Centre's Information Network). http://www.drcnet.com.cn.

—— (2000) 'Zhonghua renmin gongheguo 1999–nian guomin jingji he shehui fazhan tongji baogao' (Communiqué on the National Economy in 1999) [Internet], February. http://www.drcnet.com.cn.

State Statistical Bureau of the PRC (1998) *Zhongguo guding zichan touzi tongji nianjian* (China Statistics of Fixed Investment). Beijing, Zhongguo tongji chubanshe.

—— (1999) *Zhougguo tongji nianjian zhaiyao* (China Statistical Yearbook Abstract). Beijing, Zhongguo tongji chubanshe.

State Statistical Bureau and Ministry of Labour of the PRC (eds) (1993, 1996, 1997, 1998, 1999) *Zhongguo laodong tongji nianjian* (China Labour Statistics Yearbook). Beijing, Zhongguo tongji chubanshe.

VCChina.com (2000) *VCChina – Weixin fengxian touziwang* http://www.vcchina.com.

Wang, Xiangwei (1999) 'Free Rein, Hard Work Spur Vision towards World Elite'. *South China Morning Post*, 11 January. http://www.scmp.com.hk.

Whiting, Susan (1998) 'Exploring Performance Criteria for County and Township Officials'. Paper presented at the Workshop on Cadre Monitoring and Reward: Personnel Management and Policy Implementation in the PRC, 6–7 June, University of California, San Diego.

Wo, Willy Lap Lam (1998) 'Economic About-turn'. *South China Morning Post*, 25 February. http://www.scmp.com.hk.

Wu, Cangping (1996) *Gaige kaifang zhong chuxian de zuixin renkou wenti* (New Population Problems Emerging as Part of Reform and Opening). Beijing, Gaodeng jiaoyu.

Yang, Yiyong (1999) '2000 Nian Zhongguo Jiuye Xingshi jiqi Zhengce Xuanze' (The Employment Situation and Policy Options in China in 2000). In: Liu Guoguang et al. (eds), *2000–nian Zhongguo: Jingji xingshi fenxi yu yuce* (China in 2000: Economic Analysis and Prediction). Beijing, Shehui kexue wenxian, pp. 149–155.

Zhang, Houyi (1999) 'Zhongguo siying qiye jiben gaikuang' (Basic Situation of Private Enterprises in China). *Renmin ribao*, 20 March, p. 5.

2
CHINA'S 'COMPATIBLE OPENING'
Lessons from the Asian Crisis

Fan Gang

China has quickly opened up its economy in the past twenty years. As a result of the economic reforms, it has become the largest foreign direct investment (FDI) recipient developing country since 1993, and its trade accounts for about 40 per cent of total gross domestic product (GDP). But China is still not fully 'opened', and international pressures persist in that direction. A consensus seems to be growing within the Chinese population: China has to open its doors to catch up with the process of globalization and become a constructive and equal partner in the world market; but at the same time, China has to decide which path to choose (strategies, game tactics, etc.) taking into account its own interests, its own calculation of costs and benefits, its own capability of dealing with risks and negative impacts, and, therefore, being fully independent from the calls of multinationals, foreign powers and other international interest groups.

Globalization and the Asian Crisis

Many specialists agree that globalization provides opportunities for the developing countries to grow more rapidly, considering the increase in capital inflows and technology transfer. Nevertheless, these countries usually lack mechanisms allowing them to move more freely towards utilization of their comparative advantage (cheap labour). In economic terms, such a movement would change or more positively, would improve their resource endowments structure, implying higher levels of economic prosperity.

Nowadays, to teach the developing countries the advantages of an open economy has become obsolete. The main incentive to develop and to reform their institutions is to join the global market and become equal partners: with no opening, there can be no catching up, and the risks in being left out of the world economy increase. But why are there still so many economies that instead of benefiting from globalization have suffered continuous poverty, social instability, financial turmoil and economic crises? Looking back in history, most of the former colonial territories, which enjoyed very high degrees of commodity trade freedom, capital inflows and technology transfers, did not prosper. In fact, they still remain today as the most backward countries.

So why do the multinationals or the governments of developed countries always praise globalization, whilst the developing world is rather sceptical about it? I argue here that there is fundamentally an 'unequal footing' problem in globalization: the developing countries are constrained by their domestic problems in international competition and are subsequently more vulnerable to international market risks. In order to achieve prosperity, all countries need more than capital inflow, transferred technology and local cheap labour. Other factors matter in the production function of a nation. In fact, globalization can immediately bring in capital and technology, but can hardly develop in the short term competitive economic structures, strong institutions, market management capabilities (experience, know-how, etc.), and even basic education. All four elements are necessary for cheap labour to become a real factor of comparative advantage, and therefore to be crucial for further economic prosperity and catching up.

The developed economies have always urged the developing ones (without any explicit opposition) to reform their institutions, develop their education systems (and technology research), adjust their economic structures, learn how to manage market risks, and so on. But they have forgotten a very obvious reality: all these reforms take time. It is not a matter of just one to two years, or five to seven, but perhaps ten to twenty, or even fifty years (it took about two hundred years for the developed countries to reach their current market system). Then the real question is how can each country's domestic capacity achieve reform and development.

The 'unequal footing'

Capital and technology tend to be highly mobile as the world economy becomes increasingly globalized, while other important factors such as institutions and market management capability tend to be much less 'mobile': they are more national-specific and historically constrained. Globalization may help to improve mobility (or changes) of institutions, as the developing countries may copy laws and regulations from others, or otherwise follow the international rules when doing international business. After all, foreign investment and technology transfers bring in institutional models and management know-how. But given the nature of the institutional changes and economic development, the speed of change in such areas tends to be much slower than in other areas such as capital and technology. This is the difference and the 'unequal footing' between developed and developing countries: while the former can benefit from globalization, the emerging market economies may face higher risks and become potential losers, especially in the financial markets.

The 'incompatible opening'

The Asian Crisis in 1997 provided a cautionary tale: a developing country that goes too far in liberalizing its market, especially its financial market, may suffer global market problems more seriously than others (the Asian Crisis should be seen as an initial phase in the burst of the global financial bubble). From this point of view, the Asian Crisis was caused by the 'incompatible opening' of some developing countries. By 'incompatible opening' I refer to the incompatibility between excessive market liberalization and slowly changing domestic economic structures and institutions, as well as slowly improving market management capability.

In fact, not all markets work equally: financial markets are riskier, and therefore should be distinguished from commodity factors and service markets. Nevertheless, problems are fundamentally the same in any market, even if risks may differ: when the process of market opening is incompatible with other sectors of the economy, it will inevitably cause problems. For instance, if domestic structural adjustment has not been achieved, a fast liberalization of the commodity market may cause serious unemployment, income disparities, social unrest, and the decline of overall growth.

Speed up reform and balance globalization with domestic restructuring

The first message from the analysis above for the developing country should be not to slow down the process of opening, but to achieve quicker structural adjustment and institutional reform of its domestic economy. After all, to speed up reforms will give the country more chance to develop the process of 'compatible opening' and therefore to be able to benefit more from globalization. The concept of 'compatible opening' is about an adapable process that depends on the conditions of domestic institutional reform and capability building.

At the same time, however, it is necessary to balance the opening process with the progress of domestic reforms. Those economies having suffered from an 'excessive opening' may actually need some kind of 'retrenchment' that will allow them to move forward again more successfully. This means that market control measures ought to be implemented, especially with regards to financial market activities – at least on a temporary basis, while recovering from a crisis.

Gradual liberalization in China

Although there are 'overshooting' cases of market liberalization, China seems to remain in the category of 'compatible opening', if not 'overcautious'. Despite the negative impacts of market liberalization, these have been so far contained at a manageable level, as most economic, social and political problems have been mainly caused by domestic structural adjustment. For instance, China has not been as affected by the burst of the global financial bubble as other Asian economies. Although China shared similar problems (in some respects, these have been even worse), its financial market was not so open. There were Chinese 'domestic bubbles', without there being part of the global bubble. That is why the impacts have been manageable. In fact, the goods market follows more or less the same path. There are still various trade protections in China preventing the massive unemployment that could be caused by total trade liberalization. While 'compatible opening' is more or less a theoretical concept of the ideal situation, China's case may be defined as a 'gradual market liberalization'. The speed of gradual change may not be 'right' or 'ideal', but it is a reality.

The following sections are mainly devoted to analysing the process of China's gradual involvement in the international market: the benefits, the constraints, the difficulties and the potential problems that have prevented China from moving faster.

Opening process and benefits from globalization

China has gradually opened its economy to the world and benefits from it. Its trade dependence has risen from 17.8 per cent in 1982 to 36.7 per cent in 1997 (Table 2.1). Export/GDP ratio increased to 20.3 per cent in 1997 and contributed to over 35 per cent of GDP growth. While China had trade deficits during most of the 1980s, the next decade it had surplus.

Tariffs have been lowered down in recent years, although the average rate is still high (Tables 2.2a–c). Due to various tariff exemptions on imported equipment and production materials, the actual rate was only 3–5 per cent in the past years, according to the ratio of total tariff collected over total

Table 2.1 China's foreign trade

Year	*Trade balance*	*Trade/GDP*	*Export/GDP*
1985	−14.90	23.06	9.02
1986	−11.96	25.29	10.61
1987	−3.78	25.78	12.29
1988	−7.76	25.60	11.83
1989	−6.60	24.58	11.57
1990	8.74	30.00	16.11
1991	8.05	33.42	17.70
1992	4.35	34.24	17.56
1993	−12.22	32.66	15.31
1994	5.32	43.75	22.37
1995	16.69	40.19	21.29
1996	12.23	35.55	18.53
1997	40.34	36.05	20.27

Source: State Statistical Bureau (various years).

Table 2.2a Lowering the tariff

	1991	*1992*	*1993*	*1994*	*1995*	*1996*	*1997*
Average tariff	42.5	39.9	36.4	35.9	35.9	23.0	17.0

Source: MOFTEC internal documents, 1998.

Table 2.2b Import tariff adjustment of some electronic goods (1 April 1996) (%)

Consuming Goods	*Tariff before adjustment (preferential)*	*Tariff after adjustment (preferential)*
Colour TV	60–65	50
TV camera	85	60
Cassette recorder	90	60
Cassette videorecorder	90	60
Laser disk player	60	60
Vacuum cleaner	85	40
Electric fan	90	35
Washing machine	90	40
Household freezer	50	40
Air conditioner	90	40

Source: Customs Statistics, State Customs, Beijing, 1998

Table 2.2c Some import tariffs after adjustment (1 July 1997) (%)

	Tariff before adjustment (average)	*Tariff after adjustment (average)*
Some grains and related materials	90–120	90–120
Tobacco and cigarettes	70.0	65
TV sets	50.0	35
Buses and coaches	90.0	70
Cars and cross-country vehicles	100.0	80

Source: Tariff Adjustment Table in 1997, State Customs, Beijing, 1998.

imports. By the end of 1996, China achieved its *renminbi* (Rmb) convertibility on the current account.

China also benefits a great deal from foreign investment, especially foreign direct investment (FDI). By the end of 1997, China used about US$350 billion of foreign investment (Table 2.3). It has become the largest recipient developing country of foreign investment since 1993.

As the Chinese Rmb is not convertible in the capital account and it has a relatively closed financial capital market,[1] China has the largest share of FDI, but also less share of foreign debt or portfolio investment than most

Table 2.3 Foreign capital inflow (US$100 million)

	Total foreign investment	*FDI*	*Foreign borrowing*	*Other capital inflow*
1979–82	124.6	106.9	11.6	6.0
1983	19.8	10.7	6.4	2.8
1984	27.1	12.9	12.6	1.6
1985	46.5	26.9	16.6	3.0
1986	72.6	50.1	18.7	3.7
1987	84.5	58.1	23.1	3.3
1988	102.3	64.9	31.9	5.5
1989	100.6	62.9	33.9	3.8
1990	102.9	65.3	34.9	2.7
1991	115.5	68.9	43.7	3.0
1992	192.0	79.1	110.1	2.8
1993	398.6	111.9	275.2	2.6
1994	432.1	92.7	337.7	1.8
1995	481.3	103.3	375.2	2.8
1996	548.0	126.7	417.3	4.1
1997	644.08	120.21	452.57	71.30

Source: State Statistical Bureau (1998).

other Asian emerging market economies. Within the total foreign debt, only about 30 per cent is short-term. This has made China less vulnerable to the risks of international financial markets.

FDI[2] has made a positive contribution to China's growth, exports, employment, technology upgrading and institutional transformation. FDI was accounted as 11.7 per cent of total fixed asset investment in 1997 (Table 2.4).

Foreign funded companies, including joint ventures, have created about 6 million jobs and produced more than 14 per cent of industrial output and more than 40 per cent of exports (Tables 2.5 and 2.6). Despite the trade

Table 2.4 Contribution of FDI to the investment in fixed assets

	Total investment in fixed assets	*Investment in capital construction*	*Investment in technological upgrading*
1985	3.6	6.8	1.2
1990	6.3	13.1	4.1
1991	5.7	11.3	3.6
1992	5.8	11.1	3.6
1993	7.3	9.9	3.9
1994	9.9	14.2	7.3
1995	11.2	14.3	9.7
1996	11.7	14.3	9.8

Source: State Statistical Bureau (1997).

Table 2.5 FDI contribution to imports and exports

Year	*As % of total trade*	*As % of total exports*	*As % of total imports*
1988		5.2	
1989		9.4	
1990		12.6	
1991		16.7	
1992		20.4	
1993	34.3	27.5	40.2
1994	37.0	28.1	45.8
1995	39.1	31.3	47.7
1996	47.3	40.7	54.5
1997	47.0	41.0	54.6

Source: State Statistical Bureau (1996, 1997, 1998).

Table 2.6 FDI contribution to employment (10,000 persons)

	Total FDI	*Foreign funded companies*	*Hong Kong, Macao, Taiwan-funded companies*
1986	13	12	1
1987	21	20	1
1988	31	29	2
1989	47	43	4
1990	66	62	4
1991	165	96	69
1992	221	138	83
1993	288	133	155
1994	406	195	211
1995	513	241	272
1996	540	275	265
1997	581	300	281

Source: State Statistical Bureau (1998).

barriers, FDI brings international competition into the economy. It could well be proved that those sectors where foreign-funded companies become institutionally competitive at a faster pace end up raising the standards of business even faster. Indeed, the spill-over effects of foreign investment and the joint ventures' operations in China may be hard to measure, but they are easy to observe. People learn much more from local foreign competitors or bosses than from their overseas competitors.

In the service sector, there has been a gradual market opening. About 24 per cent of a total of 73,658 FDI projects and 40 per cent of contracted FDI capital inflows were in the service sector by the end of 1997. The figures below refer to the situation at the end of 1997, if not otherwise indicated:

1 *Banking*. A total of 132 foreign banks opened their branches in China, eighteen of which were allowed to do Rmb business in certain areas: five foreign-owned banks, seven foreign joint-venture banks, one joint-venture investment bank, and five foreign financial and accounting firms.
2 *Insurance*. Of a total of twenty-five insurance companies in China, seven were foreign-owned, five were joint ventures. The foreign companies only conducted less than 1 per cent of total business in terms of insurance payment.
3 *Commerce*. While there were only two foreign joint-venture distribution companies registered, more than 200 retail foreign or joint-venture companies were run in China with 8 per cent of retail market share.
4 *Telecommunications*. Although almost all major international equipment producers have majority shares in the industrial sector, telecommunications are still monopolized by two state companies. Joint ventures have been allowed in this area only since China's entry into the World Trade Organization (WTO) in December 2001.
5 *Foreign trade*. Foreign firms can operate in fifteen 'bounded free trade zones' in the coastal areas. Experimental projects of joint-venture trading companies have only just started.
6 *Other sectors* (tourism, legal service, accounting, advertisement). They have been more open to foreign investors and companies.

Potential negative impacts of further market liberalization

Generally speaking, the current 'negative developments' such as unemployment, income disparities, regional differences or corruption have been mainly related to domestic reforms and development, despite the impact of the market's gradual liberalization (increase of imports and FDI) at the domestic level. Yet it is hard to separate the effects of reform and opening, as they are both tightly correlated. Thus, I discuss in the following section the 'potential negative impacts' assuming that the Chinese market will be fully liberalized at a rapid pace in the near future, given other conditions, such as today's institutions and economic structure.

Unemployment in general

It is meaningless to talk about a 'boundless global economy' when no country opens its borders to Chinese migrants and no one else but the Chinese themselves have to deal with the problem of China's unemployment, just like any other country in this segmented world.

As a low income economy (US$856 GDP per capita in 2000) with the largest population in the world (almost 1.3 billion), China has the comparative advantage of low labour costs, given a certain level of education. This situation implies that China can generate new jobs in labour-intensive industries prospering through exports and FDI (Table 2.7).

Table 2.7 Comparing labour costs in Asia (average payment per week for labour in the manufacturing industry, in US$)

	China	*Hong Kong*	*Indonesia*	*Malaysia*	*The Philippines*	*Thailand*	*Republic of Korea*	*Taiwan*
Current	26.90	339.10	40.40	98.30	55.20	92.50	318.50	311.90
Cost difference (1997)*	1.00	12.60	1.50	3.70	2.10	3.40	11.80	11.60
Estimated value of 1998**	30.00	436.60	31.70	77.90	47.40	58.30	243.70	328.90
Cost difference (1998)***	1.00	14.60	1.06	2.60	1.58	1.94	8.12	10.96
Exchange rate (June 1997)	8.31	7.75	2432.00	2.64	26.38	24.70	888.00	27.81
Estimated exchange rate (1998)	8.28	7.75	3570.00	3.50	35.44	45.00	1350.00	35.50

Source: Hu (1998).

Notes:

* Payments for labour measured by local currency include wages and estimated social security expenses. Payments are calculated in US$, using the average exchange rate of June 1997.

** Ratio of average labour cost per week to that of China.

*** Suppose nominal wage growth rate is the same as nominal GDP growth rate. Local monetary cost is calculated in US$ by the estimated exchange rate of 1998.

As a potential market of 1.3 billion people, no one can afford to overlook the Chinese market. The Middle Kingdom ought to enjoy more new job opportunities created directly or indirectly by foreign investors whose major concern is long-term market shares, and not labour costs.

But no matter what the forms of market opening, trade liberalization and free foreign investment – which are crucial priorities for all countries – will have an important impact on existing domestic jobs. First, in most industries, free imports may quickly take over many domestic markets and cut the existing jobs; second, foreign investment may eliminate existing jobs if domestic firms are economically inefficient.

As predicted from the logic of political economy, we may expect more protections to emerge in the following three areas:

1 Established (traditional) industries where there are jobs and interest groups. New industries (electronics and computers), which did not exist before in China, have met less resistance to the opening process.
2 Sectors dominated by institutionally inefficient enterprises, i.e. the state-owned enterprises (SOEs). They are less competitive. Whichever form they take, either labour-intensive or technology-intensive, all other

enterprises are usually much more efficient than SOEs, but they may be forced out of business, as there is no protection against free entry.

3 Those areas that a country does not allow foreigners to dominate. The bigger the country, the more abundant these areas will be. This has much to do with national pride, ideology, and political structure.

From these points of view, China has many reasons to establish a whole set of protections, despite the consensus reached by policy-makers with regard to its position as a global player in the long run. A fast market liberalization will quickly eliminate jobs in sectors such as agriculture – which still provides more than 300 million basic low income jobs – or the traditional industries where the SOEs were established under the Soviet-type planning system for about 10 million politically and economically most prestigious state workers. The political opposition to fast market liberalization might emerge here.

With 300 million farmers working on 7 per cent of the world's cultivable land and about 0.1 acre of farmland per rural resident, it is economically difficult to use modern technologies to achieve an efficient economy of scale in China's agriculture. It is not a technological problem, but rather an employment constraint. As a result, China's rural labour productivity has been low compared with other major grain producers in the world (Table 2.8).

Table 2.8 Real agricultural growth rate, cultivated area and agricultural productivity of different countries in 1996

	Real agricultural growth rate (1990–94)		*Cultivated area per capita*		*Agricultural productivity*	
	Amount (%)	*Ranking*	*Amount (m^2)*	*Ranking*	*Amount (US$ per person)*	*Ranking*
China	4.10	2	792	36	328	42
India	2.88	9	1847	28	50	43
Japan	−2.84	38	354	42	26283	15
Indonesia	2.99	8	1582	30	767	41
Thailand	3.13	7	3543	15	825	40
France	0.40	25	3366	16	29513	11
German	–	–	1476	32	20159	20
Spain	−1.04	30	5142	7	14518	24
Russia	−0.90	28	8941	4	3753	33
Australia	–	27	26455	1	26316	14
United States	−1.15	–	7204	6	29544	10
Canada		31	15500	2	25153	16
Mexico	1.14	21	2659	24	3284	35
Argentina	1.22	19	7925	5	13160	25
Brazil	3.23	6	3226	20	–	–

Source: Institute for Management Development (1997).

Most grain prices are higher at the domestic level than in the international market. Nevertheless, domestic grain prices are still too low, considering the rural–urban income disparity. The Chinese government recently tried to change the grain procurement and distribution system in order to increase domestic prices rather than lowering them. In such a situation, it is difficult for China to further open its agricultural market in a rapid way, although the increase in imports in the long run is a policy option, as long as industrialization can draw the majority of farmers out of agriculture. Some studies show that if China liberalizes all its agricultural market now, it would lose about 20 million (19.21 million) jobs, accounting for 46.2 per cent of total farming employment.

Another reason for China to choose a self-reliance policy on agriculture is the concern about the 'food security'. With the recent memory of famine and grain embargo in the early 1960s, it is politically difficult to convince policy-makers to adopt a policy of agricultural globalization in the near future, despite the World Trade Organization's requirements.

SOEs and manufacturing industries

China has a low labour cost advantage (Table 2.7). Nevertheless, labour productivity is low in most industries, compared to other countries. Therefore, Chinese industries may not be internationally competitive except for some highly labour-intensive sectors (Tables 2.9a–b).

China developed its industrial system under the pre-reform central planning system with a high concentration of state ownership. As a result, China now faces very serious efficiency problems in many industries, as the performance of SOEs has been deteriorating (Table 2.10).

In recent years, there have been massive lay-offs of state workers as a result of structural adjustment. More lay-offs are expected in the near future: people are more convinced with the lessons from the Asian Crisis that reform has to go even further. But the demand for the protection of industries against free trade and FDI are still there and remain strong. The positive aspect is that both the central government and the local authorities have been encouraging foreign investment, hoping that it will play a constructive role in restructuring the industry with higher levels of growth without causing further unemployment. In order to deal with the increasing unemployment of state employees (Table 2.11), new programmes have been adopted since 1998, through the creation of 'urban re-employment centres'.[3]

These centres are financed by equal shares from central government, the city government and the SOEs that are laying off their workers: state workers who have not received their minimum payment (based on each city's minimum wage standard) for months or years, as their companies have been closed down or have run out of business, are now are transferred to these centres. This way, the government makes sure that the *de facto* unemployed state workers obtain their 'laid-off worker' status and get payed.

The increasing unemployment in China cannot be entirely blamed on globalization. On the one hand, the system of SOEs and state banks needs to undertake painful restructuring sooner or later. On the other hand, the growth of the domestic private sector also puts competition pressures on

Table 2.9a Manufacturing industries productivity of China, the United States and Japan

Sector	*Productivity of United States (US$) (1)*	*Productivity of Japan (US$) (2)*	*Productivity of China (US$) (3)*	*(3)/(1) ×100%*	*(3)/(2) ×100%*
Food	102,527	77,297	2,029	1.98	2.60
Beverage	183,824	173,466	2,764	1.50	1.59
Tobacco	567,568	393,587	22,277	3.92	5.66
Textile products	49,457	52,704	1,220	2.47	2.31
Garments	36,316	31,412	1,508	4.15	4.80
Leather products	45,455	51,746	1,553	3.42	3.00
Footwear	38,462	51,273			
Wood products	56,000	59,495	1,043	1.86	1.75
Furniture and decoration	44,706	63,880	1,317	2.95	2.06
Paper and related products	96,939	108,614	1,492	1.54	1.37
Printing and publishing	78,000	103,691	1,332	1.71	1.28
Industrial chemical products	191,099	250,188	2,296	1.20	0.92
Other chemical products	206,544	265,874	3,198	1.55	1.20
Petroleum and coal products	121,951	152,746	8,364	6.86	5.48
Rubber products	76,923	92,384	1,659	2.16	1.80
Plastic products	66,486	86,248	1,650	2.48	1.91
Petroleum refinery	260,274	574,827		0.00	0.00
Ceramics	54,054	59,699			
Glass and glassware	83,969	132,456			
Other non-metal mineral products	74,850	106,855	1,333	1.78	1.25

Sources: Statistics on the Third National Industry Census in 1995.

Note:
Data from the United States and Japan is for 1993; data from China is for 1995.

Table 2.9b Manufacturing industries productivity of China, the United States and Japan

Sector	*Productivity of United States (US$) (1)*	*Productivity of Japan (US$) (2)*	*Productivity of China (US$) (3)*	*(3)/(1) ×100%*	*(3)/(2) ×100%*
Iron and steel products	89,918	158,219	3,234	3.60	2.04
Nonferrous metals	73,276	109,732	2,888	3.94	2.63
Metal products	62,550	88,693	1,603	2.56	1.81
Non-electric equipment and machinery	80,436	99,101	1,573	1.96	1.59
Electric equipment and machinery	91,214	87,910	2,888	3.17	3.29
Transport equipment	101,449	121,156	2,266	2.23	1.87
Equipment for special purpose and science	104,242	73,473	1,514	1.45	2.06
Others	60,274	82,777			
Average	110,670	132,505	3,087	2.97	2.33

Sources: Same as Table 9a.

Note:
Data from the United States and Japan are for 1993; data from China are for 1995.

SOEs, forcing them to change (Table 2.12). Thus, globalization appears more as an additional factor in the process.

China's financial sector may be viewed as an 'infant industry', due to the following circumstances. First, Chinese banks only started to do real banking business recently. Before, they were rather governmental departments for financial resource allocation (Table 2.13). Second, the security market only began to develop in 1992. Third, the insurance industry launched its business less than five years ago. Fourth, many financial regulations are non-existant and the regulators are as immature as the market itself. Finally, and perhaps most important, private financial services in China have not been developed very far, and domestic competition in this industry has been very weak and has prevented the government from being confident to open the market.

Despite its shortcomings, the Chinese financial sector hires about 3 million workers, the majority of them being state employees. Foreign competition in the financial service sector has been rejected by this powerful interest group, as there is a fear that foreign banks could first draw out all the best human capital from the Chinese banks, and then swipe away their business, as they are bound to be much more cost-effective.

Table 2.10 Financial performance of major SOEs*

	1978	*1980*	*1985*	*1990*	*1995*	*1996*	*1997*
Profit rates**	15.5	16.0	13.2	3.2	1.4	0.78	0.79
Profits and taxes as % of total assets value***	24.2	24.8	23.5	12.4	6.4	7.11	7.02
Profits and taxes as % of output value	24.9	24.1	21.8	12	9.2	8.20	
Revenues from state sector as % of total budgetary revenue	n.a.		82	66.8	65.8		
Total losses (bill. Rmb)	4.2	3.4	3.2	34.9	54.1	79.68	74.44
Total losses as % of total profits	8.2	5.8	4.3	89.8	81.2	191.90	165.10
Subsidies for losses (bill. Rmb)	n.a.		32.5	57.9	32.8		
Loss-subsidies as % of budgetary revenues	n.a.	14.3	17	14.1	5.3		

Source: State Statistical Bureau (1990–96).

Notes:

* Large and medium SOEs with independent accounting.

** The State Statistical Bureau stopped providing the 'profit rate' in 1994. Thus, some figures in the table are calculated using other data available.

*** The definition of 'profits and taxes total' is different from 'pre-tax profits' because it includes all sales tax or value-added tax, and not only the income tax.

Table 2.11 Laid-off state employees in China, 1994–2000

	1994	*1995*	*1996*	*1997*	*1998**	*1999**	*2000**
Number of registered laid-off workers in urban areas (10,000 persons)**	180	n.a.	891	1,274	1,624	1,974	2,324

Sources: National Economic Research Institute (1998).

Notes:

* These three columns are estimations according to Zhang Zuoji (Head of the Ministry of Labour and Social Security).

** All figures refer to 'total layoff to date', including those who have already been re-employed after being laid-off for a while.

The Asian Crisis has made the Chinese government and the financial industry more cautious about the opening of the economy. Capital account convertibility and liberalization of the capital market have been removed from the government's agenda for the near future, although this attitude might have to change with the WTO pressures, and the banking and insurance sectors will need to be opened by 2005 or so. Once more, this proves that pressure from globalization plays a significant role in domestic reforms and development.

Table 2.12 Main indicators of the economic performance of different ownerships (%)

	Market share	*Overall productivity (Rmb/Person)*	*Ratio of return* to cost (%)*	*Ratio of return* to net assets (%)*	*Ratio of return* to gross assets (%)*
SOEs	29.31	18985.0	2.72	8.72	4.10
Privately owned enterprises	0.25	25713.7	2.56	18.51	24.58
Share holding enterprises	5.10	31435.9	8.23	10.68	10.27
Foreign funded enterprises	17.04	36154.6	4.15	8.22	7.43

Source: National Economic Research Institute (1998).

Note:

* Here 'returns' refers not only to profits, but also to 'tax payment'.

Table 2.13 Competitiveness ranking of the financial system of major economies

Economies	*Cost of capital*	*Capital efficiency*	*Stock markets dynamics*	*Banking sector efficiency*	*Performance of capital markets and quality of financial services*	*Overall national competitiveness of the financial system*
United States	5	5	1	6	1 (1)	1
Japan	3	29	7	1	5 (23)	9
Netherlands	4	1	9	7	2 (2)	6
Denmark	7	2	6	8	4 (4)	8
Switzerland	1	20	2	4	3 (3)	7
Germany	2	18	14	3	9 (7)	14
United Kingdom	6	6	3	17	8 (6)	11
Singapore	10	8	4	5	6 (10)	2
Hong Kong	19	4	8	22	12 (9)	3
Taiwan	22	34	18	12	23 (19)	23
Republic of Korea	30	44	33	41	43 (45)	30
Russia	17	46	42	46	46 (46)	46
Poland	40	45	44	44	45 (43)	43
Czech Republic	33	38	38	36	35 (36)	35
Venezuela	12	30	45	45	32 (37)	45
Argentina	43	28	28	31	31 (32)	28
Brazil	46	39	25	32	41 (41)	33
Mexico	38	41	40	43	42 (39)	40
Chile	25	19	23	27	24 (24)	24
South Africa	44	35	30	33	36 (31)	44
China	31	43	36	26	40 (42)	27

Source: Institute for Management Development (1997, 1998).

Note:

1998 Rankings are in brackets.

Inter-region and inter-group income disparity

As shown in Table 2.14, regional disparities have increased in China since the launching of reforms in the late 1970s.

It is easy to run a regression on the relationship of foreign investment, growth of export industries and regional income, proving that there is always a significant correlation. The same happens for the income disparity between different groups: foreign investment or export-related work increases the income for the highly educated urban elite, while others, especially rural labourers, remain poor. In fact, the Gini coefficient has been rising since the mid-1980's, as shown in Table 2.15.

China risks developing some sort of 'dual economy', especially if industrialization and urbanization cannot progress fast enough to involve

Table 2.14 Regional income disparity between 1988 and 1995

		1988			*1995*		
Grouped samples	*Year*	*Total disparity*	*Intra-group disparity*	*Inter-group disparity*	*Total disparity*	*Intra-group disparity*	*Inter-group disparity*
Rural–urban	1988	258.31	159.6	98.7	253.3	145.6	107.7
	(%)	(100.00)	(61.8)	(38.2)	(100)	(57.5)	(42.5)
	1995	378.41	255.9	122.5	373.14	242.3	130.9
	(%)	(100.00)	(67.6)	(32.36)	(100)	(64.9)	(35.1)
East–middle–west	1988	258.31	238.8	19.5	253.3	233.6	19.7
	(%)	(100)	(92.5)	(7.5)	(100)	(92.2)	(7.8)
	1995	378.41	343.1	35.4	373.14	336.9	36.2
	(%)	(100.00)	(90.7)	(9.3)	(100)	(90.3)	(9.7)
Six large regions*	1988	258.31	138.4	119.9	253.3	125.8	127.5
	(%)	(100.00)	(53.6)	(46.4)	(100)	(49.7)	(50.3)
	1995	378.41	206.6	171.8	373.14	202.7	170.4
	(%)	(100.00)	(54.6)	(45.4)	(100)	(54.3)	(45.7)

Source: Li et al. (1998).

Note:

* These 'Six Large Regions' are referred as eastern-rural, middle-rural, western-rural, eastern-urban, middle-urban and western-urban areas.

Table 2.15 Changes in the Gini coefficient

	1988	*1995*
Rural areas	0.338	0.429
Urban areas	0.233	0.286
National	0.375	0.445

Source: Li et al. (1998).

more rural people (200 million 'pure farmers' and 150 million rural non-farming workers), moving them to higher-income on-farming jobs, no matter where the jobs are geographically speaking, since domestic migration can play a very important and positive role in transforming the economy. But the income disparity can take place anyway, even without the effects of globalization in a country with 1.3 billion people, 70 per cent of them living in rural areas, and with a distorted allocation of resources. Globalization here is a positive change and provides an engine for economic growth and restructuring, that is, it speeds up the process.

Two economic policies adopted by the central government will effectively improve the situation, or at least prevent it from worsening: the development of the domestic market and urbanization.

In the post-Asian Crisis context, the Chinese government has emphasized the development of the domestic market, rather than pushing for more exports. As the domestic market enlargement mainly depends on the increase of the rural population's purchasing power in domestically produced goods, the macroeconomic expansionary policy will have positive impacts on further narrowing the income disparity. The efforts of the banking sector to increase loans to small businesses will also contribute to create jobs for low-income people.

Although urbanization is not a new policy, it is considered as a priority development strategy. The development of small cities and the urbanization of rural towns will create new jobs. This strategy needs to evolve with industrialization. Relaxing some restrictions, such as the urban registration system (*hukou*),[4] against domestic migration will also reduce the problem in a very positive way.

Impacts of the Asian Crisis and subsequent policies

China has been affected by the ongoing Asian financial crisis in three major areas: exports, imports and foreign investment.

1 Exports to the region in crisis have decreased. Exports to Asian countries dropped by 13 per cent (Association of South-East Asian Nations), to 31 per cent (Korea) in the first half of 1998, compared to the same period of 1999. The exports to the United States and Europe increased by 18 per cent and 17.4 per cent, respectively.
2 Imports increased. Although imports have decreased in terms of value, they have actually increased, due to the significant devaluation of Asian currencies. Smuggling also became more prominent in the first half of 1998 due to the enlarged price incentives.
3 Foreign investment from the Asian region significantly diminished, although China managed to keep FDI growing at 2.7 per cent in 1998 (Table 2.16).

Table 2.16 Foreign direct investment, 1998 (US$bn)

	Contracted $	*Growth %*	*Realized $*	*Growth %*	*% as total*
Total	24.20	5.53	20.44	−1.31	100.00
East Asia 10	12.29	−22.00	14.50	−9.10	79.30
Hong Kong	7.16	−18.20	91.06	−11.00	53.10
Japan	1.35	11.70	1.20	−28.10	8.10
Europe	3.38	65.20	19.73	28.70	6.10
US	3.21	89.20	1.73	25.90	7.90

Source: MOFTEC, September 1998, internal documents.

The main policy focuses on increasing domestic demand and controling the currency at a fixed exchange rate:

1 Fiscal expansion. About 100 billion Rmb additional government bonds have been issued to finance the public investment projects in infrastructure.
2 More policy loans have been given to infrastructure projects.
3 More loans to small private or non-state firms have been encouraged by the government.
4 Interest rates have been cut, in order to offset the impacts of deflation and to encourage consumption.
5 The foreign exchange system has been more restrictively enforced in order to reduce the capital flight resulting from the speculation on the Rmb devaluation.

The expansionary policy in 1998 was necessary to prevent the domestic market from shrinking even further. However, economic growth slowdown and deflation were mainly caused by the austerity macroeconomic policies since 1993 and the domestic problem of non-performing loans (NPLs), rather than the Asian Crisis itself. The Asian Crisis and the ongoing global market turmoil have shown that external market conditions for China are going to be less favourable than those enjoyed by Japan and the newly industrialised economies (NIEs – the 'Asian Dragons') in the 1970s and 1980s. Thus, China now has to pay more attention to the development of its domestic market.

How to achieve further 'compatible opening'

Will fast market liberalization solve the problems?

It is often suggested that China's increasing opening will be helpful in solving its economic problems. In the long run, this may be true. But in the short run, only 'compatible opening' will be effective. An 'excessive opening' or a 'limited opening' may not be desirable, after all. For example, opening even further the financial service sector to foreign banks is something strongly advocated by foreign bank managers, international organizations, and some economists in the developed countries. Nevertheless, China's current problems may not be entirely solved. When the banking sector is liberalized, many foreign banks will operate in the Chinese market. As a result, foreign investment may increase, due to the improvement of banking conditions. Some Chinese firms may also benefit from the improvement of banking services, as the financial system's development could speed up as a result of competition. But there may also be shortcomings:

1 Foreign banks will not work with heavily indebted SOEs, and may even not want to take over the insolvent state banks. The problems of most SOEs are fundamentally domestic. Thus, the solutions will remain domestic too.
2 All foreign banks coming into China will be big multinationals. As they do not provide 'micro loans', which are needed locally at the grassroots level, foreign banks will not contribute to the development of the small Chinese local private sector.
3 Meanwhile, foreign banks will kill all Chinese state banks, if full liberalization takes place. This situation will provoke massive state employee layoffs, social unrest, and therefore an interruption of the rhythm of economic growth.

In other words, the opening process is helpful, but it has to be 'compatible' with China's domestic situation.

Reforms and opening

Reforms and opening have to go hand by hand for the following reasons: first, without reforms, opening is politically impossible and unacceptable; and second, without opening, it is impossible to know what needs to be reformed in order to be competitive in the world market.

Whether or not China can speed up its opening process, such as liberalizing its capital account and service sector, will very much depend on how the SOE reforms and the state-owned and controlled banking sector evolve. In addition, the quick liberalization of the capital account in an unhealthy domestic capital market will simply lead to capital flights, to an imbalance of international payments, or even to a financial crisis, as clearly shown by some of the Asian economies or Russia.

At the domestic political economy level, as mentioned in previous sections, a quick opening would easily eliminate millions of jobs from the inefficient SOEs and insolvent state banks. Thus, a great number of SOEs ought to be closed down. But this should be done in a gradual process (it may take about five to ten years), in order to allow the economy to deal with the subsequent unemployment problem in a manageable way. The state banks should perhaps be privatized and more private or non-state banks be developed, allowing an increase in competition in the domestic banking sector: banks may then survive the competition from sophisticated and experienced foreign banks. Nevertheless, this is not a short-term issue. It might also take about five to ten years, considering the tight links between SOEs and banking reforms. Of course, these time dimensions of the reform process may be optimistic, as they are based on an optimistic scenario, without assuming major crises ahead.

The question is how can China speed up the reforms? Or otherwise stated, what should China do about the SOEs and the state banks? Although these topics cannot be addressed adequately here, I assume that reforms take time, say five to ten years, during which: (1) the size of the state sector will be gradually reduced with the privatization and dismantling of SOEs, and the growth of the private sector; (2) the non-state banks and financial firms will develop gradually, while the state banks might include partial privatization, resulting in higher degrees of domestic competition; (3) the government will gradually improve its capability of regulating the financial market; (4) the domestic capital market will develop further with the progress made in the SOE reforms and the development of a consistent legal system; (5) political reform will eventually take place; etc.

Thus, the real question is how can China go about its opening during these five to ten years, given all the above assumptions.

'Compatible opening' vs. 'sequencing'

What China should do is to continue its gradual opening process, always ensuring that it is compatible with the progress of reforms. This is in fact the main difference between the concepts of 'sequencing liberalization' and 'compatible opening'. If 'sequencing' is generally referred as to the 'you do not do B until you finish A' situation, 'compatible opening' refers to the situation in which 'you push for 30 per cent A, while you are pushing forward for 30 per cent B at the same time'.

The ideal situation should include 'enhancing and promoting each other': 35 per cent of A may speed up B, which is at a level of 30 per cent. When A is at a 35 per cent level, then B needs to go up by 40 per cent, and therefore contribute to 'pull up' A. It may not be wise to use 50 per cent of A to promote B at a level of 30 per cent, as in that case incompatibility may occur. In reality, the issue is not 'whether we should open or not', but 'how much we should open' in view of the existing domestic constraints.

Summing up, compatible opening means that both reform and opening go hand in hand: neither of them should go too fast (incompatible), or too slow (incompatible too). And they should support each other. For instance, China should not wait for SOE reforms to be accomplished and only then open its manufacturing industries. It should allow foreign direct investors to come in, first with some restrictive regulations, but then relaxing them gradually, according to the progress achieved in the reforms and the development of domestic non-state enterprises. This is what China has been doing with remarkable success in terms of both involvement of FDI and its 'spill-over effects' on SOE reforms.

China needs to allow foreign banks, insurance companies and other financial service firms to start up businesses in China from the early stage of development of the financial sector, but with no rush. It should start with a limited number of companies. Then, along with the development of local non-state banks, the state bank reforms, the improvement of the regulatory capability (regulators are at last starting to understand the functioning of the banking business and the financial market, which are still so new to them) and the legal framework, an increasing number of banks and other financial firms will gradually increase and be more competitive.

China should soon allow a selected number of investment funds to be invested in its financial market under capital control. At the beginning, the control may include a relatively long period of 'static' requirements (just as Chile has done). Then, with the development of the capital market, the SOE reforms, the banking reforms, and the risk management improvements, China may allow more investors to do business in portfolio investment and shorten the stay requirement, in order to move gradually to the full liberalization of the capital account.

Another difference between 'compatible opening' and the theoretical concept of the 'sequencing approach' is that the former may be more 'chaotic' and 'path-dependent' than the latter. It is not a well-planned process, as the reform-minded policy-makers do whatever they are able to do under the political constraints imposed by other areas. There might be no timetable at all, but when there is, it ought to be parallel to the reform process. For example, a ten-year plan for reform should be accompanied by a ten-year plan for opening.

The 'sequencing approach' has been for a long time the basic notion in the theory of market liberalization. Unfortunately, there has never been a real case of sequencing in operation, except for technical preparations involved in certain phases of market liberalization. Neither today nor in the past of China's development there has been a known case of 'sequencing'. This is perhaps due to two reasons: on the one hand, political reality never allows for well-planned sequencing, as political decision-makers are only able to do what the situation allows them to; on the other hand, those who admit the need of 'sequencing opening' usually forget it soon after. This happens for instance with 'free market advocates', who usually force developing countries to open their market in an accelerated way.

The 'sequencing approach' may also not work, as it is difficult to check if the previous step has been accomplished and the next step should be taken.

The process of reform and opening is so complicated and has so many aspects that a single 'sign' of one particular aspect may not mean much. And if we wait for all aspects to reach the 'sign', the whole process may become too cumbersome. This is also a problem for the 'compatible opening' approach, as it is necessary to know if a policy in one particular aspect is compatible with other areas. Nevertheless, 'compatible opening' requires no 'signs' to check. Instead, policy-makers need to start as early as possible to move gradually in all areas and allow the achievements to accumulate.

But is 'compatible opening' a 'half-way (or half-minded) opening'? Yes, in some sense, but this need not be a criticism. The 'half-way opening' may be a pragmatic step on the way to 'complete opening'. In fact, one of the lessons of the Asian Crisis is not that the instability was caused by a lack of opening, but that the crisis was caused by a 'complete opening' before a 'complete reform'.

The gradual approach of compatible opening may generate unfair competition and rent-seeking activities, as it is a government-managed process and may only allow a few competitors to come into the market at the beginning. However, there is nothing without costs. The only question is if this approach is more costly than others.

'Compatible opening' speed does not mean a 'slow opening'. After all, a rapid 'excessive opening' may lead to crises and setbacks that eventually make the whole process rather slower. In addition, reforms and globalization require encouragement, determination, political willingness, and the clear view of mission. The rapidly changing world pushes countries to move as quickly as possible to catch up: the developing countries should do things quicker if they want to succeed in the future. Therefore, the best policy recommendation is to react as quickly as possible in all areas, but always to keep in mind the situation of other sectors in the economy. The main point of this chapter is not that the opening process should be slow, but that speeding up the opening without considering the progress of domestic reforms would be unwise. Unfortunately, this mistaken policy has been too common both before and even after the Asian Crisis.

Timetable for opening

Setting up a timetable for market liberalization can be a very useful tool to speed up the process of reform. The pro-opening interest groups can use such a timetable to 'attack' the anti-opening groups in order to get the process to move quicker, citing 'national obligations'. It is also useful for the breakdown of bureaucratic barriers to reforms.

The key issue here is still how the timetable for opening is realistically and positively compatible with the timetable for reforms. This is not only a matter of scientific analysis, but also of conflict of interests. Interest groups may have differing opinions on the desirable speed of reform and opening, as they may be affected by the timetable differently; similarly, international players may differ from domestic groups for the same reason. A good example has been China's bid for accession to the WTO: while everybody agreed that China needed a period of transition, everybody differed on how long that transitional period should be. In the international arena, the issue of a timetable for opening is actually no more than the issue of 'international pressures'. But for the developing country, having a 'right' timetable is crucial. The problem is to get to an agreement with other international players. An excessively 'quick' timetable that satisfies foreigners' interests will not be acceptable to domestic interest groups such as workers, peasants and bank employees, and vice versa. From the policy-making and implementation points of view, an excessively slow timetable is useless, but an excessively fast one will be not useful either, as it cannot be actually implemented and may cause problems for the government's credibility. Thus, while the timetable may be an appropriate policy instrument, in reality it may not always work as expected.

There is no universal solution

It can be said that China's process of opening has so far brought some positive results. Even the negative impacts such as market competition, increasing unemployment and bankruptcy pressures can be said to have constructive aspects rather than being wholly destructive. Nevertheless, the speed of opening needs to be constantly monitored by policy-makers. An overly slow and cautious policy may be costly, but so too may be a rapid process entailing economic instability and social unrest. Specific policies leading to market liberalization need careful assessment at each stage in order to reach their long-term goal.

Notes

1 There is a small portion of 'B shares', namely the shares exclusively tradable against foreign exchange, in the stock market.
2 The concept of 'foreign investment' here refers to all 'overseas' investments, including those from Hong Kong, Macao and Taiwan.
3 Refer to Naughton, Fernández-Stembridge and Rocca in this volume for further details.
4 Most articles in this volume refer to the household registration (*hukou*), mostly in Part II.

References and further reading

Byrd, William A. and Lin, Qingsong (eds) (1990) *China's Rural Industry: Structure, Development, and Reform*. Oxford and New York, Oxford University Press.

Chen, Chien-Hsun (1996) 'Regional Determinants of Foreign Direct Investment in Mainland China'. *Journal of Economic Studies*, vol. 23, no. 2, pp. 18–30.

China Financial Statistics Yearbook (various years). Beijing, China Financial Press.

Clerides, Sofronis, Lach, Saul and Tybout, James (1996) 'Is 'Learning-by-Exporting' Important? Micro Dynamic Evidence from Colombia, Mexico and Morocco'. Working Paper no. W5715, NBER. *Quarterly Journal of Economics*, vol. 113, no. 454, issue 3 (August), pp. 903–947.

Cornia, Giovanni Andrea (1994) 'Income Distribution, Poverty and Welfare in Transitional Economies: A Comparison Between Eastern Europe and China'. *Journal of International Development*, vol. 6, no. 5 (September), pp. 569–607.

Fan, Gang (1994) 'Incremental Changes and Dual-Track Transition: Understanding the Case of China'. *Economic Policy,* issue 19 (December), pp. 99–122.

Hakimian, Hassan (1998) *From East to West Asia: Lessons of Globalization, Crisis and Economic Reform*. Working Paper no. 82. London, School of Oriental and African Studies.

He, Liping (1997) 'Taiguo jinrong weiji ji qi guoji yingxiang' (Causes of Thailand's Financial Crisis and its International Impacts). *Gaige* (June), pp. 25–33.

Hu, Zuliu (1998) 'Yazhou weiji hou de zhongguo waihui zhengce' (China's Exchange Rate Policy after the Asian Crisis). *Jinrong yanjiu*, no. 3 (March), pp. 16–19.

Institute for Management Development (1997, 1998) *The World Competitiveness Yearbook*. Cologny and Geneva, The Foundation.

Li, Shi, Zhao, Renwei and Zhang, Ping (1998) 'Zhongguo jingji gaige yi shouru fenpei de bianhua' (China's Economic Transition and the Change in Income Distribution). *Jingji yanjiu*, no. 4 (April), pp. 42–51.

National Economic Research Institute (NERI) (1998) *Zhongguo hongguan jingji fenxi* (China Macroeconomic Analysis). May Newsletter. Beijing.

Nunberg, Barbara (1989) *Public Sector Pay and Employment Reform: A Review of the World Bank Experience*. World Bank Discussion Papers no. 68. Washington DC, World Bank.

O'Cornor, David and Lunati, Maria Rosa (1998) 'Labour Market Aspects of State Enterprise Reform in China'. Working Paper no. 141 (October). OECD Centre.

Rama, Martín (1997) *Efficient Public Sector Downsizing*. Policy Research Working Paper no. 1840. Washington DC, World Bank.

State Statistical Bureau of the PRC (various years) *Zhongguo guding zichan touzi tongji nianjian* (China Fixed Investment Statistical Yearbook). Beijing, Zhongguo tongji chubanshe.

—— (various years) *Zhongguo gongye jingji tongji nianjian* (China Industrial Economy Statistical Yearbook). Beijing, Zhongguo tongji chubanshe.

—— (various years) Zhongguo gongye tongjinianjian *Zhongguo tongji nianjian* (China Statistical Yearbook). Beijing, Zhongguo tongji chubanshe.

Statistics on the Third National Industry Census in 1995 (1995). Beijing, China Statistics Press.

United Nations Development Programme (UNDP) (1996) *China: Urban Employment Promotion and Re-employment Policies*. Report prepared under UNDP Technical Support Services 1 (TSS1). New York, UNDP.

Vernon, Raymond (1996) 'International Investment and International Trade in the Product Cycle'. *Quarterly Journal of Economics*, no. 80 (May), pp. 190–207.

Wei, Shang-Jin (1993) *Open Door Policy and China's Rapid Growth: Evidence from City-level Data*. NBER Working paper no. 4602. Cambridge MA, National Bureau of Economic Research.

White, Gordon (1997) 'Social Security Reforms in China's Economic Transition: Towards "Market Socialism"?' *Mondes en Développement*, vol. 25, no. 99, pp. 57–72.

World Bank (1994) *China: Foreign Trade Reform*. Washington DC, The World Bank.

—— (1997a) *China 2020: Development Challenges in the New Century*. China 2020 Series. Washington DC, World Bank.

—— (1997b) *Sharing Rising Incomes: Disparities in China*. China 2020 Series. Washington DC, World Bank.

Part II

RESHAPING THE SOCIAL COMPACT IN URBAN CHINA

3

STABILIZING POTENTIAL INSTABILITY

Re-employment in today's China

Leila Fernández-Stembridge

After the XVth Congress of the Chinese Communist Party (CCP) in September 1997, the broadening and acceleration of a modern enterprise system – already endorsed during the VIIIth National People's Congress in March 1993 – pushed the incremental and experimental process of state-owned enterprise (SOE) reforms to be reopened in a different fashion. With the diversification and increase in competition of different forms of ownership in the marketplace, the corporate governance system functioned through the motto of 'grasping the large (SOEs), and letting the small (SOEs) go'(*zhuada fangxiao*).[1] While this approach was initially welcome, it has ultimately shown serious shortcomings. The synchronized evolution of two key elements has created obstacles to the full absorption in the labour market of those workers who were laid-off as a result of the so-called 'enterprise restructuring'.[2] First, the legacy of the deceleration of the Chinese economy – with deflation rates (−2.6 per cent in 1998 and −3.0 per cent in 1999), relatively high interest rates (around 8–10 per cent in 1998–99), low levels of domestic demand (household consumption decreased from 9.1 per cent in 1996 to 4.2 per cent in 1997, slightly recuperating to 7.4 per cent in 1999),[3] and the declining external demand caused by the Asian Crisis in 1997–98 – has entailed a slowdown in job creation. Second, the increasing level of registered unemployment in urban areas (from 2.8 per cent in 1994 to 3.1 per cent in 1999)[4] created a potential loss of social cohesion. Many would argue that these elements have been inevitably interlinked, given that a general economic recession provokes a shortage of labour demand. Nevertheless, the problem is not so much about a decreasing rate of labour demand, but rather about an inefficient allocation of labour supply.

In that sense, the Chinese labour market, which underwent considerable development during the 1980s and 1990s (mostly at the urban level), still remains somewhat stagnated. Despite the progress made at the administrative level (e.g. increasing managerial autonomy), the separation between government and enterprise still remains incomplete: SOEs are still obliged to provide social services (housing, education, medical coverage) to some of their workers – including redundant ones (*fuyu renyuan*) – and their profitability and competitiveness suffer as a result. The incompatibility between the social needs of workers and the economic requirements of SOEs is therefore still far from disappearing as a whole.

In May 1993 the State Council issued a set of regulations establishing the so-called 're-employment programme' (*zaijiuye gongcheng*) (hereafter REP) pioneered in Shanghai and identified as a set of governmental policies designed to mitigate the unemployment crisis emerging from the disproportionate number of laid-off workers (*xiagang zhigong*)[5] associated with the SOE restructuring. The REP was later extended nationwide between 1996 and 1998. While it could be argued that the Chinese government's initiative of re-employing laid-off workers is a respectable starting point aimed at alleviating the symptomatic aspects of unemployment and thereby the preventing of social instability, the key question is whether the REP has been sufficient in fully guaranteeing the reallocation of this type of labour supply, considering the present and short-term perspectives of macroeconomic growth and the unpredictable real economic conditions of SOEs. After all, SOEs are still often forced to 'internalize' the unemployment problem by providing benefits to ex-employees. In this way laid-off employees are not unleashed on the labour market and do not add to the formal ranks of the unemployed. This consititutes a new type of 'iron rice bowl' system ('*tiefanwan*' – lifetime employment),[6] even if it is under a different guise and on a transitional basis.

This chapter is divided into the following three parts: first, a brief overview of the changing process of the traditional employment system through the SOE major reforms; second, an evaluation of the effectiveness of the re-employment project; finally, a discussion of a set of long-term initiatives that could plausibly help the Chinese labour market to avoid a distorted allocation of (redundant) labour supply and the upsurge of a new 'iron rice bowl' system.

SOE reforms: from the traditional employment system to a transitional period of labour absorption

During the 1950s, a traditional employment system was set up as a result of the creation of the household registration system (*hukou*)[7] with three distinct purposes:

1 to guarantee full employment to urban workers;
2 to keep down the wage rate of urban workers;
3 to divide rural from urban labour markets.[8]

All three aspects were integrated within the so-called heavy-industry-oriented strategy, which was implemented as the economic priority of the country. The contradiction was obvious: on the one hand, as the heavy industry sector was capital-intensive, it had a very low capacity of labour absorption; on the other hand, there was no open unemployment, but rather an implicit underemployment, as the majority of urban dwellers of working age had a job, though perhaps not one fully exploiting their human capital and productivity levels. Inevitably, the prices of the factors of production were distorted, as the problem of overstaffing led to the establishment of an institutional wage, rarely reflecting to the growth of labour productivity.[9] As a result, not only was the macroeconomic policy distorted, but the planned labour system was rather neutral to the variations of the economic environment. With the launching of economic reforms at the end of the 1970s, this situation could no longer be sustained.

That is why, from then on, the Chinese government has been making special efforts to reinvigorate the deteriorated state-owned sector, and by implication, the urban employment system. These efforts have been undertaken in the following four waves of SOE reforms (Table 3.1):

1 1978–83: increase of the SOEs' managerial autonomy;
2 1984–88: introduction of the so-called contract responsibility system (implying more freedom for SOEs to hire and fire workers);
3 1989–92: slowdown of labour reforms (SOEs are pressured to increase their quotas of labour demand);
4 1993–today: creation of a modern enterprise system (launching of a corporate governance system through the '*zhuada fangxiao*' policy).

As shown in Table 3.1, during the initial stage of SOE reforms (1978–83), SOEs' managers were given more autonomy and were allowed for the first time to retain a share of their profits. At the same time, the baby-boom children of the 1950s and 1960s were entering the labour market and urban dwellers who had been sent to the countryside were returning to the cities, which altogether increased the pressures on job creation. In order to avoid higher levels of unemployment, or further overstaffing, local governments promoted employment out of the state-owned sector, encouraging the development of small businesses (*getihu*). Unfortunately, price distorsions persisted, for which levels of efficiency and resource allocation remained insufficient.[10]

While the economy was being pushed to further marketization, a second wave of SOE reforms was launched between 1984 and 1988, allowing SOEs to respond to market forces with an increasing autonomy in establishing wages according to levels of productivity. In addition, SOEs were given more freedom to hire and fire workers, following their production needs. The so-called contract responsibility system (CRS), which had emerged by 1983 and

Table 3.1 Different waves of SOE reforms and labour implications

	Traditional employment system				*Transitional absorption of labour*
	1949–1978	*1978–1983*	*1984–1988*	*1989–1992*	*1993–today*
Economic context	– Maoist Economic Heavy-Industry-Oriented Strategy: priority of capital over labour. – People's Commune System (*renmin gongshe*) in the rural areas. – Economic disasters caused by political instability (economic and political campaigns; Great Leap Forward; Cultural Revolution; etc.)	– Launching of economic reforms. – Rural decollectivization (Household Responsibility System – *baochan daohu*).	– Dual-Track System (Plan + Market) (*zhuangguizhi*). – Urban reforms and creation of SEZs. – Two crucial threats emerge: inflation and corruption.	– Tian'anmen military intervention (4 June, 1989). – Deng's Trip to the South (1992). – Introduction of new governmental policy: 'Socialism with Chinese Characteristics'.	– Fiscal reform (1994): recentralization of tax collection. – Unification of Rmb (1995). – Towards the so-called 'socialist market economy' (term adopted at the XIVth CCP Congress, October 1993). – Asian Financial Crisis (1997–98). – China joins WTO in December 2001.
SOEs and labour reforms	From a national Unified Labour Allocation System (LAS) to a centralised and arbitrary LAS.	– The autonomy of SOEs increases: they are able to retain a share of their benefits. – Employment promotion in the non-state sector. – Development of small businesses (*getihu*).	– Wages and employment decisions are decentralized (managerial autonomy). – Adoption of the Contract Responsibility System (*chengbaozhi*): freedom to hire and fire workers. – Introduction of a tax-for-profit system (*li gai shui*).	– SOEs are pressured to increase labour demand. – Labour reforms are slowed down: return to the old 'iron rice bowl' system (*tiefanwan* – lifetime employment).	– Homogeneous accounting system for all SOEs. – Hard budget constraint. – REP launching. – Launching of a new corporate governance system based on the '*zhuada, fangxiao*' system (XVth CCP Congress, September 1997).
Results	– Limited inter-enterprise and inter-regional mobility. – Establishment of an institutional wage in urban areas. – Unemployment is minimized through the reallocation of urban labour in rural areas.	– Persistence of price distorsions. – Insufficient resource allocation.	– Growth of TVEs: inter-enterprise competition. – Increase of labour mobility. – Distortion of market-determined prices (as a result of the dual-track system).	– Under-employment re-emerges. – Profits decrease. – Demand of bank credits increase.	– Unemployment is externalized. – Pressure for other reforms to be launched: finance, banking, housing, social security, pension, etc.

Sources: Hu and Li (1993: 148–153); Naughton (1995: 207–212); Lardy (1998: 22–24).
Notes: SOEs: State-Owned Enterprises; TVEs: Township and Village Enterprises; CCP: Chinese Communist Party; REP: Re-Employment Programme; SEZs: Special Economic Zones.

appeared as an incentive for enterprises to maximize their financial surplus, was replaced by the tax-for-profit system (*li gai shui* reform) until 1986, where profits were reclassified as taxes, and enterprises emerged as residual claimants on after-tax profits.[11] As this system proved to be inefficient, a more developed CRS re-emerged, lasting only until January 1994, when fiscal reforms took place (enterprise tax payments were re-centralized), and the CRS was replaced by an income tax.

With the dramatic surge of Township and Village Enterprises (TVEs) since 1984, inter-enterprise competition emerged. Between 1984 and 1988, the number of TVEs increased from almost 6.1 million to almost 18.9 million, and the number of employees rapidly rose from almost 52.1 million to 95.5 million,[12] whereas during the same period SOE employees slowly rose from 86.4 million to 99.9 million.[13] Although job creation does not represent a direct measurement of output value (after all, gross output value of SOEs was almost three times higher than the TVEs' gross output value within that same period),[14] labour costs were lower in TVEs than in SOEs, as TVEs only performed productive functions, whereas SOEs were in addition burdened with providing social services (*fuli*) to their workers. The competition caused by the growth of TVEs progressively changed the conditions of the SOE reforms, narrowing the monopoly profits of SOEs.

By 1989, SOEs had progressively lost their leading position in the national economy: in the late 1970s, they contributed nearly 80 per cent to industrial production, whereas by the end of the 1980s their contribution had declined to little more than 55 per cent.[15] In addition, the dual-track price system created a misleading trend of market-determined prices and incentives for corruption.[16] The launching of an austerity programme after the 1988 high inflation rate as measured by the consumer price index (18.8 per cent) provoked a systematic risk of social unrest, for which SOEs were pressured by the Chinese government to increase their labour demand during this third wave of reforms (1989–92) – despite their lower capacity of production – and to continue to provide, as in the past, an 'iron rice bowl' to their employees. As a result, underemployment re-emerged, profits decreased, and the demand for loans and credits increased. SOEs were again unprofitable.

By mid-1993, the situation changed, and a fourth wave of reforms was launched (1993–today). The government not only ordered all enterprises to use the same accounting system, but as a break from the past, it imposed a relatively hard budget constraint in order to stop the SOEs' indiscrimante access to bank loans, and thereby to avoid an inevitable collapse of the banking system. The breakdown of the iron rice bowl system was equally suggested: as an increase in unemployment was foreseen, an institutional watchdog had to be prepared. That is why the Ministry of Labour launched the 're-employment programme' (REP), instigating local governments to promote the development of training programmes (*peixun zhidao*) through the creation of re-employment centres (*zaijiuye fuwu zhongxin*) in order to match unemployed redundant workers with other enterprises, as well as encouraging them to be self-employed. These years could be identified as a transitional period of labour absorption, as laid-off workers have been reallocated through a transitory REP. By 1996 the REP proved to be effective and operational in 200 cities.[17] As a result, the Ministry decided to re-launch new re-employment training programmes for at least 4 million laid-off workers and 6 million unemployed from 2001 to 2003 within the current Ninth Five-Year Plan.[18]

Summing up, with the launching of SOE reforms and the more or less systematic breakdown of the traditional employment system, urban workers face today a new situation: although they no longer enjoy a lifetime job guarantee, they have become a clear target of employment regulations aimed to preserve a coherent social system. In other words, laid-off workers are in theory becoming economic units responding to market forces, but in practice they are still somehow subject, if not to a labour assignment system, at least to a labour protection/priority system, which could be easily identified as a new version (even if implicit) of the iron rice bowl system in the urban areas. Considering the REP's fundamental role in this orientation process, it remains to be seen how far this initiative is contributing to the formation of a distorted labour market.

How effective is the re-employment programme?

As a result of the gradual achievements of the state-owned sector and the progressive growth of the non-state sector,[19] the Chinese labour market has developed accordingly. In a parallel fashion, with the launching of the REP, the employment system has been undergoing a process of redistribution of the labour force within an established framework: as SOEs lay off redundant workers, the government is committed to support them.

Premier Zhu Rongji (architect of a great deal of SOE reforms) put forward the so-called '3–3–3 Plan' after 1997, entailing the unemployment compensation for laid-off workers to be supported by three financing sources: the enterprise laying off the worker, the government, and the society,[20] each of them contributing with one-third. These funds should be channelled by the re-employment centres under a system of subsidies regulated by the local authorities in which laid-off workers receive economic support for a maximum period of two years. The first year, they receive between 200 and 250 Rmb per month; the second year, almost 200 Rmb per month.[21] In addition, they theoretically obtain 25.5 per cent of their wage for their pension and medicare fund.[22] If laid-off workers have not found a job within this period, they systematically become unemployed workers (*shiye zhigong*), i.e. they no longer receive unemployment benefits from their work unit, but rather from the society as a whole.[23]

In practice, funds can have diverse origins, be differently distributed, and the re-employment centres may have heterogeneous functions, depending on the city considered (Table 3.2).

Quite clearly, the re-employment centres play a fundamental role in the development of the REP, the SOE restructuring, and the formation of a more market-oriented employment system: they are the result of the so-called 'collective digestion' (*gongtong xiaohua*) of re-employment,[24] as they do not only play an intermediate role between the enterprise and the market (reducing the overstaffing problem and low productivity levels of loss-making SOEs), but also contribute to the establishment of modern enterprises. They are generally set up by the work unit (*danwei*) that has laid off the workers, they supervise and keep records of laid-off workers, search for

Table 3.2 Re-employment centres in Beijing and Shanghai: definition and sources of financing

Different perspectives (expressed by)	*Definition (functions played by these centres)*	*Sources of financing (who finances the funds?)*
Shanghai Labour Bureau	'Administrative and social entities' ('*guanli yu shehui danwei*') with two defined functions: 1. management (to guarantee the minimum wage to the worker); 2. training (to create government supported 'education schools' within the enterprises).*	1/3: Enterprise laying off the worker 1/3: Government 1/3: Society
Beijing Ministry of Labour	'Institutional entities operating as independent legal persons' ('*duli faren zige de shiye danwei*')	40%: Local Labour Bureau (*shi laodongju*); 30%: Local Bureau of Finance (*shi caizhengju*) 30%: Each of the three economic sectors (*jingji hangye*)

Source: Interviews at the Shanghai Labour Bureau and Beijing Ministry of Labour. June and July 1998. Information updated in 2001.

Note:

* A Shanghai Labour Bureau representative added to this definition the interest in following the German model: if these 'education schools' can reallocate laid-off workers in the labour market, the government will be willing to pay extra money. This initiative could create stronger competition, and the incentives for a better quality in training would therefore be much higher.

alternative jobs for them, and organize training programmes. Thus, they are the main instruments of reallocation (*fenliu*) of laid-off workers into the growing labour market, and contribute somehow to a deeper sense of labour force competition.

Nevertheless, the reallocation of laid-off workers is fairly 'selective'. After all, 'these workers have been serving the State, and cannot be thrown out to the market without any protection' ('*you yao caijian renyuan, you bu tuixiang shehui*').[25] Indeed, local governments are applying preferential policies both for laid-off workers and the enterprises hiring them. For instance, in general terms (although it may not always be the case), if a married couple works in the same work unit, only one can be dismissed; disabled workers and model workers (*laodong mofan*) cannot be fired; if a laid-off worker wants to create his/her own business (e.g. retail selling), the government will give him/her 10,000 Rmb and tax exemption for three years; if an enterprise hires a laid-off worker, it will receive between 4,000 and 6,000 Rmb, as long as the newly employed worker signs a contract for two years minimum; etc.[26]

In addition, the reallocation of laid-off workers is fairly dependent on age and working experience (measured by length of time spent at the work unit). For instance, laid-off workers under 35 years old will have to enter the labour market, without any explicit financial or social support; those between 35 and 45 years old are encouraged to be re-employed through the so-called collective labour export institutions (*guli kaizhan cheng jianzhi de jiti laowu shuchu*); those who are five years below the established age of retirement can still receive a wage from their work unit, working less hours, only with the consent of the centre and their work unit; and those who are within the retirement age will systematically be retired.[27] This preferential system is understandable, as the older working age groups have a lower capacity to adapt themselves to the new labour environment. After all, the majority of laid-off workers are far above 35 years old, as they belong to the young generation working during the Maoist employment system, and are therefore the 'iron rice bowl babies' who have now matured in age, but probably not so much in job experience.

The general profile of laid-off workers could be defined as a middle-aged woman with a low education level and scarce professional skills. As shown in Table 3.3, there are more women than men that are being laid off: women tend to be concentrated in the state-owned textile and traditional industrial sectors, which presumably have now the highest unemployment rate.[28]

With such a prospect, the REP's challenge is enormous. There is not only a qualitative problem, but also some uncertainty as regards the quantitative phenomenon. In fact, the estimates and true magnitude of unemployment are all too vague: first, it is not always clear whether all redundant workers (*fuyu renyuan*) become laid-off workers (*xiagang zhigong*) and ultimately unemployed (*shiye renyuan*); second, the REP is still in a transitional period, for which the results are difficult to estimate on an accurate basis.

Table 3.3 Laid-off workers: general profile (%)

Characteristics	*Laid-off workers (within the total urban unemployed persons)*
Gender	
Male	40.0
Female	47.3
Education	
Illiterate and semi-illiterate	0.5
Primary school	8.2
Junior secondary school	54.9
Senior secondary school	33.1
College and higher level	3.2
Age	
25–29	40.8
30–34	60.1
35–39	68.1
40–44	74.7
45–49	77.1
50–54	61.2
55–59	70.4

Source: Zhongguo tongji nianjian (China Statistical Yearbook) (1999: 175–176).

Note:

The total percentage of laid-off workers as part of the urban unemployed persons is 43.8 per cent. Notice that all percentages are individually related to the total amount of urban unemployed persons, and *not* to the total amount of laid-off workers. This means, for instance, that within the total urban unemployed, 40 per cent are male laid-off workers.

According to nationwide official sources, in 1997, amongst the 12 million urban SOE employees who were laid off under the reform policy, 6 million were re-employed.[29] A year later, stated differently, amongst all unemployed workers, 43.8 per cent were laid off from SOEs.[30] In informal conversations with Chinese scholars, many of them estimated the nationwide number of laid-off workers to be around 8 million in 1998, 12 million in 2000, and 15 million in 2001. Non-mainland journals declare this number to be between 20 and 30 million in 1997–98.[31] According to the local official sources, in Beijing, between 1995 and 1998, the 360,000 Beijing workers that lost their jobs were all re-employed by the end of 1998, either in or outside the industrial sector. During the first quarter of 1998, about 38,000 workers were laidoff and were not re-employed by mid-1998. In addition, these same sources forecasted an increase of 160,000 between 1998 and the end of year 2000.[32] With regard to Shanghai, it would seem that during the Eighth Five-Year Plan, amongst the 861,000 workers that were laid off, around 664,000 were reallocated, either through an early retirement or after having found a job in the informal sector. In 1996, 1,090,000 were laid off, and more than 75 per cent found a new job.[33] The discrepancy in quantitative estimates is therefore pretty evident.[34]

But more important than the data information for the REP to succeed – which is often more a matter of propaganda and sensationalism than a reality – is the response laid-off workers give to the unemployment benefits they are offered. As mentioned earlier, the re-employment centres help laid-off workers to find alternative jobs by compelling them to participate in the training programmes included within the so-called '10 Million in 3 Years' re-employment training plans (*san nian qian wan zaijiuye peixun jihua*), launched first as an aim to provide occupational guidance and training services to 10 million people in a period of three years between 1998 and 2000, renewed now for the period 2001–3.[35]

Up to now, the results have not always been as expected. Laid-off workers tend to be rather conservative, as they do not develop a competitive attitude towards job seeking. The centres push laid-off workers to attend specific training programmes aimed to help them adapt to the new demands in the market, but many of these workers systematically refuse to attend them. Participating in them entails a complete rupture with their former work unit, when they were reallocated in a job using their newly acquired skills. Most of the jobs they are being trained for are based on short-term or long-term contracts, for which the workers lose their feeling of 'belonging' to their work unit, while their iron rice bowl is being smashed into pieces.

Nevertheless, this smashing may only be apparent, as SOE (redundant) workers continue to be protected by the state and are therefore part of a new type of iron rice bowl mechanism. Otherwise, it is difficult to explain the relative success the REP has had in preventing instability in China's economic reforms and social transformations: launched as a temporary instrument, it has become an important intermediator between the economic restructuring of SOEs and the social equilibrium of urban employees. But is preventing instability the only possible way of succeeding? Are there not better and less temporary choices, such as the formation of a true labour market and a more stable adjustment to the economic and social reality? This might avoid the current unemployment problem becoming a 'political/state problem', which could ultimately contribute to the creation of a 'disguised' iron rice bowl system.

How to avoid a distorted allocation of labour supply and a disguised iron rice bowl system

In theory, the current wave of SOE reforms is contributing to an improvement of the labour allocation system, growing out of the traditional employment system and pushing it into the establishment of a more market-oriented labour distribution with the help of the instrumental variables launched by the REP.

In practice, the employment administration model of the traditional planned system has not yet fully disappeared and continues to affect the people's attitude toward the employment situation (e.g. refusing to perform certain types of jobs), which by implication means a rejection of the newly established labour policies. This is why it is necessary to resort to alternative options.

To encourage the growth of the service sector in general and the informal economy in particular seems to be a way of solving the problem: not only it is a convenient re-employment measure, but it also promotes economic growth creating further demand and supply dynamism. Since the public sector's restructuring in recent years, the Chinese authorities have tended to identify the informal sector as a 'district (or community) service' (*shequ fuwu*). Within this context, the so-called informal jobs (*fei zhenggui jiuye*) often include low-skill jobs such as the domestic service sector (*jia zhengfu*), hourly work (*xiaoshigong*), or garbage recycling (*feiping shougou*), etc.[36] Due to analytical shortcomings, I prefer to identify this sector as part of the 'newly established sector', i.e. the non-state sector (as opposed to the state-owned sector, or 'traditional sector'), where labour absorption is based on human capital values (and not on a discretional labour assignment) and income is determined according to market forces and labour productivity levels (no institutional wage resulting from the state monopoly).[37]

No matter what definition we give it, what is interesting to notice here is that this 'newly established sector' gives laid-off workers the opportunity to feel 'useful', as they can contribute to the urban community's economic growth: yesterday, they made a living and ate from their iron rice bowl for the sake of the 'nation's wealth'; today, they can help society to evolve thanks to their active participation in social services, receiving on most occasions the state's support. In fact, as a result of the propaganda, the encouragement mechanisms used by the local authorities, and the preferential system given to laid-off workers to establish their own businesses, there has been a considerable increase of the self-employed in the (non-state) service sector, ranging from 10,000 in 1978 to about 4.5 million in 1999 (Figure 3.1).

At the beginning, the governmental authorities tended to consider the trend toward 'informality' as a temporary solution and a guarantee for the reallocation of laid-off workers. Now, it seems to have become a potential sector responding to the imperatives of demand and supply forces, in parallel with the increasing living standards of the Chinese urban population in general. This means that, as laid-off workers are given the freedom to find alternative jobs, they have more incentives to create their own businesses (as they rarely find an ideal job position), and ultimately become citizens with the same rights and privileges as the rest of the workers: 'once the fish have been nourished, they will gain weight, and will end up contributing to the economic and social growth' (*fangshui yanyu*).[38]

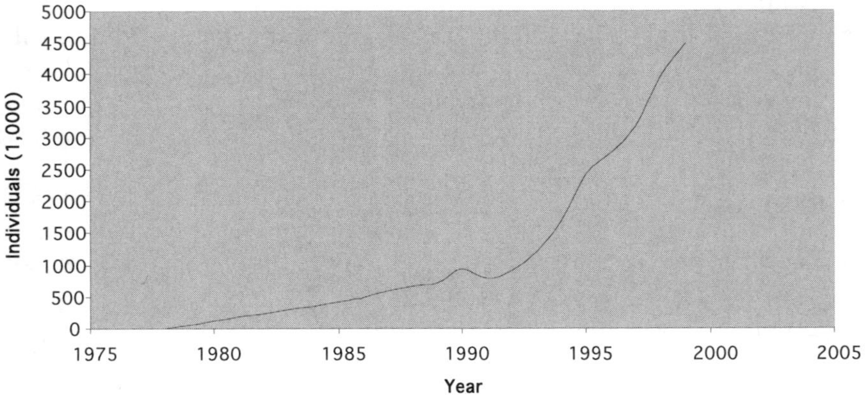

Figure 3.1 Self-employed individuals in social services.
Source: Zhongguo tongji nianjian (China Statistical Yearbook) (2000: 138).

As a result of the current transitional process, many laid-off workers can subsist with small jobs, often without 'declaring' them, while they are receiving at the same time subsidies from the re-employment centres. At first sight, this trend may contradict the essence of the governmental policies and, by implication, the (implicit) purpose of perpetuating the iron rice bowl of redundant workers: work unit A (enterprise of origin) supports the worker through subsidies, while enterprise B (new enterprise) offers a new job (obtained normally through social networking, *guanxi*). Although the authorities are fully aware of this situation, not much has been done to stop it. Quite the contrary: as workers are gradually beginning to understand the rules of the market, there is a generalised hope that the planned system will be finally eroded. Besides, as the re-employment situation is considered to be temporary, performing one, two or even three extra jobs is simply viewed as an 'inevitable result of transition' (*guodu jieduan*).[39]

Despite the tacit governmental acceptance that laid-off workers may perform unstable jobs while they are receiving unemployment subsidy, the governmental authorities have long considered increasing unemployment subsidies to about 450–500 Rmb per month (more than 100 per cent increase). Theoretically, this initiative aims to end the temptation of having extra sources of income and, more important, it guarantees acceptable living conditions to laid-off workers. The key is how to find enough financial sources to do so: the establishment of a valid nationwide social security system is, no doubt, an essential part of the solution.

In the traditional employment system, the lack of an effective social security system hindered SOEs from freely laying off workers, and thus prevented their restructuring. After all, medical care was provided by the work unit. Thus, if workers were laid off, they systematically lost this coverage, inevitably causing social discontent.

During what I call the transitional period of labour absorption – i.e. job reallocation of laid-off workers through the REP – SOEs have not yet developed a system in which workers contribute to the social security on a regular basis. As long as this problem is not fully solved, the progress of SOE reforms will remain insufficient, as SOEs keep many redundant workers, and therefore internalize the unemployment pressure at the expense of efficiency.[40] One possible solution to this problem could be to charge new taxes at the national level, not only to enterprises, but also to workers, according to their level of wages: if workers contribute to the social security system and to other taxes (for instance, fuel taxes),[41] unemployment insurance expenses (minimum living standards, medical care and pension funds) could possibly be covered. This way, the social obligations of the state and the individual responsibilities of workers will be more balanced.

All this is easy to say, but maybe not so easy to apply. The current unemployment problem is evidently transforming the Chinese labour market into a puzzle of challenges. Indeed, the unallocated labour supply (laid-off and/or unemployed workers) cannot indefinitely depend on a maintenance system that is effectively a transitional (almost empty) iron rice bowl, as this is likely to have an effect on workers' motivation to find new jobs. The Chinese economy has long suffered from this phenomenon. It would be unwise to repeat this process, even if it is under a different guise.

That is the reason why I include here four long-term initiatives aimed to avoid both structural unemployment and the stagnation of China's labour market in the context of today's SOE reforms.[42] These policy initiatives could be useful in a broader study of how economic reforms affect the structure of urban labour, and how urban labour alters the social welfare system in today's China.

How to avoid the upsurge of a new iron rice bowl system: long-term initiatives

Adjustment of human capital

It is true that workers are not being laid off from SOEs because of their skills, but rather because of the enterprise where they work.[43] Nevertheless, it seems quite clear that SOE workers need to readjust their working skills to the new labour demands. Returns to education are generally low (the rate of return has rarely been above 4.5 per cent)[44] and workers need further incentives to remain in high-skill positions within the state-owned sector, or otherwise to be able to compete for the non-state sector.

The training programmes offered by the re-employment centres are a positive step but would need to be applied, not when workers have been laid off, but rather when workers are still in their jobs, on a regular basis (once every two months, for instance). China's most clear comparative advantage is its abundant cheap labour force, but this does not mean that quantity and quality cannot clearly compensate each other, as long as labour costs do not increase excessively (as it could negatively affect higher employment opportunities). It is up to the market forces to compete for lower labour costs in this case.

Adjustment of the industrial structure

The industrial system is persistently distorted as a result of the incompatibilities between large SOEs and (state-owned) small and medium enterprises (SMEs): whereas large SOEs continue to receive subsidies disguised as banking credits, SMEs are still unable to receive credits to finance new investment projects (presumably changeable under the World Trade Organization umbrella). They only receive credit support to cover social costs of laid-off workers – thus, the political slogan applied since 1994: 'to swim or to drown'.[45] Subsequently, SMEs are the big losers of reforms: although enterprise mergers are encouraged and bankruptcy procedures are supposed to be standardized,[46] they tend to be under-capitalized and often survive only thanks to local protectionism.[47] As long as large SOEs do not effectively modify their distorted corporate system and enhance an independent enterprise management, the establishment of a competitive mechanism for the survival of the fittest companies (through the diversion of laid-off workers, the encouragement of the REP, or the downsizing of staff) will not become a reality.

In a parallel fashion, there is a clear tendency of labour rejection (*xiagang*) in the secondary sector and labour absorption (*shanggang*) in the tertiary sector. This effectively corresponds with economic fundamentals: the industrial sector is capital-intensive, whereas the service sector is labour-intensive. As stated earlier, this situation did not apply before the SOE reforms were initiated. But even if the industrial sector is now undergoing a transformation, we cannot expect the heavy-industrial sector to disappear fully. Instead, it will need to re-adapt its infrastructure and capital input, in order to be increasingly competitive with foreign products, especially considering China's recent membership of the WTO.

Since the launching of economic reforms in the late 1970s, China has been relying heavily on foreign direct investment, probably not so much for the development of new products and the stimulus for job creation, but mostly for an apprenticeship in the distribution and utilization of capital. If the lesson has been adequately learnt, the Chinese industrial sector should then be adjusted to the progressively sophisticated domestic and external demands. Demand being more stimulated, the inherited macroeconomic slowdown presumably comes to an end, entailing a more adequate labour supply distribution.

A better balance between the state-owned and the non-state-owned sectors

Although large SOEs are now being targeted as economies of scale and small SOEs are starting to be a little more competitive and flexible, the state-owned sector has not fully changed the structure of its assets. It continues to be a capital-intensive sector. The non-state sector, in contrast, is proving to be much more labour-intensive and has therefore a larger elasticity in its employment. Thus, despite the wave of unemployment externalization, many SOEs are still internalizing their redundant workers, for which they have to bear a heavy social burden: they are being both a cause and a rescuer of the emergence of a higher unemployment rate. In addition, and despite the amendment of the Constitution in 1999 accepting the existence of the private sector in the Chinese economy, it is still seriously constrained by the limited knowledge of, and access to, the financial system, preventing it from actively participating in a genuine competitive economy.[48]

Inter-enterprise competition is being increased with the rapid growth of TVEs. But what needs to be further enhanced is inter-ownership competition, as SOEs would be under the real pressure of attenuating their labour costs, and therefore guaranteeing wages dependent on labour productivity levels. The competition between both sectors appears therefore as an appropriate instrument for higher levels of employment creation.

Breakdown of the persistent dualism between rural and urban workers

Despite the relaxation of China's preferential urban registration system (*chengshi hukou*), which since the Maoist period has been guaranteeing high wages and material benefits to all urban workers (regardless of their labour productivity), the distinction between rural and urban workers is still far from disappearing. Rural workers have been relatively free to migrate to the cities since the introduction of economic reforms, excluding some moments of retrenchment by the end of the 1980s. However, once arriving in the cities, their job mobility is restricted: they are forced to perform certain types of jobs (low-paid, unskilled, dirty, physically demanding) traditionally rejected by local workers. In addition, ever since the launching of the REP, local governments have developed a whole set of discriminatory policies in favour of laid-off workers and to the detriment of migrant workers, giving preference to the former during reallocation.[49] The lack of vertical labour mobility is therefore evident.

In economic terms, this initiative proves to be an important impediment for further labour flexibility. Considering the shortage of labour demand, the authorities try to solve the problem of laid-off workers by persuading them to perform similar jobs to migrant workers, if they want to make a living. Nevertheless, not only do urban workers show reluctance in this regard, but the majority of enterprises have a clear segmentation structure: they hire migrant workers at the bottom level and hire local workers at the highest levels. If the enterprise is compelled to hire more local workers, the general level of wages will need to be increased and the enterprise will then have to bear excessive labour costs. From this point of view, migrant workers have certain influence on laid-off workers, but it is rather small, due to this segmentation structure.

In social terms, the general profile of migrant workers rarely coincides with the characteristics of laid-off workers. As proved by different works on migration,[50] migrant workers tend to be fairly young (18–25 years old), both female and male, not too highly educated (secondary level of education) and, most important, incredibly adaptable to labour market demands: as local authorities increase the administration obstacles for them to settle down in the city, many will simply migrate to different areas. Migrant workers are therefore proving to be much more flexible than the local authorities, with their segregative actions. Not only do these restrictive policies delimit an important source of demand in urban areas, and prevent a higher savings rate (e.g. remittances sent back to the province of origin), they also push enterprises to hire migrant workers in an undeclared way, following the motto '*shang you cengce, xia you duice*' ('policies are above, correct methods are below')[51] in order to lower their labour costs and not lose their competitive power, while contributing to a more precarious situation for migrant workers. Despite the lack of empirical evidence proving how the REP has influenced the evolution of the urban unemployment rate, and the difficulty in estimating its effects on this persistent dualism, it is quite clear that the increasing discrepancies between both labour profiles only contribute to hinder the evolving process of today's economic transition.[52]

Concluding remarks

The '*xiagang* generation' is seemingly an unfortunate generation: not only did they go through extremely difficult moments such as the post Great Leap Forward famine, or the Cultural Revolution, but they now have to pay for the economic imbalance inherited from the Maoist years. The least they can hope for is a guarantee of long-term social stability, with comprehensive support from the authorities, the media – although they often excessively use the propagandistic instrument of the so-called 'laid-off workers stars' (*mingxing xiagang*) – and the rest of the society. But this support needs to be envisaged as a truly transitional process, avoiding therefore the establishment of a new type of iron rice bowl that could entail a parasitic system unresponsive of the emerging market forces.

Considering the temporary character of the current re-employment initiatives, it is still early to draw a conclusion. But what seems evident is that China is now a victim of a triple-edged controversy. First, laid-off workers are unfairly compelled to give up their jobs for the sake of microeconomic equilibrium and macroeconomic stability; second, SOEs do not always necessarily improve their productivity levels, as they are often pushed to 'baby-sitting' their redundant workers in order to preserve social stability at the local and national levels; third, the current treatment given to laid-off workers is provoking a long-term structural problem of labour supply allocation, affecting therefore labour flexibility.

No doubt, the Chinese labour market is now being strongly influenced by China's WTO membership. In the short run, the unemployment rate's increase will be inevitable, as competition increases, specialization develops, and the non-productive SOEs will necessarily have to be entirely dismantled. But in the long term, labour perspectives are seemingly positive, as China will have more open access to new technologies, and foreign direct investment will recover again from the slowdown it underwent in the late 1990s. This way, the implications of higher unemployment rates may be more controllable, as new economic sectors (services, tourism, etc.) will absorb the unemployed in the long term. Nevertheless, as long as human capital value is not adjusted, the industrial structure is not rearranged, the state-owned and non-state-owned sectors are not better balanced, and the persistent dualism between rural and urban workers does not disappear, it will be difficult to eliminate the persistence of the traditional employment system and to envisage a genuine breakdown of an already rusty iron rice bowl.

Notes

1 This policy can be summarised as follows: over 10,000 large and medium SOEs remain under the Central Government's control and are often converted into shareholding companies, or otherwise loss-making SOEs merge with profitable ones. In parallel, more than 100,000 small SOEs are privatized, either merging with other non-state enterprises, forming joint ventures with foreign enterprises, or leasing assets to workers. Xin (1998) and Lardy (1998: 24).

2 The 'enterprise restructuring', which includes the development of a 'new system', and not so much the restructuring of the 'old system', started around 1993, under the initiative of local governments. As it proved to be quite successful in terms of social stability, it was then fully legitimized at the XVth Congress. For a detailed explanation, refer to Fan (1997) and Naughton (1998).

3 *Zhongguo tongji nianjian* (2000: 70, 289). Hereafter *ZTN*.

4 *ZTN* (2000: 115). The disparities between official and non-official data are quite considerable, as informal sources estimate urban unemployment rate to be around 20 per cent.

5 The idea of 'laid-off worker' (*xiagang zhigong*) is different from 'unemployed worker' (*shiye zhigong*), or from 'person waiting to be employed' (*daiye renyuan*). Although the *xiagang zhigong* theoretically leaves his/her job on a temporary basis, he/she continues to belong to the work unit (*danwei*), for which the labour contract is still in force. In other words, 'the worker leaves the business, but not the factory' ('*li shang, mei li chang*'). *Xiagang zhigong* can also be said *xiagang*

gongren or *xiagang renyuan*. To simplify, I use here the English term of 'laid-off worker'.

6 Mao launched an economic policy based on preventing unemployment and safeguarding the urban workers' standard of living and right to work through the establishment of the work unit (*danwei*) and its inherent iron rice bowl, guaranteeing the workers their basic necessities (accommodation, education and medical coverage). Thus, regardless of their productivity levels, urban workers had job insurance, contributing to the nation's wealth, and therefore to the stability of the party.

7 The household registration system (*hukou*), officially created in the late 1950s, was first set up as a way of distinguishing the inhabitants of the rural areas from those of the urban areas. Later on, it became a method of control, impeding the free movement of peasant workers wanting to move to the cities.

8 Cai (1998a).

9 For a more detailed view about the relationship between institutional wage and labour productivity, see Cai (1998a: 7).

10 Lardy (1998: 23) and Johnston (1998).

11 For a more comprehensive view on the *li gai shui* reform, refer to Naughton (1995: 183–187).

12 *Zhongguo nongcun tongji nianjian* (1996: 327 and 329).

13 *ZTN* (1995: 84).

14 For SOEs' gross output value of industry, refer to *ZTN* (1998: 435). For TVEs' gross output value, refer to *ZTN* (1995: 365).

15 *ZTN* (1995: 377).

16 China's reform strategy since 1978 has often been described as a set of policies following a double track, implying the conjunction of a traditional planned system and a tendency towards a market economy in the allocation of economic resources. With this system, SOEs can sell that output exceeding the quotas established at a market price and plan their levels of output according to the response shown by the market. A great bulk of this system is characterized by the coexistence of two types of prices: one being established by the state (low) and the other one by the market (high). The effects of this strategy become more evident by the end of the 1980s (high inflation rates, corruption, etc.). Lin, Cai and Li (1996: 291–292) and Naughton (1995: 7–8, 114).

17 Johnston (1998).

18 Jin (2001).

19 The non-state sector includes urban collectives, community-owned rural industries, household agriculture, private enterprises, self-employment, joint ventures and wholly foreign-owned enterprises. The central government has no authority over their assets. The non-state sector has rapidly spread since the 1990s: by 1999, it provided almost 80 per cent of industrial output and created about 59 per cent of new jobs at the urban level. *ZTN* (2000: 115 and 409).

20 The concept of 'society' (and the funds originating from it) is difficult to define. Here, there are two possible ways of defining it: (1) social insurance compensation (in theory, workers should contribute with 1 per cent of their monthly wage to the unemployment insurance); (2) administration fees payed by migrant workers. This last idea is often espoused by the local governments

themselves – interviews at the *Shanghai laodongju guanli zhiye bumen* (Shanghai Labour Bureau Administrative Employment Department) in May 1998; and at the *Beijingshi rencai (shichang) fuwu zhongxin* (Beijing Service Centre for the Talent (Market) in July 1998 – and clearly appears in Chinese documents ('Shanghai: Chengshi . . .' 1998: 99–110). Paradoxically, although immigration is a clear financial support for local laid-off workers, it has also become a target of the discriminative policies aimed to give priority to local workers.

21 Notice that this plan was launched when China's GDP per capita was approximately 6,000 Rmb (US$720) (i.e. around 500 Rmb (US$60) per month).

22 Although this percentage is effectively declared by some local authorities, it remains often at a theoretical level, as the work unit or even the government cannot provide the economic support in an immediate way. As a result, many laid-off workers do not receive this compensation on a regular basis. Only if a laid-off worker has medical expenses will he/she presumably be compensated. I thank my Chinese colleagues for commenting on this aspect.

23 I.e. 'the people will feed the people' ('*yimin yaomin*'). Interviews, Beijing and Shanghai, 1998.

24 Hou (1998: 23).

25 Interview, July 1998.

26 These are some of the regulations set up in Beijing, Shanghai or Jinan local governments. Interviews, Beijing, Shanghai and Jinan, 1998.

27 'Guanyu jin . . .' (1998: 12). Like the Social Security Reform, the Pension Reform is now a major focus of attention in Chinese policy.

28 The textile sector's labour costs are pretty high, considering it is a labour-intensive sector. Although the traditional industrial sector is capital-intensive, competition with foreign products is far too strong, which makes it difficult to offer good quality and cheap products at the same time. Its high unemployment rate results in this case from the market situation. Interview, Shanghai Labour Bureau, June 1998. The exact unemployment rates of both sectors were not given in the interview and do not appear in any data source.

29 State Council's document published in the *Renmin ribao*, 23 June 1998, quoted from Xin (1998).

30 *ZTN* (1999: 175).

31 'The Worsening Problem of Unemployment' (1998: 75).

32 Interview at the Beijing Talent Labour Market, July 1998.

33 'Shanghai: Chengshi . . .' (1998: 100).

34 Naughton, Rocca and Bakken also offer unemployment statistics in this volume.

35 'The Worsening Problem . . .' (1998: 85).

36 'Zaijiuye si zhong xin qudao' (1998: 73).

37 This new definition is included in my doctoral thesis on 'Migration and Labor Mobility in China's Economic Transition: Migrant Workers vs. Laid-Off Workers', defended at the Economics Department, Universidad Autónoma de Madrid, Spain, May 2001.

38 'Shen cheng . . .' (1998: 3).

39 Interview at the re-employment centre for the heavy industrial sector in Nanshi District (Shanghai), June 1998.

40 Cai (1998a).

41 This idea is clearly stated in Liu (1998). According to his calculations, contributing to social security and paying for fuel taxes will loosely cover the unemployment insurance expenses.
42 Refer also to Cai (1998a)
43 Xin (1998).
44 Byron and Manaloto (1990) and Maurer-Fazio (1995).
45 Huchet and Richet (2000).
46 An initiative encouraged by the Chinese government through the Decision of the Central Committee of the Communist Party of China on Major Issues Concerning the Reform and Development of State-Owned Enterprises (adopted at the 4th Plenum of the XVth CPC Central Committee on 22 September 1999).
47 Huchet and Richet (2000).
48 Quite clearly, the Chinese financial sector is fragmented: even if SOEs in the industrial sector merely represent 40 per cent of the total industrial production, they continue to absorb 70 per cent of the credits conceded by the banks to the enterprises. Huchet and Richet (2000).
49 For a more detailed view on this problem, refer to Fernández-Stembridge (1999: 29–33).
50 The analysis of rural-urban migration is fairly extensive. For an overview, refer to authors such as Elisabeth Croll, Cai Fang, Bai Nansheng, Cindy Fan, Ma Xia, Kenneth Roberts, Scott Rozelle, Dorothy Solinger, or Wang Feng, amongst many others.
51 'Shanghai: Chengshi . . .' (1998: 105).
52 In August 2001, Beijing introduced a regulation establishing three categories of residents: those staying in the city for more than three years (category A); those staying less than three years (B); and those staying those staying less than one year (C). This new regulation was issued while the local government pressured enterprises to hire workers ignoring their *hukou*: both rural and urban workers can be hired on an equal basis. It needs to be noted here that this significant step applies mostly to the educated migrant sector (the so-called *rencai* population, i.e. those with a university education level).

References and further reading

'Article Views State Enterprise Problems and Remedies' (1995). *Zhenli de zhuique*. In *Foreign Broadcast Information Services*, 3 April, pp. 41–44.

'Benshi fei zhenggui jiuye zoushang zhenggui' (1998) (Moving Toward the Correct Path of Local Informal Employment). *Xinmin wanbao,* 25 May, p. 1.

Broadman, Harry G. (1995) *Meeting the Challenge of Chinese Enterprise Reform*. World Bank Discussion Papers. Washington DC, World Bank.

Byron, Raymond P. and Manaloto, Evelyn Q. (1990) 'Returns to Education in China'. *Economic Development and Cultural Change*, vol. 8, no. 4, pp. 738–796.

Cai, Fang (1998a) 'Options of Employment Policies in Transitional China: Getting Institutions Right'. Paper presented at the International Symposium on 'China: Public Policy Choice Toward the XXIst Century'. Beijing, 27–28 November.

—— (1998b) 'Eryuan laodongli shichang tiaojian xia de jiuye tizhi zhuanhuan' (The Transition of the Employment System Under the Dual Labor Market). *Zhongguo shehui kexue*, vol. 2, pp. 4–14.

Fan, Gang (1997) 'Restructuring of Ownership: The New Stage of Gradual Reform in China'. Unpublished paper, October.

Fernández-Stembridge, Leila (1999) 'Nongcun liudong laodongli de wugong jihui – Lun chengshi laodong shichang de wanshan' (Labour Opportunities for Rural Migrant Workers – On the Process of Maturity of the Urban Labour Market). *Zhongguo renkou kexue*, vol. 2, no. 71 (1 April), pp. 29–33.

'Guanyu jin yi bu jiazhang wo shi zhongdian hangye, qiye kaizhang zaijiuye shidian gongzuo de yijian' (1998) (Some Suggestions Related to the Experimental Efforts for the Re-enforcement of Key Sectors and Enterprises in the City of Beijing). *Jing laojiufa*, no. 51, pp. 12–13.

Guoyou da zhong xing qiye jianli xiandai qiye zhidu he jiaqiang guanli de jiben guifan (2000) (Basic Norm for Establishing the Modern Enterprise System and Strengthening Its Management (on a Trial Basis) for Large and Medium SOEs). Beijing, Zhongguo falü chubanshe, 28 September.

Hou, Yafei (1998) ' 'Tuoguan': Guoyou qiye fuyu zhigong liudong mushi tansuo' (An Approach to the Levels of Fluidity of Redundant Workers in State Owned Enterprises). *Zhongguo renkou kexue*, vol. 3, pp. 18–25.

Hu Teh-wei and Li, Elizabeth Hon-ming (1993) 'Labor Market'. In: Walter Galenson (ed.) *China's Economic Reform*. San Francisco, The 1990 Institute, pp. 148–163.

Huchet, Jean-François and Richet, Xavier (2000) 'Entre bureaucratie et marché: Les groupes industriels chinois à la recherche d'un nouveau gouvernement d'entreprise (1)'. *Perspectives chinoises*, October. http://www.cefc.com.hk/english/ressources/wp2/.

'Infatuation's End' (1999). *The Economist*, 25 September, pp. 85–91.

Jin, Baicheng (2001) 'Project Helps Train Laid-off Workers'. *China Daily*, 30 January. http://www.chinadaily.com.cn.

Johnston, Michael (1998) 'Friction in the Black Box'. Forging Consensus for the Lay-off and Re-employment Policies of State-Owned Enterprise Workers'. Unpublished paper, April.

'Journal Analyzes Urban Unemployment' (1998) *Zhongguo Gaige*, 13 February. In *Foreign Broadcast Information Services*, April 3 pp. 37–41.

Lardy, Nicholas R. (1998) *China's Unfinished Economic Revolution*. Washington DC, Brookings Institution Press.

Lin, Justin Yifu, Fang Cai, and Zhou Li (1996) *The China Miracle: Development Strategy and Economic Reform*. The Chinese University of Hong Kong, Chinese University Press.

—— (1998) 'China's Economic Reforms: Some Unfinished Business. Competition, Policy Burdens, and State-Owned Enterprise Reform'. *The American Economic Review*, vol. 88, no. 2 (May), pp. 422–427.

Liu, Shaojia (1998) 'Zhongguo shifu neng yongyou yige wanshang de quanguo tongchou de chengzhen shiye shehui baozhang tixi?' (Can China Have a Nation-wide Social Security System for Urban and Suburban Unemployed Workers?). Unpublished paper, July.

Maurer-Fazio, Margaret (1995) 'Labor Reform in China: Crossing the River by Feeling the Stones'. *Comparative Economic Studies*, vol. 37, no. 4 (Winter), pp. 111–123.

Naughton, Barry (1995) *Growing Out of the Plan: Chinese Economic Reform, 1978–1993*. New York, Cambridge University Press.

—— (1998) 'China: Domestic Restructuring and a New Role in Asia'. Paper presented at the Conference on 'The Asia Economic Crisis'. University of Washington, 30 October–1 November.

OECD (2000) *China in the Global Economy: Reforming China's Enterprises*. Paris, OECD.

Pudney, Stephen (1992) 'Social Security Reform in Urban China: The Case of Shanghai'. Discussion Papers on Economic Transition. University of Cambridge.

Sachs, Jeffrey and Wing Thye Woo (1995) 'Understanding China's Economic Performance'. Unpublished paper.

'Shanghai: Chengshi zhigong yu nongcun mingong de fenceng yu ronghe' (1998) (Shanghai: Stratification and Unification of Urban and Rural Workers). Beijing daxue zhongguo jingji yanjiu zhongxin chengshi laodongli shichang keti zu. *Gaige*, vol. 4, pp. 99–110.

'Shen cheng "fei zhenggui jiuye" fangxing wei ai' (1998) (Explaining the Process of Development of the Urban 'Informal Employment'). *Xinwenbao*, 21 May, p. 3.

'The Worsening Problem of Unemployment' (1998). *Inside Mainland China*, vol. 20, no. 8 (August), pp. 72–76.

Watson, Andrew (1998) 'Employment Policy During Economic Transformation: Issues of Equity and Regional Disparities', Paper presented at the International Symposium on 'China: Public Policy Choice Toward the XXIst Century'. Beijing, 27–28 November.

Xin, Meng (1998) 'Recent Development in China's Labour Market'. Unpublished paper. 'Zaijiuye si zhong xin qudao' (1998) (Four Types of New Channels for Re-employment). *Zhongguo jingji xinxi*, vol. 6, no. 136 (June), p. 73.

Zhang, Xinhua (1998) 'Zhongguo nongcun laodongli liudong yu qiye rongyuan zaijiuye' (China's Rural Migrant Labour and Re-employment of Redundant Workers). In *Renkou daguo: Chengshihua zhilu*. Beijing, Zhongguo renkou chubanshe, pp. 209–222.

Zhongguo nongcun tongji nianjian (1996) (Rural Statistical Yearbook of China). State Statistical Bureau, Zhongguo tongji chubanshe.

Zhongguo tongji nianjian (1995, 1997, 1998, 1999, 2000) (China Statistical Yearbook). State Statistical Bureau, Zhongguo tongji.

4

OLD WORKING CLASS, NEW WORKING CLASS

Reforms, labour crisis and the two faces of conflicts in Chinese urban areas

Jean-Louis Rocca

Since the end of 1993 and the call for the creation of a 'modern enterprise system', the reform of the state-owned sector has led to a complete reshaping of the structure of urban employment. The separation between ownership and management rights, the spreading of the shareholding system, and the emphasis on the financial profitability of enterprises have all gradually destroyed the paradigm of urban socialist employment. This paradigm was based on an ideological principle: the urban enterprise must not be merely an economic entity, it has to assume social and political responsibilities. Most urban workers were employed by enterprise units (*qiye danwei*) in charge of every aspect of their social lives. Not only were workers enjoying a life tenure job but they were also provided with a wide range of welfare facilities in different sectors of social life (housing, health, pension, etc.). Apart from these social functions, the *danwei* system operated as a political entity, further controlling its employees' lives.[1] Andrew Walder has defined the labour relations produced by the *danwei* system as neo-traditional. The monopoly on the distribution of material rewards and the total control of cadres over the mechanisms of social promotion led to the appearance of an 'organized dependence', structured through clientelist networks between workers and cadres.[2] Unlike what has emerged in Western capitalist countries, the relations between workers and management were not based on the general principle of labour exploitation and a clear conflictual frame of organic ties connecting workers and power.[3] This left the door open to conflicts, but conflicts which were themselves developing within the political apparatus and solved through internal bargaining.[4]

At the same time, the *danwei* system and the paradigm of urban socialist employment were highly fragmented. The splits involved the working class (old qualified workers/contractual young workers, big enterprise workers/

small enterprise workers, etc.) and the status of the *danwei* (central/local units, big/small units).[5] Moreover, it is important to observe that urban areas were not entirely devoted to public employment. In fact, a small minority of workers were not enjoying the benefits provided by the *danwei* system. Employees of collective small-scale enterprises enjoyed the same working conditions as contractual workers forming altogether a new type of Chinese proletariat. The *danwei* and the socialist employment systems represented the general framework in which the relations between workers and cadres functioned during the Maoist period. Every *danwei* constituted a 'small society' (*xiao shehui*), a 'village within a city' dominated by the feeling of belonging to a community.[6]

The reshaping of labour relations started in 1986 with the introduction of the labour contract, abolishing the life employment system and allowed the enterprise to fire and hire people according to economic rationality. Besides, the *danwei* welfare system was replaced by a state welfare sytem.[7] The objective of the reform was to alleviate the social and political burden of state-owned enterprises (SOEs) with the aim of improving their financial situation.[8]

Since 1994, the pace of restructuring has increased to a great extent. This acceleration does not have its origins in policies and regulations adopted by the central government, but rather in official declarations allowing local authorities and enterprises to transform general orientations into practical decisions.[9] In addition, local authorities and enterprises have largely used these new opportunities to reshape the structure of urban labour and to redefine labour relations through a commodification of the workforce. Henceforth, as a commodity, the workforce must have an economic utility and create wealth.[10] This radical change has led to a massive phenomenon of redundancies. According to the Research Institute of the Commission of Planification, 13 million people were laid off in 1997.[11] Other sources give 12 million people laid off in 1998 and 11 million in 1999.[12] Quite clearly, there is a complete withering of the *danwei* system of protection (including payment of pensions) and, as a result, an impoverishment of an important portion of the urban population. In recent years, a significant number of demonstrations, petitions, sit-ins and violent actions have taken place in most big cities, protesting against the degradation of living conditions of certain elements of the working class.

This kind of phenomenon is quite common in both developed and developing countries. But, because of the particular position that the urban working class occupies in the Chinese political scene, the situation of these industrial workers deserves special attention. As seen above, the Chinese urban working class is different from the 'classic' working class. Its insertion within the political apparatus and its dominant position in the cities has lead to its protests generating immediate political outcomes. This social unrest has raised two sets of parallel questions. First of all, are conflicts challenging the organic ties which have linked the urban working class and the socialist state since 1949 to such an extent that urban workers could develop autonomous political actions?[13] Do they represent a danger for social stability? Secondly, is the state able to change as a result of the new situation, and in which direction?

In order to answer these questions it is necessary to insist on regional variations. The proportion of SOE employees in the workforce, the size and scope of redundancies, the strategic importance and financial availabilities of the place are some elements, amongst others, which determine the behaviour of the different actors. In this chapter, the main hypothesis is that urban China is living a double phenomenon. In certain regions, mainly the coastal provinces, where the opportunities for re-employment exist, a new kind of labour relations is emerging alongside a process of 'normalization' of working conditions, labour conflicts and the relations between the state and the workers. The second phenomenon concerns industrial provinces and cities of the northern and central regions. In this case, not only are redundancies very important but the prospects for employment are very grim. In such a context, the local state (mainly the municipal authorities) is involved in a socialization of its modes of actions and of its ways of functioning in order to 'soften' the social consequences of reforms. At the same time, far from breaking organic ties with the political apparatus, workers try to preserve a new kind of dependency based no longer on the enterprise, but directly on the state. This attempt leads to a 'ritualized social bargaining' in which people in need organize themselves (through regular and peaceful demonstrations and reasonable demands) in order to maintain a constant, non-political but efficient pressure on local governments. Nevertheless, here also the regional variations are very important and the conditions of bargaining are highly differentiated from place to place.

The social consequences of restructuring

Although unemployment is the most important social outcome of SOE reforms, it is very difficult to evaluate the unemployed population. Despite the numerous declarations concerning redundancies, the official number of the registered urban unemployed (*dengji shiye*) remains quite stable: 4.76 million people in 1994 (unemployment rate:[14] 2.8 per cent),[15] 5.53 million in 1996 (3 per cent),[16] 5.77 million at the end of 1997 (3.1 per cent)[17] and 6 million at the end of 1998 (3.5 per cent). Moreover, not only has the number of staff and workers (*zhigong*) remained stable between 1994 and 1997 (148 million against 146 million) but the number of SOE staff and workers remained unchanged during that same period (108 million against 107 million).[18] This apparent paradox can be easily explained by the fact that Chinese statistics have a very restricted approach to unemployment. The unemployed population comprises only urban people fired by bankrupt enterprises benefiting from unemployment insurance funds. Apart from this population, Chinese officials and enterprises have invented some particular categories of people who have no job but are not considered as unemployed. According to the regime, China remains a socialist country and unemployment cannot structurally exist. Thus, to be without a job is necessarily a temporary situation.

Most redundancies take the form of laid-off employees (*xiagang*) who no longer work but are supposed to continue to receive part of their income, for which they are accounted as staff and workers. That is why they are not considered to be unemployed but rather of temporary non-working status. They are supposed to be re-employed shortly after being laid off. Needless to say, it is difficult to give an evaluation of this population category. If the numbers vary according to different sources, it is mainly because of the evolution of the meaning of the term *xiagang* itself. In fact, this status is becoming gradually less temporary. On that point, it is interesting to notice that some local authorities have set up 'laid off certificates'[19] in order to provide preferential opportunities to the *xiagang*. This kind of 'labelling' reveals the fact that the laid-off status is no longer provisional.

Although the different figures available are contradictory, most of them conclude that the proportion of re-employed *xiagang* is quite small. According to surveys done by the State Council and other labour departments, until 1997, 20 million people were laid off, and 70 per cent of them were re-employed or forced to go on early retirement by 1998.[20] Other sources estimated then the rate of re-employment to be 60 per cent.[21] The scenarios given by other researchers are much grimmer. For instance, in 1996, laid-off workers remained, on average, for three years and nine months without a job, and at the end of that same year, only 26 per cent of *xiagang* were re-employed.[22] In the case of Shanxi, about one-third of laid-off workers were re-employed,[23] while in Liaoning it was about 25 per cent.[24] Even in Shanghai, where the problem of employment is less serious than in other parts of the country, 34.8 per cent of *xiagang* waited for one year before finding a new job, 24.1 per cent between one year and two years, 18.2 per cent from two years to three years, and 22.9 per cent more than three years.[25] It is very difficult to estimate the number of re-employed workers, given that most of the re-working *xiagang* are involved in self-subsistance activities (*zimo zhiye*), i.e. petty and unstable jobs like peddling, repairing, shoe-shining, etc. For instance, already in 1997, amongst the 4.8 million *xiagang* who got a job that year, 2.8 million of them were employed in the private sector (with about 1.9 million of them being in the 'self-subsistance sector').[26] The majority of laid-off workers lack qualifications and therefore have serious difficulties in finding a new job.[27] In addition, some of the *xiagang* people are forced to go on 'early retirement' (*tiqian tuixiu*), contributing therefore to an artifical decrease in the real number of *xiagang* workers. Table 4.1 gives a general estimation of unemployment.

Table 4.1 Unemployment estimates

Years	*1994*	*1996*	*1997*	*1998*	*1999*	*2000*
Numbers*	6.5	13.5–15.5	14.7–17.2	16–19	15–20	22–25
Proportions**	3.4	6.6–7.6	7–8.2	7.6–9	7–9.3	10–11.3

Sources: 'Xiagang zhigongde shenghuo . . .' (1997); Sun (1998); Ma (1998); Li (1998); Fan (1998).

Notes:

* Registered unemployed plus laid-off without having been re-employed yet (in million).

** Proportions of the unemployed population to urban unemployed persons and employed persons (in %).

According to Chinese researchers, 'hidden unemployment' (*yinxing shiye*), i.e. the surplus workforce, was 35 million in 1996[28] and 30 million in 1997.[29] Numbers from the Statistical Bureau (quoted by a Hong Kong review)[30] estimate that between 550,000 and 600,000 people were fired every month in 1997 and 1998, and both the unemployed and the *xiagang* reached 37 million people (35 per cent of workers and employees). Obviously, this figure takes into account the re-employed laid-off.

In order to give a more precise picture of the situation of unemployment it is important to include in our estimations another kind of people: the victims of partial or delayed payment of wages (*touqian gongzi*). These workers have a job but no salary and often do not work any more or only part-time. Under such circumstances, they can be considered as an alternative type of unemployed, as employers break the labour contract by stopping or reducing the payment of labour. Most of the time, this phenomenon is a consequence of financial difficulties, according to some sources, some enterprises take advantage of the official declarations on the necessity of reshaping urban labour in order to diminish wages, without firing an extra amount of workers. For instance, in Jixi (Heilongjiang), 440,000 workers from the Bureau of Mining received about 40 Rmb per month in the mid-1990s.[31] According to a paper published in April 1994, 80 working units had not paid wages and bonuses to 300,000 employees since November 1993 and 180,000 other workers had received only one-third or two-thirds of their wages.[32] About 300,000 workers from the four most important mining plants of Heilongjiang had not been paid at all for several months.[33] In 1995, more than 70 per cent of SOEs put off, at varying degrees, the payment of wages.[34] In Taiyuan, some people were not paid for fifteen months in 1995.[35] In 1996, Hugang (Huhehot Steel Company) employees only received 50–70 per cent of their wages for eight months.[36] At the end of June 1996, in the whole of Liaoning, 7,847 companies, or 14.2 per cent, were behind with salaries (7,000 in October 1995). This lack of payment concerned 1,702 million workers for a total amount of 2.81 billion Rmb (or 1,650 Rmb per head), which represents an increase of 170 per cent and 290 per cent respectively compared with the previous year.[37] In the north-eastern provinces, 4.26 million workers and retired people lacked an income because of delays in payment in June 1996.[38] In Zibo (Shandong), 44.8 per cent of workers no longer received an income.[39] By 1998, 12 per cent of Chongqing employees did not receive any income at all.[40]

Nationwide figures confirm this whole phenomenon. According to trade unions, 10 million workers were victims of delay in payment of wages in 1995[41] and more than 70 per cent of SOEs put off at varying degrees the payment of wages.[42] Vice-Premier Wu Bangguo estimated at 11 million the number of Chinese workers not having been paid or only partially paid in the first four months of 1997.[43] According to another official source, 12.8 million retired people and workers were in that situation in 1996 and 13.8 million people in the first nine months of 1997.[44]

The blurred nature of Chinese statistics on unemployment reflects the difficulties faced by the Chinese authorities in dealing with the question of jobless people in a unified and transparent manner, both for ideological reasons (because China remains socialist and therefore cannot produce non-workers) and for pragmatic reasons (because of the socio-political danger of a 'head-on' attack). It is therefore a matter of making the reshaping process acceptable by dividing it up, by fragmenting the problem while multiplying policies or even leaving the companies to sort themselves out, as with post-poned wages. That way, the Chinese authorities can maintain the fiction of a non-violent transition from the socialist paradigm to the new 'modern labour market'. The problem is that the victims of the SOE restructuring do not live in a fiction but rather in a (difficult) reality.

Apart from redundancies, urban dwellers are also struck by two additional problems. The first one concerns the reform of the welfare system. In most places, the previous system – based on the payment by the enterprises of health expenses and pensions – is collapsing while the new one is far from being able to establish a social security net. The old age protection system (*yanglao baozhuang zhidu*), the health protection system (*yiliao baozhang zhidu*), as well as the unemployment protection system (*shiye baozhang zhidu*),[45] are all based on the contributions of enterprises and workers to funds managed by local authorities, but are unable to assume a universal protection. First of all, the enterprises are not willing to pay the due contributions, as some of them do not have enough funds, and others prefer to save money for investment purposes. Second, the total wages on which the contributions are calculated have declined in certain regions.[46] Third, as funds are badly managed, it is not rare to discover that large amounts of money have disappeared or have been been transferred to private accounts. For instance, in 1998, 8.2 billion Rmb devoted to the payment of 1.8 million retired workers were embezzled.[47] As a result, the urban population has experienced for several years a neat decrease in social security: many urban dwellers have not had their health expenses reimbursed,[48] *xiagang* people and a proportion of registered unemployed have not received any money at all, and millions of retired people have suffered delays in the payment of their pensions.

The second problem lies in the commodification of previously freely provided social facilities like schooling and housing. For several years, school fees and vents have increased to a great extent.

Social unrest and regional variations

Already in 1993, more than 6,300 strikes of different forms involving some 320,000 people, 440 cases of disturbances of the public order and 210 cases of rebellion occured in different cities.[49] Another source quoting a document from the Ministry of Labour included 12,000 conflicts and 2,500 sit-ins, destructions of machines, strikes and detentions of cadres.[50] In 1995, about 480,000 persons attended more than 3,700 meetings, strikes, petitions and demonstrations in enterprises, administrative organs, mining plants and working units all over the country.[51] According to an internal report published by a Hong Kong review concerning 120 cities, 1,520 demonstrations, protest meetings and petitions gathering 1.85 million signatures occurred from January to September 1996. On 52 occasions the troubles led to violence, and 820 people were injured (citizens, state and party officials, and policemen). That same year, 1,740 strikes and 370 attacks on state and party organs occurred.[52] In 1997, the situation worsened (455 strikes and demonstrations broke out). This increase in social instability seemed to be linked to the sudden acceleration of the reforms after the XVth Party Congress. Local authorities used this opportunity to eliminate small and medium sized enterprises, forcing workers to resign, to go on early retirement or to buy shares of unprofitable enterprises.[53] From January to October 1997, 115 cases of attacks on party and governmental buildings were reported. These numbers seem to be below those of 1996 but the incidents were more violent: 320 cadres were injured and 10 killed.[54] In 1998, about 3,300 demonstrations, protest meetings and petitions took place, 400 of them leading to violence.[55]

Social unrest in urban areas is usually viewed as a direct result of political instability. But in order to measure its political impact, it is necessary to measure the nature and meaning of protest movements. In fact, it appears that behind social unrest lay very different social and geographical situations. Due to the limited available local monographes on urban social problems, it is rather difficult to draw a precise picture of local variations. Although internal provincial differences between cities are certainly very significant, the analysis needs to be limited to general and rough statements at the regional level. First, it is helpful to distinguish two geographical groups. The first one could be named the 'labour post-crisis' group, including the developing coastal provinces (Guangdong, Fujian, Jiangsu, Zhejiang and Shanghai). The second one includes most of the central and northern provinces (Liaoning, Jilin, Heilongjiang, Sichuan, Hunan, Shandong, Shanxi, Shaanxi, Hebei, Hubei, Henan), where SOE restructuring takes the form of a labour crisis.

The differeences between these two groups are based on three aspects of protest movements. First of all, trouble cases are far more significant in the second group.[56] In cities like Shenyang or Wuhan, troubles occur on a nearly daily basis in certain periods. Second, in the first group of provinces, protest movements are limited to an enterprise whereas in central and northern regions social unrest involves social categories. Finally, in coastal provinces, conflicts generally concern working conditions and labour payment. In other provinces, the question at stake is living conditions in post-reshaping urban society. This is probably the most important point, as it is directly linked to the status of labour in post-socialist China. From this point of view, it is possible to distinguish two different Chinas, one where labour supply remains important (although under new conditions), and another one where finding a job is a rare opportunity.

But before going deeper into this matter, it is necessary to note that the variations in the status of labour depend on different factors, particularly the proportion of employment in SOEs before the restructuring process. In the north-eastern regions (Heilongjiang, Jilin and Liaoning), 65 per cent of the urban workforce was working in SOEs in 1994. In Sichuan, Henan and Shaanxi, the proportion was respectively 68 per cent, 71 per cent and 77.5 per cent against 53.4 per cent, 52.7 per cent, 50.8 per cent in Fujian, Guangdong and Zhejiang.[57] As a consequence, the size of surplus workforce and the number of redundancies vary to a great extent between the two groups of provinces. In 1997, amongst the 13–14 million laid-off, 1.6 million were living in Liaoning province. At the end of 1997, nearly 13.7 per cent of the Chinese *xiagang* who had not yet obtained a new job were living in Liaoning.[58] A second factor concerns the extent of re-employment. In coastal provinces, economic growth offers more opportunities to the *xiagang* to find new jobs in foreign investment factories or even in modernized enterprises. In Fujian, there were only 140,000 *xiagang* without a job[59] by the end of 1997, against 710,000 in Shandong and 1.23 million in Liaoning.[60] In Shaanxi province, only one-third of laid-offs got a new job.[61] Even in Shanghai where the proportion of SOE employees was quite high (67.3 per cent), 1.1 million laid-off were re-employed from a total of 1.3 million.[62] Moreover, the 'jobs' obtained in the two groups after being laid-off were not always the same kind. Most of the new occupations in the second group were self-subsistance activities (*zimo zhiye*). The working conditions in coastal provinces are certainly very bad but the fact that workers are so numerous at least allows them to develop solidarity.

Towards post-socialist labour conditions

Most conflicts which have taken place in coastal provinces concern wage levels and working conditions. The enterprises involved are usually Hong Kong, Korean, Taiwanese and Japanese-invested factories, or otherwise collective, private and SOE enterprises working as subcontractors for foreign companies.[63] For instance, in May 1994 there was a strike at the Hong Kong-invested Weiwang Company in Zhuhai: over 2,000 workers asked for an increase in wage of 30 per cent in order to compensate for an inflation rate of 21 per cent.[64] In Zhuhai Meida Cassettes Factory, some workers went on strike to protest against new regulations imposing fines for late working, forcing workers to supervise each other.[65] In March 1996, 600 workers of the Xiede Hardware Manufacturing Factory, set up by a Hong Kong businessman, went on strike. The demands were reasonable (an increase of 1 to 3 Rmb per hour), but the boss refused, and the workers were beaten by the police.[66] In July 1998, over 200 workers from the Hong Kong-owned Chong Xing Qiu Spectacles Factory took part in a collective protest in front of the Cha Shan government officies. The workers had not been paid for three months.[67] Protest movements also take place in SOEs, although they take the form of collective inaction like 'collective goldbricking, withdrawal of effort, spontaneous work stoppages and quasi sit-ins'.[68]

According to Lee Ching Wan, the collapse of the neo-traditional 'organized dependence' in Guangzhou has led to the emergence of a new dependence she names 'disorganized despotism'. Despotism 'denotes three aspects of labour management relations: labour's institutional dependence on production work for livelihood, imposition of coercive modes of labour control and workers' collective apprehension of such control as violations of their material interests and moral precepts'.[69] The term disorganized 'refers to the disarticulation of diverse reform measures as providing the institutional context for a despotic regime'.[70] In the same spirit, Anita Chan uses the term 'bonded' labour market[71] to describe the new kind of labour relations which is appearing in the non-state as well as the state footwear industry. The workers have to pay a 'bond' (*yajin*) and to accept low wages and bad working conditions.[72]

What is emerging behind these developments is a new labour status – and even a new working class. In reading reports concerning working conditions in the SOEs, collective, private or export-oriented foreign controlled enterprises, one is struck by similarities with nineteenth-century European factories or today's developing countries' export sector: 'Young women forced to work seven days a week, 12 hours a day, earning as little as 12 to 18 cents an hour with no benefits, housed in cramped, dirty rooms, fed on thin rice gruel, stripped of their legal rights, under constant surveillance and intimidation'.[73] Many workers have been victims of factory explosions and fires, as in Jinjiang city (Fujian), where 32 workers locked in a dormitory were killed.[74] These young women are often migrants coming from remote rural areas, with no protection, and are fired as soon as they develop serious health problems.

The presence of migrant workers in most coastal cities is crucial: in Guangzhou, more than one-third of urban employees are registered migrant workers,[75] and in Dongguan nearly 90 per cent of production line workers are migrants.[76] This situation contributes to a general reassessmemt of wages and working conditions. Those workers who remain in SOEs are compelled to accept a new labour relationship based on exploitation.[77] They have to behave as normal workers paid to create revenues for the owner of the capital. It is not surprising that, at the same time, they are discovering what the European working class has practised for a long time: everyday forms of 'resistance of the weak'[78] as well as embryonically organized collective actions, such as spontaneous strikes. From such a perspective, social unrest in coastal provinces could be the prelude to the emergence of workers' movements as an answer to the development of 'disorganized despotism', but this is very difficult to gauge at present. According to publications from dissident organizations, the number of trade unions in coastal provinces is increasing. But other sources of information note the development of secret localistic groups[79] that try to protect the interests of their members in organizing different forms of collective actions, often using blackmail, extortion and violence.[80]

Whatever the evolution of the labour conflicts may be, it is clear that the neo-traditionalist 'organized dependence' is collapsing. It is striking to notice that the local authorities rarely interfere in the new labour relations set up between workers and enterprises. Not only do governments, labour bureaus and trade unions hardly ever intervene during conflicts,[81] they rarely try to protect the workers' rights. In fact, they often even tend to suppress any attempt to form independent trade unions.[82] Thus, workers feel that trade unions are on the side of the capitalistic entrepreneurs and are more interested in doing business with Hong Kong and Taiwan people than in defending their workers. When protest movements succeed, it is generally because workers have to fight against both the enterprise management and the local labour bureau and trade unions.[83] Local authorities content themselves in taking general measures in order to limit social instability. For example, it is forbidden in Guangzhou to fire a worker whose spouse is unemployed or who has been in the job more than ten years and is within a five-year period of retiring.[84]

However, at the very same time, new kinds of dependence are emerging. The bonded labour market and disorganized despotism contribute to the fragmentation of the new working class. The social and geographical origins of the workers determine their status, their working conditions and their income level. Urban SOE workers experiment with new labour relations, but they are better treated than migrants.[85] They can use social relations (*guanxi*) and protections to limit the consequences of the normalization of the working class. Within the migrant population itself, the status of the different local groups depends on their ability to protect their interests and to weave relations with the local powerholders.[86]

Conflicts and socialization of the state

What is most striking in the protest movements in central and northern SOEs is their standardized aspect.[87] Whatever the cause of the incident, it usually starts with people gathering in the centre of the town in front of the municipal government building. This fact witnesses the growing importance of municipal authorities as the main interlocutors of the angry population. The protesters block a main crossroads in order to be received by the officials, giving them a petition or a set of documents including their demands. The incident usually lasts for a short time, either because the officials agree to receive the representatives and deal with the problem, or because the police intervene and disperse the crowd, usually in a peaceful way. But in other cases, the scenario may be quite different. According to the Hong Kong press, in 1997 riots took place in Zhengzhou, Kaifeng (Henan) and in Jinan (Shandong), where buildings were looted and police cars set on fire by protesters. Over 500 persons were injured in front of the party committee of Hebei province during fights between petitioners and the police.[88] In Shaoyang (Hunan), 1,000 laid-off workers looted the director of the local police administration's office in order to protest against the arrest of five of them, who were suspected of attacking the party committee building and the office of a factory boss.[89] Sichuan is the province where the most violent incidents occured. In July 1997, according to dissident sources, over 100,000 Mianyang protesters were brutally dispersed by the police: about 100 people were injured and 80 arrested. According to Sichuan officials, only 700 citizens attended the demonstration and 9 were put into custody. According to them, the financial problems facing the employees of an enterprise on the verge of bankruptcy were at the origin of unrest in the city.[90] In October 1997, the Hong Kong media reported fights between the police and 300 workers from the Radio Factory in Zigong. They had not been paid since the year before. The protesters blocked a crossroads for three hours.[91] The authorities admitted the incident but they claimed that the protesters were only 30 retired people who had not received their pensions and denied that violence occured.[92] Because of the very grim situation in the region at the time, it is possible that the sources described different movements taking place simultaneously. Demonstrations broke out again in Zigong in March and April 1998, but this time with no violence. The protesters were *xiagang* and retired workers who no longer received any money from their enterprises. They demonstrated and blocked the streets in the centre of the town.[93]

However, apart from these cases, the troubles are dealt with by relatively 'soft' means, especially if we compare them with the way the authorities deal with rural troubles. In urban areas, the authorities seem to prefer to negotiate. Even in Shaoyang where the troubles were particularly violent, the local government played the card of moderation and ordered to free the five detainees. Local authorities try to calm the protesters down and to satisfy some of their demands, promising for example the payment of due wages and pensions or giving emergency aid to the people in need. Arrests are not frequent except when the protest is violent – but even in this case only the leaders are usually put into custody – or when dissidents are involved.[94]

Most movements are spontaneous and lack any form of organization. Very few sources provide examples of organized strikes and demonstrations by structured organizations.[95] However, if they exist, they do not seem to have developed to a great extent as they remain very discrete and are rarely noticed even in internal documents and informal discussions with researchers. For reasons explained below, they probably do not represent an important force among workers for the time being.

The demands of the protest movements are usually not connected with political objectives. Even when the redundancies or closures are contested (which is rarely the case), the aim is not to contest the policies themselves but rather the social consequences of the SOE reshaping, such as the non-payment of wages and pensions, or the absence of social and financial protections for the laid-off.[96] There is no question of really defending the old system or opposing the reforms. Most of the slogans are pragmatic: 'we want to eat',[97] 'we want food and work',[98] 'we must exist, we need justice', 'save the people',[99] 'we want wages', 'respect for the old workers', 'we need money to live', 'we want our pensions',[100] etc. These demands reveal in fact the appearence of a 'new poverty' phenomenon in urban areas as a result of the increasing unemployment rate.[101]

Leaving aside certain periods (notably the Great Leap Forward), poverty has always been limited to a fringe group of the population, seen as 'the enemies of the regime' and to a minority which had no access to the system of public employment. Even though the urban population affected by poverty is still limited, the fact that millions of urban citizens are meeting growing difficulties in their daily life is a real shock for urban society. Official statistics classified only 12 million urban residents as poor,[102] and 8 per cent of workers were considered to have encountered difficulties in their daily life in 1994, against 5 per cent in 1993.[103] In 1996, the number of urban poor was contained between 12 to 20 million.[104] Actually, these estimates only concern the absolute poor (*juedui pinkun*), i.e. those whose income does not enable them to buy basic essentials.[105] Other figures include people suffering relative poverty (*xiangdui pingkun*), i.e. people whose income is largely below the average income. According to Zhu Qingfang, there were 30.8 million poor people in 1995: 12.4 million people in absolute poverty, 11.5 million unpaid workers and retired people, 4.9 million unemployed and 1.9 million old and handicapped. In 1996, the average income per capita of poor people decreased by 12 per cent, reaching 1,321 Rmb per year (30 per cent of urban average income), and 90 per cent of people in absolute poverty lived in the centre and the west. In fact, 30 per cent were poor due to delays in wage payment, 20 per cent because of unemployment, 17 per cent for not having received their pensions, 10 per cent for earning low wages, 10 per cent because of inflation and 5 per cent because of being old or handicapped.[106] In 1995, the employed represented 53.9 per cent of the poor and the retired 16.7 per cent.[107] In 1997, 85 per cent of poor families lived in the centre and the west, among whom 38.4 per cent lived in the three north-western provinces (Heilongjiang, Jilin, Liaoning).[108]

This rapid increase in poverty is parallel to an increase in the gap between social categories. In 1995, 41 per cent of urban dwellers saw their income decline,[109] and in 1997 the number increased to 45 per cent.[110] Obviously, the emerging social polarization has increased the resentment of people in need against the undesired consequences of reform.

But even if political questions are not totally absent, the protest movements do not seem to develop a critique of the regime. For instance, social problems are often connected with corruption, although under what could be identified as a 'populist' approach: the protesters demand honest leaders; they criticize managers who lay off people but spend money in travelling and banquets; they criticize the individual entrepreneurs (*getihu*) who are supposed to make easy money or peasants who come in town and sell vegetables at (supposed) expensive prices; etc. But, as in 1989, no political position is assumed except a defence of the socialist roots of the regime. According to internal sources, leftist slogans have been shouted during demonstrations: 'long life to socialism' (*shehuizhuyi wansui*), 'we want a true socialist system not a false one' (*yao shehuizhuyi, bu yao jia shehuizhuyi*), 'against the new bureaucratic capitalistic class' (*dadao xin guanliao zichanjieji*). In particular, many old workers feel betrayed by the party, stating the following: 'we gave our youth to the party and now it has abandoned us, we ask our children for help, but they have been fired'.[111]

So, it seems that there are neither signs of contestation of the regime nor a tendency towards the development of a political movement. Unlike what is happening in rural areas, protest movements rarely try to popularize their struggle by contacting the media or referring to the law in order to justify their demands. In other words, protesters do not seem to have the intention of breaking the organic ties which link them to the regime. The reason for this conservative approach is quite simple. It seems that very few people consider that the reshaping of urban employment is avoidable. Most workers seem to accept the idea that political decisions have to be based, not on political principles, but rather on the socio-economic interests of 'society'. This fact suggests that China is experiencing what Hannah Arendt calls 'the rise of the social', i.e. 'the emergence of society – the rise of housekeeping, its activity, problems, and organizational devices – from the shadowy interior of the household, into the light of the public sphere'.[112] The notions of economic rationality, production efficiency, profit law, accumulation, income, consumption, investment and poverty tend therefore to be put right at the centre of political action.

Thus, the question at stake now is no longer whether the socialist system needs to be replaced, but rather how to cope with the consequences of the depolitization of politics. In such a context, the most rational and pragmatic form of protesting is to 'blackmail' authorities. In order to reach this objective, workers can play two cards: first, the ideological card (as the regime is still pretending to be socialist, it cannot refuse to help the workers), and second, the 'socialist stability' card (in most places, SOE workers or former workers still represent the great majority of the population, so in order to protect social stability, local authorities must limit the consequences of the SOEs restructuring). This latter tactic is quite efficient. Not only do local authorities try to avoid violent confrontation,[113] but they are usually very keen on reaching an agreement with the protesters. The fact that the negotciations take place at the grassroots level eases the dialogue and improves the efficiency of popular pressure.

The reluctance of workers to develop political autonomy can be explained by a parallel evolution in the political apparatus itself. As a result of unemployment and poverty crisis, local governments have been compelled to adopt new attitudes and new policies. In that sense, the urban society is experiencing something very close to the double phenomenon which Jürgen Habermas identifies with modernity, i.e. an 'etatization' of the society and a socialization of the state. 'Etatization' of the society means that the state takes on a growing number of social duties and then creates a state dependency. This is precisely the case of urban China, as the withdrawal of the social burden by enterprises compels the local state to be in charge of the social reproduction of part of the urban population through charity activities. Socialization of the state means that the state gradually orients its policies toward the satisfaction of social needs and delegates to society a number of activities it previously assumed.

In many places the struggle against unemployment and the support of the poor have become the two main concerns for local authorities. Grassroots administrations like labour bureaus, street bureaus or residents' committees, as well as mass movements like the women's federation and the trade unions, have gradually abandoned their political duties and concentrated their efforts on solving unemployment and organizing charitable work. The re-employment programme (*zaijiuye gongcheng*) set up by the Labour Bureau has been aimed to stimulate the supply of jobs through different means (training programmes, development of a labour market, creation of new jobs, especially in the service sector, etc.) in order to redeploy the laid-off.[114] Within the framework of this programme, trade unions have set up 100 technical and professional training centres, local labour bureaus have created 4,000 employment agencies, and the mass movement street bureaus, and residents' committees have set up 50,000 employment service centres.[115] In

May 1998 there were 30,000 training centres in China.[116] Thanks to this programme 4.3 million jobs have been created and 34,000 institutions have helped 8.7 million people to be re-employed. Moreover 3 million persons have attended professional training sessions.[117]

The enterprises engaging laid-off workers enjoy preferential tax policies.[118] Those *xiagang* who want to set up a business receive some financial support. In Shenyang and in Hunan, authorities have set up a '*xiagang* card' including different advantages.[119] For instance, Shenyang's Planning Department lends land and the Trade and Industrial Department (concentrated on patents and market management) charges them half of the management tax (*guanlifei*).[120] In fact, Shenyang's street offices (*jiedao banshichu*) seem to play a determining role in the creation of street markets, where most of the traders are *xiagang*. One of these offices spent 6.5 million Rmb in the creation of six street markets (flea markets, agricultural product markets, etc.), employing 3,500 *xiagang*.[121]

The implementation of an 'anti-poverty policy' is another way of describing how the state is considering its functions in urban areas. Unlike the situation during the Maoist period, the problem of poverty concerns too many people and is too serious to be met with only the help of friends and relatives, and thus the state has been compelled to promote the creation of a welfare system for urban poor. The first initatives took place in Shanghai in 1993 and then in Xiamen, Fuzhou, Guangzhou, Qingdao and Wuxi. The main measure has been to set up a guarantee system of a minimum basic income (*zuidi shenghuo baozhang zhidu*).[122] The head of a family in this situation has to contact the residents' committee and the street office which are entitled to check the case and to approve the demand. The file is transmitted to the Ministry of Civil Affairs (*mingzheng bu*), which pays subsidies through the street office.[123] The minimum basic income was 114 Rmb per month in 1993, 136 Rmb in 1994, 155 Rmb in 1995 and 164 Rmb in 1996.[124] These represent an average income, as every city can determine its own amount. In 1995, 100 cities had established a minimum income of between 96 and 170 Rmb.[125] In 1997 the figures were respectively 200 cities and between 80 and 250 Rmb.[126]

Finally, state and grassroots institutions have also put in place a charity system in order to struggle against the newly emerged poverty. The trade unions play a leading role in the 'programme for providing warmth' (*song wenhuan gongcheng*) approved in 1994, whose objective is to collect funds to help urban dwellers in need. The funds are used to pay emergency aid, to distribute basic essentials, to help people paying electricity bills, etc.[127] According to a vice-president of the Chinese trade unions, they set up 17,000 local branches of this programme, with a budget of 2 billion Rmb. Four million families benefited from the programme subsidies in 1997.[128] Apart from the trade unions, every institution is supposed to help the poor. For instance, in Shanghai, 50 working units gave 2.9 million Rmb to workers in necessity, so that they could enjoy the New Year Festival. National leaders visit regularly poverty-stricken cities, bringing comfort and money to people.[129] However, this phenomenon does not lead to the creation of non-governmental organizations or associations which would be the last stage of the socialization of the state. Since new orientations of the different institutions have been adopted as an attempt to survive in the new environment, there is no question of them accepting outsiders. Citizens can take initiatives to help people getting jobs but under the control of local institutions and within the framework defined by them. Rich entrepreneurs can give money to poor people but charity must remain 'public' and must follow the official channels.

Confrontation and ritualization

Apart from the standardized modes of action, the analysis of protest movements brings another process to light: a ritualization of social anger. It would seem that protesters have adopted a mode of action based on frequent and peaceful demonstrations in those provinces where the SOE restructuring was launched earlier than in the rest of the country. In particular, in north-eastern China's industrial cities and in big industrial centres like Wuhan, protesters have tended to gather in front of municipality buildings or in the centre of the town on a weekly and even on a daily basis. According to internal sources, from January to September 1998, there were between fourteen and fifteen protest movements in Wuhan.[130] In Shenyang, the same frequency was noticed.[131] Their tactic consists of putting the retired on the front line in order to deter repressive measures, as well as being present as often as possible in order to create a quasi-permanent pressure on officials. The demands are very simple: the protesters claim for money and food. As the protest discourse relies on the official ideology, retired people become very useful: they are the living examples of the contradition of the regime, as China is not only supposed to be a socialist country giving priority to the people's interest, but the government's policy ought to provide for those who have given their lives to socialism. The tactic seems to be relatively effective. In many big cities of central and northern China, wages, pensions and subsidies are distributed in a ritual way three or four times a year, in particular before the New Year and the National Day.[132]

Although the places which have this ritualization are by far the most stricken by unemployment, the social situation there does not seem particularly unstable. It is possible to explain this apparent paradox precisely by the fact that the seriousness of the social crisis created by SOE restructuring has forced local authorities to 'socialize' their policies more than elsewhere. For example, Liaoning is one of the first provinces to have implemented the reform of SOEs. It is also a province largely devoted to heavy industry and therefore especially concerned by 'hidden unemployment'. As a result, at the end of 1997, nearly 13.7 per cent of the Chinese *xiagang* who had not yet obtained a new job were living in Liaoning.[133] In 1997, there were 430,000 registered unemployed (3.7 per cent of the urban active population)[134] and 1,230 million *xiagang* without jobs (10.6 per cent),[135] giving an unemployment rate of 14.3 per cent excluding workers without wages. As a result, local authorities had to emphasize social work, allowing even the development of small business, including often prostitution.[136]

In other provinces like Sichuan the situation is quite different. The reshaping has started later and SOE employment and heavy industry are of less importance. In these provinces, redundancies began around 1999 and protesters still hope to protect their jobs by limiting their demonstrations against the closing down of enterprises.

Hence the forms of social unrest can be seen to reflect the process of reform. According to researchers and officials, the first years of restructuring (1994–96) seem to have been years of confrontation. The protest movements took the forms of strikes and violent demonstrations aiming to preserve the socialist employment paradigm. In a second stage, when it appeared that the SOE restructuring was unavoidable, bargaining, blackmailing and constant pressure took the lead in the means of contest. In central provinces, the evolution seemed to follow the same logic. However, ritualization of protest and socialization of the state have depended on the ability of local authorities to collect funds in order to ease the social outcomes of the reform. These funds can have several origins. They can be collected from successful enterprises (if they exist). They can also be obtained from local banks with the central government's authorization, or directly from the public budget. In this case it is not only the economic situation which is at stake but the political status of the region.[137]

Ritualization and socialization depend also on the existence or not of other problems with which local authorities have to deal. In Liaoning, the unemployment problem is essentially urban, whereas in Sichuan the surplus rural workforce represents another and not less important battlefield. Quite clearly, analysis at the provincial level makes any predictions highly hypothetical. The evolution of the double process depends on various local factors. For example, one year after the Mianyang events, Chinese newspapers echoed a propaganda campaign aimed to prove that all problems had been solved. Efforts were made to stimulate the economy and the growth rate reached 15 per cent in 1997, nearly double the national figure. Undoubtedly, central authorities played a determinant role in this success, probably in providing funds to 'stimulate the economy' but also in intervening directly in the local economic policy. The city government spent 15,000 Rmb to help every *xiagang* to find a job and the local re-employment programme costed 200 million Rmb. The origin of this huge amount of money was justified by the municipality saving money in public infrastructure expenses.

Moreover, it is striking to notice that the Changhong Group, one of the most successful examples of SOE modernization, is based in Mianyang and has the financial and political ability to stimulate local business: 300 new enterprises (many of them subcontrated) have set up a business in Mianyang.[138]

Concluding remarks

Despite its limited scope, the analysis of urban conflicts seems to reveal that the Chinese working class is experiencing two different sets of conditions. The first one concerns the coastal provinces in which the question at stake is not the elimination of a working class but the emergence of a new one. In these regions, not only has the public sector never played an important role in employment but the economic growth which has taken place in the last fifteen years has radically changed the situation of employment. In the 'reformed' SOEs and in foreign investment enterprises, conflicts are of a post-socialist nature. Here, social unrest takes place in a context of deterioration of labour conditions and of income reduction. The new demands witness the 'normalization' of the working class after three decades of socialism. As regards the state, it appears that local authorities have largely withdrawn from the economic field and have cut organic ties with the workers. The passive behaviour of trade unions and local administrations during the conflicts reveal that they do not even have a role of go-between between employers and employees.

In most other provinces, the scenario is completely different. The old working class is on the verge of being liquidated and the prospects for employment appear very gloomy. The opportunities to get a proper job are very small, and many laid-off workers have to rely on personal relations and petty activities to survive. The nature of conflicts has changed along the way. During the first years of the employment reshaping, protest movements were marked by violence and the determination to avoid being laid off, but the recent conflicts reveal resigned behaviour in the workers' ranks. The reshaping of urban employment has ushered in a new phase in coastal provinces, while workers of industrial cities have entered into a political dependence which is, however, less demanding than the previous one.

In comparative terms, China seems to be following the path of many developing countries where a small part of the territory is devoted to export manufacture and the greatest part to the 'second economy', the 'informal sector' or criminal activities.[139] In fact, the picture is quite different. It is true that workers in coastal provinces are the victims of exploitation in similar ways to European workers during the nineteenth century and most workers of the developing countries today. However, the situation in many central provinces displays a double process which changes the perspective. On the one hand, local authorities have socialized their policies in order to compensate the withdrawal of the enterprises from the welfare sphere. The adoption of anti-poverty policies, the emphasis on the re-employment programme, the importance devoted to charity activities by grassroots administration and mass movements witness this orientation. As a result, workers no longer depend on the *danwei* but on the local state. On the other hand, workers tend to ritualize their protest in order to make it more effective. In being dismissed from the *danwei*, workers lose what has crystallized their social identity, i.e. their belonging to a labour community.[140] The old working class is therefore becoming a social group that has to fight to get means of subsistence.

Workers will only enjoy a good position within the process of income redistribution as long as they preserve privileged relations with the local authorities and they prevent conflicts from being solved in the public sphere. As during the 1989 movements, they have no interest in having a public debate. This is probably why conflicts generally do not enter the political field and the democratic movement has few echoes among protesters. Democracy implies the determination of the public interest on the basis of social interests when the old working class, in losing its firm position in the production process, has lost a large part of its social legitimacy. Subsequently, workers prefer to keep clientelist relations and remain within the political apparatus, thus avoiding calling into question the bargaining deal (social stability against benefits).

By accepting the dependence on the state, urban workers can maintain a privileged position. Not only do they escape from 'slavery income', but they rarely fall into extreme poverty (begging is not a common activity in industrial cities and beggars are usually rural migrants). Nevertheless, the socialization of the state has changed to a great extent the relations between local cadres and the population. It is easier for people to put pressure on grassroots officials and on municipal officials than on the 'state' as an autonomous entity like during the socialist period. Moreover, the legitimacy given to social demands – through 'the rise of the social' – compels cadres to try to reach clear and accountable targets: new occupations, professional training, charitable actions, etc. They are to a certain extent supervised by the urban population. But only to a certain extent, as the socialization of the state is often limited to a form of corporatism in which 'the state recognizes one and only one organization . . . as the sole representative of the sectoral interests of the individuals, enterprises or institutions'.[141] In other words, mass movements have changed their activities (from political control to social work), but not their nature. They continue to have the monopoly of the intermediation between the urban population and the political apparatus.

The general impression is that the Chinese state seems 'to live on credit' in trying constantly to find resources to cope with the worsening of social problems. Until now, a major social crisis has been avoided because the local state has been able to assure social reproduction of urban dwellers. However, this analysis gives only a static picture of the situation. The two scenarios concerning the old and the new working classes are based on highly unpredicable factors and first of all on the continuation of economic growth. The ritualized social bargaining costs a lot of money. In recent years, the state has spent 1.15 billion Rmb per year to finance funds devoted to the guarantee of a minimum basic income[142] and trade unions have spent 2 billion Rmb to help urban households in need in 1997.[143] The sum is far from being sufficient. The amount per head of the benefits is not very high and few people are affected.[144] In 1997, an official source estimated at 4.2 billion Rmb per year the necessary funds to help poor urban citizens.[145] However, even this sum seems insufficient if we take into account the number of people in need. Besides, though the re-employment programme represents a heavy burden for local and central finances, its efficiency is highly questionable. For example, it is not uncommon to see managers engaging *xiagang* 'to take advantage of preferential tax policies and firing them after a while'.[146]

But not only are funds insufficient, the uncertainties of employment prospects may also compel authorities to provide more and more money to support the victims of the labour crisis. Local authorities have therefore two means to cope with this growing burden. One consists in relying on public finance through bank loans and emergency funds coming from the centre; the other one by increasing local tax revenues. These two means depend on two unpredictable elements: the continuation of a high level of economic growth and the ability of the central government to guarantee an efficient redistributive system between the different regions. The latter is a recurring problem. Since the begining of the 1980s, the government has tried to increase the level of fiscal redistribution in order to limit the disparities produced by the reform policy. It seems that until now these efforts have remained unsuccessful: despite the anti-poverty policy, coastal provinces still enjoy a privileged position. As stated earlier, the first attempt to set up a welfare system for the urban poor took place in coastal cities. Moreover, of the 2 billion Rmb distributed to poor households in 1997 by trade unions, 20 per cent were given to Shanghai families.[147] Quite clearly, the reluctance of the richest regions to redistribute economic gains contributes to create an inequality as regards poverty.

Finally, it is interesting to note that China's economic development has become increasingly dependent on exogeneous and 'volatile' factors, mostly since the Asian Crisis. No doubt, Asia's economic recovery calls into question the existence of millions of urban dwellers among the ranks of the new working class.

Notes

1 For a more precise description of the *danwei* system, see Lü and Perry (1997); Whyte and Parish (1984); Womack (1991); Yang (1989); Blecher and White (1979); Henderson and Cohen (1984).

2 Walder (1986).
3 Perry (1992).
4 Perry (1995).
5 Lü and Perry (1997); Perry (1995); Chan (1993).
6 Lü and Perry (1997).
7 On this question, refer to Wong and MacPherson (1995).
8 For more details on SOE reforms, refer to Naughton and Fernández-Stembridge in this volume.
9 For example, the XVth Congress in mid-September 1997 confirmed the principle of opening up the capital of the SOEs and the shareholding system without really defining the methods, the process and the conditions of implemenation of this reform.
10 And not only for strictly economic purposes. As we will see, the labour market is still constrained by different social elements.
11 *Liaowang* (5 January 1998: 10–11).
12 *Agence France Presse* (Hereafter *AFP*), 28 February 1998.
13 Referring to what happened during the Tiananmen movement in 1989, see Perry (1992).
14 The urban unemployment rate refers to the ratio of registered unemployed persons to the sum of employed persons and the registered unemployed persons. It is however necessary to note that if we use this method, the ratios given by the Chinese statistics are wrong.
15 *Zhongguo tongji nianjian* (1995).
16 Li Peilin (1998).
17 *Xinhua* cited in *Summary of World Broadcasts, Far East* (hereafter *SWB*), 3255, S1/1–2, 17 June 1998.
18 *Zhongguo tongji nianjian* (1998: 127).
19 In Hunan (*Xinhua* cited in *SWB,* 3104, S1/3, 17 December 1997) and in Liaoning (Interview, Liaoning Academy of Social Sciences, 1998).
20 *Jingji cankao bao* (1998).
21 Sun (1998).
22 Ma (1998).
23 Watson (1998).
24 Kernen and Rocca (2000).
25 In 1996, see Tian and Yuan (1997).
26 *AFP,* 2 February 1998 and 4 March 1998, *Xinhua* cited in *SWB*, 3168, S2/3, 6 March 1998. See also other surveys in Kernen and Rocca (2000); *Shehuixue yanjiu,* (1997); *Jingji cankao bao* (7 February 1998: 1).
27 Watson (1998); *Xiaofei jingji* (1997); Tian and Yuan (1997); Jiang (1998).
28 Zhu (1998: 62–66).
29 Shen (1997).
30 *Zheng ming*, no. 245 (March 1998: 24).
31 That is about 10–15 per cent of the average wage. *Dangdai* (1994–B).
32 *Zheng ming*, no. 198 (April 1994: 30–31).
33 *Ming bao* (5 January 1995: B1).
34 *Jiushiniandai* (1995).
35 Li Meifeng (1996).
36 Wang Junmin (1997).

37 Jin (1997).
38 Zhu (1998).
39 *Zheng ming*, no. 248 (June 1998: 50–51).
40 *AFP*, 28 January 1998.
41 Zhu (1998).
42 *Jiushiniandai* (1995: 31).
43 *Xinhua* cited in *SWB,* 2950, S1/1–2, 20 June 1997.
44 Zhu and Jiang (1997: 221–233).
45 For more details, see the article in two parts written by Ge (1998); World Bank (1997).
46 Ge (1998); Wang Junmin (1997).
47 *AFP*, 25 July 1998.
48 Zhu (1998: 62–66).
49 *Zheng ming*, no. 198 (April 1994: 21).
50 *Dangdai* (1994b: 21).
51 *Zheng ming*, no. 216 (October 1995: 12–13).
52 *Zheng ming*, no. 230 (December 1996: 11–13).
53 *Zheng ming,* no. 242 (December 1997: 16–18).
54 *Zheng ming,* no. 242 (December 1997: 23–24).
55 *Zheng ming*, no. 247 (May 1998: 17–18).
56 *Zheng ming*, no. 230 (December 1996: 11–13); *Zheng ming*, no. 200 (June 1994: 9–10); *Wen Weipo* cited in *SWB/FE*/2144, S1/2–3, 4 November 1995.
57 *Zhongguo tongji nianjian* (1995: 84).
58 Xu, Cao and Zhang (1998).
59 *Xinhua* cited in *SWB,* no. 3143, S1/13–14, 5 February 1998.
60 *Xinhua* cited in *SWB,* no. 3163, S1/6–7, 26 February 1998.
61 Watson (1998).
62 *Xinhua* cited in *SWB,* 3129, S1/9, 20 January 1998.
63 Chan (1994); *Dangdai* (1994a); *Dazhong ribao* in *SWB*, no. 2039, G/12–13, 5 July 1994.
64 China Labour Education and Information Centre (1996).
65 *Ibid.*
66 *Sing Tao Jih Pao* cited in *SWB/FE*/2577, G63, April 1996.
67 *China Labour Bulletin* (hereafter *CLB*), no. 43 (July–August 1998: 16).
68 Lee (1998a).
69 Lee (1998b).
70 *Ibid.*
71 Chan (1998).
72 In a Taiwan-fund shoes factory, the workers had levied 500 Rmb deposit. The net monthly amount paid to new recruits, after deduction for meals and accommodation, was only 20 Rmb (*Zhongguo xinwenshe* cited in *SWB*, 3016, G/6, 5 September 1997).
73 Kernaghan (1998). See also China Labour Education and Information Centre (1995a, 1995b); and information published by the Hong Kong reviews *Change* and *China Labour Bulletin*, Hong Kong.
74 *SWB*, 3016, G/6, 5 September 1997. Two similar cases have recently taken place in a Japanese-invested factory in Huizhou (Guangdong) and in a tennis table factory in Yiwu City (Zhejiang), *CLB,* no. 42 (May–June 1998: 17).

75 Lee (1998a).
76 Li Cheng (1996).
77 Lee (1998a).
78 Scott (1985).
79 Perry (1995); Lee (1998b).
80 *Dangdai* (1998a). In Fujian province, the Taiwanese businessmen were complaining in 1994 about the racket they suffered from local gangs. *Zhongguo xinwen she* cited in *SWB FE*/1969, G11, 12 April 1994.
81 Chan (1994); *Dangdai* (1994a).
82 Lee (1998b).
83 *Ibid.*
84 *Xinhua* cited in *SWB*, 3104, S1/3, 17 December 1997.
85 Chan (1998)
86 Solinger (1991); Solinger (1995).
87 The following statements are based on the analysis of over one hundred cases of protest movements taking place in 1996, 1997 and 1998 in over thirty towns. It is only a small sample of the impressive number of incidents reported by witnesses. Cases are limited, as I have chosen them through different means (Chinese and Western newspapers, internal documents, interviews), reducing therefore the possibilities of having a wider range. The following incidents took place in Nanchong, Dujiangyan, Zigong, Yibin, Suining, Mianyang and Chengdu in Sichuan; Achang, Jiamusi, Qiqihaer, Mudanjiang and Yichun in Heilongjiang; Anshan, Fushun and Shenyang in Liaoning; Zhengzhou, Xudang and Kaifeng in Henan; Changsha and Shaoyang in Hunan; Baoji and Xi'an in Shaanxi; Taiyuan and Datong in Shanxi; Hefei in Anhui; Lianyungang in Jiangsu; Wuhan in Hubei; Zunyi in Guizhou; Shizuishan in Ningxia; Anyuan in Jiangxi; Jinan in Shandong; Maotai in Guangdong; Baotou in Inner Mongolia; and Shijiazhuang in Hebei. The frequency of incidents varies greatly according to different places. In certain cities like Wuhan, Shenyang or Fushun, troubles are very frequent. In other places like Mianyang or Zigong, they have been very specific but violent. Some cities or regions included within the first group are probably in a similar situation as the second one, and vice versa.
88 *Zheng ming*, no. 242 (December 1997: 23–24).
89 *Zheng ming*, no. 250 (August 1998: 27). Between 25 November 1997 and 3 January 1998, many incidents took place in Qiqihaer, Jiamusi, Mudanjiang and Yichun (Heilongjiang). About 15,000 workers, cadres and citizens looted the party committee building and the headquarters of the enterprises. They set police, party and government cars on fire and attacked police headquarters, custody centres and airports. Around 70 people were injured (amongst them 25 policemen), 4 people died and 150 people were arrested. *Zheng ming*, no. 243 (January 1998: 18–19).
90 *AFP*, 17 July 1997; *Zhongwen xinwen she* cited in SWB, 2976, G/4, 21 July 1997.
91 *Hong Kong TV* cited in *SWB*, 3049, G/4, 4 October 1997; and *AFP*, 12 October 1997.
92 *Zhongwen xinwen she*, cited in *SWB*, 3053, G/6, 18 October 1997.
93 *CLB,* no. 42 (May–June 1998: 13–15).
94 This is the case of Tan Li in Guangzhou and Tu Guangwen in Jiangxi. *CLB*, no. 43 (July–August 1998: 10–13).

95 According to *Zheng ming*, several secret organizations of workers were born in different places. *Zheng ming*, no. 230 (December 1996: 11–13). See also *Zheng ming*, no. 241 (November 1997: 36). Hong Kong press includes certain cases of terrorism. Refer to *Ping Kuo Jih Pao* cited in *SWB*, 2873, G/5 (21 March 1997).
96 See for example *Hsin Pao* cited in *SWB*, 2826, G/8, 25 January 1997; *AFP*, 18 June 1997; *Hong Kong TV* cited in *AFP*, 3 December 1997; *AFP*, 9 December 1997; *AFP*, 5 January 1998; *AFP*, 16 March 1998; *SWB*, 3244, G/6, 4 June 1998; *Ming bao*, 3 June 1998: A15; *AFP*, 1 July 1998; *CLB*, no. 43 (July–August 98: 23).
97 *AFP*, 1 July 1998.
98 *Ming bao* (3 June 1998: A15).
99 *AFP*, 19 September 1998.
100 Internal documents and interviews in 1997 and 1998.
101 On the 'new poverty' phenomenon see Ge (1997).
102 *Zhongguo xinwen she agency* cited in *SWB/FE/*2175, G/3, 10 December 1994.
103 *Zhongguo xinwen she agency* cited in *SWB/FE/*2211, G/5, 1 February 1995.
104 *Guanli shijie* (1997).
105 Shen (1997).
106 Zhu (1998).
107 *Guanli shijie* (1997).
108 Zhu and Jiang (1997).
109 *Guanli shijie* (1997).
110 Zhu and Jiang (1997).
111 See for example *AFP*, 18 April 1998.
112 Arendt (1958).
113 The repression is far from being absent of the strategies of control of social unrest. For instance, Zhengzhou authorities set up anti-riots corps composed of young soldiers. See *Henan Ribao* cited in *SWB*, 2960, G/5, 2 July 1997. According to internal information, similar corps have been set up in Sichuan and Liaoning. Nevertheless, the objectives of these institutions are less to 'militarize' society than to isolate the protesters in order to avoid the spreading of unrest
114 *Renmin ribao* (23 March 1995: 2).
115 *Xinhua* cited in *SWB,* 3244, S1/4–5, 4 June 1998.
116 *AFP*, 18 May 1998.
117 *Xinhua* cited in *SWB*, 3255, S1/1–2, 17 June 1998; Kernen and Rocca (2000).
118 Watson (1998); Kernen and Rocca (2000).
119 *Xinhua*, *SWB,* 3104, S1/3, 17 December 1997.
120 Liaoning Academy of Social Sciences. Interviews, July 1997 and September–October 1998.
121 *Shenyang ribao* (24 July 1997).
122 *SWB/FE/*2637, S1/2–3, XH, 13 June 1996.
123 *Renkou xuekan* (1998).
124 *Xiaofei jingji* (1997).
125 *Xinhua* cited in *SWB/FE/*2637, S1/2–3, 13 June 1996.
126 Zhu (1997).
127 Jin (1997).
128 *CLB*, no. 42 (May–June 1998: 15). *Xinhua, SWB*, 2810, S1/3, 7 January 1997.
129 Like Zhu Rongji in Jiangxi. *Xinhua*, *SWB,* 3116, G/5–6, 5 January 1998.

130 For some examples see *AFP*, 13 April 1998; *Sing Tao Jih Pao* cited in *SWB*, 3253, G/4, 15 June 1998; *AFP*, 18 September 1998.
131 *AFP*, 3 May 1998 and internal documents.
132 *Sing Tao Jih Pao* cited in *SWB*, 2824, S1/3–4, 23 January 1997.
133 Xu, Cao and Zhang (1998).
134 *Ibid.*
135 *Ibid.*
136 In Shenyang, there are increasing numbers of venues offering karaoke, massage and saunas.
137 Liaoning is of great strategic importance. It is a military base (including many army enterprises) and a communication junction between China, Korea and Russia. Therefore, to preserve social stability in Liaoning is crucial.
138 *Renmin ribao* (9 June 1998: 4).
139 Guangdong and Fujian, Liaoning and Shandong are particularly struck by smuggling.
140 The similarity with what happened in European countries during the 1980s is obvious. In France and in Great Britain, workers lost a great part of their contesting strength when they were laid off within the framework of the so-called 'industrial restructuration'.
141 Unger and Chan (1995).
142 *Zhongguo shehui bao* (1998).
143 *CLB*, no. 42 (May–June 1998: 15).
144 The 1.15 billions have been distributed to 2 million people, i.e. 575 Rmb per person.
145 *Xinhua* cited in *SWB,* 2906, S1/3, 30 April 1997.
146 *Xinhua* cited in *SWB,* 3241, G/7, 1 June 1998.
147 *CLB*, no. 42 (May–June 1998: 15).

References and further reading

Arendt, Hannah (1958) *The Human Condition*. Chicago and London, University of Chicago Press.

Blecher, Mark J. and White, Gordon (1979) *Micropolitics in Contemporary China: A Technical Unit During and After the Cultural Revolution*. Armonk NY, M. E. Sharpe.

Chan, Anita (1993) 'Revolution or Corporatism? Workers and Trade Unions in Post-Mao China'. *Australian Journal of Chinese Affairs,* no. 29 (January), pp. 31–61.

—— (1994) 'L'agitation ouvrière derrière le "made in China"'. *Perspectives chinoises*, no. 24 (July–August), pp. 10–13.

—— (1998) 'Chinese Factories and Two Kinds of Free-Market (Read Bonded) Workforces'. Paper presented at the Annual Meeting of the Association for Asian Studies, Washington DC, 26–29 March.

'Chengshi pinkun he zuidi shenghuo baozhang zhidu' (Urban Poverty and Basic Living Allowances System) (1998) *Renkou xuekan*, no. 2, pp. 23–28.

Chengzhen pinkun wenti ketizu (Study Group on Poverty in Urban Areas) (1997) 'Chengzhen pinkun ji youguan de tizhi jianshe wenti' (Urban Poverty Related to the Construction of a System of Organization). *Guanli shijie*, no. 3, pp. 192–200.

Chengzhen qiye xiagang zhigong zaijiuye zhuangkuang tiaocha kejizu (Study Group of Research on the Situation of Re-employment of Xiagang People from Urban Enterprises) (1997) 'Kunjing yu chulu' (Difficulties and Ways Out). *Shehuixue yanjiu*, no. 6, pp. 24–34.

China Labour Bulletin (1998a) no. 40 (January–February), pp. 2–6.

—— (1998b) no. 42 (May–June), pp. 13–15 and 17.

—— (1998c) no. 43 (July–August), pp. 16 and 23.

China Labour Education and Information Centre (1995a) 'Behind the Boom: Working Conditions in the Textile, Garment and Toy Industries in China'. Hong Kong.

—— (1995b) 'Women Workers in China'. Hong Kong.

—— (1996) 'The Flip-side of Success: The Situation of Workers and Organising in Foreign-invested Electronics Entreprises in Guangdong'. Hong Kong.

Dangdai (1994a) no. 38 (15 March), pp. 38–39.

—— (1994b) no. 38 (15 May), p. 21.

Fan, Hailin (1998) 'Lun shiye baoxian yu zaijiuye fuwu' (On Unemployment Protection and Re-employment Services). *Renkou xuekan*, no. 2, pp. 29–32.

Ge, Yanfeng (1997) 'Chengzhen pinkun wenti baogao' (Report on Poverty in Urban Areas). In Jiang Liu, Lu Xueyi and Dan Tianlun (eds), *1996–1997–nian Zhongguo shehui xingshi fenxi yu yuce: shehui lanpishu* (Blue Book: The Situation of Chinese Analysis and Prediction). Beijing, Zhongguo shehui kexue chubanshe.

—— (1998) 'Gaige yu fazhan guocheng zhong shehui baozhang zhidu de jianshe wenti' (The Problem of Construction of a System of Social Protection in the Process of Development and Reform). *Shehuixue yanjiu*, no. 1, pp. 98–109 and no. 2, pp. 93–98.

Henderson, Gail and Cohen, Myron S. (1984) *The Chinese Hospital: A Socialist Work Unit*. New Haven, Yale University Press.

Jiang, Ping (1998) 'Bu zaiye renkou tedian ji chengyin' (Composition and Characteristics of the Inhabitants Without Job). *Funü yanjiu luncong*, no. 1, pp. 21–25.

Jin, Si (1997) 'Chengzhen zhigong fupin xianzhuang ji duice yanjiu' (The Present Situation of Urban Poverty and the Study of Countermeasures). In *1996–1997 nian Liaoning sheng jingji shehui xingshi fenxi yu yuce* (1996–1997 Liaoning Province Economic Social Situation Analysis and Prediction). Shenyang, Liaoning renmin chubanshe, pp. 328–339.

Jingji cankao bao (Economic Information Daily) (1998). 'Yao duqudao anzhi xiagang zhigong' (We Must By All Means Find Jobs for *Xiagang* People), 7 February, p. 1.

Jiushiniandai (1995) no. 311 (December), p. 31.

Kernaghan, C. (1998) 'Behind the Label: Made in China', a special report prepared for the National Labor Committee, March.

Kernen, Antoine and Rocca, Jean-Louis (2000) 'The Reform of State-Owned Enterprises and its Social Consequences in Shenyang and Liaoning'. *China Perspectives*, no. 27 (January–February), pp. 35–51.

Lee, Ching Wan (1998a) 'The Labor Politics of Market Socialism: Collective Inaction and Class Experiences Among State Workers in Guangzhou'. *Modern China*, vol. 24, no. 1 (January), pp. 3–33.

—— (1998b) 'Disorganized Despotism: Transition From Neo-Traditionalism in Guangzhou'. Paper presented at the Annual Meeting of the Association for Asian Studies, Washington DC, 26–29 March.

Li, Cheng (1996) 'Surplus Rural Laborers and Internal Migration in China'. *Asian Survey,* vol. 36, no. 11 (November), p. 1132.

Li, Meifeng (1996) 'Neilu gongye chengshi xinsheng pinkun renkou de fenbu, chengyin ji shehui yingxiang' (Distribution, Composition and Social Influence of the New Poor People in Inland Industrial Cities). Taiyuan Academy of Social Sciences, 20 July.

Li, Peilin (1998) 'Laogongye jidi de shiye zhili: hou gongyehua he shichanghua' (Old Industry and Unemployment Administration: Post-Industrialisation and Marketization). *Shehuixue yanjiu*, no. 4, p. 12.

Lü, Xiaobo and Perry, Elizabeth J. (eds) (1997) *Danwei: The Changing Workplace in Historical and Comparative Perspective*. Armonk NY and London, M. E. Sharpe.

Ma, Mingjie (1998) 'Zhongguo chengshi zhigong shenghuo zhuangkuang baogao' (Report on the Living Situation of Workers and Employees in Urban China). *Gaige zongheng*, no. 1, pp. 36–37.

Perry, Elizabeth J. (1992) 'Casting a Chinese "Democracy" Movement: The Roles of Students, Workers and Entrepreneurs'. In Jeffrey N. Wassertrom and Elizabeth J. Perry (eds), *Popular Protest and Political Culture in Modern China: Learning from 1989*. Boulder, Westview Press, pp. 146–164.

—— (1995) 'Labor's Battle for Political Space: The Role of Workers in Contemporary China'. In Davis Deborah (ed.), *Urban Spaces in Contemporary China. The Potential for Autonomy and Community in Post-Mao China*: Cambridge, MA, Woodrow Wilson Centre Press and Cambridge University Press, pp. 302–325.

Scott, James C. (1985) *Weapons of the Weak*. New Haven CT, Yale University Press.

Shehuixue yanjiu (Sociological Studies) (1997) 'Chengzhen qiye xiagang zhigong zaijiuye zhuangkuang tiaocha', Kejizu (Study Group of Research on the Situation of Re-employment of *Xiagang* People from Urban Enterprises) '*Kunjing yu chulu*' (Difficulties and Ways Out), No. 6, pp. 24–34.

Shen Hong (1997) In Jiang Liu (ed.), *Zhongguo shehui xingshi fenxi yu yuce* (China Social Situation Analysis and Prediction). Beijing, Shehui kexue wenxian chubanshe, pp. 90–105.

Solinger, Dorothy J. (1991) *China's Transients and the State: A Form of Civil Society*. Hong-Kong Institute of Asia-Pacific Studies, Chinese University of Hong Kong.

—— (1995) 'The Chinese Work Unit and Transient Labor in the Transition from Socialism'. *Modern China*, vol. 21, no. 2 (April), pp. 155–183.

Sun, Zhigang (1998) 'Bian zaijiuye wei zai chuangye' (From Re-employment to Entreprises Re-creation). *Zhongguo gongye jingji*, no. 5, pp. 41–45.

Tian, Bingnan and Yuan Jianmin (1997) 'Shanghai xiagang renyuan de tiaocha yanjiu' (Study on Shanghai Xiagang People). *Shehuixue*, no. 2, pp. 7–12.

Unger, Jonathan and Chan, Anita (1995) 'China, Corporatism and the East Asian Model'. *Australian Journal of Chinese Affairs*, no. 33 (January), pp. 27–53.

Walder, Andrew (1986) *Communist Neo-Traditionalism: Work and Authority in Chinese Industry*. Berkeley, University of California Press.

—— (1992) 'Urban Industrial Workers: Some Observations on the 1980s'. In Arthur Rosenbaum (ed.), *State and Society in China: The Consequences of Reform*. Boulder, Westview Press, pp. 103–120.

Wang, Junmin (1997) 'Cong gongzheng yu minzhu de jiaodu kan changzhen dishouren qunti wenti' (The Collective Problem of People with a Low Level of

Living Standards Viewed from the Point of View of Democracy and Justice). *Lilun yanjiu*, no. 3, pp. 34–38.

Wang, Peixuan, (1998) 'Chengshi pinkun wenti de zhentan duan' (Diagnostic on Urban Poverty). *Nanjing daxue xuebao*, no. 1, pp. 141–148.

Watson, Andrew (1998) 'Entreprise Reform and Employment Change in Shaanxi Province'. Paper presented at the Annual Meeting of the Association for Asian Studies, Washington D.C, 26–29 March.

Whyte, Martin K. and Parish, William L. (1984) *Urban Life in Contemporary China*. Chicago, University of Chicago Press.

Womack, Brantly (1991) 'Transfigured Community: New Traditionalism and Work Unit Socialism in China'. *China Quarterly*, no. 126 (June 1991), pp. 313–332.

Wong, Linda and MacPherson, Susan (eds) (1995) *Social Change and Social Policy in Contemporary China*. Aldershot, Avebury.

World Bank (1997) *China 2020, Pension Reform in China. Old Age Security*. Washington DC, World Bank.

'Xiagang zhigong de shenghuo zhuangkuang ji qi shehui zhichi' (Social Support and Living Conditions of the *Xiagang* People) (1997). *Xiaofei jingji*, no. 1, pp. 47–51.

Xu, Jiwu, Cao Xiaofeng and Zhang Zhuomin (eds) (1998) *1997–1998 nian Liaoning sheng jingji shehui xingshi fenxi yu yuce* (1997–1998 Liaoning Province Social and Economic Situation Analysis and Prediction). Shenyang, Liaoning renmin chubanshe.

Yang, Mayfair Mei-hui (1989) 'Between State and Society: The Construction of Corporateness in a Chinese Socialist Factory'. *Australian Journal of Chinese Affairs,* no. 22, pp. 31–60.

'Yao duqudao anzhi xiagang zhigong' (We Must by All Means Find Jobs for *Xiagang* People) (1998) *Jingji cankao bao*, 7 February, p. 1.

Zheng ming (1994) no.198, April, p. 21 and pp. 30–31.

—— (1994) no. 200 (June, pp. 9–10.

—— (1995) no. 216 (October), pp. 12–13.

—— (1996) no. 230 (December), pp. 11–13.

—— (1997) no. 241 (November), p. 36.

—— (1997) no. 242 (December), pp. 16–18 and 23–24.

—— (1998) no. 243 (January), pp. 18–19.

—— (1998) no. 245 (March), p. 24.

—— (1998) no. 247 (May), pp. 17–18.

—— (1998) no. 248 (June), pp. 50–51.

—— (1998) no. 249 (July), pp. 10–11.

—— (1998) no. 250 (August), p. 27.

Zhongguo shehui bao (1998) 8 January, p. 3.

Zhongguo tongji nianjian (China Statistical Yearbook) (1995, 1998). Beijing: Zhongguo tongji chubanshe.

Zhu, Qingfang and Jiang Liu (eds) (1997) *Zhongguo shehui xingshi fenxi yu yuce* (Analysis and Prediction of China's Society). Beijing, Shehui kexue wenxian chubanshe.

Zhu, Qingfang (1998) 'Chengzhen pinkun renkou de tedian, pinkun yuanyin jiekun duice' (Characteristics of Urban Poverty, Poverty Reasons and Anti-Poverty Policies). *Shehui kexue yanjiu*, no. 1, pp. 62–66.

5

THE DEVELOPMENT OF THE URBAN HOUSING MARKET

Social implications

Brian Hook

The context for the 1998 reform: proposals and intentions

The reform of the housing system was among the important matters discussed at the first session of the IXth National People's Congress (NPC) in March 1998. The newly elected Premier Zhu Rongji confirmed at a press conference at the time of the Congress that housing development would become a new national economic growth point.[1] This policy had already been alluded to in the Report on Work of the government by the outgoing Premier Li Peng. That document comprised three sections: a review of the work over the past five years; suggestions by the State Council on the work of the government for 1998; and the international situation and diplomatic work.[2]

There is a brief reference to progress in (*inter alia*) urban housing reform in the first section reviewing the achievements in the past five years.[3] The second section, conveying suggestions by the State Council on the work envisaged for 1998, contains the following explicit references to housing: 'The construction of ordinary civil housing should be accelerated. We must press ahead with the reform of housing, taking effective measures to promote its commercialization and making the construction of civil housing a new point for economic growth.'[4]

The suggestions of the State Council conveyed by Li Peng in his report were set out in one of the eight sub-sections: agriculture, state-owned enterprises (SOEs), the objectives of macroeconomic control, opening up to the world, scientific and cultural issues including education and technology, livelihood issues, government restructuring and reunification. The foregoing references to housing were incorporated into the third sub-section in the context of achieving an economic growth rate of 8 per cent in 1998 through 'appropriately increased investment'. In the general context of housing reform it is perhaps equally significant that the preceding sub-section, dealing with the reform of SOEs, includes the following important passage: 'Personnel of enterprises should change their thinking so that production, operation and internal management can meet the needs of the market, and government at all levels should actively help enterprises divest themselves of social functions. Enterprises should accumulate more funds and operate their assets more advantageously.'[5]

The need to accelerate both the construction of urban housing and the reform of the housing system were also subjects referred to in the Report on the Implementation of the 1997 Plan for National Economic and Social Development and on the Draft 1998 Plan. Chen Jinhua, the minister in charge of the State Planning Commission, having drawn attention to conspicuously unsound aspects of the economic structure, referred to the need to 'reconcile the relationships between income and social wealth'. Regarding new points for economic growth in 1998, he stated: 'Focusing on accelerating the construction of urban housing, we should speed up the reform of the housing system'. In the passage of his report on fixed asset investment in 1998, he indicated that of a total amounting to 2,785 billion Rmb, 355 billion Rmb would be for real estate development. He cited agriculture, forestry, water conservancy, railways, roads, environmental protection, the application of high technology to production and urban housing as priority subjects for fixed asset investment.[6]

These documentary references indicate both the main trends in and the strategic rationale for the housing policy. The main trends are increased investment and construction together with systemic reform. The strategic rationale of the policy is to meet the social demand for more and better housing by extending the existing limited market in housing while reducing the overall burden of state institutions, including enterprises, in providing and administering housing. The first part of the rationale is not new. A limited market in housing had emerged in the course of protracted attempts since 1980 to reform the housing system.[7] There had been some improvements over almost two decades, but save for experimentation, the chief characteristic of the old system remained. That was the link between the work unit, the *danwei*, and the construction, allocation and administration of housing. The reference in the report delivered by Li Peng to the need for enterprises to 'divest themselves of social functions' and (here I paraphrase the text) to concentrate on 'core activities' signalled the intention to end a housing system whose provenance was in the socialist economy of the 1950s.

The second part of the rationale indicated by the documents is therefore new; both its economic and social implications must be factored into assessments of enterprise and housing reform in China. The end of what is officially referred to as the welfare allocation of housing[8] was reported on 21 July 1998. The State Council announced that the welfare allocation (*zhufang shiwu fenpei*) would cease during the second half of the year and be replaced by the commercialization (*zhufang huobihua*) of housing.[9] The communiqué granted the various levels of government some latitude in the pace and scope of implementing the policy, but affirmed that with the cessation of the welfare allocation system, all new housing would be sold and not rented. This policy, it appears, would accompany an intensification of the existing policy to sell existing public housing (*gong fang*). The main sources of finance for the transactions were cited as wages, housing accommodation funds, individual housing loans, and funds left over in housing construction subsidies. The intention appeared to be to extend the practice of establishing housing accommodation funds and to establish minimum rates of contribution by the end of 1999.

The baseline for the 1998 reforms

China has been in a state of political, economic and social flux since it embarked unequivocally on the Dengist reform programme in the early 1980s. The administration of housing has been part of this scene. There has, in practice, been a slow and uncertain transition from the pre-existing housing system to the housing system as it existed on the eve of the 1998 reforms. It may be useful, as a measure for assessing the social implications of the implementation of these reforms, to map in some of the chief features of this passage. It seems evident that while the 1980–98 period was one of slow and uncertain transition in the housing system, it was not one of transformation. By this, one implies that the baseline for the 1998 reforms remained generically identifiable with that of the pre-transition system. That system had its provenance in the socialist political-economic system established in the 1950s. Consequently, on the eve of the 1998 reforms, the chief characteristics of the traditional housing system remained substantially and effectively in place.

What were these generically identifiable characteristics? One key characteristic is conveyed by the term adopted to describe the housing system, namely welfare housing allocation (*zhufang shiwu fenpei*).[10] This concept was based on the imperatives of the socialist political economy of the 1950s. These included the appropriation by the central government of funds to be allocated to local governments and enterprises for the construction of urban housing for their employees. The work units involved then allocated the housing to their employees through a housing committee, whose procedures were normally frustratingly tortuous, singularly opaque and consequently generally unpopular. Such procedures would purport to apply objective criteria in allocating accommodation but by repute, they were frequently induced to pursue subjective agendas.

In a study of relations between workers, managers and the state towards the end of the first decade of the reforms, Andrew Walder was able to capture the atmosphere generated in enterprises by the welfare allocation of housing:

> The allocation of factory housing has become easily the greatest source of conflict in factories in the 1980s, and as such it throws into bold relief the way in which the abuse of power and privilege by even a small minority of factory cadres can create seemingly insoluble conflicts and deep-seated antagonisms. In the Mao era, housing assignments were often given preferentially to cadres and their loyal followers in the factory, but the decisions were made behind closed doors, one at a time, and were not announced publicly. In the reform decade, however, managers commonly sought to defuse conflict over housing allocations by creating more 'democratic' forums to make even-handed decisions based on such 'hard' criteria as years on the waiting list, seniority, and metres per person in the current apartment. The members of these 'housing allocation committees' (*fenfang weiyuanhui*) are chosen in a wide variety of ways, and the proportion of workers and managers who sit on them, and the criteria they employ to allocate new apartments, also vary considerably. However, the new committees have instead often heightened worker anxiety over housing allocations and their awareness of cadre privilege. This is so for two reasons. First, the committees have turned the periodic allocation of apartments into a public spectacle, in which the attention of the majority of the workforce is for several weeks focused firmly on the decision-making process and the name list that results. Secondly, regardless of the integrity and good will of some cadres, there seem always to be others who cannot resist manipulating the process to the advantage of their families and friends. The consequence, of course, is to make cadre privilege and abuse of power more transparent than before, and since this is open subversion of the democratic process promised by the committees, it may make cadre privilege appear to be even more illegitimate and intolerable than in the past.[11]

The account included the following examples. In one, a Beijing factory created a committee to assign new housing. The committee adopted a complex points system based on criteria such as current space per person and number of generations in the present accommodation, whether the spouse worked in the same unit or had personal unit-allocated accommodation, seniority and status. The outcome of deliberations was that despite the admirable points system, ultimately most of the apartments went to middle-level cadres (who were awarded supplementary points for their status). Predictably a row ensued. It was settled by reallocating the apartments being vacated by the fortunate cadres to the vociferous protesters.[12]

In another remarkable account, on this occasion of an ultimately failed and, in retrospect, predictably doomed attempt to improve the work of the housing allocation committee, Walder quoted verbatim from interview notes. The episode concerned an individual who had been promoted to be director of his enterprise. During his rise through the ranks the enterprise had conducted three housing distributions. On the first occasion, when he was without authority, the committee had been nobbled by cadres. The new apartments went to their young relatives. On the second, by which time he had authority, he kept the cadres at bay and achieved what he perceived to be a relatively smooth distribution of fifty apartments. After the event, however, he discovered that the cadres had pre-emptively set aside six apartments for 'special cases'. On the third, in 1987, when he had become director and was shortly to be transferred, the committee was out of his hands. The vice-director who had succeeded him forced through the allocation of apartments to two young sons of officials in the company and bureau above the enterprise.[13]

The popular reaction provoked by the third example illustrates an important aspect of the link between the social issues generated by the welfare housing allocation system and the economic performance of the work unit:

> When the drivers heard about this, there were about three days or so when no work was done at all. The unit was thrown into confusion. Everybody did nothing except talk about the housing decisions, from the top of the unit to the bottom. The two vice-directors had a lot of people run to their office to complain and yell, cry, and try to reason with them. About six or seven got really angry and yelled. The two cadres said it wasn't their decision, it was the committee's, and they couldn't interfere in the committee's decision. No one listened to me, or came to complain to me, because they knew I was almost gone. After I left, the unit began to lose money for the first time, and I think this was mainly because of the cadres' workstyle problem and the workers' anger about it . . . This is also a major reason why the drivers began to demand tips all the time from the customers.[14]

There are of course arguably even more important aspects of the link between social and economic issues generated by the welfare housing allocation system. Among them is the degree of dependency of the household on the work unit and conversely the degree of control exerted by those in authority in the work unit over individuals in the household. Until relatively recently, and certainly well into the current reform period, despite the increasing dependence of enterprise managers on workers' performance in meeting the demands of a marketized economy, this dependence or control remained absolute for some and very extensive for others.

Accordingly, when the abolition of the welfare allocation of housing was announced, those in authority in the unit were still able to affect the quality of life of most individuals. They might exercise discretionary authority over access to facilities in education, health, food, clothing and entertainment, permission to marry and start a family, and the location and quality of accommodation for the household.

Until the 1998 decision, reforms in the housing system could therefore be characterized as change within tradition. Nothing that had been adopted appeared likely to replace or even irreparably weaken the dependency of the household on the unit exercising the authority over housing through the welfare allocation system. Despite the market reforms, the shifting imperatives of the workplace, higher wages and salaries, less political pressure, the demise of the traditional household registration system and the advance of consumerism in China, the nexus between the welfare allocation of housing and the role of the work unit has remained, arguably, the chief characteristic of social organization.

I suggest, therefore, that between 1980 and 1998 there has been a transition in the housing system, but until the announcement of the decision to abolish the welfare allocation in 1998, there has been no prospect of a transformation. Take, for example, the main elements of the system: funding for construction, allocation, rent, maintenance, management and ownership. Until enterprises were permitted to divert profits into housing construction and privately funded construction became possible, housing was funded through appropriations by the central authorities for allocation to local governments and enterprises. The retention of profits enabled profitable enterprises to invest in housing but unprofitable enterprises were clearly not so beneficially placed.[15]

The system of allocation, as shown by Walder, remained potentially vulnerable: at best to unscrupulous manipulation and at worst to corruption. The principle on which the rent was calculated did not change radically over the years. On the premise of a socialist economy envisaging low incomes and low expenditures (*di shouru, di xiaofei*) with implicit rather than explicit taxation, there was a comprehensively subsidized system. Accordingly, the practice of providing housing at nominal rents was largely unchanged. Even with a significant growth in real household income, rents remained low.[16]

It follows from the low rent system that there has been minimal provision for maintenance and property management. In fact, the conspicuous feature of the exterior of much work unit housing in China was, until recently, its low levels of maintenance and estate management. Such housing is characterized by pervasive dilapidation, decay and an absence of the spontaneous spirit of self-help and community which, cynicism aside, ought to be axiomatic in this environment. In this respect, it must be said, public housing in China appears to suffer the same syndrome as that in many countries, except that the general material conditions are worse.

Regarding ownership, all land in China is owned by the state and ownership of the public housing constructed on it is vested in the relevant unit.

From 1980 onwards, an effort has been made to sell existing public housing (*gong fang*) at discounted prices. Under this scheme, buyers acquired the right to use the property (*shiyong quan*) with the right to sell it subject to restrictions. This did not amount to a full property right since the land right was not conveyed nor was the price of land factored into the selling price. Thus, in such transactions, a link to the original owner has been retained.[17] Clearly, not all of the private housing has its origins in this scheme. It has become possible, for example, for private developers to acquire the same level of land use rights as enterprises and housing bureaus, albeit at higher prices. When they build, these additional costs are factored into the selling price. Accordingly, prices for private housing with full property rights, as distinct from the right to the use of the property, are much higher than those for the original scheme.

These variations are responsible for a multiple pricing system which, at the lower end of the range, has led to the disposal of a relatively small proportion of the highly-subsidized, low-quality, poorly-maintained public housing stock, and, at the high end of the range, has led to the development of a real estate market restricted by affordability to a few. Accordingly, by 1998, almost two decades after the initial reforms had been launched, the housing system had indeed undergone a transition, but it had yet to be transformed.

There appear to have been three key factors inhibiting its transformation. First, as Aimin Chen shows,[18] there remained a persistently high ratio of price to rent which, save for the disposal of the old public housing stock, discouraged private ownership. Second, in the emerging commercial market, as indicated earlier, the ratio of price to income rendered most housing unaffordable save for rich entrepreneurs, Chinese living overseas and households with one or more members working for foreign companies. Third, the government, possibly fearing the social implications of such a step, had yet to adopt policies that would induce the marketization of urban housing. The government appears to have overcome this inhibition and this implicit calculation is the subject of the concluding section of this chapter.

The social implications of the 1998 reform policy

The new housing reform programme contains five complementary measures, the first of which is the key to the transformation of the existing system:

1 the end of the welfare allocation of housing with no new apartments allocated according to the old system;
2 a substantial increase in rents and the provision of housing allowances to encourage the purchase of the apartments;
3 the availability of loans to facilitate the purchase of housing by individuals;

4 a depreciation allowance based on an employee's length of service and the age of the property to reduce the price of public housing sold to individuals;
5 the right to re-sell public housing after five years subject to the original unit retaining the right of first refusal enabling it to share in any increase in value.[19]

Before discussing the social implications of the reforms, it is necessary to make some general assumptions about the likely speed and intensity of their implementation. Clearly, if they remain merely on paper there will be little change and no effect. There are good reasons to believe this will not be the case.

First, the economic imperatives are self-evident. At stake is the opportunity to boost growth, to remove some of the non-core activity of SOEs, enabling them to improve their competitiveness at a critical conjuncture in national and international economic development. Second, there is an urgent problem posed by the demographic profile: the number of couples requiring housing in the foreseeable future. Third, although there are risks in promoting marketization, it is evident that a regulatory framework is in place, based on experience gained from experimentation and advice from abroad, and the banking system has been prepared for the change. The question remains, however, whether the preparations will be sufficient to cope with the demands of the market.

What will happen next? The new policy marks the end of the welfare allocation system based on the time-honoured concept of 'production first, living standards second, high accumulation and low consumption'. Housing will no longer be allocated according to length of service, status, number of dependants, their age and so forth. The government seeks to reduce the housing burden on the exchequer and on the SOEs by shifting it to householders.

The official view is that direct subsidies to financial departments for maintenance and management cost some 5 billion Rmb annually. The State Economic and Trade Commission has calculated that from 1992 to 1994 the average annual input by SOEs to housing construction and maintenance cost 140 billion Rmb. If the policy remained unchanged, these costs would rise due to demand from a net increase in the urban population and the implementation of the policy of providing 12 m^2 of living space for each person. The funding implications are put at an annual investment of 200 billion Rmb.[20]

The government view of the need to transform the old system is supported by other arguments. These include the tendency in many units to abuse the system, as shown by Andrew Walder in the passage quoted earlier. This has led to quantities of welfare housing being under-used while many deserving families are inadequately accommodated and, consequently, dissatisfied. At the same time, the government notes a rising demand for commercial housing and a commercial housing glut caused by unaffordable prices.[21]

Against this background, the official view is that the needs of the state system and the welfare of the individual can be best met by the creation of an integrated housing market. The commercial market is being stimulated by the availability of loans at affordable prices. At the same time, the public housing market is being given a major stimulus by, on the one hand, the provision of loans, and on the other, the implementation of a policy to raise rents. A 1997–98 survey of some 48,800 residents in major cities by a unit of the State Statistical Bureau indicated 33 per cent of families were owner-occupiers while 49 per cent rented houses from their units.[22] The latter, together with newly-weds, will be among those most affected by a policy which seeks to stimulate both the primary and the as yet undeveloped secondary market in housing. The optimum result, from the point of view of the government, would be the provision of a housing ladder allowing residents a considerable freedom of choice based on affordability and preference.

Some of the social implications of the new policy have already been alluded to in this and earlier sections. The government hopes that its citizens will be attracted to the concept of owner-occupiership. For its part, it will be aware that a level of confidence in the state system, its economic prospects, the rule of law and social stability are pre-conditions for the individual to make the necessary investment in property. There is some justification in such hope in that a significant proportion of old public housing (some 33 per cent, if the survey results are reliable) is currently owner-occupied.[23] If the current price–rent ratio for public housing is further adjusted to encourage buying and discourage renting, and a secondary market develops, the extent of owner-occupation will increase eventually.

The social implications of a substantial increase in owner-occupancy could be far-reaching for the existing state system. By requiring householders to shoulder greater responsibilities, the government will in turn be expected to deliver an enhanced system of state administration, including improvements in the provision and management of infrastructure and facilities. Investment by a majority of urban residents of life savings in their own accommodation, with the prospect of rising values and moving up a housing ladder, will generate a practical reason for closer scrutiny of China's urban governance. Those circumstances could not exist under the welfare allocation of housing.

In urban Hong Kong, on which to some extent China's real estate practice and legislation is based, the prelude to political activism for many activists was the formation of management committees in multi-storey buildings. The colonial authorities encouraged the formation of such committees for sound administrative reasons. Some of the members cut their political teeth on the pressing issues of managing multi-storey housing. The task of managing such densely populated buildings is clearly currently beyond the capabilities of units. Once owner-occupiers envisage a pecuniary interest in the functioning of their building, its infrastructure, its immediate environment, including the proximity of services and schools and so forth, they are likely to develop a rapid and profound mutual interest in the enhancement of the value of their investment.

There is, of course, no certainty that the authorities in China would permit such a trend to emerge. It could, however, be difficult to resist. If the authorities tried to cage the residents by containing legitimate livelihood grievances, there would be a slow and uncertain response to the current sales pitch. The most serious consequence would be that the state would have to continue to shoulder the burden it manifestly wishes to shed. It is no more than speculation, but the present leadership in the State Council might actually envisage citizens' demands for greater administrative efficiency and government transparency as a useful by-product of the housing policy.

Clearly, in the circumstances, if the new policy were to succeed to any significant degree, the transformation of the urban housing market would have its main social impact initially on the traditional role of the *danwei*. A radical change in the role of the *danwei* could not happen overnight, but given the present economic imperatives in China, it appears a likely outcome occurring progressively within an overall time-frame of five years. If this were so, the social implications would be far-reaching.

Among the most obvious social implications are a reduction in the levels of dependency and clientelism generated by the *danwei* system, enhanced levels of independence and individual responsibility, and opportunities for greater labour mobility. This multiple prescription will not be universally welcome but, driven by economic imperatives, it may be a medicine that in various doses everybody must, over time, accept.

The most reluctant to accept it could be cadres whose own livelihood within the social ambit of the non-economic *danwei* system would be directly affected. Within enterprises, they are the modern successors of the often vilified 'cadres divorced from production' (*tuo chan ganbu*) of the Cultural Revolution period. There is already evidence of the reluctance of cadres in the *danwei* or the housing bureaus to sever the link between enterprise or ministry and its housing stock sufficiently to stimulate the development of a secondary market.[24]

The reasons for cadres to resist the policy are twofold. First, they are aware of the level of emancipation for unit members implicit in it. Second, they act on behalf of the enterprise in preserving its share in the windfall profits that could be enjoyed once the primary and secondary property markets become integrated.[25] Meanwhile, however, with the weight of State Council authority behind a policy consistent with national and international policy affirmed at the XVth National Party Congress and, as indicated earlier, at the IXth National Party Congress, it is unlikely that such resistance will prevail over a full-five year period.

Once the key role of the *danwei* in providing accommodation changes, and in parallel a proper housing market from which owners can profit develops, there should be much greater labour mobility. This will benefit both the employees who wish to change jobs and the employers who wish to recruit staff with particular qualifications and skills from other local enterprises or if necessary from other cities. Initially, such improvements in labour mobility and human resource optimization are more likely to emerge in the major conurbations such as Shanghai, Beijing, Tianjin and Guangzhou. Here, the levels of educational achievement, by virtue of the existing concentration of education facilities and human resources, exceed those in other parts of China.[26] The result is they are hubs for the development of the modern economy. Consequently, they are also likely to lead the way in labour mobility, human resource optimization and the development of an integrated housing market.

A reluctance to implement the new housing policy may not be exclusively confined to cadres who fear the loss of vested interests in the existing system. It is evident that the changes proposed may be less acceptable to the older generation than to the younger generation. The former, people aged over forty, tend to be more conservative. Among them could be many who resent the replacement of a system with which they are at least familiar by another with which they are unfamiliar. 'Better the devil you know' could be their likely response. Among the younger generation, however, those aged between twenty and forty, in particular those aged between thirty and forty, the new housing policy should prove popular, since, for many, it comes at a time when they can take advantage of the freedom it offers.

An issue that has to be addressed is what proportion of each generation would be able to afford to enter the new housing market? Clearly, old public housing, being sold at 135 Rmb per m^2 for 60 m^2 apartments, with special subsidies for older residents, loans and incentives, including the threat to raise rents, is an inducement many can afford to take. But even at that level there could be resistance. While the concept of owner-occupancy may appear, at first glance, to be a good deal, in practice it may not be so good; once the extent of the responsibilities such as maintenance are known, the enthusiasm may wane. Much may depend on the levels to which the authorities consider rents may be raised.

Under the new housing policy, all new housing will be sold. As prices must reflect construction costs, site development and land fees, they will unavoidably be considerably higher than old public housing. Encouraged by the new policy, state-owned construction companies and private developers, many of whom are said to be linked to state-owned concerns, are constructing apartments of some 100 m^2 for sale at 300,000. Rmb. And 80 per cent mortgages repayable over twenty years are said to be available from banks and housing accumulation funds operated by work units to promote the sale of these apartments, provided that the purchaser can put down a deposit of 60,000 Rmb.[27]

Such developments appear to be precisely what the leadership has in mind for the new policy. They are a rapid response to the need for a new economic growth point, since they stimulate a range of industries besides construction, are popular and affordable. The downside may be that the emphasis on quantity, together with the setting of a 3 per cent profit margin for developers, could be a prescription for the use of inferior raw materials and fittings. The result could be buildings that deteriorate relatively quickly.

This should not be the case for the purely commercial developments whose buyers are the new affluent urban middle class. Among them are entrepreneurs, staff working in foreign enterprises, and young professionals in high technology companies, banking and finance, particularly where there are two household incomes from such sources. Foreign companies can also buy or lease such apartments for expatriate staff. There is a range of prices for apartments of 150 m^2 that would be classified as either good or very good accommodation in cities in Western Europe.

The price range for such housing is from 2,000 to 9,000 Rmb per m^2, depending on criteria such as location, floor level, car parking and security. Purchase prices range from 300,000 Rmb to 1.35 million Rmb. It is evident that there is some concern over security since prices can be notably higher for developments with high levels of security to deter unauthorized entry, and notably lower where there is none. Security is regarded as necessary close to zones where a large number of migrant workers are located. At present, there is over-supply and insufficient demand at the top end of the market. There is more demand for commercial housing at the lower end of the market where prices are more affordable. Financing is readily available with bank mortgages available from banks such as the Bank of Construction and the Industrial and Commercial Bank of China, and downpayment facilities are often provided by developers.

Conclusions

The housing policy adopted in China in 1998 had the potential to transform the housing system, implying therefore significant social implications in the longer term. As it has been implemented in recent years, there has been a visible increase in owner-occupancy and a transfer of responsibility within the housing system, generating important changes in the role of the work unit. There is documentary evidence that this has been the intention of the current leadership in the SOE reforms. By divesting the latter of their social functions, the prospects for enhanced levels of productivity and competitiveness are progressively becoming a reality.

To the extent that owner-occupancy rises within the current housing system, it is expected there will be a more direct interest in urban governance. Those with a stake in urban property will be more concerned with the provision of facilities, infrastructure and in the protection of the environment. Multi-storeyed owner-occupied housing normally requires residents' committees to coordinate responses to local government. This was the case in Hong Kong. They were vehicles for one of the earliest forms of political activism there. A similar trend may occur in China. The process may be more acceptable to the authorities given the likelihood of its being based in specific livelihood issues rather than abstract ideological issues perceived to be challenging the role of the Chinese Communist Party.

The increase in owner-occupancy could significantly reduce the dependency of the individuals on the work unit and the phenomenon of clientelism within units. It should lead to greater labour mobility and a more efficient labour market. It is expected that these changes will be more appealing to adults under forty than those over forty. The reason for this is, on the one hand, a natural conservatism among the older generation and, on the other, a sense of opportunity among the younger generation.

Regarding demand in the housing market, it is expected that this will continue to be stimulated by a combination of measures such as mortgage and loan facilities to facilitate the purchase of property, and rent increases to alter the price–rent ratio in favour of purchasing. The emerging market will be more integrated than that under the old system but it will remain segmented by price. The large housing developments under construction are a response to the 1998 policy and apartments are available at affordable prices. Although there are reservations about the quality of the construction, the market response is favourable. If development continues and demand remains at a reasonable level, a housing ladder should emerge comprising primary and secondary housing markets. Sustained over the current five-year time-frame, the positive effect on the economy will be significant as corresponding consumer demand for fittings and decoration for old property is generated. The social implications of such a transformation in the housing market are impossible to predict with precision. Provided there is sustained and uninterrupted development of the housing market, it could contribute to a significant advance towards the emergence of aspects of civil society in China.

Notes

1 Kou (1998).

2 Li (1998).

3 *Ibid.* It was noted that average urban per capita disposable income reached 5,160 Rmb and housing 8.7 m^2. The latter reflects the more generous conditions in small cities and towns rather than the cramped conditions in the municipalities.

4 *Ibid.*
5 *Ibid.*
6 Chen, J. (1998).
7 Chen, A. (1998).
8 The term is derived from the practice of providing accommodation, taking into account needs, at a nominal rent within a low wage and low expenditure economy such as that in China before the impact of the Dengist reforms.
9 Xinhua (1998).
10 Kou (1998).
11 Walder (1996: 56).
12 *Ibid.*
13 *Ibid.*
14 Walder (1996: 58). The author is quoting verbatim from an interview conducted in 1990 in the United States with an émigré production worker who had advanced from repair worker to manager over an eighteen-year career.
15 Chen, A. (1998). Between 1979 and 1988, due to developments in small cities and towns, the central government share in housing investment fell from 90 to 16 per cent. At that juncture, SOEs, individuals, local governments and collectives accounted for 52, 20, 6 and 6 per cent respectively.
16 *Ibid.* Rounding off data from the State Statistical Bureau (1981), in 1981, annual urban wages averaged 772 Rmb per worker, living expenses 457 Rmb per person, living space 4 m^2 and rent 636 Rmb; in 1994, similar annual measures showed wages at 4,500 Rmb, expenses 2,852 Rmb, space 7.8 m^2 and rent 29 Rmb.
17 *Ibid.* Based on figures in the *Urban Construction Annual Report* by the Jianshebu Zonghe Jihua Caiwusi, in 1993, over 68 million m^2 of old public housing had been sold at an average price of 135 Rmb per m^2. The total urban housing stock was over 2,595 million m^2 of which 1,307 million m^2 was owned by enterprises, 425 million m^2 by city housing bureaus and 863 million m^2 was privately owned.
18 *Ibid.*
19 Kou (1998).
20 *Ibid.* The estimated increase in the urban population 1996–2000 is 10 million. Four million urban households have less than 4 m^2 per person.
21 *Ibid.* In 1997, there was a 15.7 per cent increase in sales but an increase of 23.7 per cent in unsold space. There was some 70 million m^2 of empty commercial accommodation at the end of 1997. 30 per cent of the real estate developers were operating at a loss.
22 Wei (1998). The author discusses data compiled in a survey by the China Economy Monitor Analysis Centre of the State Statistical Bureau.
23 *Ibid.*
24 Seidlitz andMurphy (1998).
25 *Ibid.*
26 See for example Hook and Lee (1998).
27 See Seidlitz and Murphy (1998).

References

Chen, Aimin (1998) 'China's Urban Housing Market Development: Problems and Prospects'. *Journal of Contemporary China*, vol. 7, no. 17 (March), pp. 43–60.

Chen, Jinhua (1998) Speech at First Session of the 9th National People's Congress (6 March). In *Summary of World Broadcasts*, Part 3, Asia Pacific, FE/3171.

Hook, Brian and Lee, Wing-On (1998) 'Human Resources in Beijing and Tianjin'. In Brian Hook (ed.) *Beijing and Tianjin Towards a Millenial Megalopolis*. Hong Kong, Oxford University Press, pp. 104–133.

Kou, Zhengling (1998) 'Welfare Housing Allocation will Become History'. *Beijing Review*, vol. 41, no. 44 (2–8 November), pp. 13–16.

Li, Peng (1998) Report on the Work of the Government, 5 March. Text from live TV roadcast, British Broadcasting Corporation (BBC). In *Summary of World Broadcasts*, Part 3, Asia Pacific, FE/3168.

Seidlitz, Peter and Murphy, David (1998) 'State's Dead Hand Holds Back Property Sector'. *South China Morning Post*, 23 November.

State Statistical Bureau of the PRC (1981) *Zhongguo tongji nianjian* (China Statistical Yearbook). Beijing, Zhongguo tongji chubanshe.

Walder, Andrew G. (1996) 'Workers, Managers and the State: The Reform Era and the Political Crisis of 1989'. In Brian Hook (ed.), *The Individual and the State in China*. Oxford, Clarendon Press, pp. 43–69.

Wei, Bian (1998) 'City Dwellers Survey on Consumption'. *Beijing Review*, vol. 41, no. 36 (7–13 September), pp. 23–24.

Xinhua (1998) 'Guanyu jinyibu shenhua chengzhen zhufang zhidu gaige jiakuai zhufang jianshe de tongzhi' (Information on the Further Deepening of the Reform of the Urban Housing System and on the Acceleration of the Construction of Housing). 21 July, Beijing, Xinhuashe.

Part III

SOCIAL CONFLICTS, CONTROL AND COHESION

6

NORMS, POLICE AND THE PROBLEMS OF CONTROL

Børge Bakken

On the inner cover of a 1997 official report from the Chinese Ministry of Public Security about police work there is a full-page picture of a policewoman carrying a little girl on her back through the water in a flooded area. The text accompanying the picture reads *yu-shui qingshen*, the old slogan of the party (here substituted by the police) and the people 'being as close as fish and water'. It is accompanied by an English caption saying 'Police–people intimacy'. The rest of the report is constantly referring to 'mobilizing the people' in crime prevention and 'the masses guarding and controlling' (*qunfang qunzhi*) the public order.[1] The armed police has set up different 'help-the-poor activities', and more than 12,000 'learn-from-Lei Feng groups' in urban and rural areas are 'taking care of more than 30,000 elderly, widows, orphans and the handicapped'.[2]

However, in police manuals where the new strategies and methods of maintaining public order are being discussed we see quite another and considerably less intimate reality presented. Here we experience an explicit emphasis on a reduction of citizen intervention. Formerly it was the rule that crowds should themselves assist the police in upholding social order. The 'support of the masses' should be utilized in police work. Now police manuals instead explicitly encourage police personnel to disperse crowds instead of asking for assistance in cases where quarrels or fights occur in a public place.[3] Instead of the 'support from crowds' policy formerly advocated, the 'fear of crowds' seems to have taken over. It is becoming increasingly unclear in what way citizens should intervene or if they should intervene at all. Intervention should be done by professionals only, goes the argument.[4] The idyllic picture of intimacy is in contrast to reports of the treatment of demonstrating peasants, such as in Qidong County in Hunan in November 1996 where public security forces employed tear-gas grenades to disperse the demonstrating peasants who had gathered to demand a cutback in exorbitant taxes and levies.[5] Several reports on police–civilian clashes in Guangdong in 1997 and 1998 gained the interest of the Central Military Commission, which ordered an investigation of the matter. Deng Zuxuan, police commissar of Guangdong Provincial Armed Police corps, could report back that 'the few cases of police–civilian conflict' were 'not as serious as reported outside' and that they were 'trivial'.[6] The problem is, however, that the People's Armed Police is led by the Central Military Commission, and there is no independent investigation into matters like this. The police has a legitimacy crisis on its hands, and in 1998 it even got a Chinese version of a 'Rodney King case' to deal with when a video photographer managed to capture on video police officers beating up and torturing suspects during their interrogations at the police station at Ruijin Second Road, Luwan District in Shanghai. Again, 'no evidence has been found', according to the official investigation report. The report was written by the local Luwan Public Security Sub-Bureau in Shanghai.[7]

Whilst the community control system is still upheld in theory, the distance between police and public is increasing and popular support is being sought not first and foremost through 'police–people intimacy' but through a more direct and alarmist fear of crime and the criminal. The arguments about mass participation and community policing stand in contrast to the view of professionalization and militarization of the police force and the organs of control. The opposing positions reflect the dilemmas of control in a changing Chinese society. The 'hard' methods of militarization and professionalization will mean increased distance between people and police. At the same time there is a dilemma linked to the 'soft' methods of control as well when community turns into domination.

Community, nostalgia and norms in a changing society

If we go back to the modern 'classics' of the People's Republic like the *Communist Manifesto*, we may remember the famous passage where Marx describes the modern world as a monster, a process where everything stable 'evaporates' (*verdampft*) and where 'everything solid melts into air'. Without nostalgia for the old society, Marx describes modern society as a sorcerer no longer able to control the powers of the underworld conjured up by his spells.[8] In some ways the words of the manifesto have caught up with the reality of Chinese authorities, which intensely fear losing control of the powers of the reforms conjured up by their own political spells.

Over the centuries the Chinese elite has shared a common pattern of thought, the fear of *luan* or disorder, and the knowledge that if you start losing the hearts and the minds of men, you are in real trouble. In the present context I will look at the waning effect of community control and the urge to strengthen the police force and to professionalize and militarize the apparatuses of control. For a system without legal checks and balances, based on the power of morality (*de*) rather than law (*fa*) and the strength of the exemplary norm, the effect is particularly disastrous. The norm is a measurement and a means of producing a common standard, but such a standard may be constituted in various ways. Models have been used to set standards and to increase the salience of norms. Norms can be enormously durable. Here we may recall Edward Shils's remark that the normative core of tradition is the inertial force which holds society in a given form over time.[9] That the norm is linked to inertia and durability, however, does not necessarily mean that norms will remain consistent over time. On the contrary, norms are inconsistent almost by definition. Even if norms might have moved slowly in a traditional context, their inconsistency wins out in the long run. A norm cannot bind anyone for an indefinite period, as law in principle can.[10] The norm establishes itself as an order, and the whole society is defined by this order.

The norm is thus important in upholding order, and the modern Chinese sorcerers have upset the public who not only appreciate what modernity can deliver but also fear the dangers of modernity. The Chinese communist term for 'comrade' – *tongzhi* – might shed light on this dilemma. The expression literally means 'common will'. This 'common will' forms one of the prerequisites for Ferdinand Tönnies's theory of community or *Gemeinschaft*. Tönnies claims that among kinsmen, neighbours and friends no weighing of advantages is necessary. They act under the impact of 'a common will [*gemeinsamer Willen*] or spirit which surrounds the individual like a living substance [*ein Lebenselement*]'.[11] *Tongzhi* concerns the socialist promise of a development combining the memories and the securities of the past with the utopian dreams of a future society. Peter Berger has pointed out that socialism can be understood as a faith in renewed community, and that in its mythic form it has the capacity to combine modernizing and counter-modernizing traits.[12] This socialist myth absorbs central themes of modernity, among them the progress of history and the changeable character of man, as well as a utopian view of the socialist society as a renewed community pointing back to the memories of the past. Socialism also presents itself as a solution to the problem of anomie, as it 'promises to reintegrate the individual in all-embracing structures of solidarity'. And further, 'if modernization can be described as a spreading condition of homelessness, then socialism can be understood as the promise of a new home', Berger and his associates claim.[13] For many Chinese the modernizations have represented such homelessness. Anomie has often been interpreted as 'normlessness', and this is precisely what Chinese criminologists claim to be a main characteristic of criminals. Another definition of anomie focuses on the abundance of norms rather than lack of norms. There is no longer a common standard for the wide range of new and modern norms in a modern society, and many people react against this state with anxiety.[14] As I will argue, the Chinese crime wave has been described in very alarmist ways, and the debate about control has been based on this common fear of the new and modern developments in society. Although there has arguably been a dramatic rise in crime in China, this reaction might partly be seen as a moral panic. More important is the fact that for the regime legitimacy flows not only from the regime's ability to mobilize economic resources and to achieve growth, but also from the success the regime has in implementing order in society. The aim of the regime is to establish legitimacy through growth and order. The regime thus has an interest in focusing on its ability to control disorder and to legitimize itself through such claims. In the Durkheimian sense it needs disorder and the criminal to regain the hearts and minds of the people.

The social fabric in socialist China was built on traditionalistic structures with a promise and the practice of community. Ferdinand Tönnies made the famous distinction in sociology between community and society, or *Gemeinschaft* and *Gesellschaft*.[15] Claiming that China resembled a form of *Gemeinschaft* should not be misinterpreted in utopian terms, and the social form of *Gemeinschaft* should least of all be romanticized. Rather it should be seen in light of Tönnies's additional concepts of '*Herrschaft*' and '*Genossenschaft*'. By *Herrschaft* he means authoritarian domination, by *Genossenschaft* egalitarian fellowship or comradeship. Both possible subtypes of *Gemeinschaft* could be found in the Chinese socialist state. *Herrschaft* operates as a communal kind of authoritarian domination, as in vassalage, contrary to the contract defining a *Gesellschaft*. These are all forms of social relationships. Chinese comradeship could probably explain some of the success of the initial phase of Chinese communism, but is hardly valid as an explanation of the community structures under Chinese socialist rule. The ideologically defined *Genossenschaft* from the Cultural Revolution was often experienced as a harsh *Herrschaft*, and the community solutions from those days make it easy to understand the quest for professionalism, although it is equally hard to defend the arguments of technologies of militarized policing.

Ideology and 'spiritual civilization' (*jingshen wenming*), however, are not lost from the Chinese debate at all, and sometimes appear in the expression 'cultural policing' or 'cultural defense' (*wenming baowei*). The present regime, like former regimes both during and before the formation of the People's Republic, repeatedly stress the learning of models, and the soldier hero Lei Feng still leads the army of exemplary models whom the citizens should strive to emulate. The campaigns even concern emulating the good policeman. One of them, like Tianjin people's policeman Dai Chengjian, reached the front page of the *People's Daily* where he was reported to have moved people to tears through his good and heroic deeds.[16] He 'drew a clear line between public duties and private gains', and 'safeguarded the purity of the national emblem on his cap' by refusing to accept the smallest bribe, and 'doing innumerable small and ordinary things' to serve the people. Of course the model was launched to counter the trend of corruption in the police force and the growing distrust of the police among people.

In people's minds, however, the good cop seems more and more to lead a life in the shadow of the bad one. The police force as well as the army has seen widespread corruption in its ranks, smuggling has been a particularly big problem, and popular support is fading. A recent report from the Ministry of Public Security revealed that more than 130,000 police were caught breaking the law in 1998, according to the special supervisory units set up to discipline the force.[17] Public complaints against police included use of violence, abuse of power, receiving bribes, protecting criminals and corruption. If we believe the official reports, the proportion of police caught breaking the law could be nearly as high as 10 per cent of the total police force.

The problem about the present attempts to set up exemplary models is that there is less and less consensus between the values and norms of the state and those of the smaller community. The exemplary 'models' (*bangyang*) or 'heroes' (*yingxiong*) in China, and the method of educating the masses through the use of exemplary model personalities, have been widespread, and should be seen in the perspective of general social control. Models, however, can be part of a culture, and models can be imposed from above. The ideal of modelling theory is still that models should emerge from below. Models coming from below have social and cultural moorings, making them extremely stable and effective in holding society together. The imposed model, by contrast, lacks such moorings: it is a figure constructed 'outside' society itself. In China, we can find examples of both these approaches of models and modelling. Tracing the cultural basis of educational development, LeVine and White have explored the roots of what they call the 'agrarian concept of virtue'. In the process they come close to Chinese thinking about morality and model learning:

> What is most important about agrarian concepts of virtue, is not that they are used to punish deviants and reward conformists to community standards in the manner of a legal code that is being enforced, but that they offer rich models of the good life and the good person that inspire identification in boys and girls and motivate adults to realize the cultural ideals in their own lives.[18]

These cultural influences are effective because the models are reinforced by experience, and are so deeply grounded in the pragmatics of the agrarian family situation as to be consistent with common-sense conclusions of nearly any member of that community. The symbols contained in traditional models are also more elaborated conceptually and more appealing emotionally than those of an ideology coming from outside the community itself. It is vital that the ideals embodied in such local models can be viewed as locally realizable. Without this concrete and realistic approach, models can even become counter-productive. The politically correct 'exemplary norms' have few or no moorings in the local community any longer, and such norms could be termed 'super-social' norms rather than social norms.[19]

There is a lot of cynicism linked to such norms – in particular after the Cultural Revolution and since the start of the economic reforms.[20] The Chinese regime has to think about ways of control in a situation where it gets little for free in the form of the social moorings of norms.

The waning of community control

There has been a big change of the social landscape since the beginning of the reforms in 1978, and former methods of keeping order have been challenged in many ways, leading to a crisis in policing and penal strategies. Changes both in organizational structures and in norms and values complicate the picture of control. As a result of the reform there has been a break-up of the collective, community-oriented vision of society. The structural and social manifestations of a break-up of collective and community values are side-effects of the economic forces unleashed by the processes of reform. China before the reforms had a highly regimented sense of community with strict prohibitions of internal migration reinforcing a traditional, highly sedentary and stable sense of moral community. Centralized planning, a high level of state ownership of industry and an economy organized on the basis of a state plan reinforced such tendencies and also offered a space for prison rehabilitative programmes to stretch beyond the prison and into the community. Local industries were asked not only to follow the plan, but to take the employees they were allocated by the plan. This included taking former employees who had committed crimes back after the completion of their prison terms. The inmates thus returned to their former communities and through the methods of *ganhua* and 'reintegrative shaming' and a coersive programme of monitoring and surveillance they were effectively supervised and reintegrated into their former communities, with low recidivism rates as a result.[21] Official recidivism rates are still reported to be very low in China, but one Chinese researcher could tell me that he was not allowed to publish his findings anywhere since he found high recidivism rates (up to 60 per cent) in poor areas in Anhui as well as in rich boomtown-type areas on the east coast.

One of the structural preconditions for this successful rehabilitation was the tight demographic policing of the population. The economic reforms and the following massive shift in the demographic situation have made it much harder for the police to monitor and control temporary migration. The population is no longer static and stable. Figures ranging from 70 to 210 million indicate the scope of the present migration of mostly (60–70 per cent) rural people taking up urban jobs for which urban residence permit (*hukou*) holders could not be found. This 'floating' population (*liudong renkou* or *liumin*) typically makes up about 20–30 per cent of the permanent population in China's biggest cities today. In Guangzhou one-third of the population is floating.[22] Most goods, including grain, have become available without coupons, making it possible to move around in a way not formerly seen in China. Regional variations in economic development have become far more pronounced as the reforms tend to be more successful in the coastal areas. There have been initatives to put the State Planning Commission in charge of *hukou* transfer policy, but the *hukou* registration system is still administered by the police, and handbooks of registration administrators are devoted to the use of registration data in crime prevention and in hunting criminals. The great attraction of urban status is another type of more subtle control upheld by the *hukou* system.[23]

While the *hukou* system remains a prime example of administrative control, in post-reform China the conditions for a tight demographic policing linked to the residence permit are about to wither away. The reforms demanded a mobility among the workforce that was formerly unheard of in China, and the state therefore needed to relax the tight demographic policing procedures to allow the economy to develop freely. The state has been forced by economic necessity to allow a 'controlled' migration since the rigidities of the registration system prevented a competitive labour market from taking shape. The 'control' is slipping, however, and rules are bent in all directions as the flow of *liudong renkou* or *liumin* – the floating population – increases.

The *hukou* system is not dead, but in terms of policing the new realities have led to crucial changes in methods. First the police need to target special groups and special areas instead of relying on the all-round demographic control system. In police terminology we talk about a 'focal population' (*zhongdian renkou*) as the focus of special police attention. This focal population consists of a range of 'suspicious' or 'potentially suspicious' characters or 'risk groups' who could be dangerous to the public order. Groups of special interest in this respect are teenagers, the mobile or floating population and the temporary resident population. The most obvious 'focal group' is of course those who have been released from prison and criminal detention.[24] The police seem to be particularly interested in what has been termed people 'with three no's'. That is people without legitimate identification cards, fixed residences and proper jobs or incomes. Preliminary figures showed that only in Guangdong there were 600,000 people 'with three no's' in 1996.[25] Most of these people have come from rural areas and flooded into large and medium cities and economically developed areas. The police also target groups – particularly so called 'transient criminals' (*liucuanfan*) – gathering along railroads and highways, and preventive measures are taken to control the growing population of beggars and to strengthen management of room rentals and temporary shack accommodation. During the 'hard blow' campaign of 1983 gang leaders as well as transient criminals were the main targets of attack.

Then there is the social control of key areas (*shehui kongzhi mian*). The areas to be targeted are places known to be frequented by criminals, but there is also a clear tendency to concentrate the police force in the cities, and leave the counryside to the mobile police and the militia. The main geographical 'target' is now the urban centres and the eastern coastal region of economic growth. This means that police are partly withdrawing from rural areas. At the same time crime is spreading to the countryside, where nearly half of the criminal cases reported to the police now occur. Since reporting crime is more difficult in the countryside, the real percentage of crime is perhaps even larger here than in the cities. One-third of reported serious crime now takes place in the countryside.[26] Public security forces in the cities now concentrate their work inside and outside big- and medium-size state owned enterprises. Because of the relatively high rates of juvenile crime, public security work in areas around middle and primary schools has also been tightened.[27]

The performance of police stations is now being measured by success in surveilling the targeted population of key areas. Conditions have changed so much that tight demographic control even over these groups has become difficult for the police to enforce. The new rehabilitative strategies send the ex-criminal back to the streets or in the best cases set him up with a stall to be an entrepreneur. Shanghai has had a successful programme of turning ex-criminals into self-employed entrepreneurs. In 1993 as many as 4 per cent of the new self-employed enterprises in Shanghai were formed by the demograhically microscopic group of released prisoners.[28] Tight community surveillance is no longer implemented in the way it was, and the police seem to have withdrawn into the control of targeted groups and targeted individuals. The policy of 'targeting' in many ways symbolizes the withdrawal of the central police force.

Fear, community and the alleged 'crime-wave'

There is much talk of crime in China, and one often feels in the midst of a crime-ridden environment when listening to the talk only. The increase, however, has more to do with the relative increase rather than with a real existing 'crime wave' in the Western sense of the concept. International statistics on crime such as those compiled by Interpol are virtually unannotated, leaving us completely uninformed about national differences with respect to reporting practices, laws, different methods of calculation, or different nations' definitions of crime. Nevertheless, the Interpol data provide a rough indication of where China stands internationally in terms of crime.[29] Reports from 113 countries from the late 1980s on rates of crime list only two countries with a lower crime rate than China.[30] A more reliable measure than overall crime rates is provided by homicide statistics. Internationally, homicide reports follow a fairly uniform pattern, as all countries view homicide as a serious crime. The Chinese homicide rate in 1986 was 1.1 per 100,000 population, giving it a ranking of 103rd among the 113 countries reported.[31] The homicide rate, however, indicates that there has indeed been a considerable rise in crime since the mid-1980s. The homicide rate stood at 1.25 in 1987, increased to 1.92 in 1990 and stood at 2.18 per 100,000 population according to the 1998 criminal statistics.[32] Still the internal crime wave is indeed modest compared to international crime rates. In comparison, a group of Western countries in 1995 had an average crime rate nearly sixty times higher than China's.[33]

The 'crime wave' of the early 1980s that triggered off the harsh anti-crime campaigns in 1983 meant an overall crime rate of less than 90 per 100,000 population. The rate reached a peak of 210 in 1991. Due to a redefinition of theft, the overall crime rate now stands at about 135 per 100,000 population, and has decreased slightly since this redefinition of crime was established in the early 1990s.[34] Still only a fraction of the Western crime rates, the most disturbing aspect of the Chinese crime profile is the fact that the percentage of 'serious crime' is growing steadily. From 1981 to 1994 it increased from only 7 per cent to 25 per cent of the total number of reported crimes. However, because several types of petty theft were omitted from the statistics in 1992, and no longer termed 'criminal', the situation is not as bad as it looks. The official crime rates are most probably too low. Files of criminal cases are not set up truthfully. Officials now openly admit that because too many criminal cases are embarrassing for local police or cadres in charge of crime prevention, there are 'risks' of official and public criticism to bear if files of criminal cases are set up truthfully. In Shanghai, the absolute figures of criminal cases on file are reported to have increased dramatically, not because of a general rise in crime, but simply because of more truthful and accurate reporting.[35] This phenomenon might also explain the unnaturally high increase in reported crime just after 1989 when the control climate was changed abruptly as a political reaction to the 'turmoil' of that particular year. Some calculate that the real crime rates in China are as much as three to four times higher if all the criminal cases which do not reach the courts and are summarily dealt with by the police are included.[36] Under-reporting of crime is a similar problem to a lesser or greater degree in all countries.

Despite the reported increase in crime over the last fifteen to twenty years, the official approach to crime in China has been exaggerated and alarmist.[37] International comparison has highlighted that there are indeed very low rates of crime in Chinese society. The tough reaction there to all forms of crime cannot be rationally explained on the basis of these low rates. It seems extraordinary that such rates can trigger harsh and brutal methods of deterrence, particularly since the methods fail to deliver. The campaign-style policing used in 1983 and in later anti-crime campaigns has not been effective. The 'hard blows' (*yanda*) campaign in 1983 was not primarily a reaction against rising crime rates. The crime rates had gone down for two successive years when the campaign started. Instead it was a face-saving operation from the security forces, and a demonstration that they were capable of upholding order in society.[38] The criminal and his destruction became a symbol of both transgression and defence of social and cultural boundaries. The drama conducted by the public security organs is meant to show to a broader audience the themes of social order and cultural danger. Whether this produces more or less crime is secondary to its symbolic meaning and its assumed overall educational effect.[39] Deterrence theory holds that increasing the penalty for an offence will decrease its frequency, while decreasing the penalty will result in increased violations. As many criminologists critical of deterrence theory and capital punishment have pointed out, however, a brutalizing effect is the more likely outcome, as confirmed by the findings after the 'severe blows' campaign.[40] It is still common practice to parade criminals through the streets, although some restrictions have recently been put on such practices. It is usual that persons with a 'problem' of some sort in their file are 'for educational reasons' the first to be sent from their work units to be spectators at big sentence pronouncements or execution rallies. The method of public execution rallies is said to be effective over the short term, but if the increase in crime that followed in the wake of the 'severe blows' campaign teaches us anything, it is that deterrence does not work over the long term. The short-term effect of control in such campaigns pays the heavy debt of a brutalized crime scene. But such campaigns might have an 'educative' effect, showing a resolute regime aimed at upholding order in society. As a 'parading of power' the campaigns might well have a positive propaganda effect for the regime. The recent 'Law on Penal Procedure' has, however, made some police districts abandon the practices of parading convicts awaiting execution and holding public executions.[41] The abolishment of parading might even be a case of security since reports can tell of riots against police forces parading criminals. The most serious incident of this kind took place in Yining, a major city in Ili prefecture in Xinjiang in February 1997. About one thousand citizens went into the streets to intercept the motorcade taking prisoners to the execution ground. The clash between civilians and the armed police left at least twelve people dead.[42]

Viewed from an international perspective, the Chinese crime wave constitutes a mere ripple in a pond, but this comparative finding does not lessen the anxieties in China about crime. We need to focus attention on the fact that reactions against crime in Chinese society might not be rationally based on, or at least limited to, the wish to solve the problem of crime as such. These reactions have to be seen in terms of defending the social and moral order in a society undergoing rapid transformation. In order to gain legitimacy, the 'hard blows' against crime have been an important resource. This should not only be seen as reactions from the repressive state against its people, as there is much popular support for harsh police methods in China. The fear of crime is a useful source of legitimacy for harsh reactions and the building of a strong police force and control apparatuses. A survey among 15,000 people from 1991 showed that nearly 60 per cent of the respondents answered that they found the existing laws 'too lenient' (*guokuan*). Only about 2 per cent found the laws 'too strict' (*guoyan*).[43] Surveys show that there is much support from the grassroots for the harsh methods of crime control and the widespread use of the death penalty in China today.[44] In some ways the regime has a clear interest in upholding an alarmist view of the crime situation in the country. At the same time it needs to show that it is in command, and that it is able to uphold order.

In spite of the huge social changes we have seen over the last two decades of the twentieth century, the attitudes and strategies of keeping social order still seem to reflect the values which originated in a situation that is no longer there. According to some observers the old structure of mass line policing is but a 'formal shell' in today's China, and the social climate that once made *ganhua* a viable form of control is no longer there.[45] *Ganhua* is a word that often reappears in the vocabulary of prison education. The word has the meaning of 'helping somebody to change by persuation and education'. When the White Paper on Criminal Reform in China was released by the State Council in August 1992, a whole chapter was given to stories about successful rehabilitation and the task of changing prisoners through methods of persuasion. In particular the 'beneficial effects which the personal examples and words of the prison staff have on the prisoners in their care' is stressed here.[46] The talk of *ganhua* has today become a much more idealistic notion without moorings in the surrounding society, as the economic reform programme has eroded the structural bonds that tied communities together and once produced the space of *ganhua* to operate beyond the prison walls. Local security committees have rehabilitative functions in this respect, but they are more in a social vacuum now than ever before.

The reforms have increased wealth as well as polarization in society and thereby increased the opportunity structure for crime. Meng Qingfeng, the head of public security in Shandong province, claims that reforms have opened up new spaces for crime and that reform has brought about a change in lifestyle that cannot easily be controlled in the old ways.[47] For instance, the phenomenon of night life was something virtually unknown before the reform period started. I still remember Beijing twenty years ago when the streets were empty after nine o'clock in the evening. People's feeling of community is also withering away. The new high rise apartment buildings do not have the same type of community feeling that the old *siheyuan* and the local *hutongs* could offer. Residents care less for each other, Meng maintains, and even in the countryside families only care about their own individual families after the responsibility system was introduced. There is clearly a nostalgia back to the old community control in the writings of this public security cadre, as exists also among large groups of the population. Fear for one's own security is also a feeling that in particular urban citizens in China see as more and more troublesome. A survey on people's attitudes towards public security in Beijing in 1991 showed that nearly one-third of respondents answered that they were 'very afraid' or 'afraid' when asked the question: 'Are you afraid when a stranger calls at your door?'[48] The *China Youth News* asked the same question in 1995, and found that more than 40 per cent of respondents answered that they were afraid. Some 53.3 per cent now felt that they lived in an 'unsafe' environment. The percentages of people feeling insecure had gone up since a similar survey was conducted in 1993, and the issue of social order had jumped from seventh to fourth rank in a list of most important issues in 1995.[49] In the well-promoted model village of Tengzhou in Shandong province similar questions were asked. As many as 95 per cent of the inhabitants answered that social control and safety were either 'very good' or 'good'.[50] Like so often in Chinese propaganda, the model is strikingly different from the normal trends in Chinese society. The educative model of Tengzhou, however, is a nostalgic attempt to re-establish the glory of former successes of community control.

The Academy of Social Sciences in Shandong, promoting the Tengzhou model of community control, takes care to explain that control has to utilize the surrounding community (*shequ huanying*) and the community culture (*shequ wenhua*) to be effective.[51] State policies must be carried out through local community organizations, and a system of 'villagers' self-control' (*cunmin zizhi*) should be implemented. The crucial point here is that state values and state policies should correspond to the values of the community. If there is such a correspondance, then community control is effective.

The ironfist of policing – the People's Armed Police

Already in 1980 the new slogan of 'comprehensive control of social order' (*shehui zhi'an zonghe zhili*) was formulated, and later written into a directive of the Central Committee in 1982. The new approach should be 'comprehensive' because it should include all relevant means of control to uphold social order. After 1989 the comprehensive control or comprehensive management of crime came to represent the 'basic approach' to public order in China. The regime needed to show that it was in charge, and it was stressed that control should be achieved both through 'hard blows' and other methods, meaning both deterrence and community control.[52] The police force was meant to be the locomotive of this struggle.

The professional people's police (*zhiye xing renmin jingcha*) under the Ministry of Public Security includes public security police, traffic police, patrol police, fire prevention police and the household registration police (*hukou jing*). Then there is the People's Armed Police (*wuchang jingcha*) (PAP) and the judicial police (*falü jingcha*) under the control of the Supreme People's Court and the Supreme People's Procuratorate.[53] Ordinary police work is done by the first category, but the police force is reportedly plagued by a lack of recruits, funding and quality, and there are regularly reports of poorly equipped police. Many rural districts today do not have a police station at all, and only about a quarter of a million police are assigned to police station duties.[54] In many places the police are still organized to handle a static society and rather ill-equipped to handle the new challenges of a modern society. Some of the criticisms in the force are real enough, but some use the ill-equipped old-style community police as a pretext for professionalization and restructuring of the police in line with an entirely new concept of control and efficiency.

If we use the latest available official data from 1993, China does not have a large police force in relative terms, with an average of 128 police personnel per 100,000 population. These figures are about half of the world average ratio. These figures might be too low as police personnel on the work units' payrolls are simply listed as regular staff in the statistics. The recent increases in the PAP force increases the number considerably, and a Hong Kong journal in 1994 reported a new plan to increase the police force by the end of the century to around 3.6 to 4 million.[55] The estimated number of police within the force today stretches from a low 800,000 up to 1.3, 1.8 and 2.2 million.[56]

During the 'hard blow' campaigns in the mid-1990s there was considerable criticism within the police force against campaign-style policing. The force seemed to be plagued by fatigue, and some complained that they had no days off and no time for their families, commenting that 'some men can't even find time to see their wives if they're sick'.[57] Even in the internal police journals we find criticism of the 'hard blows' campaign-style policing methods.[58] The politicized anti-crime campaigns, however, are continuing in order to 'curb the rising crime rate and maintain a sound and safe social order', according to Luo Gan, China's top law enforcement official and State Councillor. Neighbourhoods have to be mobilized and more should be done to build 'safe and civilized' communities, Luo adds.[59]

The People's Armed Police was originally the guard unit protecting the party leaders, formed already in 1927, but the new PAP force is a product of the reforms, and was established as recently as 1982. It was controlled by the new Ministry of State Security, a force linking public security and intelligence. A near total reshuffle occurred after the 1995 scandal when Li Peiyao, vice-chairman of the National People's Congress Standing Committee, was killed by a PAP officer. As a result, the force came under the leadership of the Central Military Commission in August 1995. The criticism against the force was devastating. Not only was it behind the killing, it was involved in the beating of the mayor of Xiamen, hired prostitutes and engaged in armed struggles. It was described as a 'loose, unruly, lordly and luxury loving' force where some elements 'became "bandits" who did whatever they liked'.[60] Jiang Zemin had himself selected the responsible PAP commander Ba Zhongtan, who was now severely criticized and made responsible for the mess. Ba was removed from office and took nearly all leading figures of the PAP with him in his fall from power. Jiang, however, regained authority as the chairman of the Central Military Commission, and managed to counter opposition from within the army. Some 500,000 men were removed from the army to revitalize and strengthen the PAP. The implementation of that decision has probably strongly enhanced Jiang Zemin's power in controlling the army.[61]

Although an official part of the public security force, the PAP is now a mixture of army and police.[62] Certain key tasks have recently been handed over to People's Liberation Army (PLA) units that have just been turned into armed police. Although there is no direct relation between the PAP and the PLA, the two organizations often cooperate in military operations. The PAP is now modelled after the army, and PAP soldiers enrol for compulsory service like the soldiers of the PLA. Mobility is a keyword for PAP work, and units have been deployed in cities as well as in 'unstable areas'. They regularly take part in large-scale anti-riot exercises, and have been used to suppress popular resistance and separatist insurgencies both in Tibet and in Xinjiang. The PAP was also active in suppressing the protest movement in Beijing in 1989, but the corps then failed to obey orders – a matter that led up to the corps' first reorganization after 1989 when the force was equipped to face demonstrations. Part of the army corps that participated in the Tiananmen suppression has been transferred to the PAP.

In 1995 the PAP Headquarters ordered each county and city PAP squadron to establish an anti-riot squad.[63] This force was developed further after the reshuffle, and a 'quick response force' is now the principal force in dealing with riots. Highly trained ten-man squads are to be equipped with the best vehicles and weapons available, and their rapid-reaction and mobile fighting capability is stressed in particular. The mobility of the force is also functional in the sense that they do not develop sympathy with the local people and therefore refuse to carry out orders. One might say that the mobile PAP units are the direct opposite of the local community police, and that this type of policing follows a directly opposite line of thought. The corps is also used for border immigration control, anti-smuggling and anti-narcotics work.

The most important task for the PAP is to assure internal security and to prevent social instability, but there are also economic tasks for the PAP. At the XIVth Party Congress in 1992 it was stated that: 'The most fundamental task for the PAP . . . is to ensure the political and social stability of the country and unswervingly escort the cause of economic development'.[64] The PAP was therefore heavily involved in business activities, operating as one of the big entrepreneurs on the Chinese market.[65] This trend of course made the PAP more vulnerable to corruption within its own ranks, thus making the corps even more unpopular among the public. After the reshuffle of the PAP came probably the most important reform of the armed forces since the start of the economic reforms. A circular from the Chinese Communist Party Central Committee, the State Council and the Central Military Commission from July 1998 banned both the PLA and the PAP from engaging in any economic activities.[66] Although it is not easy to implement the directive immediately and in full, it has made it much more complicated for the armed forces to engage in corrupt activities. Prior to the ban on business activities, there had merely been sporadic crackdowns on police corruption, mainly focusing on changing police norms. Those initiatives included a moral development programme to teach policemen how to improve themselves, not to accept bribes and not to bully people. The closest one came to a business ban was a warning to policemen not to get involved in the entertainment business.[67]

There is much talk of the quality of the PAP and the police in general, and some advocate a stronger emphasis on education and technologically advanced equipment for the force. The debate has revealed a lot of scepticism towards security teams and local volunteers, and it has also stressed that the quality of the armed police is far too low. Reports that police work has now become the favourite job choice for university students is mainly propagandistic and wishful thinking.[68] Still ideology and politics are regarded a priority in the efforts to improve the educational level of the force, according to the newly appointed commander, General Yang Guoping, and Political Commissar Xu Yongqing.[69]

The *Herrschaft* of 'soft' community policing

Community control used to be fairly successful in China, but facing the situation of changing demographic realities and social norms, what will be the likely future of this type of control? Chinese observers themselves point to the tendency of breakdown in the community control systems. Meng Qingfeng considers that in the cities the space and opportunity structure for criminal activities are expanding, and in the countryside peasants operate on the basis of individual families, which makes community control far more difficult.[70] Population migration might not necessarily be a direct cause for increased crime, but undoubtedly it forms an important basis for the growing opportunity structure for crime in China during the reforms.

The 'soft' community approach is not necessarily as soft as we like to think, but before we explore that matter closely we should look at the state of the mass public-security network. It was in a rather messy state during the first decade of the reform period. In 1988 it was reported that only 20 per cent of the local security committees (*zhibaohui*) were efficient.[71] From 1989 on, the control system was strengthened, but still public security personnel cannot carry out community control the way they used to. One report from 1992 states that the security committees in the cities were security committees in name only.[72] In 1996 the Ministry of Public Security officially set the number of people involved in community security committees at 1,190,000.[73] These committees patrol the neighbourhood, supervise households and courtyards, and play a role in prevention of fires, crime and accidents. They are also involved in the registration of the floating population and in general crime prevention. In the countryside, however, the local security offices only have two or three people working for them, and one security officer has to take care of a population of 10,000 all by himself. In the cities one household registration officer often has to take care of a population as big as that formerly controlled by three or four neighbourhood committees.[74]

The new police strategy means a partial withdrawal from the countryside. The community control system was dismantled, but is now being reorganized. From 1986 to 1989 the number of village committees fell somewhat while there was a slight increase in the number of urban security committees. The number of urban public security small groups (*zhibao xiaozu*) grew by more than 20 per cent during this period, while the village security groups fell by nearly 30 per cent.[75] In terms of number of persons involved in the committees, however, there is a falling tendency in the cities, while it grew by more than 30 per cent in the villages. The average number of participants per committee thus decreased from an average of about six to four in the cities, while it increased from about four to five in the rural areas.[76] The observation made by some scholars that urban neighbourhood committees and groups were growing and active while the rural committees and groups were in decline during the late 1980s does not apply to the restructuring of public security after 1989, but the slight growth in the countryside came while the regular police was weakened and concentrated even stronger in the main urban areas.[77] A community control system is still emphasized both in the cities and in the villages, but its social moorings are considerably weakened.

So-called basic level security networks (*jiceng zhi'an wangluo*) have been set up, and security patrols (*zhi'an xunluodui*) operate in counties, townships and villages. Each township has established a comprehensive control office, and security household groups (*zhi'an lianhuzu*) have been formed to keep social order, patrol the area and reform offenders. There is still talk of the 'mass prevention and mass security groups' (*qunfang qunzhi duiwu*), but the local police stations (*paichusuo*) are being described as the central coordinator, and the 'dragon head' of such work. In some places a rural registration system similar to that of the cities is also implemented in an attempt to take back the demographic control lost during the reforms. The recent attempts to strengthen the community control system, however, do not have support in the general community structure. The 'residents' committees' which were supposed to assist in keeping order in the local neighbourhood are in decline, and support from the general public is waning.

The police have ordered work units to set up internal 'security sections' (*baowei ke*) under the supervision of the local security police. Some factories have established their own offices of internal security (*neibao bu*). This security corps does not wear uniforms, and the system of internal security has been commercialized. We have recently seen the establishment and rapid growth of work unit and factory uniformed vigilante groups and companies. In Shandong in 1992 there were about 560 so called 'economic people's police groups' (*jingji minjingdui*) consisting of as many as 23,800 men. Another growing industry is the security company (*bao'an gongsi*). This is a type of half-private half-collective commercialized community control, very useful for local police stations, which take part of their income from such companies. In 1992 this type of company was just emerging in China. About forty companies were set up in Shandong that year, and about 5,000 people worked within these companies then. In addition about 110,000 work unit security guards work within the unit itself.[78] These are often categorized as 'factory guards' (*huchang renyuan*), 'mine guards' (*hukuang renyuan*), 'campus guards' (*huxiao renyuan*), etc. Over the last four or five years there are reports that the security companies are a fast-growing type of enterprise in the country, particularly in the developed areas. Figures from the Ministry of Public Security from 1996 estimate the number of such companies to be 1,500 with a staff of about 250,000. The official Ministry of Public Security report states that such companies are 'an important accessory to police organs'.[79]

The idyllic picture of intimacy with the people and the happy *Genossenshaft* is again challenged by the night activities of these companies. There are several reports about the brutality of internal security guards (*neibao*). A common complaint is the constant bullying of the workers. Workers are woken up in their dorms in the middle of the night by security guards checking for illegal guests. There are frequent checks for residence cards and so on. Some of the guards beat up workers at will, and even use handcuffs and cattle-prods to punish them for violations of factory regulations.[80]

In one instance in Zhaoqing City, the Zhaojie Footwear Company had hired more than one hundred security guards (*bao'anyuan*) to keep the workers within the walls of their work unit during their work-hours as well as in their spare time. The workers are not allowed to leave without permission from the factory leadership, who keep back wages as well as resident permits to prevent workers from escaping. There is extensive overnight work at the factory, and the armed security guard patrols run the factory like a prison. Workers are beaten, and sometimes even tortured. This particular factory was disciplined by the Provincial Labour Bureau after an investigation team was sent there and found out that the company violated the Labour Law.[81] In another company in Yangsheng village so-called *dashou* – thugs hired by labour contractors – regularly beat up workers who protested against the company rules. Workers were not allowed to talk to each other, and like in the Zhaoqing factory they were not allowed to leave their work place. Two workers who tried to escape were beaten with iron bars and were seriously injured. In this instance the local police arrested eleven of the *dashou*, and set the workers free.[82] In both these instances the stories reached the press, and in Yangsheng the local police caught the factory thugs. Many workers are not that fortunate, and often the local police see the emergence of factory guards and factory thugs as an important supplement to their own income and funding.

The companies are an increasingly important source of income for the public police forces, and they are well paid to keep order at the factory level. The link between the security companies and the local police is more and more often of an economic kind rather than a controlling or supervisory kind, and the police earn money by leasing out vehicles and uniforms. The number of labour disputes has risen sharply. During just one year from 1993 to 1994 an increase of 155 per cent was reported throughout the country.[83] Labour unrest has increased even further with the reform of the state-owned enterprises and the rapid increase of laid-off workers. Official estimates on unemployment are a mere 3.5 per cent for the whole country, but 9 per cent in the cities. Affecting 50 million households, the unemployment rate now stands three times as high as in 1993.[84] The official estimates are far too low as many workers are never registered in those statistics, and unemployed workers 'waiting for jobs' (*daiye*) are not regarded as jobless according to the statistics. Even officially it is being admitted, however, that China's unemployment rate is now the highest in fifty years.[85] Often the regular police force is hired to take care of labour disputes. In one instance an enterprise had hired the section chief of the local public security bureau to settle labour disputes within the company, and the local police arrested striking workers on his orders.[86] Since there is virtually no trade union organization taking care of workers' interests and workers' unrest, and even the capacity of the local police is limited, the security vigilantes have become the ruling force of order in many factories. Their nightsticks and cattle-prods now define the rules of order in many an enterprise.[87] Security guards even use their position to earn private money under the pretext of 'security'. Factories use punishment by introducing excessive fees for workers who fall asleep at work or arrive late, and such punishment is enforced by security guards who often pocket the money themselves.[88]

Some representatives from the security forces whom I talked to in the summer of 2001 voiced fear about the development of security companies. In a situation where the public security organs are withdrawing from the countryside and 'targeting' areas and groups, the growth of commercial security companies could weaken the central security apparatus and their monopoly of control. Even if the security companies should be nominally supervised and approved by the central public security forces, the reality was that there was no interference as long as they paid well. In this case we do not see a democratization of control, rather the vigilantes might in a worst case scenario instead represent some sort of warlordism eating away at the social cohesion and stability of Chinese society. The paradox here is that the very apparatus of social order could be an important incentive to disorder and upheaval. This is not community control, but on the contrary, a beginning of the rule of police and vigilantes.

Conclusion

In China we have seen the beginning of a breakdown in what used to be regulation through norms and communities. The effectiveness of the norm in regulating society is obvious. A discipline based on the norm is more durable than one based on outer force only because it seeks to bind people to society with their own ideas. It is linked to power in a way less likely to manifest force or violence. Regulation through the norm is more based on willed consent, and functions more like a positive restraint. In China, regulation through the norm is still of strategic importance for the programme of spiritual civilization, and defines a main approach to the regulation of order. This 'spiritual' regulation is fading and becoming less and less efficient, however, and an 'outer' approach to control and a more professionalized regular apparatus of force and violence is gradually taking the upper hand. The methods of 'targeting', the development of mobile armed police forces, the growth of commercial security companies and vigilante groups, and the reorganization of the community control system are forms of policing that have grown out of the demands for control in the economic reform period. The regime is today faced by a new social milieu, and the situation both in terms of structures and values has changed rapidly during the economic reforms. The community control system is waning because the support for the police among the general public is diminishing. The social fabric, the social norms and the social atmosphere have all changed, and so has the apparatus of control and the methods of policing.

There is no such thing as the 'rule of law' – a system of law protecting a pluralist civil society against the state – in China today, but liberals and non-liberals alike would agree that formal law is necessary when community breaks down. Instead there is a 'rule *by* law' in China, but this is often brutal and arbitrary, and the situation can be dangerous since the regime is about to 'lose community' and thereby the ability of community control from below.[89] There is also not much community spirit in the new commercialized security companies and their form of '*Herrschaft*', and the community spirit shown by armed police through sporadic 'learn from Lei Feng activities' can hardly be taken for more than a social theatre performance. Despite trends to the contrary, the big anti-crime campaigns that we have seen recurring after 1983 and the widespread use of the death penalty have probably come to stay for a long period of time. Such campaigns might not be productive in preventing crime in the long term, but they might be important for the regime in terms of enhancing its legitimation in the short run. In this respect the support from below for harsh reactions against crime should not be underestimated. The developments in policing and social control that we have seen in China are very different from a scenario that sees liberalism, democracy and the 'rule of law' as the inevitable outcome of market economic reforms. These are rather tendencies to the contrary, and the 'invisible hand' has so far often been represented by a very visible fist.

Notes

1 Ministry of Public Security of the PRC (hereafter MPS) (1997). Flood relief is being extensively used in the propaganda to emphasize the close relations between the people and the armed forces in general. 'Wherevener there is flood there are soldiers', says the *China Youth Daily* in an article praising the armed forces' involvement in the battle against flooding. See *Zhongguo qingnianbao* (1 August 1998). See also for the same date a commentator's article on 'Salute to the Heroic People's Army'.
2 *Summary of World Broadcasts-Far East* (hereafter: *SWB-FE*) (1999a).
3 See Nie (1989) and Song (1989).
4 See Einwalter (1996).
5 *Yuegang xinxi ribao*, report quoted in *SWB-FE* (1996c: G/4).
6 *SWB-FE* (1998c: G/3).
7 The footage was captured with a hidden camera from a building across the street, and was made by a Canadian Television (CTV) crew, making the issue an international scandal. The Foreign Ministry held a press conference stating that extraction of confessions through torture is prohibited by Chinese law, but that no evidence had been found in the Luwan branch case. See *SWB-FE* (1998d: G/8) and *SWB-FE* (1998e: G/5–6).
8 Marx (1971: 529, 531).
9 Shils (1971: 122–159).
10 See Ewald (1990: 156).
11 Tönnies (1929: 195).
12 Berger (1977).
13 Berger, Berger and Kellner (1973: 124).
14 For an analysis on anomie in China, refer to Fisac's chapter in this volume.
15 See Tönnies (1931: 34–73).
16 *Renmin ribao* (8 May 1994: 1).
17 *Renmin gong'an banyuekan* (1999). The number included 27,638 police engaging in improper conduct and who broke disciplinary regulations.
18 LeVine and White (1986: 35).
19 See my discussion in Bakken (2000).
20 I have discussed the breakdown of exemplary norms and heroic figures in my book: Bakken (1993: 135–68).
21 Dutton and Xu (1998: 11).
22 In Beijing the floating population made up 22.03 per cent of the total population in 1991, in Shaghai 26.18 per cent, in Wuhan 21.79, and in Chengdu 24.88 per cent. See Gu (1991: 135), quoted from Li (1998).
23 On the development of the *hukou* system in present-day China see Mallee (1995: 29). See also Liu (1992).
24 Meng (1992: 15).

25 *SWB-FE* (1996a: G/13) and *SWB-FE* (1998j: G/1–3).
26 Some 46.6 per cent of criminal cases reported to the police in 1993 occured in the countryside. *Dagong bao* (10 October 1994), p. 9. Quoted from *China News Analysis*, no. 1536, p. 4.
27 These priorities are stressed by the Central Committee for Comprehensive Management of Public Security (CCCMPS), now a regular organization of the Chinese Communist Party's Central Committee. See *SWB-FE* (1998a: G/7).
28 Chen (1994: 14). I am indebted to Professor Li Cheng for making me aware of this source.
29 See Organisation Internationale de Police Criminelle (1990). The numbers quoted in this article are based on the 1985–86 and 1987–88 statistics, thus supplementing the 97 countries in the 1985–86 statistics with an additional 16 countries from the 1987–88 statistics. (I have omitted the South African 'homelands' from this list.)
30 Only two countries – Mali with 11.08 cases per 100,000 population, and Nepal wilh 33.29 cases – have a lower reported crime rate than China's 51.9 cases per 100,000 population in 1986.
31 It shared the place with Finland. Only Saudi Arabia, Indonesia, Norway, Congo, Ireland, Cameroon, Argentina, Burkina Faso, and Mali had lower reported homicide rates, ranging from Saudi-Arabia's 1.02 to Mali's 0.01 at the bottom of the list.
32 *Zhongguo falü nianjian* (1986: 818, 827). *Zhongguo falü nianjian* (1991: 942, 952) and *Zhongguo falü nianjian* (1998: 1244, 1251).
33 The fourteen countries were: West Germany, England, Italy, France, Spain, USA, Canada, Belgium, Norway, Denmark, Sweden, Finland, New Zealand and Australia. The average crime rate for these countries was about 8,000 per 100,000 population.
34 *Zhongguo falü nianjian* (1998: 1244, 1251).
35 See interview with Shanghai Public Security Bureau Director Liu Yungeng, *Ming bao* (2 February 1999: A13). See also *SWB-FE* (1999c: G/7–8).
36 Between 1986 and 1988, a national research project was undertaken to find the real crime rates in China. It concluded that the actual crime rates where three to four times higher than the official statistics. Dai (1989), quoted from Dutton and Lee (1993: 318).
37 Bakken (1993: 29–58).
38 The security forces were especially humiliated by the two gangster brothers Wang (Erwang) who shot several policemen as they escaped all the way through China after a murder in Harbin. The two were killed in a shoot-out with the army after a long period on the run, nearly gaining mythical status among the general population in the process. On the Erwang, see Xin, M. (1991).
39 See *ibid.*
40 The same brutalizing effect was illustrated on a wider scale by Archer and Gartner (1984). Their evidence from a cross-national sample also showed, in contrast, that abolition of capital punishment was in most cases followed by absolute decreases in homicide rates, not by the increases predicted in deterrence theory.
41 *SWB-FE* (1997a: G/10) and *SWB-FE* (1997b: G/7).
42 The prisoners being paraded probably involved members of the pro-Xinjiang independence movement. An account of the event can be read in the Hong Kong newspaper *Ming bao* (1999).

43 Public Security Research Institute (1991).
44 For a more detailed discussion of this topic, see *ibid.*
45 See Dutton (1995: 437). On *ganhua*, see the discussion in Dutton and Xu (1998).
46 See *Renmin ribao* (*haiwai ban*) (12 August 1992: 3) and *SWB-FE* (1992: C1/1–10).
47 Meng (1992: 15).
48 Public Security Research Institute (1991: 60).
49 *Zhongguo qingnian bao* (11 March 1995: 1), quoted in *China News Analysis* (1995: 7).
50 Xin, G. (1992: 37).
51 Chen and Liu (1992: 19–23).
52 State Council of the PRC (1991: 197–9) and *Renmin ribao* (21 January 1991). See also Qiao Shi's report in *SWB-FE*/0976 (22 January 1991: B2/4–6).
53 According to the 1993 *Law Yearbook of China* the police force then counted 1,484,000 people, of whom 854,000 worked in the professional people's police force, and 623,000 worked for the PAP, while an additional 7,000 worked as judicial police. The more recent issues of the *Law Yearbook* have omitted the number of people's police and the PAP from their tables. See *Zhongguo falü nianjian* (1993: 946). The figures are actually taken from the end of 1991. There have been no tables on the development of the police force in the yearbook since then. The judicial police is listed under 'Personnel of the country's procuratorial organs' and is still retained in the 1995 edition of the yearbook. The force grew from 7,018 people in the 1993 yearbook to 10,451 in the 1995 yearbook, an increase of nearly 50 per cent in two years. See *Zhongguo falü nianjian* (1993: 940; 1995: 1068).
54 *Renmin ribao* (21 January 1991).
55 See 'A New Script for Public Order' (1994) and *Zheng ming* (March 1994: 18–19).
56 The highest of 2.2 million is given by *Dongxiang* (1996: 8). See *China News Analysis* (1998: 7) for sources on the number of police within the PAP. The official prison population of 1,244,000 makes 107 prisoners per 100,000 inhabitants, slightly higher than the world average of 105. Estimates made by Western scholars, however, set the Chinese prison population at 166 per 100,000 population, still a relatively modest number. See *SWB-FE* (1994a: G/12), and Seymour and Anderson (1998: 219).
57 *SWB-FE* (1996c: G/9).
58 See Zhang (1995: 37–40).
59 See *SWB-FE* (1998i: G/6). Luo Gan, member of the C political bureau and a hardliner linked to Li Peng, has gained power through his election as secretary of the Central Commission of Political Science and Law (CCPSL). These and other readjustments have been made to eliminate the influence of Qiao Shi and to smoothen Li Peng's replacement of Qiao Shi as chairman of the National People's Congress. See *SWB-FE* (1998c: G/12–13).
60 *SWB-FE* (1996c).
61 *SWB-FE* (1996b: G/9).
62 See 'The People's Armed Police' (1993).
63 See *Ding* (1995: 130–1).
64 *Renmin ribao* (14 October 1992: 3).
65 *Jingji ribao* (11 September 1992: 2) quoted from *China News Analysis* (1992, no. 1482: 8).

66 See *SWB-FE* (1998h: G/2).
67 *SWB-FE* (1998f: G/6).
68 *SWB-FE* (1994: G/10).
69 *China News Analysis* (15 May 1998, no. 1610).
70 Meng (19962: 15).
71 Hua (1988: 11–13). The security committees are mass organizations that maintain basic supervisory work at a street and work-unit level, find work for former inmates, organize mass public-security campaigns, etc. They are led by small groups of citizens cooperating with the police and other organs of the public security bureaus.
72 See Guo (1992).
73 MPS (1997: 11–12).
74 Meng (1992: 15).
75 See Dutton and Lee (1993: 328) and Dutton (1995: 433).
76 *Zhongguo falü nianjian* (1991: 947; 1992: 866; 1993: 946). The yearbook stopped publishing such data from the 1994 issue.
77 See Dutton and Lee (1993: 328).
78 Meng (1992: 16).
79 MPS (1997: 11–12).
80 See *Gongren ribao* (27 March 1996: 7).
81 Chan (1998: 58–61).
82 *Pingguo ribao* (21 June 1996). I am indebted to Jiang Kelin for showing me these sources on security guard violence.
83 *1994~1995–nian: Zhongguo shehui xingshi fenxi yu yuce*. Beijing, Zhongguo shehui kexueyuan chubanshe (1995: 297).
84 *SWB-FE* (1998g: G/9) and *SWB-FE* (1998k: G/7–8).
85 *SWB-FE* (1998b: G/13) and *SWB-FE* (1999b: G/9).
86 *Gongren ribao* (11 November 1993: 2).
87 According to an interview with trade union cadres at the Trade Union College (Gongyun xueyuan) in Beijing in 1994, the central All China Federation of Trade Unions (ACFTU) had no contact whatsoever with as much as 70 per cent of the rural enterprises in the country.
88 This is a clear violation of the labour law, but is according to some reports a quite common practice. In one Henan factory the standard punishment for arriving late grew from 2 to 100 Rmb over three years. See *Gongren ribao* (20 June 1995: 5).
89 On the distinction 'rule of law' and 'rule by law' in the Chinese context, see Baum (1996).

References and further reading

'A New Script for Public Order' (1994) *China News Analysis*, no. 1447, 11 August, p. 8.

Archer, Dane and Gartner, Rosemary (1984) *Violence and Crime in Cross-National Perspective*. New Haven, Yale University Press.

Bakken, Børge (1993) 'Crime, Juvenile Delinquency and Deterrence Policy in China'. *Australian Journal of Chinese Affairs,* no. 30 (July), pp. 29–58.

—— (2000) *The Exemplary Society: Human Improvement, Social Control and the Dangers of Modernity*. Oxford, Oxford University Press.

Baum, Richard (1996) 'Modernization and Legal Reform in Post-Mao China: The Rebirth of Socialist Legality'. *Studies in Comparative Communism*, no. 2, pp. 69–103.

Berger, Peter L. (1977) *Facing up to Modernity*. New York, Basic Books.

Berger, Peter L., Berger, Birgitte and Kellner, Hansfried (1973) *The Homeless Mind*. Harmondsworth, Penguin Books.

Chan, Anita (1998) 'The Conditions of Chinese Workers in East Asian-Funded Enterprises'. *Chinese Sociology and Anthropology*, vol. 30, no. 4 (Summer).

Chen, Baorong (1994) 'Jiushi niandai Shanghai geti siying jingji fazhan yanjiu' (Study of the Development of Private Economy in Shanghai in the 1990s). Unpublished paper, Shanghai.

Chen, Jian and Liu, Minan (1992) 'Shequ kongzhi yu Tengzhou moshi' (Community Control and the Tengzhou Model). *Qingshaonian fanzui yanjiu*, no. 11 (November), pp. 19–23.

Dai, Wendian (1989) 'Dui wo guo xianjieduan fanzui wenti yanjiu de yixie sikao' (Some Reflections on the Research into Current Problems of Crime in China). *Zhongguo xianjieduan fanzui wenti yanjiu (di yi ji)* vol. 1, pp. 1–11.

Dagong bao (1994) 10 October, p. 9.

Ding, Arthur S. (1995) 'Jiang Zemin Inspects Armed Police Corps'. *Issues and Studies*, vol. 31, no. 11 (November), pp. 130–131.

Dongxiang (1996) no. 8, p. 8.

Dutton, Michael (1995) 'Dreaming of Better Times: "Repetition with a difference" and Community Policing in China'. *Positions*, vol. 3, no. 2, pp. 415–417.

Dutton, Michael and Lee, Tianfu (1993) 'Missing the Target? Policing Strategies in the Period of Economic Reform'. *Crime and Delinquency*, no. 3, pp. 316–336.

Dutton, Michael and Xu, Zhangrun (1998) 'Facing Difference: Relations, Change and the Prison Sector in Contemporary China'. In Robert P. Weiss and Nigel South (eds) *Comparing Prison Systems: Toward a Comparative and International Penology*. Newark NJ, Gordon and Breach Publishers, pp. 289–336.

Einwalter, Dawn (1996) 'Selflessness and Self-interest: Public Morality and the Xu Hong Campaign'. Unpublished paper.

Ewald, François (1990) 'Norms, Discipline, and the Law'. *Representations*, no. 30 (Spring), pp. 138–161.

'Gaining Importance: The People's Armed Police' (1998) *China News Analysis*, no. 1610, 15 May.

Gongren ribao (1993) 11 November, p. 2.

—— (1995) 20 June, p. 5.

—— (1996) 27 March, p. 7.

Gu, Shengzu (1991) *Feinonghua yu chengzhenhua yanjiu* (A Study of Non-agriculturalization and Urbanization). Hangzhou, Zhejiang renmin chubanshe.

Guo, Fengxiang (1992) 'Rudong xian nongcon Fangcui tuanhuo de tedian he yuanyin' (The Characteristics and Causes of Rural Gang Crime in Rudong County), *Qingshaonian fanzui yanjiu* (Research in Juvenile Crime), no. 2, pp. 9–12.

Hua Nianlun (1988) 'Shehui zhi'an wenti toushi' (Perspectives on Social and Public Security Problems). *Liaowang*, no. 50, 12 December, pp. 11–13.

Jiang Liu, Lu Xueyi and Shan Tianlun (eds) (1995) *1994–1995-nian: Zhongguo shehui xingshi fenxi yu yuce* (1994–1995: Analysis and Prediction of the Social Situation in China). Beijing, Zhongguo shehui kexueyuan chubanshe.

Jingji ribao (1992) 11 September, p. 2.

LeVine, Robert A. and White, Merry I. (1986) *Human Conditions: The Cultural Basis of Educational Development*. New York and London, Routledge & Kegan Paul.

Li, Cheng (1998) 'Surplus Rural Laborers and Internal Migration in China: Current Status and Future Prospects'. In Børge Bakken (ed.), *Migration in China.* NIAS Report no. 31. Copenhagen, NIAS Publishing.

Liu, Guangren (ed.) (1992) *Hukou guanlixue* (Household Registration Management). Beijing, Zhongguo jiancha chubanshe.

Mallee, Hein (1995) 'China's Household Registration System Under Reform'. *Development and Change*, no. 1 (January), pp. 29–40.

Marx, Karl (1971) 'Manifest der Kommunistischen Partei' (Communist Party's Manifesto). *Die Frühschriften*. Stuttgart, Alfred Körner Verlag, pp. 529–531.

Meng, Qingfeng (1992) 'Jiaqiang jiceng wangluo jianshe, tigao shequ kongzhi nengli' (Strengthen the Construction of Basic Level Networks and Increase the Capacity of Community Control). *Qingshaonian fanzui yanjiu*, no. 11, pp. 15–18.

Ming bao (1999) 2 February, p. A13.

Ministry of Public Security of the PRC (1997) *Zhongguo gong'an gongzuo* (Policing in China), Beijing, Ministry of Public Security of the PRC.

Nie, Shiji (1989) *Gong'an baowei renyuan shiyong zhishi shouce* (Handbook for Public Security Protection Workers). Chengdu, Sichuan renmin chubanshe.

Organisation Internationale de Police Criminelle (1990) *Statistiques criminelles internationales 1985–1986* (International Criminal Statistics 1985–1986). Lyon, Saint Cloud, Le Secretariat General de l'O.I.P.C. – Interpol.

Pingguo ribao (1996) 21 June, p. 1.

Public Security Research Institute, Ministry of Public Security of the PRC (Gong'anbu gonggong anquan yanjiusuo) (1991) *Ni ganjue anquan ma?* (Do you Feel Safe?). Beijing, Chunzhong chubanshe.

Qiao, Shi (1991) Report. Quoted in *Summary of World Broadcasts – Far East*, no. 0976, 22 January, pp. B2/4–6.

Renmin gong'an banyuekan (1999) 25 January, p. 1.

Renmin ribao (1991) 21 January, p. 1.

—— (1991) 1 November, p. 3.

—— (1994) 8 May, p. 1.

Renmin ribao (haiwai ban) (1992) 12 August, p. 3.

'Salute to the Heroic People's Army' (1998). *Renmin ribao*, 1 August, p. 1.

Seymour, James D. and Anderson, Richard (1998) *New Ghosts: Old Ghosts. Prison and Labor Reform Camps in China*. Armonk NY, M. E. Sharpe.

Shils, Edward (1971) 'Tradition'. *Comparative Studies in Society and History*, vol. 13, no. 2 (April), pp. 122–159.

'Social Order and the Police' (1995) *China News Analysis*, no. 1536, 1 June, p. 4.

Song, Zhansheng (1989) *Zhongguo gong'an baike quanshu* (China Public Security Encyclopedia). Guilin, Guilin renmin chubanshe.

South China Morning Post (1999) 12 January. <http://www.scmp.com>.

Summary of World Broadcasts – Far East (1992), no. 1458, 13 August.

—— (1994) no. 1987, 3 May.

—— (1996a) no. 2638, 14 June.

—— (1996b) no. 2705, 31 August.
—— (1997a) no. 2807, 3 January.
—— (1997b) no. 2825, 24 January.
—— (1997c) no. 2908, 2 May.
—— (1998a) no. 3150, 13 February.
—— (1998b) no. 3155, 19 February.
—— (1998c) no. 3175, 14 March.
—— (1998d) no. 3234, 23 May.
—— (1998e) no. 3235, 25 May.
—— (1998f) no. 3238, 28 May.
—— (1998g) no. 3261, 24 June.
—— (1998h) no. 3293, 31 July.
—— (1998i) no. 3332, 15 September.
—— (1998j) no. 3401, 4 December.
—— (1998k) no. 3402, 5 December.
—— (1999a) no. 3464, 20 February.
—— (1999b) no. 3478, 9 March.
—— (1999c) no. 3499, 2 April.

State Council of the PRC (1991) *Guowuyuan gongbao* (State Council Bulletin), no. 6. Beijing, State Council of the PRC.

'The People's Armed Police' (1993). *China News Analysis*, no. 1482, 1 April, p. 4.

Tönnies, Ferdinand (1929) *SoziologischeStudien und Kritiken; Dritte Sammlung* (Sociological Studies and Critics. Third Compilation). Jena, Verlag von Gustav Fischer.

—— (1931) *Einfhrung in die Soziologie* (Introduction to Sociology), vol. 2. Stuttgart, Ferdinand Enke.

Xin, Ming (ed.) (1991) *Fanzui xue* (Criminology). Chongqing, Chongqing chubanshe.

Xin, Yi (1992) 'Guanyu Tengzhou shi nongcun shequ gongcong anquan gan de diaocha' (Survey on the Sense of Security in the Rural Community of Tengzhou Municipality). *Qingshaonian fanzui yanjiu*, no. 11 (November), p. 37.

Xingdao Ribao (1996) 30 August, p. 4.

Zhang, Daohua (1995) 'Cong fumian kan "yanda"' (Looking at the Negative Side of the 'Hard Blows'). *Gong'an yanjiu*, no. 6, pp. 37–40.

Zheng ming (PRC) (1994) no. 3, March, pp. 18–19.

Zhongguo falü nianjian (various dates). Beijing, Zhongguo falü nianjian she.

Zhongguo qingnian bao (1998) 1 August 1998, p. 1.

—— (1995) 11 March, p. 1.

7

SOCIAL ANOMIE AND POLITICAL DISCOURSE IN CONTEMPORARY CHINA

Taciana Fisac

In 1976 Mao Zedong died. This marked the end of an era whose darker side is becoming more and more evident. His successor, Deng Xiaoping, opted for pragmatism and for two decades was the leading force behind the current social and economic reforms.[1] Although the death of Mao revealed political errors which, among other consequences, had led to serious famine and situations of chaos among the Chinese population, the death of Deng in February 1997 happened at a time of growing prosperity. After the Chinese Communist Party (CCP)'s XVIth Congress on October 2002, the so-called Deng Xiaoping Theory continues to be in force.

Throughout the process of what can be termed liberalization, Mao's ideological framework had little by little been eroded. Deng Xiaoping's theses proposed that Marxism-Leninism and Mao Zedong thought should be adapted to the specific reality of China, depending on the necessities and practical results of the reforms in progress. This was done with the aim of getting away from Mao's approach, but without totally rejecting him. When the reforms were launched in 1978 with the objective of achieving the modernization of the country, it was difficult to foresee the extent of subsequent changes and the impressive economic growth which was to occur. These transformations have undoubtedly meant an improvement in the living standards of a large part of the population, but they have also caused important social problems. As it usually happens when there are rapid structural changes, together with a clear lack of state control in some areas, there has been a noticeable loss of ideological direction and a common feeling that previously prevailing moral values are disappearing.

The general perception today is that there is a lack of shared norms likely to inform individual attitudes and behaviour and this becomes evident in conversations with local people during fieldwork in China. Those who are familiar with the current situation of the country admit that a significant breakdown has taken place in the former normative frame of reference. Some of these perceptions are clearly shown by a change in the lifestyle of the Chinese people. An explicit example, which is perceptible just walking along the streets, is the lack of respect for traffic regulations. But there is also, for instance, a clear lack of formal regulation in different aspects of social life.

This chapter endeavours to analyse this lack of a normative frame of reference which has come about in today's Chinese society. For that purpose, use has been made of a sociological concept, namely the concept of anomie. Thus, before proceeding further, a brief definition of anomie must be given so that its application is sufficiently clear.

The etymology of the term anomie evokes the absence of norms or rules. The French sociologist Emile Durkheim (1858–1917) first used the term in his work *De la division du travail social,* originally published in 1893, and later developed it in another masterpiece completed in 1897, *Le Suicide.*[2] In the latter work, Durkheim argues that the wellbeing of the individual is only possible when there is a balance between his desires and the means at his disposal to achieve them. Human desires are, of course, unlimited, but the means are not. The limits to desires are imposed socially through a normative framework which obliges the individual to adapt his or her desires to aims that have a greater probability of being reached. When this collective framework is broken or disappears, the resulting situation is one of anomie. According to Durkheim, suicide would be one extreme but typical manifestation of an anomic situation.

Durkheim's concept of anomie was later redeveloped by the North American sociologist Robert K. Merton, who included it in a general theory of deviant behaviour.[3] Later, other social scientists also went back to this theory and redeveloped it. My application of this notion to contemporary Chinese society and political discourse takes as a reference Durkheim's idea of anomie as a state of society characterized by the lack of a consistent compulsory normative structure. It is important to mention that the lack of normative structure is always to be understood as a question of degree, as well as relative to the context of a given society. In my opinion, it is of special interest to apply the concept of anomie to contemporary Chinese society so as to explain certain matters which have become increasingly serious as a result of the rapid social and economic changes.

There are certain phenomena which may be considered to be indicators of social anomie in the People's Republic of China (PRC). Of these, I address two distinct social phenomena: corruption and suicide. In addition, I consider the political discourse and the re-emergence of nationalism as two indicators of sustained anomie from the political power itself. My analysis supposes a continuum from the Mao period to that of Deng or post-Deng. My starting point is also a hypothesis stated by Peter Waldmann, Professor of Sociology at the University of Augsburg, which deals with the question of whether dictatorial regimes do in fact maintain the external aspects of norms, understood as laws, and especially those related to the maintenance of security and public order thanks to their repressive potential. Under a dictatorship, however, one would also perceive a tendency towards the erosion of the ethical, moral and even linguistic basics of a general normative consensus, and the very members of the society affected would, on occasions, be aware of this. The behaviour resulting from the social anomie generated would become patent precisely during processes of regime liberalization and transition from dictatorial rule. Although we cannot speak of democratization in the case of China, the important process of change and liberalization after the death of Mao Zedong, on the one hand, and the evident resulting process of social anomie on the other hand, provide sufficient conditions to utilize this interesting hypothesis insofar as it is possible. This is the task I intend to address in this chapter.

Corruption: from Mao to the present

In today's China, all kinds of statements relating to widespread corruption are common. The media report news on this phenomenon almost every day. This trend could indicate the progressive increase and spread of such a pathology, which is intrinsically linked to party bureaucracy. Corruption in China appears in a wide range of practices from the clearly illegal to those that aim to create a relationship of compromise in order to obtain a mutual benefit. In China this is called *guanxi*.[4] Although several definitions and classifications have been given, I would like to underline what the people in general and the media in the PRC understand by corruption (*fubai*). Corruption appears in a wider range of activities than those in Western literature. The reason why I have chosen this reference is because the official definition of corruption included in the legislation of the PRC is still very ambiguous.[5] Moreover, this ambiguity can be extended to cover the application of the law in the fight against corruption. Popular culture provides a varied range of sayings and jokes, specifically satirizing what are considered to be the most common practices of corruption. As an example, the four cardinal principles are reworded as follows: 'Basically do not spend your wages, do not touch your wife, do not buy tobacco and alcohol, and all objects are presents'.[6] In addition, there is a number of books on the market that reveal abuses committed by important members of the CCP and their relatives, and these seem to have a large following of avid readers.[7]

According to some Chinese sources, corruption exists in at least thirteen groups of activities:[8]

1 First, moral degeneration, i.e. the use of power positions in order to establish a sexual relationship, to obtain the services of prostitutes, to rape women, and to spread obscene objects;
2 Taking bribes, i.e. to accept money, goods or gifts as a reward for a job carried out (this is generally termed *ruihua qian* or speedmoney);

3 Demanding bribes, i.e. to demand money, goods or gifts as a necessary condition for carrying out a job;
4 Embezzlement (*tanwu*), i.e. when a civil servant acquires state or collective property administered by him/her through deceit or some other strategy;
5 Misappropriation or acquisition of public property, i.e. when a civil servants uses his/her situation in order to illegally acquire public property;
6 Squandering of public goods;
7 Rechannelling state funds in order to obtain profit for individuals or small groups;
8 Perversion of the course of justice;
9 Taking a political decision or offering a service partially, i.e. when an official takes a decision giving priority to his/her own interests or to those of relatives and friends;
10 Acquiring additional benefit for relatives and friends, to use power and position illegally so as to satisfy the wishes of relatives and friends;
11 Having two jobs simultaneously, a public post and another one in a private company, in order to acquire additional gain;
12 Public bribery, i.e. when a small group or a government organism at an inferior level bribes those at a superior level in order to obtain benefit for its work unit;
13 To impose fines arbitrarily with the intention of obtaining sums of money from companies, employees and rural workers.

Although this is not an official definition, it is particularly interesting, as it includes all cases that are generally understood by Chinese society to comprise corruption. Undoubtedly, it implies a very wide definition of these so-called yellow crimes. At any rate, the activities listed can be identified in China, but it is very difficult to obtain real data on which to quantify them. However, it can be said that, in relative international terms, China was considered to have one of the highest corruption levels in 1995. The situation has improved in recent years, but corruption is still a serious problem.[9] Definite data on the current magnitude of the phenomenon is not yet available. Among the indicators commonly used to measure corruption are the number of cases investigated by the CCP's Central Disciplinary Committee, as well as the number of party members condemned for what are termed as economic crimes.[10] In 1995, some Chinese sources indicated that the number of party members condemned for economic crimes between 1987 and 1988 was 210,625, of which 32,994 were for bribery.[11] In 1995, a total of 155,485 cases had been reviewed, from which 147,132 persons were sentenced, 5,333 of them belonging to levels above the county (*xian*) and the department (*ju*). In 1996, the number of executive members sentenced reached 6,358, and in the first half of 1997 there were already 21,000 executive members and 78 were from provincial or ministerial institutions.[12] In the last few years several anti-corruption campaigns investigated and sentenced corrupt officials at the departmental and provincial levels. All this information has been systematically published in the media.[13] Table 7.1 includes data from various sources. Naturally, such data have to be considered with caution.

Chinese public opinion now tends to believe that corruption generally appeared during the period of reforms launched by Deng Xiaoping, but the facts suggest otherwise. Corruption has a long tradition in China. I am not going to deal with the Imperial period nor the first half of the twentieth century, but I will make some brief references to the period of supremacy of the CCP. Table 7.2 shows all the campaigns in which the fight against corruption has been, in one way or the other, explicitly announced since the foundation of the PRC until today.

It is interesting to trace how corruption and the official campaigns launched to fight against it have been interpreted in different ways, and this has varied with the Chinese political system. The fight against corruption throughout the Maoist period was one of the instruments used in the power struggle. Examples are the 'Three-Anti' Campaign of 1951, against corruption and other abuses of party executive members and state officials, and the 'Five-Anti' Campaign of 1952, against bribery, tax evasion, theft of state property, cheating on government contracts and the abuse of state economic information. The use of corruption as a tool for the struggle among factions within the party indeed became evident in the Mao and post-Mao period.[14] Quite a significant example would be the accusations of corruption against Zhao Ziyang, members of his family, and political allies after the massacre of Tiananmen in 1989.[15]

Table 7.1 Number of corruption cases reviewed and number of CCP members condemned for economic crimes, 1981–1999

Year	*Members condemned or expelled*	*Cases reviewed*
1981		30,000 (Fujian)
1983–1987	150,000	
1987–1988	210,625	
1988	25,000	
1990	79,000	
1991–1992	154,289	
Sept. 1993–June 1995	237,627	244,913
1995	147,132	155,485
1996	6,358 executive members	
First half 1977	21,000 executive members 78 provincial or ministerial institutions	
1990–1998	1,1 million corruption cases	
1999	132,000	130,000

Source: Baum (1994: 140, 168, 317, 428); Tsao and Worthley (1996: 22); Zheng (1997: 209); Xin (1998: 474); Li (2000: 13).

Table 7.2 Campaigns which involved the fight against corruption, 1951–2000

	Denomination	*Aim*
1951	The 'Three-Anti' Campaign	Against corruption, waste and bureaucratism
1952	The 'Five-Anti' Campaign	Against corruption and other abuses by executive party members and state functionaries
1953	New 'Three-Anti' Campaign	Corruption, leftist trends and functionalism
1957	Party Rectification	
1957–1958	Anti-Rightists	
1959–1960	Anti-Rightists Deviation	
1961	Reeducation of Party Members	
1963–1964	'Five Anti' Campaign	
1964	Party Rectification	
1964–1966	Socialist Education	
1969	Party Rectification	In coastal cities
1981	Anti-Bourgeois Liberalization	In Special Economic Zones
1982	Anti-Corruption Anti-Economic Crimes	Against corruption, abuse of power and bureaucratism, as well as decadent elements
1983	Party Rectification Anti-Spiritual Pollution	Elimination of a series of new unhealthy tendencies
1983–1987	Party Rectification	Against corruption, including waste and extravagance
1987	Anti-Bourgeois Liberalism	Drive to clamp down on economic crime and corruption
1987–1988	Anti-Corruption Reforms	Campaigns to build a clean
1989	Against Bourgeois Liberalism	government and curb corruption
1989–1992	Anti-Corruption Drive	
1993–2000	Anti-Corruption Campaigns	

Going back to the initial period of the transition after Mao Zedong's death, we can remember a journalist who provoked great social commotion. I am referring to Liu Binyan, who returned to the literary scene with the publication of a report (*baogao wenxue*) in September 1979 which caused an enormous impact on Chinese society. In 'Between People and Monsters' (*Ren yao zhi jian*), Liu Binyan described the underworld of corruption which was normal amongst the bureaucracy of a district in north-east China. The report was extremely detailed and the charge of corruption went back to the periods of famine after the Great Leap Forward. The report ended with the following words:

> The trial of Wang Shouxin on corruption has begun and she is under arrest. But have the social conditions that allowed Wang Shouxin to exist and evolve undergone any change? Is it not true

> that in each corner there are great and small Wang Shouxins, who continue to rot socialism, who continue to corrupt the party and receive no punishment from the dictatorship of the proletariat? People, we must be alert! The time to claim victory has not come yet.[16]

Not only did the author speak out against corruption but he also expressed his conjectures regarding the social and political mechanisms which allowed such occurrences. The criticism of a system, where monsters like the corrupt Wang Shouxin were born and lived, led this literary work to be considered as one of the most controversial of the post-Mao period.

'Between People and Monsters' had an open ending. Nothing was said about the result of the trial of Wang Shouxin and her gang. The trial had been announced a few months before in the *People's Daily*, and was presented as a lesson for other high-ranking party officials who might feel inclined to dishonesty.[17] The definite recognition of the veracity of the accusations of corruption, at both the official and the popular level, was not just the condemnation of Wang Shouxin, but rather the fact that 'Between People and Monsters' received the National Literary Prize for reports (*baogao wenxue*) in 1979. Nevertheless, the controversy arising around Liu Binyan led to his expulsion from the CCP in January 1987.[18]

Undoubtedly, corruption cannot be fully explained as an unexpected consequence of the economic reforms, as some authors have argued.[19] Nor can it be considered as one of the diseases of bourgeois liberalization proceeding from beyond China's borders, as some conservative members of the CCP have put forward.[20] Corruption, in China and elsewhere, can be explained as the conjunction of various circumstances. Corruption is not exclusively a Chinese phenomenon. It is spread and persists throughout the world. Thus, to my way of seeing things, the conditions facilitating the particularly high level of corruption in the Middle Kingdom are to be found in the system implanted during the time of Mao, when the abuse of political and administrative power structures furnished many opportunities for both minor and major corrupt practices. As has been pointed out in previous studies, circumvention or manipulation of regulations by officials were common in Maoist China, as in many other communist states.[21] Clientelism was also important in a world where political favours, and not economic values, were crucial for survival. Time and transparency will certainly reveal more evidence of all of this. Meanwhile, the CCP continues to show its reverence for the past, together with its incapacity and indecision in the fight against corruption.

Suicide

In Durkheim's work, suicide rates were considered to be an indicator clearly associated with social anomie. In *Le Suicide*, Durkheim makes a distinction between three types of suicide: egoistic, altruistic and anomic.[22] When talking about anomic suicide, Durkheim mainly analyses its occurrence during periods of economic change, both of crisis and of prosperity, which he conceives as 'disturbances of the collective order'.[23] If we apply suicide rates as an indicator of social anomie to contemporary China, the result – expected, if we take the initial hypothesis into account – is still surprising. According to Chinese official data, the country has today one of the highest suicide rates in the world.

With regard to statistics on suicide, apart from the elaboration problems they entail in any part of the world, there are also problems which are particular to China. As any specialist knows, statistics issued in the PRC should be interpreted very carefully. In fact, concerning the contemporary period, it is almost impossible to obtain sufficiently reliable statistics on suicide until 1987. The reasons are mainly of a political and technical nature. During the Maoist period, suicide was considered to be an act of betrayal against the people.[24] It appears that all the information on suicide was considered to be sensitive and even today Chinese researchers themselves cannot always easily have access to it. There is doubt as to whether the information was in fact gathered at the time. In aggregate statistics on death caused by injuries during the Maoist period, deaths by suicide were likely to be included.

Table 7.3 offers data from a report of the Chinese Ministry of Health. The data on urban areas are from a sample of what the Chinese call 16 large cities and 25 medium and small cities. The data on rural areas up to 1993 are taken from a report on 87 counties, while the data for 1994 and 1995 include 14 provinces and a total of 104 counties. Most probably, the data in the table underestimate the real extent of suicide. This fact has been noted by the Chinese researchers themselves.[25]

According to specialized studies, the most common method for committing suicide in rural areas is by consuming toxic substances. Thus, as part of the agricultural reforms, rat poison has gradually been substituted by insecticides.[26] The study of the traditionally high rate of suicide observed among Chinese women in comparison with that of other countries in the world would deserve a chapter to itself.[27]

All these data mean that, for example, in 1994 the suicide rate in rural China (32.00) was almost 300 per cent greater than the average of the European Union (12.05).[28] According to some reports, China, with approximately 21.5 per cent of the world's population, accounts for more than 40 per cent of the suicides worldwide.[29] It is in the rural areas of China where we find a particularly high suicide rate. The most updated data show a decreasing tendency.[30] Some studies have underlined that Chinese culture shows a predisposition to suicide, but comparing data from Hong Kong, Taiwan and Singapore prove that other factors, more related with socio-economic or psychological aspects, must be considered.[31] The comparison

Table 7.3 Chinese suicide rates in urban and rural areas, 1987–1995

Age	*1987*		*1988*		*1989*		*1990*		*1991*		*1992*		*1993*		*1994*		*1995*	
	Urban	*Rural*	*Urban*	*Rural*	*Urban*	*Rural*	*Urban*	*Rural*	*Urban*	*Rural*	*Urban*	*Rural*	*Urban*	*Rural*	*Urban*	*Rural*	*Urban*	*Rural*
1	0.00	0.00	0.00	0.35	0.10	0.06	0.05	0.53	0.00	0.03	0.00	0.05	0.03	0.00	0.03	0.17	0.00	0.25
5	0.05	0.13	0.14	0.33	0.05	0.17	0.05	0.20	0.02	0.32	0.09	0.13	0.00	5.10	0.19	0.26	0.12	0.03
10	1.41	2.75	1.21	2.35	0.84	1.40	0.88	1.67	1.11	1.88	1.13	1.43	0.71	1.29	1.14	2.20	1.02	1.35
15	9.82	28.81	7.90	22.49	6.52	22.23	5.48	16.69	6.01	20.48	4.48	14.47	3.09	11.11	3.23	13.84	3.22	10.40
20	12.69	57.36	11.84	52.48	11.97	51.24	10.41	34.94	11.94	47.78	11.14	37.54	6.79	32.94	6.22	35.49	7.26	26.65
25	8.00	24.79	7.66	28.93	8.65	32.70	9.02	28.67	9.54	36.83	8.25	32.13	6.27	35.16	7.17	35.32	8.05	31.67
30	8.48	27.38	8.11	25.45	9.23	26.71	7.74	21.40	6.56	26.91	7.12	24.51	6.08	25.70	6.29	27.55	6.65	27.27
35	8.72	26.06	8.36	25.91	9.58	30.11	8.69	20.96	8.93	26.52	7.72	24.60	6.82	23.19	6.58	24.31	7.32	21.28
40	8.41	25.03	7.66	28.93	9.35	27.05	7.50	19.65	8.76	26.54	8.73	23.46	7.62	25.35	8.27	28.01	8.17	26.25
45	8.70	28.94	8.36	25.91	8.76	27.53	8.49	22.35	9.29	30.33	8.79	27.16	7.91	30.26	8.33	30.28	9.18	26.19
50	11.87	30.63	10.25	30.97	9.69	33.55	8.99	27.65	10.03	36.10	10.58	31.65	7.62	34.62	7.24	30.83	7.03	29.15
55	12.73	37.39	12.00	38.60	12.75	40.95	11.18	32.09	11.39	39.59	11.53	33.74	8.44	39.13	7.64	37.33	8.50	33.18
60	17.53	58.54	16.00	58.84	15.07	53.87	14.57	48.21	15.23	63.05	15.43	52.89	10.82	57.67	10.25	57.87	13.46	51.52
65	26.11	67.81	22.44	61.72	25.01	63.95	18.97	53.26	20.33	70.11	19.57	62.74	15.93	68.21	2.85	67.03	14.46	61.80
70	38.17	94.65	32.58	91.62	33.32	90.96	27.91	80.70	30.99	110.86	28.47	94.63	20.34	109.42	21.67	116.57	23.39	97.70
75	45.85	85.85	45.87	94.10	41.52	102.16	44.02	84.16	42.77	109.52	33.33	99.21	31.22	113.40	30.70	106.39	33.23	99.72
80	67.85	117.11	62.25	119.61	61.09	122.85	58.67	112.19	55.79	133.09	48.59	103.32	47.49	123.53	36.94	132.13	43.15	139.32
85	83.41	145.68	72.95	144.04	82.62	149.10	67.49	132.59	59.37	142.31	65.03	129.06	46.46	113.76	48.39	125.13	43.73	127.65
Total	9.80	27.69	9.02	17.49	9.39	27.21	8.57	22.46	9.05	29.10	8.46	25.43	6.72	25.49	6.74	27.05	7.42	24.05

Source: Yang (1997: 225)

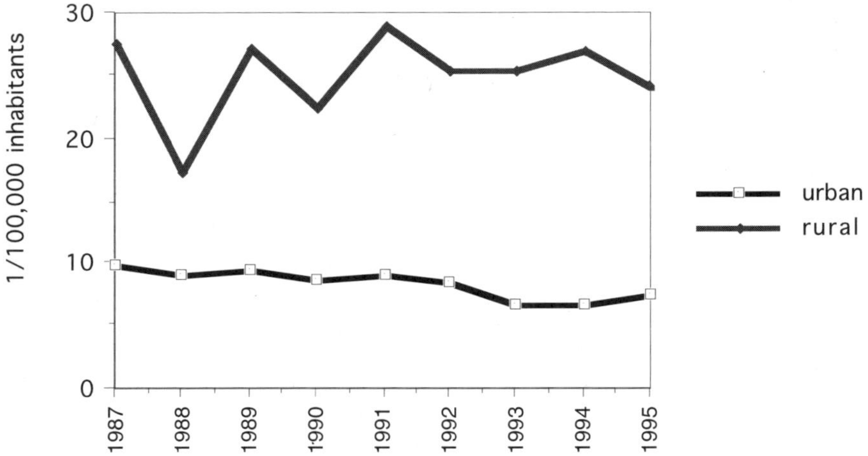

Figure 7.1 Evolution of suicide rates in rural and urban areas of the People's Republic of China, 1987–1995.

Source: Devised by the author from the data included in Yang (1997: 225).

between data of different regions of the world proves that only Hungary (33.5) and several countries of the former Soviet Union have a higher suicide rate than that of rural China. Interestingly enough, all these countries have undergone comparatively rapid socio-political and economic changes during the last two decades. Some additional data provided by the World Health Organisation 1995 Report is shown in Figure 7.2. For comparative purposes, the figure includes, among others, the three European countries with higher suicide rates (Finland (26.4), Denmark (17.3) and France (19.8)), two countries with a low rate (Spain (6.6) and the United Kingdom (7.2)) and other countries or territories with Chinese population (Hong Kong (12.9) and Singapore (13.6)).

As far as the Maoist period is concerned, there is no quantitative data indicating the number of suicides within the whole population. However, a qualitative analysis of the history of those years leads one to assume that there was no likelihood of a break between the Maoist and the post-Mao period. It is possible that at certain stages the suicide rate was even greater. For example, there is some agreement on the fact that during the first phase of the Cultural Revolution, between 1966 and 1968, suicide rates increased.[32] These suicides were frequent in urban areas, mostly among those who were labelled as capitalists and intellectuals. In some cases these suicides were interpreted as a final and definite form of dissent.[33] But, going beyond supposed protest behaviour, it is surprising how in different biographical narratives written in the years under Mao, reference is repeatedly made to suicide, either successful[34] or frustrated attempts,[35] as a way out of great

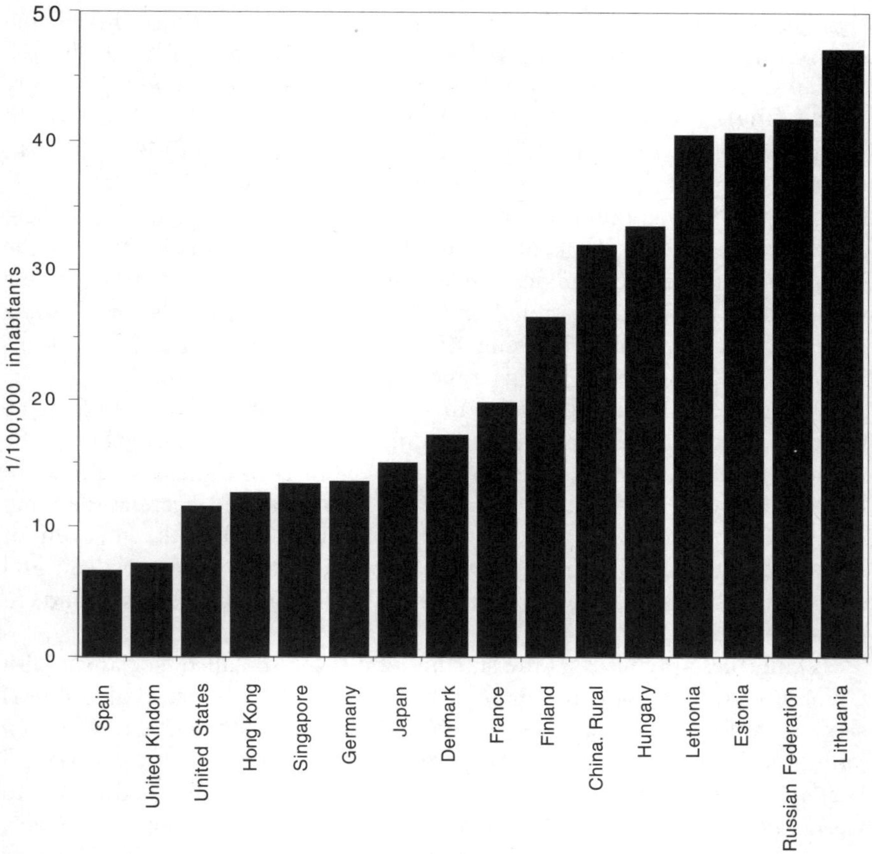

Figure 7.2 Suicide rates in rural China and other countries in 1994.

Source: Devised by the author, using data from World Heath Organization (1996: 1998). The data published for Spain and United States are from 1992, while for France they are from 1993.

despair and confusion.[36] Many testimonies lead one to consider that suicide rates were similar to the present ones, if not higher, especially during the Cultural Revolution.

Anomie and political discourse

The levels of corruption and especially the data available on suicide certainly indicate that we can speak of the existence of social anomie in present-day China. I would now like to spend some time on a brief analysis of what could be the causes and manifestations of anomie in the political discourse. By political discourse I refer mainly to the official discourse of the CCP, but also to the political discourse of several intellectuals who have reached a significant audience in the country. In terms of the official political discourse, the ideological and normative changes have been justified through the so-called 'socialism with Chinese characteristics' (*zhongguo tese shehuizhuyi*). The term and its conceptualization are attributed directly to Deng Xiaoping, who supposedly began to draft it at the Third Plenum, XIth Central Committee, held in Beijing on 18–22 December, 1978. It appears explicitly in the inaugural discourse of the XIIth Party Congress, held in September 1982.[37] A look at the official documents which refer to the invention of this expression only underlines its versatility. According to some of the latest official versions, the theory of 'socialism with Chinese characteristics' appeared in Deng Xiaoping's work, mainly in his writings between 1982 and 1992. Deng argues that, since the second half of the 1950s, all the communist parties in the world were forced to reflect the difficulties faced by socialism. According to the 'master designer of the reforms' (*Zhongguo de zong shejishi*), from 1958 to 1978 China's development had been slowed down mainly because class struggle had become the main focus. However, in the opinion of the Chinese leader, the mission of socialism is the development of production potential. True socialism and communism are not poverty but the search for the fastest road to development.

Taking these premises as the starting point, the so-called 'socialism with Chinese characteristics' began to take shape and led to several political slogans. Among these were: 'Economic construction as the nucleus' (*yi yingji jianshe wei zhongxin*); 'The strategic aim for development in three stages' (*sanbu fazhang zhanlue mubiao*); 'Reform, liberalization and dedication to work' (*gaige kaifang gaohuo*); 'Adherence to the four basic principles' (*jianchi si xiang jiben yuanze*); 'The four guarantees' (*si xiang baozheng*); 'The four have's' (*si you*); 'Seize with both hands' (*liang shou zhua*); 'Science and technology form the backbone of production' (*kexue jishu shi di-yi shengchanli*); 'An independent foreign policy with control of the initiative' (*duli zizhu de heping waijiao zhengce*); 'One country, two systems' (*yi guo liang zhi*); and so on.[38] In the discourse of both the CCP leaders and the officially controlled mass media, the expression 'with Chinese characteristics' has become a rhetorical formula with a multiplicity of uses which is untiringly employed to justify any practices and positions.

A variety of explanations are provided by ordinary people in an attempt to clarify the meaning of the expression. For some, it means the flexibility to apply reforms with no need to attend an established legal framework. Others explain it as referring to a kind of social behaviour which in contexts alien to China, especially in Western countries, would be considered irregular or undesirable. Totally different examples are given in this respect, such as the lack of awareness of environmental problems among the people or the illicit use of public funds for private ends by the leaders, including payments to prostitutes. The media apply the expression also in a variety of ways, but it is used abundantly in political manifestos.[39] At any rate, its full content is never explained with precision. This ambiguity might well be interpreted as the way in which the political discourse justifies the wide leeway it allows itself in a situation where there is an absence of a widely shared legal framework, lack of normative structure or, relatively speaking, normative insufficiency. To my way of thinking, twenty years ago it served to legitimate change without having to fall back on a radical disqualification of the past and it also served to restrain the internal tensions within the party. Nowadays, this kind of political discourse serves to sustain social anomie.

When there is a situation of generalized social anomie, individual and collective reactions that attempt to offset its effects are likely to exist. In other words, situations of uncertainty may lead to a type of flight forward or an attempt to recuperate security through past ideas and attitudes which are perceived as more comforting. A tendency to find solutions in extremist approaches is also more likely to happen. In today's Chinese society it is clear that one of the reactions that has taken shape is the call for a return to a Maoist type of social control and the idealization or reasserting of the Maoist period – so-called Mao fever (*Mao Zedong re* or *Mao re*), which reached its zenith at the centenary celebrations of Mao's birth in December 1993. Another reaction is the nationalistic glorification which has occurred throughout the 1990s and which will be dealt with below.

The call for social order

A book that should be mentioned in the context of the Mao fever and which had an important influence when it was published is *Seeing China Through the Third Eye* (*Di-san zhi yangjing kan zhongguo*). This book was published on the Chinese mainland in mid-1994, and its authorship was falsely attributed to a German scholar (*Luoyiningge'er*), while a Chinese citizen, identified as the work's translator, was in fact the real author. His name was Wang Shan, assistant manager at the Opera Theatre in Beijing. One reason for highlighting this work is the fact that it has been read avidly by many young people, especially, though not only, in university circles. Some of these young university readers believed, and continue to believe today, that it is an exact, objective work which puts forward a serious, impartial social analysis. At least, this was the opinion I was personally given by many of them.[40]

Seeing China Through the Third Eye is divided into six chapters. The first one criticizes foreign intervention in Chinese affairs. Dealing with all the points would require too much space, but among the most outstanding is the idea that Chinese tradition and the social situation of the country require a strong power which can impose the necessary social order and stability. Along these lines, it defends the fact that Mao Zedong, who is described as a leader with a spirit of optimism, heroism and romanticism,[41] acted rightfully when he understood that the rural workers had to be confined to the land, as their mobility was the cause of chaos and lack of control. A complete section is also dedicated to the assertion that the increase in the rate of delinquency is due to the migration of rural workers but no evidence is provided. He states that official statistics on the matter have not yet been made public.[42] Perhaps one of the chapters which most clearly reveals the author's position is that one dedicated to the intellectuals. The harshest criticism is aimed at them, as can be found in the following excerpts:

> Only one response is possible. After ten years, the rebellion of the intelligentsia has not been successful. Mao Zedong continually repeated this classic maxim, which, in fact, shows the tragic history and traditions of Chinese intellectuals, because they are only a deplorable, spoiled group, the instrument or ornament of one or other social layer. For some time now their wills have been castrated, as they have never been an independent part of social production.[43]

Those intellectuals who propose some type of democratization are described by the author as narrow-minded, since their proposals are considered to be destabilizing and a true incitement for the return of the so-called ultra-left of the Cultural Revolution.[44] These are some of the most relevant paragraphs included in the text:

> After the fall of the Gang of Four, they are the opposition to the practice of going in through the back door [*zou houmen*] and the loudest outcry of the popular democratic movement against privilege. During the incidents in Beijing in 1989, these were the problems which caused most indignation on the university campuses.
>
> Leaving political problems apart, and starting from the standpoint of conscience and social sentiment, we discover that in the opposition to privilege there is a relationship between the ultra-left and the current popular democrats which fits together in a very precise way. If we attempt for a deeper more serene analysis, we can reach the following conclusion: the popular democratic conscience, which has existed for some time, is the best breeding ground to ensure that the ultra-left of the Cultural Revolution come to power. Thus, the current democratic movements and their ideology clearly bear the legacy of the Cultural Revolution.
>
> Based on this conclusion and going one step further, making a logical deduction we can obtain an answer which involves a clear warning. If a reform of the social order cannot be carried out, in such a way as to direct it towards stability and democracy, based on competition, equality and risk, and it is left at the mercy of the changes in power, it is possible that the popular democratic conscience and extremist ideologies will arise together. But do the

> Chinese want to undergo the experiences of the Cultural Revolution again? Deng Xiaoping's change of attitude as regards the wall of Xidan shows the realistic style of an eminent politician in extremely difficult situations of choice.[45]

This last part, of course, refers to the fact that Deng Xiaoping forbade the so-called democratic wall of Xidan in 1979.

Concerning the student demonstrations of 1989, the author openly defends the army intervention as he believes that if this had not happened, China would have entered a period of anarchy and disintegration. Thus, it is understandable that the book was praised by the current General Secretary of the party, Jiang Zemin, as stated in the edition published in Hong Kong in January 1995. Although the book also criticises the abuse of power among local Party officials, as a whole it defends the need to strengthen control over the Chinese population, fundamentally the rural workers and the intellectuals, in order to recover from the loss of order and prevent a state of chaos. Thus, no doubt, social anomie plays for the author an important role in legitimating political control.[46]

The return of Maoism

The discourse of other intellectuals makes a much more explicit reference to how much the Maoist period is commemorated.[47] One author who is considered to write serious or pure literature (*chun wenxue*), Zhang Chengzhi, has also become a strong supporter of Maoism. Born in 1948 in Beijing, he belongs to the Hui ethnic group, i.e., he is a Chinese Muslim. In addition, two items of his biography should be highlighted: he coined the term Red Guard (*hongweibing*) during the Cultural Revolution, and in the post-Mao period he rediscovered his ethnic, cultural and religious roots as a member of a Muslim collectivity. In an interview published in 1994 in English, Zhang Chengzhi firmly asserted that literature must be a religion and that anybody who could not demonstrate the same attitude of sincerity towards literature as towards religion should not write.[48] Zhang Chengzhi was given the chance to stay in Japan as a visiting scholar on two occasions, and ever since these trips, especially the second one at the start of the 1990s, he has explicitly expressed xenophobic opinions. Zhang Chengzhi has stood out in public discussions due to his extreme defence of the writer's social responsibility. He pleads for the return to a normative literature. In some way he shares the idea of literature at the service of the people, and he agrees that its major function is to educate the people, the same as during the Maoist period.

Zhang Chengzhi's ideas make up an explosive mixture, converging in the same direction with totalitarian Maoism and religious fundamentalism, together with explicit xenophobic attitudes.[49] Perhaps for those who have not read the novels he published at the beginning of the 1980s, set in the vast prairies of Central Mongolia, these assertions might seem too strong. Therefore, it might be helpful to quote the exact words of the author, published outside of China and referring to Mao Zedong. I transcribe here some paragraphs of an article written by Zhang Chengzhi in 1993:

> With his death, China's age of great men came to an end. The masses felt a sense of loss. They have not yet found an alternative. That is to say, that despite the passing of time, when the masses feel themselves discriminated against and oppressed, they can think of no other leader than Mao Zedong.
>
> Despite all the talk of international peace for our ancient motherland of China, the New World Order is a pitiless killer and every Chinese person will have to face its onslaught one day. In the future, world justice will continue to be frustrated and there will be no such thing as compassion; nor will anyone stand up for the dispossessed.
>
> The name Mao Zedong will remain eternally a symbol of rebellion against this new order. His prestige may well rise gradually among the masses once more. Of course, Mao Zedong must be criticised in human terms, but ironically, for those Chinese like me who continue to oppose neo-colonialism, the international balance of power makes it necessary for us to look at him as a bastion of human dignity.

It is in this light, for the people of China and the poor nations throughout the world who are confronted with the new international scene, that it is possible that the influence and significance of Mao Zedong will gain a new lease of life.[50] Some may interpret this pro-Mao reaction as something quite natural, since it comes from a very significant ex-Red Guard. Nevertheless, this has not been the attitude of other fervent Red Guards who stood out during the Cultural Revolution, as for example Zheng Yi, who has revealed episodes involving cannibalism in Guangxi province during the Cultural Revolution. He adopted a much more critical stance towards Mao Zedong as a person and his policies.[51]

But this longing for Maoism can be seen in many other circumstances. Throughout 1997, and coinciding with the return of Hong Kong to China, two films were screened almost simultaneously for the first time: *The Opium War* (*Yapian zhanzheng*) and *Those Days with Lei Feng* (*He Lei Feng zai yiqi de rizi*). As we all know, Lei Feng was a soldier presented as being completely dedicated to the revolutionary cause and to others. He felt the love and gratitude for the CCP that a good son feels for his mother in the finest Confucian tradition. Lei Feng is and was the ideal model symbolizing blind faith in Mao and the party. It should be remembered that, at different times during Deng's period, campaigns were again launched proposing him as a model to imitate. In a conversation held with the writer Dai Qing, she made comments on the impact of both films. She believed that the film on

Lei Feng had a greater emotional effect on the audience than *The Opium War*. Dai Qing explained that ordinary people sought to recuperate the lost values reflected in his character.[52]

The resort to nationalistic glorification

If, as we have seen, a response used in order to adapt to uncertainty might be a return to the figure of Mao Zedong or to other emblematic models of the Maoist period, another possible one is the nationalistic glorification which has occurred throughout recent years in the PRC. Faced with the loss of image due mainly to the scourge of corruption, and aware of what happened in the Soviet Union and some East European countries, the CCP has tried to rearm itself with a type of extreme nationalism that has deeply influenced the population. The denunciation of a neo-imperialism coming from abroad has logically led to more internal cohesion. In this way, nationalism, with its multiple applications, has become a necessary piece in the party's propaganda arsenal.

The legacy of Mao has been the source of many controversies, but the majority of the Chinese people have hardly ever questioned the idea that thanks to the Great Helmsman, as he was known, the PRC recovered its national pride and won the recognition it deserves internationally. This is repeated even by young Chinese who were born during Deng's era. Currently, the strengthening of national identity has again become an instrument for the self-assertion of China in the world.[53] Nationalistic glorification is especially evident in attitudes towards cultural imperialism by foreign powers, and takes shape in specifically anti-American and anti-Japanese movements. I do not wish to focus on the nationalism that has been promoted from the Propaganda Department of the CCP and in the discourse of the top leaders since the foundation of the PRC and especially during the 1990s, but rather to draw attention to expressions of nationalism which are apparently more popular, but undoubtedly also sustained by the CCP. This is, to give an example, the case of one of the most controversial best-sellers in the country, which appeared in 1996. I refer to a book entitled *China Can Say No* (*Zhongguo keyi shuo bu*), which, according to several press articles appearing both on the mainland and in Hong Kong, had important social repercussions. I came to the same conclusion once I had checked that in Beijing most people with a certain level of education knew of the book or had leafed through it. Only young university students admitted having devoured the book, which they considered as good, pleasing to read and even convincing. Nevertheless, after a deeper conversation they admitted that the book was one of nationalistic glorification, although this was no impediment to considering its arguments to be convincing.

It was also praised by various levels of the party. The book is a compilation of several brief texts with a shared theme of criticizing the United

States, although it does also criticise other Western countries. The authors list what they consider to be serious insults and humiliations from the United States. Among the various conspiracies attributed to this country in order to degrade China, the authors mention its criticism of the Chinese situation regarding human rights and birth control.

The language of the book is indeed direct and extremist. One of the chapters is entitled 'Contempt for that class of Chinese people' (*Wo tuoqi nazhong zhongguoren*).[54] Briefly, it describes a Chinese called Wang who has a foreign friend, an Englishman from Oxford, no less. Wang cannot help but talk of his foreign friend all the time. His name is Mark and he turns out to be both a womanizer and a drinker, as well as the son of a famous nuclear physicist. After giving a frightful description of the Englishman, as well as a Chinese girl with a fascination for the United States, the author finishes off with the following words: 'That type of Chinese! That type of Western slave! The face and behaviour of that type of Western slave! I despise them all! Ah! Bah!' Among the different terms the author could have used for 'despise', he chose a very specific one (*tuoqi*), composed of the character for 'to spit' and the character for 'to reject'.

Another text from this same book is entitled 'Detain your filthy hand: we do not welcome your sexual harassment' (*Nakai ni angzang de shou: women bu yao xing saorao*). This text maintains that sexual harassment is a common practice undergone by Chinese women in foreign enterprises operating in China. It cannot be denied that such harassment might happen, as it does in every country, but the vocabulary and the stance taken to argue the point denote rather more than the denunciation of sexual harassment in Chinese society. In fact, these are some of the sentences stated by a foreigner who defends a colleague who has committed sexual harassment:

> China is not an open country, it has no brothels, (he) has no outlet for his sexual appetite, there is no respect for human rights.[55]

Another foreigner states literally:

> This is the price one has to pay for economic development. If you did not let them harass women, they would not want to come to your country, and if they did not come, it would be difficult for you to achieve the objective you have fixed in order to attract foreign capital and technology. That is the way China is being developed, don't look so surprised and don't think it so strange.

It continues by attributing the following statement to a Western sinologist:

> Sexual harassment will not subjugate the country. What can subjugate it is economic backwardness. If the English fought against

> you and the Japanese invaded your territory, it was because the economy was underdeveloped. From this viewpoint, to exchange sexual harassment for economic development is the exchange of something small for something big.[56]

Another section of the book is entitled 'The West does not shine, the East does' (*Xifang bu liang dong fang liang*). Here, the general tone of the book is well summed up in a demagogic tone using the most vulgar arguments in order to discredit everything foreign and praise what is genuinely Chinese. The impact of the book and the acceptance of the arguments it puts forward amongst many sectors of the Chinese population leads us to believe that this encouragement of nationalistic glorification constitutes the offer of a collective identity, and its success migh be attributed to the uncertainty generated by the rapid process of social and economic modernization in progress, together with the collapse, to a great extent, of the preceding ideological framework.

Concluding remarks

There are indicators of social anomie in today's People's Republic of China. According to official data, the suicide rate is truly high, especially in the countryside. Corruption is also widespread. These two indicators of anomie undoubtedly have their roots in the Maoist period, but it was especially during the process of social and economic modernization in the Deng era that they became more evident to the population as a whole, together with a general sense of change in the daily life context. This situation of social anomie is sustained by the discourse of the CCP in that, on the one hand, it legitimates the need for state social control, and on the other hand, it is used to solve the struggle amongst the various factions in the party. In addition, it enables us to understand why Chinese society is more likely to accept discourses such as the longing for the times of Mao and nationalistic glorification. No doubt, the sustainment of current levels of anomie in Chinese society may continue to provide us with quite a few surprises.

Notes

1 There is abundant academic literature regarding the changes which took place once Deng Xiaoping had launched the reforms. Among these, see: Aubert et al. (1986); Barnett and Clough (1986); Hamrin (1990); Baum (1991).
2 The editions used of both texts are Durkheim (1998 and 1997).
3 Merton (1957).
4 For a definition and classification of corruption in China see White (1996: 41–42).
5 For a review of the anti-corruption legislation in the PRC, see Kolenda (1990: 187–232).

6 According to the official doctrine and the Constitution of the CCP, revised at the XVth National Congress and adopted on 18 September 1997, the construction of the country is based on four principles: the socialist road, the people's democratic dictatorship, the CCP leadership, and Marxism-Leninism and Mao Zedong thought.

7 Two examples of this are Fang (1996) and He and Gao (1996). The first one practically became a bestseller and novelizes the scandal that erupted in the Beijing town hall and ended on 29 August 1997 with the expulsion of Chen Xitong (Beijing's Mayor) under the accusation of serious crimes of corruption. The second text deals with the illicit amassing of wealth by the wives and children of renouned members of the party. Although this latter book was acquired outside China, several people on the mainland informed me that they were waiting for copies to circulate so that they could buy it and read it.

8 Xin (1998: 456–459).

9 According to a survey carried out in 1995 by *Transparency International,* businessmen considered Indonesia and then the PRC to be the two countries with the highest level of corruption in the world. See *TI, Press Release* (1995: 3), quoted in Cabestan (1996: 663). The 2001 Corruption Perceptions Index shows that a deterioration has been perceived in China from 1980 to 1996 and again a certain improvement from 1996 to 2001. All this information and more was included in Transparency International's webpage on 28 October 2001. Refer to: htpp://www.transparency.org/.

10 Tsao and Worthley (1996: 22–23).

11 *Ibid.* (1996: 22).

12 Xin (1998: 474).

13 For instance the report published in *Beijing Review*, 22 May 2000.

14 See Lo (1993: 195–209).

15 *Ibid.* (1993: 204–205). Zhao Ziyang was appointed Secretary General of the CCP since 1987 but was then relieved of all official posts for the support he gave to the 1989 student movement.

16 The text was originally published in *Renmin wenxue*, no. 9 (1979). The version I have used was published in Huang, D. (1980: 128).

17 Among others, see Heilongjiang sheng . . . (1999: 2) and 'Jianchi shehuizhuyi . . .' (1979: 2).

18 Published in *Renmin ribao*, 25 January 1987.

19 For instance, see Gong (1993: 311–327).

20 See Levy (1995: 1–25).

21 See the interesting article by Oi (1989: 223–225).

22 See Durkheim (1997). There is a fourth type of suicide, the fatalistic suicide, that Durkheim mentions in a footnote on page 311.

23 *Ibid.* (1997: 271).

24 See Yang (1997: 224).

25 *Ibid.* (1997: 226).

26 See He and Lester (1998).

27 The seriousness of the problem is shown by facts such as that one included in the magazine *Rural Women Knowing All* (*Nongjia nü baishi tongi zazhi*) sponsored by the All China Women's Federation, which publishes special sections for the prevention of women's suicide.

28 According to the *Eurostat* published by the Statistical Office of the European Union (1997), the average rate for European Union countries was 12.05. The comparison between European and Chinese statistics is complicated since the Standard Populations sample used, i.e. world or European, is probably not the same. This is not mentioned in the Chinese statistics I had access to.

29 The magazine *Time Australia* in its section on Asia published the following information on 2 February: 'A 1995 World Mental Health Report put the overall suicide rate in China at 17.1 per 100,000 people, which is among the highest in the world (Hungary ranked no. 1). Last year a study achieved by the World Bank, the World Health Organization and Harvard University put the rate at 30.3 per 100,000, compared with 10.7 for the rest of the world. That study estimates that China, with 21.5 per cent of the world's population, accounts for a staggering 43.6 per cent of the 786,000 suicides worldwide. Allowing for some of those officially listed as accidents, the study suggests that more than 300,000 Chinese kill themselves every year.' In any case, says Michael Phillips, a Canadian researcher at Beijing's Hui Long Guan Hospital, 'We're talking about pretty damn big numbers. It's a huge health problem. Particularly for women.'

30 See World Health Organization's data on the website in October 2001: http://www.who.int/mental_health/Topic_Suicide/suicide1.html.

31 See Phillips et al. (1999: 25–50)

32 Yang (1997: 233). In an interesting study by White III (1989: 276–279), suicides during this period are even described as anomic.

33 See Thurston (1990: 162–166).

34 Cheng Naishan in Leung (1994: 37–38), Chen Yi in Leung (1994: 266); Feng Jicai in Martin (1992: 16), Gu Hua in Martin (1992: 97) and Lao She in Martin (1992: 267); Wen Jieruo in Lau and Goldblatt (1995: 706).

35 Shen Congwen in Martin (1992: 289).

36 Wang Ruowang in Martin (1992: 7–8); Liu (1990: 118). In his memories, Ji Xianlin mentions not only his thoughts about commiting suicide, but also the suicide of professors and cadres at Peking University. See Ji (1998: 71–82).

37 Huang, Y. (1998: 595–616).

38 *Ibid.* (1998: 604–605).

39 For example, in the numerous articles that appeared before and during the XVth Congress of the CCP in September 1997. Nearly every day there appeared an article with this expression. Among others see: *Renmin ribao*, 1 September 1997; *Renmin ribao*, 13 September 1997; *Renmin ribao*, 19 September 1997, and many more that could be quoted.

40 These opinions were expressed during informal interviews while on a trip to Beijing in August and September 1997.

41 The version I have used is Wang (1995: 264).

42 *Ibid.* (1995: 71–82).

43 *Ibid.* (1995: 107).

44 *Ibid.* (1995: 83 et seq.).

45 *Ibid.* (1995: 145–146).

46 See Lo (1993: 195–196).

47 The glorification of the Mao period appears continually in popular magazines with numerous photographs and stories of the revolution such as *Jiefangjun shenghuo*.

48 Leung (1994: 225).
49 These xenophobic attitudes are even involved in his condition as *Hui* and his attitude towards the *Han*.
50 Originally published in the Japanese magazine *Sekai*, the English version is included in Barmé (1996: 274).
51 Zheng, Y. (1993). A reduced version of the book has been published in English.
52 Personal interview held with Dai Qing in Beijing, 28 August 1997.
53 There has been extensive literature on Chinese nationalism in recent years. Standing out among other texts is Unger (1996).
54 Song et al. (1996: 55).
55 *Ibid.* (1996: 295).
56 *Ibid.* (1996: 295–296).

References and further reading

Aubert, Claude, Chevrier, Yves et al. (1986) *La société chinoise après Mao. Entre autorité et modernité*. Paris, Fayard.

Barnett, Andrew D. and Clough, Ralph N. (eds) (1986) *Modernizing China: Post-Mao Reform and Development*. Boulder and London, Westview Press.

Barmé, Geremie R. (1996) *Shades of Mao*. Armonk NY, M. E. Sharpe.

Baum, Richard (ed.) (1991) *Reform and Reaction in Post-Mao China*. New York and London, Routledge.

—— (1994) *Burying Mao: Chinese Politics in the Age of Deng Xiaoping*. Princeton, Princeton University Press.

Cabestan, Jean-Pierre (1996) 'Chine: Un état de lois sans état de droit'. *Revue du tiers monde,* no. 147 (July–September), pp. 649–668.

Durkheim, Emile (1978) *De la division du travail social*. 10th edition. Paris, Presses Universitaires de France.

—— (1997) *Le Suicide*. 9th edition. Paris, Presses Universitaires de France.

Fang, Wen (1996) *Tian nu* (Heaven's Rage). Beijing, Yuanfang chubanshe.

Gong, Ting (1993) 'Corruption and Reform in China: An Analysis of Unintended Consequences'. *Crime, Law and Social Change*, vol. 19, no. 4, pp. 311–327.

Hamrin, Carol Lee (1990) *China and the Challenge of the Future: Changing Political Patterns*. Boulder and London, Westview Press.

He, Pin and Gao, Xin (1996) *Zhongguo 'daizi dang*' (The Chinese Commmunist Party's 'Heirs Kinfolk'). Hong Kong, Minjing chubanshe.

He, Zengke (2000) 'Corruption and Anti-Corruption in Reform China'. *Communist and Post-Communist Studies*, vol. 33, pp. 243–270.

He, Zhao-Xiang and Lester, David (1998) 'Methods for Suicide in Mainland China'. *Death Studies*, vol. 22, no. 6, pp. 571–579.

'Heilongjiang sheng pohuo yiqi yanzhong tanwu jiduan anjian' (Prosecution Case of the Discovery and Arrest of a Group Committing Serious Corruption in Heilongjiang Province) (1979) *Renmin ribao*, 23 April, p. 2.

Huang, Dazhi (ed.) (1980) *Zhongguo xin xieshizhuyi pinglun xuan – Liu Binyan ji qi zuopin* (Selected Comments on China's New Realism: Liu Binyan and his Works). Hong Kong, Bowen shuju chuban.

Huang, Yepin (ed.) (1998) *1978–1998 Zhongguo da juece jishi* (China's Greatest Political Decisions, 1978–1988), vol. 2. Beijing, Guanming ribao chubanshe.

Huang, Zhiling (1997) 'Battle to Stamp Out Corruption Purifies Country'. *China Daily*, 9 September, p. 4.

Ji, Xianlin (1998) *Niupeng zayi* (Memories of the Stall). Beijing, Zhonggong zhongyang dangxiao chubanshe.

'Jianchi shehuizhuyi, daji tanwu daoqie' (Keeping Firm in Socialism, Striking Corruption and Theft) (1979) *Renmin ribao*, 23 April, p. 2.

Kolenda, Helena, (1990) 'One Party, Two Systems: Corruption in the People's Republic of China and Attempts to Control it'. *Journal of Chinese Law*, vol. 4, no. 2 (Fall), pp. 187–232.

Lau, Joseph S. M. and Goldblatt, Howard (eds) (1995) *The Columbia Anthology of Modern Chinese Literature*. New York, Columbia University Press.

Leung, Laifong (1994) *Morning Sun: Interviews with Chinese Writers of the Lost Generation*. Armonk NY and London, M. E. Sharpe.

Levy, Richard (1995) 'Corruption, Economic Crime and Social Transformation since the Reforms: The Debate in China'. *Australian Journal of Chinese Affairs*, no. 33 (January), pp. 1–25.

Li, Rongxia (2000) 'Inflicting Severe Punishment on Corruption'. *Beijing Review*, 22 May, pp.12–15.

Link, Perry, Madsen, Richard and Pickowicz, Paul (1989) *Unofficial China: Popular Culture and Thought in the People's Republic of China*. Boulder, San Francisco and London, Westview Press.

Liu, Binyan (1990) *A Higher Kind of Loyalty*. New York, Pantheon.

Lo, T. Wing (1993) 'The Politics of Social Censure. Corruption and Bourgeois Liberation in Communist China'. *Social and Legal Studies,* vol. 2 (June), pp. 195–209.

Lü, Xiaobo (1999) 'From Rank-Seeking to Rent-Seeking: Changing Administrative Ethos and Corruption in Reform China'. *Crime, Law and Social Change*, vol. 32, pp. 347–370.

'Major Corruption Cases' (2000) *Beijing Review*, 22 May, pp. 14–17.

Martin, Helmut (1992) *Modern Chinese Writers Self-Portrayals*. Armonk NY and London, M. E. Sharpe.

Merton, Robert K. (1957) *Social Theory and Social Structure*. New York, Free Press.

Oi, Jean C. (1989) 'Market Reforms and Corruption in Rural China'. *Studies in Comparative Communism*, vol. 21, no. 2/3 (Summer/Autumn), pp. 221–233.

Phillips, Michael R, Liu, Huaqing and Zhang, Yanping (1999) 'Suicide and Social Change in China'. *Culture, Medicine and Psychiatry*, vol. 23, pp. 25–50.

Song, Qiang et al. (1996) *Zhongguo keyi shuo bu* (China Can Say No). Beijing, Zhongguo gongshang lianhe chubanshe.

State Statistical Bureau (1998) *Zhongguo tongji nianjian* (China Labour Statistics). Beijing, Zhongguo tongji chubanshe.

Statistical Office of the European Union (1997) *Eurostat Anuario 1997*. Luxemburg, Official Publications of the European Union.

Thurston, Anne F. (1990) 'Urban Violence During the Cultural Revolution: Who is to Blame?' In Jonathan Lipman and Steven Harrell (eds), *Violence in China*. Albany NY, State University of New York Press.

Transparency International (2001) 28 October. http://www.transparency.org/.

Tsao, King K. and Worthley, John Abbot (1996) 'China: Administrative Corruption-

Experience in a Comparative Context'. *Australian Journal of Public Administration*, vol. 55, no. 4, pp. 22–29.

Unger, Jonathan (ed.) (1996) *Chinese Nationalism*. Armonk NY, M. E. Sharpe.

Wang, Shan (1995) *Di-san zhi yangjing kan zhongguo* (Looking at China with the Third Eye). 4th edition. Hong Kong, Ming bao chubanshe youxian gongsi.

White III, Lynn T. (1989) *Policies of Chaos: The Organizational Causes of Violence in China's Cultural Revolution*. Princeton, Princeton University Press.

White, Gordon (1996) 'Corruption and Market Reform in China'. *IDS Bulletin*, vol. 27, no. 2, pp. 40–47.

World Health Organization (1996) *World Health Statistics Annual 1995*. Geneva, World Health Organization.

—— (1998) *World Health Statistics Annual 1996*. Geneva, World Health Organisation.

—— (2001) 28 October. http://www.who.int/mental_health/Topic_Suicide/suicide1.html.

Xin, Xiangyang (1998) *Hong qiang juece* (The Politics of the Red Wall). Beijing, Zhongguo jingji chubanshe.

Yang, Zi Hui (1997) 'The Study of Suicides in Chinese Cities and Rural Areas'. *Chinese Journal of Population Science*, vol. 9, no. 3, pp. 223–238.

Zheng, Shiping (1997) *Party vs. State in Post-1949 China*. Cambridge, Cambridge University Press.

Zheng, Yi (1993) *Hongse jinianbei* (Scarlet Memorial). Taipei, Huashi wenhua gongsi.

8

OVERSEAS CHINESE ASSOCIATIONS BUILDING UP A NATIONAL IDENTITY

Specific cases in Spain[1]

Gladys Nieto

Introduction

Building up identities in general, and national identities in particular, takes place in specific contexts of unequal power relationships. Building up an identity implies an agreement between different social actors involved in it. Dominant groups in possession of greater power are able to define certain identities which are taken up by other groups as their own. In that sense, it is important to identify which actors produce identities, and for what reason they build them.[2] The state constitutes one of the main agents in the construction and transmission of a national identity. In the particular case of China, such state identity transmission is not only limited to citizens living inside its borders, but it also extends to Chinese communities outside the country, i.e. the Chinese diaspora.

This chapter analyses two aspects of this issue. First, it examines the present processes of the extension of Chinese pan-nationalism and national identity from the motherland towards the overseas communities. Second, it emphasizes how the elites of the Sino-Spanish community build up their national identity through their associations.

The associative renaissance

Some *huaqiao* dwellers in Spain consider their community to be relatively new when compared to those of South-East Asia and the United States, which have a long history of settlement and development. If we evaluate their demographic dimensions, it is possible to state that in the last fifteen years the Sino-Spanish community has reached significant proportions and a relative maturity. Towards the mid-1980s and 1990s, the Chinese community living in Spain witnessed a significant growth in size. The peaks of this 'demographic explosion' took place in 1986 and 1991, coinciding with the two policies launched by the Spanish government regulating the situation of illegal migrants. In those years, the community grew by 54 per cent and 58 per cent respectively. In 1997 and 1998 there were also significant increases of the Chinese population as a result of family regrouping processes and the granting of immigration applications. In 1998, the number of Chinese residents, according to official statistics, reached approximately 21,300 people. Amongst these, the vast majority, about 20,690, came from the People's Republic of China (PRC), and only 612 originated from Taiwan.[3] The real extent of the Chinese population, which includes a significant number of people not having legalized their residence in Spain, is difficult to establish accurately. There is a large number of estimates, from the Chinese and Taiwanese embassies, and from the Chinese associations or intellectuals, who hardly ever mention their sources of information. Amongst these estimates, there are figures that are two or three times greater than the official figure. The growth of the Chinese population in Spain is related to the rapid economic growth that placed Spain amongst the most developed countries in the world during the 1980s. Chinese emigrants in search of new opportunities in non-exploited areas where they can develop their businesses have found the appropiate conditions in Spain. This could be compared to the emigration that occurred from Eastern Europe after the collapse of the Communist Bloc. The population growth in Spain was generated by means of the reactivation of the emigration networks of residents who brought their relatives mainly from the district of Qingtian in Zhejiang province (south-west of China). Within Europe, Spain is the favourite destination for the Qingtianese, and some 15,000 have established their new residence there.[4]

The Chinese in Spain are presently a more diversified community than when they began to arrive. They have a history of settlement that stretches back approximately eighty years to the pioneering emigration of a group of Chinese workers who were hired during the First World War in order to perform jobs related to the front, and who later moved to other European countries. As mentioned earlier, several of the first immigrants came from the district of Qingtian in Zhejiang province.

At the same time, as the Sino-Spanish community was growing numerically at the beginning of the 1990s, a significant process simultaneously took place: the emergence of a massive number of Chinese voluntary associations. Whilst in the 1970s the Association of Chinese Restaurants of Madrid, a pioneer group of owners of Chinese restaurants in Spain, was founded, in the 1980s the Association of the Chinese in Spain, which is one of the two most important national Chinese voluntary associations, was created. There are now 34 Chinese associations in the country in which migrants from the PRC and Taiwan tend to concentrate. Approximately 76 per cent of these were created after 1991, more than half of which were launched right after 1995 (see Figures 8.1 and 8.2).

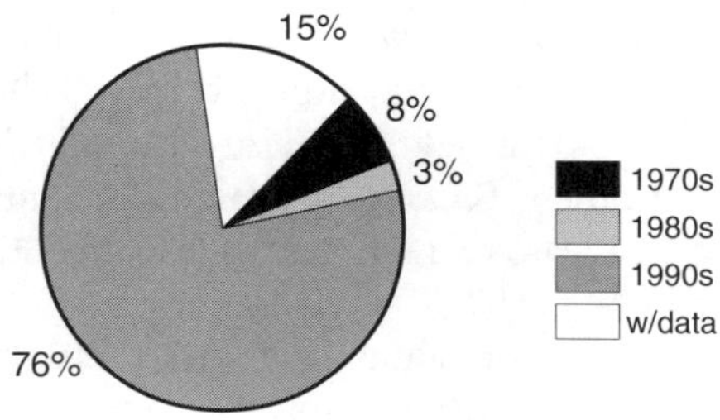

Figure 8.1 Chinese associations according to the decade in which they were created.
Sources: Ministry of Public Security and Chinese voluntary associations.

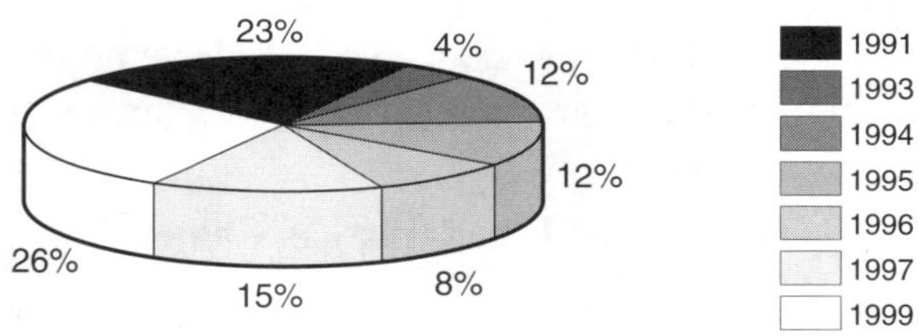

Figure 8.2 Chinese associations in the 1990s according to the year of creation.
Sources: Ministry of Public Security and Chinese voluntary associations.

The Spanish Chinese association movement includes not only the previously mentioned associations, but also others with a religious or political character, those formed by businessmen engaged in gastronomy, those engaged in an economic cooperation between China and Spain, those establishing a cultural exchange between the two countries, associations of friendship and charity, professional groups related to artistic and academic production, associations formed by young Chinese, women or students, as well as those related to Chinese schools set up in the Spanish territory. The Chinese voluntary organizations work at a local, regional and national level. The two most important associations at the national level are the aforementioned Asociación de los chinos en España (Association of the Chinese in Spain) and the Organización General de Chinos en España (General Organization of the Chinese in Spain).

The renaissance of associations in recent years has also included the establishment of schools for the Chinese migrants' children, as well as the publication of Chinese newspapers. In 1992, a Chinese school was founded by Taiwanese migrants in Madrid. This school was the only one of its type in the whole country. In only a few years, particularly between 1995 and 1999, Chinese language schools depending on the voluntary associations grew from one to eight. At present, there are three in Madrid and one in each of the following cities: Barcelona, Valencia, Malaga, Granada and Sevilla. There are now at least two Chinese newspapers that circulate within the Chinese community.[5]

The development of Chinese voluntary associations and the emergence of *putonghua* schools and community newspapers cannot be interpreted merely as a natural phenomenon resulting from the maturity of this migrant community.[6] It is connected with the current political alignment originating from the motherland, encouraging a sense of patriotic or national loyalty. Similar processes can be observed in other European countries in which Chinese communities exist. The modernization project in the mainland and the so-called consolidation of the political and economic project of Greater China, which includes the 'rebel' province of Taiwan as well as the overseas Chinese, represents a framework through which one can understand the proliferation of Chinese voluntary associations, newspapers and Chinese schools in Spain.

The state and the Overseas Chinese

One of the aspects that usually stands out amongst the overseas Chinese communities is their relative independence from the societies in which they are living. This distinctive feature is sometimes mentioned in the academic sphere, with descriptions that highlight the invisibility of this type of migration within the framework of some destination countries.[7] More particularly, in Spain, this collective 'invisibility' and self-sufficiency is re-emphasized by the institutions of social welfare, as a result of the infrequency of demands from the Chinese compared to other migrant communities from the Third World. The fact that this group does not present itself as one requiring help from the Spanish social services is seen as an anomalous situation and as a latent threat. Furthermore, in recent years, the increase of criminal incidents that have involved some Chinese residents in the country have prompted the media to reinforce this characteristic of a self-sufficient community, combined with stereotypes associated with criminal activities.[8] The most common image of the community is its organization according to its own internal norms, with its own justice and law, and over which the host state has little control.

This idea that overseas Chinese communities are almost autonomous and self-governing has already been analysed in the segmentary organization model.[9] According to this model, the *huaqiao* organize themselves abroad in a similar fashion to the traditional urban population in China, running their own businesses without the interference of governmental institutions. In the case of the large *huaqiao* communities, especially in the United States and

South-East Asia, the same hierarchical segmentary structure of the group acted as their own political and administrative system. The complex structure of these communities, their extension and the increasing social mobility of Chinese migrants enable their leaders to play a mediating role between their own community and the host state, particularly when certain members of the community have gained substantial economic power.

This typical model of self-government, which is common to groups from South-East Asia, cannot be applied to the case of Spain for various reasons. In the first place, the *huaqiao* in Spain are a relatively newly formed community, small in number when compared to those Chinese communities in the United States and South-East Asia. We also have to take into account that migrants only represent 2.96 per cent of the total non-local population in Spain, a very low figure when compared to other European countries such as France or Great Britain.[10] Second, and probably most important, the Sino-Spanish community cannot be treated as a single collective unit. In recent years, internal conflicts have emerged between the leaders of the Chinese associations (especially those originating from the PRC), in the search of a legitimacy that could lead to the establishment of one organization representing the whole community. Thus, even if the host society views the Chinese as a corporative group, the Chinese associations have been involved in internal struggles.

The fact is that the Overseas Chinese show some kind of self-government capacity: as they find themselves living in a foreign country, they need to adjust their organization according to the laws of the destination country. But is the *huaqiao*'s capacity of self-government linked to the lack of control from the motherland? How far do the *huaqiao* enjoy relative independence from the destination country as well as from the motherland? Finding an answer to each of these questions may help us understand how the Overseas Chinese build up a national identity.

The *huaqiao* are, and have been historically, under the influence of the motherland and its dominant political or economic processes. Historical and emotional ties create a strong sense of loyalty to China and an interest in its national identity and national projects.

Although a certain consensus exists between social scientists in considering nationalism as a modern political phenomenon, associated with the appearance of nation-states and with an ideological origin rooted in the late eighteenth century, this consensus is not as great as it seems. Nationalism can be interpreted as a national feeling, a nationalist ideology, certain nationalist movements or an identifying language.[11] As well as the problem of defining nationalism, the case of Chinese nationalism has a particular complexity. Patriotic Chinese feelings include a mixture of political nationalism, an ethnic *han* identity, and a cultural pride in Chinese civilization.[12] The Chinese vision of the world is formed not only by cultural constructions but also by historical or racial myths, leading to an image of the difference and unity of the Chinese nation.

In order to apply the idea of nationalism as a modern phenomenon to the Chinese case, we can go back to the establishment of the Republic of China in 1912, at the risk of excluding certain historical, racial, cultural or symbolic factors that help create a sense of nation. The strict distinction between certain ideas gathered under the idea of 'culturalism' (essential in traditional China) and a modern nationalism that replaced it with the arrival of Western imperialism, provoking a new way of thinking and a national identity, is the basis of the thesis of 'culturalism to nationalism' in the explanation of nationalist phenomena in China. This theory has been analysed in order to show its range and limitations, as well as to propose a more viable alternative to this proposition.[13] The most valuable part of this theory is that it highlights the change in beliefs of the elite and the official doctrine about the nature of the Chinese community and its place in the world, bringing together the previous culturalism and the later modern nationalism. These two doctrines are presented as incompatible: culturalism emphasizes the cultural factors in the definition of the community, while modern nationalism defines the community as a territorial state aiming to achieve its political integration. Essentially, here we have two visions, one ethnic-oriented and the other state-oriented. The first one defines the nation as a large ethnic group with a common culture and ancestry, and nationalism as a cultural movement. The second one understands the nation as a territorial and political entity, and nationalism as an aspiration towards self-government.

The weakness of the theory of 'culturalism to nationalism' is that the clarity and the entirety of the change are exaggerated, either disregarding the existence of a premodern nationalism in the imperial era or otherwise underestimating the existence of culturalism in the modern era. According to this view,[14] culturalism coexists with other ideas of the state and the nation. Culturalism and modern nationalism have been doctrines linked to the elites in their respective areas but have never monopolized the ideas explaining the various factors in the formation of the Chinese nation.

This analysis helps us to understand the development of a national feeling the overseas Chinese communities have, as this feeling is not limited to a sense of patriotic loyalty, but also includes a sense of belonging to a bigger cultural and ethnic community defined by a common line of descent – especially by means of allusions to the first ancestor, the Yellow Emperor. In the creation of national identities, it is not only certain cultural aspects that come into play, but also a certain sense of racial belonging that is one of the basic foundations of national identity in Eastern Asia in the twenty-first century.[15]

Let us go back then to the ways in which the Chinese state has positioned itself in relation to the communities of migrants. Historically, the ties between the state and the Chinese that live abroad have gone through stages that Wang Gungu[16] defines as a cycle of strong–weak–strong:

1 During the Qing dynasty, the lack of government support to Chinese traders resulted from the fact that they functioned with a high degree of independence and searched for trust within their own community. This lack of government interest in the future of the *huaqiao* represents a weak stage in the cycle.
2 Between 1840 and 1949, while the Republic was divided by the wars and the Japanese invasion (identified as a strong stage), the call towards the *huaqiao* was understood as part of the need to save the nation, to bring about the revolution or to express love for the country. The Chinese government guaranteed recognition of the Overseas Chinese, hoping for their loyalty and economic support.
3 The Maoist stage between 1949 and 1976 is recognized as a new weak stage. In this stage, some emigrants returned to the country while others migrated abroad. The government maintained an indifferent attitude towards the Overseas Chinese. After 1955, as China aimed to keep good relations with the South-East Asian countries, the overseas communities, which were fearful of the triumph of the communist revolution, expressed their loyalty towards the countries in which they lived, adopting their own laws and customs. As a result, they changed their identity from *huaqiao* (a term with a strong connotation of patriotism towards China) to *huaren* (ethnic Chinese).[17] These policies led the Chinese communities to develop a certain self-sufficiency and autonomy with regards to the motherland.
4 The present stage stemming from the more open policies of the PRC in 1978 is characterized by a renewed search for support from the *huaqiao*, in return for their recognition. The call from the mainland to the overseas Chinese communities is focused on the search for economic participation by means of capital investment, contributing to the construction of Greater China. Greater China aims to achieve not only economic integration but also the political reunification of the Chinese international community, which involves the recovery of lost territories, the support of the *huaqiao* communities and the efforts to maintain territorial unity, which could potentially be threatened by the peripheral nationalism of Tibet, Xinjiang and Taiwan. Greater China is a project that can be summarized as China's claim in the world, expressing its pride in becoming an economic power and confirming its superiority in relation to Western countries.

The success of these calls from the state's point of view, that is to say that Overseas Chinese accept them, depends, to a certain extent, on how the participants see themselves as part of the national project. In other words, their loyalty depends on their sense of collective identity. But the construction of collective identity is a complex affair, influenced by different players in unequal relations of power. Indeed, certain types of collective identities can be distinguished.[18] There are, for instance, those that aim to extend or reinforce the dominance of certain groups over others; there are identities of resistance formed in opposition to dominant groups; there are identities produced as a result of important issues or social changes, and so forth. If the state is the agent promoting these collective identities, that will entail certain advantages over other groups deprived of the necessary power.

We can examine, therefore, the way in which a form of legitimate identity has been extended to the Overseas Chinese. The Chinese Communist Party and the Nationalist Party have promoted over the course of time a 'state version of identity',[19] i.e. certain actions originating from the state tending to produce a political-ideological sense of national belonging inside or outside its frontiers.

Chinese newspapers and schools provide ideal channels to transmit the state version of identity and to reinforce the patriotic links with the motherland. That is why the teaching of the language is one of the pillars on which the policies towards Overseas Chinese have been based. This expressed itself most strongly during the years of the Republic and the anti-Japanese war. The teaching of the language, specifically Mandarin, was the keystone of the policies of the nationalists towards Overseas Chinese.[20] This is such that there are declarations stating that without a Chinese education there could not be Overseas Chinese. The loyalty towards China and the Nationalist Party were created and encouraged in the classroom. In the 1920s, various schools were set up across South-East Asia and many teachers left China to teach in them. Later, around 1937, during the anti-Japanese war, loyalty was based on the necessity to expel foreign powers from China.

The interest on the part of the Chinese state in promoting a national identity among its citizens overseas supposes that they support certain national projects. The hope for political loyalty is based on a common cultural, historical and racial inheritance, in which all the Chinese belong to a great community towards which they should direct their effort. As already noted, China's relationship with its overseas communities has varied over the years. If in some historical periods the *huaqiao* were the people who could save the country, in other periods they constituted anti-patriotic elements which instead of staying in the country to help for its reconstruction, for example after the Maoist triumph, they decided to migrate. We will therefore analyse the way in which the state version of identity influences the stance adopted by the Overseas Chinese, putting special emphasis on the specific role that the Sino-Spanish associations occupy in relation to the new project of national development.

The expressions of loyalty

The present modernization in China, with its promise of giving the PRC a leading role in the international order (lost as a result of historical concessions towards the Western imperialistic powers), and the attempts at the political reunification of the international Chinese community, is the context in which the overseas Chinese are included. The support of the *huaqiao* in the establishment of Greater China depends in great measure on the range of their attitudes towards the motherland. Overseas Chinese are not a compact and homogeneous group. They come from diverse origins, and can adopt different forms of loyalty to the nation as well as different forms of national identity. In the case of the call for economic investment in the motherland, it has been seen that the *huaqiao* have given a mixed response.[21] Participation in the development of Greater China may be tempting, but it also requires caution. This caution is mainly the result of the political system in the PRC, and uncertainty regarding the business climate there. There are Overseas Chinese who have very strong ties with China and identify themselves closely with the destiny of the country. Meanwhile, a large part of the *huaqiao* limit their participation to the political sphere and to commercial and community associations. Finally, other groups have broken their links with China, recognizing themselves as nationals of other countries, not allowing themselves to be treated as Chinese, and not wishing to be recognized as loyal Chinese nationals.

As the focus here is on the transmission of national identities, it is interesting to see how those Overseas Chinese who are most closely linked to the political negotiation interact using one very specific instrument: their associations. The Chinese voluntary associations enjoy high status within the community mainly because of their wealth. These sectors of the community elite include businessmen who can combine their business in both the destination country and the motherland. Their contacts with both European and Chinese businesses can bring about the formation of networks that facilitate information exchange and investment opportunities. Finally, the transnational character of the associations leaders' political links contributes to the growth of their economy and culture. Within the hierarchical structure that is common in overseas Chinese communities, the fact that leaders participate in the associations gives them a privileged position in the social scale, the chance to act as intermediaries between the least prestigious groups of their own community abroad and certain political groups in the motherland. The associations participate in the political arena as they have the power to make final decisions that concern the overseas community and take on the role of transmitting values to this group. In their typical role, the associations appear as moral arbiters in the resolutions of conflicts within the community, and they define the limits of behaviour that the members of the group should follow. Some of these roles still exist in the new associations that have emerged in Spain since the 1990s. For example, one of the aims of the Association of Fellow-Countrymen from Wenzhou was 'to encourage the Chinese to understand that they cannot do what they want, that there is room for the association to solve conflicts'.[22] In that sense, the association act as a type of mediating force through which migrants could solve their disputes. This role was evident, for example, in February 1998 during the production of a Spanish film that included depictions of the Chinese mafia. About sixteen Chinese associations produced a statement in which they encouraged the boycott of the film, due to the damage it did to the prestige and life of the Chinese community. This resulted in the pressure on Chinese migrants not to participate as extras in the film.[23] Both the Embassy of the PRC in Madrid and some official sectors in Qingtian supported this action, citing the moral damage to the Chinese image.

But this event cannot be understood in isolation. In recent years, the Chinese associations have not only linked themselves, in different ways, with the officialdom of the motherland, influencing the growth of a dominant state rhetoric, but they have also acted in ways to express their loyalty to their country of destination. Some of the new associations have emerged in Spain at times when the Chinese community has seen its businesses threatened by a poor image. During the last few years, the media has dwelled in a sensationalist way upon an image of migrants associated with mafias and international criminal networks, blackmail of restaurants, and murders within the community. Together with this comes a silence that protects such criminal activities. State control began through inspections and raids on restaurants and sweatshops, sometimes with the subsequent expulsion of those migrants who had not legalized their residence in the country. In this context, several Chinese associations were formed, not only in an attempt to re-establish a positive collective image, but also to try to solve the conflicts within the community. They were also trying to avoid more serious consequences for the already depressed restaurant business that was suffering severe fluctuations in the number of customers as a result of critical newspaper articles. That is why the associations began to affirm their loyalty to their country of residence, searching for channels of communication with the host society, by means of an 'integrating' discourse with the Spanish society and 'respect of its laws and customs'.

The interest of the Chinese state in encouraging migrants to identify with the Chinese modernization project has been re-emphasized in recent years by means of a series of institutions promoting this vision. Nyíri explains it in this way:

> Since the mid-1980s, the PRC leadership has embarked on a path of economic, political and military expansion. It increasingly aims to replace nominal marxism with an etatism composed largely of elements of traditional morality and early-twentieth-century nationalism. As a result, the PRC has become increasingly interested not only in securing Overseas Chinese investment but also in resuscitating the national loyalties of Overseas Chinese, much in the same way as the Nationalist government did in the years before the

> Second World War. Since 1984, a number of political bodies have been revitalized or created to serve this purpose. These include the National Association of Overseas Chinese, Returned Overseas Chinese, and Dependents of Overseas Chinese (*Quanguo Huaqiao Guiqiao Qiaojuan Lianhehui*), the Overseas Comission (*Huaqiao Weiyuanhui*) of the National People's Congress, the Overseas Chinese Affairs Bureau (*Qiaowu Bangongshi*) of the State Council, the China Overseas Exchange Commission, and the equivalent of these bodies at lower administrative levels. If current trends continue, we are likely to see more and better organized links between the PRC and the Overseas Chinese'.[24]

The majority of Sino-Spanish associations emerging during this period searched for legitimization from the motherland and closer links with Chinese associations in other European countries. The fact that the leaders of the associations are involved in a wide range of businesses means that they have to operate in a dualistic fashion, being aware of the circumstances in which they live, as well as paying attention to the demands of loyalty coming from China. In general, the associations are linked with the official Chinese representatives who participate in their community events. During these events, which bring together the most important associations at the national level (coming both from the PRC and Taiwan), the representatives of the embassies of the motherland are present, and at times give speeches about the political and economic situation. The linkage between the associations and the officialdom of the motherland promotes the extension not only of the state ideology but also of cultural, historical and ethnic ideas associated with the present national project. The idea of a Chinese pan-nationalism mobilizing the overseas communities is becoming stronger with more diverse roots. Chinese identity is one of these roots, based on the idea of a common racial origin amongst the *han*, descendents of the Yellow Emperor. In addition, the Confucian tradition constitutes another element of this pan-nationalism by means of the moral rules that define a harmonious social order and the hierarchical positioning of individuals on a family and social scale.[25]

As previously stated, the periods of strong state demands from China towards the *huaqiao* communities, both in the Republican period and now, imply the promotion of a national identity and the use of idealistic methods in order to make it effective, i.e. through the schools and newspapers. The proliferation of Chinese schools in Spain as well as the publication of various Chinese newspapers appears to be connected with this new strong cycle of the extension of nationalism among overseas Chinese communities. This nationalist renewal expresses itself in an ideological reaffirmation and in the strengthening of a national identity, including an element of anti-foreign rhetoric.

Newspapers and schools depend on the voluntary associations and a sector of the community elite: they are strongly influenced by them. The fact that the new associations are looking for official Chinese support for their legitimization makes them likely to tow the official line. This is expressed, for example, in their views on the role that schools and newspapers play in transmitting a strong national feeling:

> At the same time that the Sino-Spanish people make an effort to integrate themselves into Spanish society, they also try to maintain their own culture and keep the ties with the motherland. This can be demonstrated mainly by the publication of Chinese newspapers.[26]

> Far from the native place, we can feel nostalgia; we know how important the country is in our hearts. The patriotic feeling of the Chinese in overseas countries can be reflected in the teaching of the Chinese language to children. It is a common desire amongst overseas Chinese to make sure that their children learn the Chinese language and understand the culture of their country.[27]

The teaching of the language and the publication of newspapers can be seen as ways of expressing love for the country. But what motivations lie behind such loyalty? First let us consider some of the ways in which the feeling of national belonging is transmitted by the schools and the Chinese press.

Teaching to be Chinese

In comparison with the North, the South of China, the main source of international migration, has a significant linguistic diversity. Chinese migrant residents in Spain, because of their different origins, use their local dialects. The fact that the vast majority come from the region of Qingtian (Zhejiang province) means that the local dialect (*qingtianhua*) is the most spoken within the community. There are also other groups of migrants that speak *wenzhouhua*, *shanghaihua* and *guangdonghua*, amongst others. Except for the older generation – the first generation of migrants – they use their own dialect and the language of the country or *guoyu*. The bond achieved by the use of the same dialect is the basis for some associations, especially in the case of compatriots or *tongxianghui*.

Within the second generation of Chinese migrants, the use of *putonghua* is quite mixed. This may be because they receive a Spanish education and speak Spanish, or because in their homes they only speak the dialect from their area of origin, or otherwise because they can understand Chinese or the dialect but cannot speak it, etc. The recent establishment of Chinese language schools for the children of migrants has been well received within the community, as shown by the growing number of children and teenagers attending them. On occasions, the study of Chinese language does not really appear to appeal to the children, who speak Spanish to each other in their breaks and do not see homework as a useful task. If they already have homework set from Monday to Friday by the Spanish school, the Chinese school takes up all of Saturday and in addition they have to do extra preparation at home. But for their families, learning the Chinese language is of great importance, a cultural asset essential for their children. A teacher from one of these Chinese schools explained it in this way: 'Parents pressure their children so that they do not lose their Chinese skills and they ask the teachers to give them a lot of homework, but everything really depends on the pupils'.[28]

Language is one of the most powerful instruments in the construction of an identity, and more particularly in the construction of national identities. This is why linguistic policies play a fundamental role in the agenda of nationalist projects. The relationship established between identity and language is so close that it includes the transmission of cultural values associated with each language in particular. The passive acceptance of a second language can result in the progressive loss of history or the common cultural values. Thus, certain ethnic minorities disagree with learning the Spanish language, in order to maintain their own cultural identity. In the Qingtianese migrants' history in Spain, during the first decades of the twentieth century, there was certain resistance to learning the Spanish language, as there was a general fear of betraying their ancestors by learning a language that did not belong to their own 'civilization'.[29] This contrast has been expressed in terms of both linguistics and identity, for example in Singapore, where there is immigration from the South of China that corresponds with Hokkien and Cantonese dialect groups. The extension and promotion of Mandarin as a 'mother' language, on the one hand, seems to relegate dialects to a position of secondary importance and encourage other types of identities, because those who do not know the national language cannot be considered as completely Chinese.[30] Local dialects find a channel of direct communication with their native place in the recreation of the identities linked to it. On the other hand, the national language results in a large community, called motherland or nation. The increase of Chinese schools in Spain can be seen as a way in which the unifying language of the country acts as an element in the Chinese community, offering a national identity that dominates over local identities. But if the traditional aims of schools and newspapers are the development of a national identity and an increase of the feelings of loyalty towards the motherland, these forms of promotion exist at the same time as a call for local identities and links between migrants and their *qiaoxiang* (native place), as explained below.

As previously stated, nationalism is culturally and politically established amongst all the individuals involved, but what is really important is how and why it is established. We have focused on a particular group within the *huaqiao*, the association elites, whose privileged status, due to their power (as a result of their close relationship with the official institutions in the motherland, as well as their ability to carry out certain tasks within the community), enables them to promote and legitimate an identity.

A patriotic viewpoint that comes from both cultural and racial constructions, in which all the Chinese are included in an ethnic community, appears for example in the motto of one of the Chinese schools set up in Barcelona: 'Yellow skin, black hair and eyes are symbols passed on by our ancestors. No matter where or when, you will always be descendent from the Chinese people.'[31] Even if the characteristics of a Chinese national identity have been developed historically and reinforced by the state, nowadays it can also be part of a real sense of belonging among the Chinese people that they recovered for themselves and with which they can identify. That explains, to a great extent, the Chinese migrants' interest in their children learning the language, as shown by the great support for Chinese schools in Spain.

Being Chinese is the basis of this national identity. According to Wu's interpretation,[32] the characteristic of being Chinese corresponds to the traditional vision of China as the centre of existence, beyond which the barbarians lived. Chinese were part of a unified civilization with centuries of history. In this respect, for this author, the methods of identification amongst Overseas Chinese oscillate between two positions, one of which we can see as 'political', integrating the Chinese people (a modern patriotism or nationalism), and the other we can see as 'cultural', concentrating on the cultural inheritance transmitted by ancestors and the essential difference of this culture from the non-Chinese. In today's context, we find a reaffirmation of Chineseness, with language as the most important channel. One of the teachers (Taiwanese) from the fourth level at the Chinese school in Barcelona explained her experience of 'teaching how to be Chinese' with an interesting illustration:

> We try to teach the children how to be Chinese, as they all speak Spanish. For instance, no matter where you were born, and even if you do not have Chinese citizenship, as long as you understand how to read and write Chinese, you are already 50 per cent Chinese. Writing requires concentration, in whatever language, but even more in Chinese. You should sit straight, not leaning like this (she imitates bored children, resting her head on her hands). I tell them off when they do this. The handwriting must be harmonious with square letters. They should respect the size of the characters. The same applies to life, it should be straight and harmonious. It is something philosophical. I make them repeat the characters one, twenty, or a hundred times when they are not well written.[33]

According to the above description, both Chinese identity and moral character seem to be transmitted through the everyday teaching of the language. The most outstanding aspect of this account is that being Chinese is taught physically, through the identification of a straight position of the body with correct moral behaviour. During my observations of the youngest children in their first year of school, this tendency was indeed visible. In order to physically 'straighten' the students, one of the teachers stood behind those who were not sitting properly or were playing with their pencils and gently sat them correctly, moving their heads so their eyes went directly to the textbook, trying to make them concentrate.

The transmission of national identity in schools is not limited to language learning, but also includes other practices. Children sometimes take part in singing or reading recitals at community events organized by the Chinese associations on their anniversaries, the Chinese New Year or some special occasions, such as the celebration of Hong Kong's return to the PRC some years ago. In addition, children occasionally take part in cultural events organized by government institutions from the motherland, not only in Spain but also in other European countries. An example is the exhibition 'Beloved China', in which Chinese history and culture were presented by means of pictures and texts, referring to the role of the Overseas Chinese in the present project to modernize the country. It was organized by the Historical and Cultural Committee of Zhejiang for the People's Consultative Political Conference.

In order to explain the processes of transmission of national identity through Chinese schools, this chapter has concentrated on those organized by the migrants' associations from the PRC. The migratory communities from Taiwan, although sharing some common aspects with those from the PRC, have been established in different historical periods and function as autonomous sectors, with their own associations, even if some migrants take part in Chinese organizations at a national level. The only school organized by Taiwanese migrants is established in Madrid. There, Chinese language with traditional characters is taught, as well as handicrafts, poetry, dance and other activities. The establishment of two Chinese schools in Madrid, run by migrants from the PRC, is resulting in a process of selection: while the children from Zhejiang province study in schools run by associations from the mainland, those from Taiwan, Hong Kong, South-East Asia and a few from the PRC study in the Taiwanese school.

Although both schools from the mainland and the one from Taiwan share the aim of transmitting a sense of being Chinese, there is some competition between them, particularly as regards the transmission of 'true values' from Chinese culture, especially through handwriting in traditional characters.[34] Nevertheless, it is difficult to establish how successful the schools are in generating national feelings and a love for the motherland in their pupils. Maybe parents' desire for their children to feel both part of Greater China and also integrated into their host country can be ascribed to their need for cultural continuity between generations, made possible by the ancestral language.

Loyalty towards the *Qiaoxiang*[35]

As already stated, nationalism is transmitted through Chinese schools and newspapers. As far as schools are concerned, national identity is understood to derive from a common historical, cultural or racial origin shared by all Chinese, in which the language is the unifying element. Nevertheless, the articles presented in Chinese newspapers include a stronger promotion of local identity derived from the native place of the majority of the Chinese people in Spain: Qingtian.

In recent years, some articles outlining the history of Qingtianese migrants in Europe, and especially in Spain, have been published in newspapers. These accounts describe the pioneering migrants and the hard conditions they had to struggle against in the new social environment. These historical descriptions include an interesting trend: they are based on prestigious members of the group, such as those who established the first businesses in Spain, those who received a higher education in China, the leaders who organized the associations, etc. Even if the Sino-Spanish community includes groups from different origins, history claims a unique linkage with Qingtian: 'At present, the Chinese migrants in Spain are Qingtianese. Thus, if somebody refers to the history of Qingtianese migrants in Spain, it is the same as if we refer to the Chinese migrants in Spain.'[36]

Concentrating specifically on the press descriptions, Qingtian is held to strongly influence the behaviour and the character of the inhabitants of the region, and even more so amongst those who migrate. The outstanding qualities of this group and their ability to overcome difficulies are related to the physical and geographical characteristics of a hostile and beautiful motherland. Examples of these comparisons between the local features and the character of the group are: 'Qingtianese living there are tough as mountains. Precisely because of this resistant spirit, people from this region go overseas and manage to succeed despite all the difficulties';[37] 'Parental links are a logical consequence of the natural conditions found in Qingtian';[38] 'When the morning mist dissipates or when the night falls, smoke rising up in columns towards the sky suggests a peaceful and tranquil ambience. Influenced by a land like this, people are natural, friendly, down to earth, and even naive.'[39]

Qingtian with its scarp mountains and little arable land is a poorly endowed environment and does not provide enough to satisfy the basic needs of its inhabitants. But this hostile environment, sometimes a disavantage for the group, also provides the force from which their spirit of adventure and their ability to set up businessess abroad emanates. Ultimately this collective virtue stands out above the common Chinese character, highlighting a specific local identity based on a feeling of solidarity expressed as follows:

> This is possibly the most important characteristic differentiating Qingtianese from people from other regions. The Chinese capacity to overcome difficulties and anxieties and their spirit of adventure

> seem to be part of a collective character. But the spirit of mutual aid and self-Qingtianese is outstanding . . . The Qingtianese society seems to be like a huge tree with many intertwined branches, which cannot be cut, broken or separated without affecting the whole.[40]

The relationship linking the land and this group is the basis of the love for the *qiaoxiang* and the deep nostalgia of whose living far from it. No doubt, the native place greatly influences the nature of migrants' identity. It is the place where the initial family links and origins were historically constructed. Without underestimating the importance of this reality, it is interesting to look at the people promoting this loyalty, the form it adopts, and its aim.

The most prestigious sectors within the Chinese community are those in charge of the internal newspapers. This instrumental power gives them the ability to define and extend the symbolic contents of 'visions of the world'. As far as this 'vision of the world' is concerned, loyalty is not towards an abstract homeland, but rather towards a specific surrounding: the native place. The native place is where the migrants' duty is concentrated and where the expression of their affection, by means of economic support, is directed. Here are some examples of these sentiments:

> Just like the Fangshanese [from Fangshan, Qingtian] from different places, those from Barcelona who are far from their homeland always have their heart in the native place and a constant concern for everything happening there.[41]

> He honestly said, after being informed of the disaster in our native place, the *huaqiao* residents in Spain were very affected, shocked by this calamity . . . everyone contributed to this donation as a proof of our sympathy. The amount reached 100,000 Rmb in order to support the people from our native place to help for its reconstruction . . . The generosity shown by the *huaqiao* in Spain in making this donation will always be remembered in the hearts of the *huaqiao*'s homeland.[42]

The aid and support given to the homeland is based on the love of migrants for their native place. At the same time, these actions increase the social prestige of their leaders. The creation of schools, parks, bridges, hospitals, donations in the case of natural disasters, or the participation in charitable social programmes in the homeland constitute social responsibilities to the elites of the Overseas Chinese. Leaders should not only be able to accumulate wealth, but should also express great generosity and social sensibility. This generosity represents a return of their wealth by means of the circulation of the accumulated assets. Throughout the examples of charity, the circulation of wealth is compensated by the respect and gratitude of their fellow-countrymen and their equals in the host country. In that sense, the native place is where migrants redirect their love for their land, and also where they feel recognized by their original fellow-countrymen.

At present, the richest sectors of Overseas Chinese contribute not only with charitable donations to their native places, but also business investment. Although investment is not linked so closely to the love for the *qiaoxiang* (according to the articles issued by the media), it is understood by the local Chinese bureaucracy as material proof of the patriotic devotion of the Overseas Chinese and has great symbolic importance in the discourse of the overseas elite. With this, they contribute to the reinforcement of a legitimate and dominant identity. Perhaps this is merely politically correct rhetoric aimed to impress Chinese officials, or maybe there is a genuine wish to repatriate wealth obtained abroad, and thereby to obtain gratitude and recognition. Altruistic acts of giving can bring compensation in the form of prestige, recognition and social acceptance. The role adopted by the elites of the Sino-Spanish community in the nationalist project of the motherland is therefore two-way: they promote a state version of national identity and loyalty to the motherland; and in return they reap great social and economic capital.

In conclusion, nationalism and nations possess their own life independent of the state, although they are influenced by cultural constructions and political projects. Identities are formed in certain contexts of inequality of power. That is why the state's influence in the development and promotion of a national identity is not the same as that of a less powerful group. But in reality, lesser social actors play a role in identifying and promoting the symbolic contents of these identities. This chapter has focused mainly on the transmission of a national feeling in Chinese schools and newspapers in Spain dependent on voluntary associations, within the context of political negotiations originating from China. But this negotiation takes place within a historical framework in which Overseas Chinese know that the Chinese state at present is interested in their participation in the construction of Greater China, but tomorrow may abandon them. In that sense, the strength of the linkage encouraged by the present nationalist project in China will depend on the way migrants understand the nation and what they expect from it.

Notes

1 This research has been done thanks to the finantial support of the CICYT, Spanish Education Ministry (2FD97–0874).

2 Castells (1998: 54).

3 Ministry of Home Affairs of Spain (1999).

4 According to the versions of the Qingtian Returned Overseas Chinese Association (*Zhejiang sheng Qingtian huiguo huaqiao lianhehui*) (25 June 1998).

5 The only two newspapers that are actually edited by Spanish *huaqiao* are the *Chinese News* (*Huaxin bao*) and the *Chinese Information* (*Xizhong dao bao*).

During the 1990s some newspapers were founded such as *The Voice of the Chinese in Spain* (*Xihua zhi sheng*), *Weekly News for Chinese* (*Xibanya huaqiao xinwen zhoubao*), *The Chinese Voice in Europe* (*Ouzhou huasheng bao*) and *The Chinese* (*Zhongguoren*), but none of them are published at present.

6 To conclude that the emergence of these associations is the logical result of the development of the Chinese society and an objective reflection of the social, economic and cultural state of the Chinese migrants in this period is common to certain sectors of the community's elite.

7 Some examples of this type of description in academic publications can be seen in Campani and Maddii (1992), Robinson (1992), and Campani, Carchedi and Tassinari (1994).

8 Aparici and Nieto (1994).

9 Crissman (1967).

10 In France the Chinese population amounts approximately to 120,000 and in England to 162,000 people. Pan (1999: 306, 312).

11 Hutchinson and Smith (1994: 4).

12 Townsend (1996b: xvii).

13 Townsend (1996a: 2).

14 Townsend (1996a: 23–24).

15 Dikötter (2000: 166).

16 Wang (1993).

17 Beltrán (1997: 169).

18 Castells (1998: 30).

19 Wu (1991).

20 Pan (1994: 206).

21 Wang (1993).

22 Fieldwork Registration No. 35 (Valencia, 19 May 1996), p. 4.

23 Ahrens (1998); Tristán (1998).

24 Nyíri (1998).

25 Christiansen (1997: 4).

26 Ma (1996d).

27 Ma (1996e).

28 Fieldwork Registration No. 32, p. 3.

29 Ma (1996c).

30 Lim (1993: 213).

31 Ma (1996e).

32 Wu (1991).

33 Fieldwork Registration No. 32 (Barcelona, 30 March 1996), p. 3.

34 Nieto (1998).

35 Native place.

36 Ma (1996c).

37 Ma (1996a).

38 Ma (1996b).

39 Ma (1996f).

40 Ma (1996b).

41 Ma (1996f).

42 Xihua zhi sheng (1996).

References and further reading

Ahrens, J. M. (1998) 'La colonia china boicotea el rodaje de una película sobre la mafia china. Los actores y el director han sido amenazados' (Chinese Community Boycotts the Filming of a Movie on the Chinese Mafia. Actor and Director Have Been Threatened). *El País*, 20 February, pp. 1 and 3.

Aparici, Roberto and Nieto, Gladys (1994) *Inmigrantes en España: La construcción del 'otro' a través de los medios de comunicación* (Migrants in Spain: The Construction of the 'Other' Throughout Mass Media). Report, General Direction of Migrations, Ministry of Social Affairs (unpublished).

Beltrán Antolín, Joaquín (1997) 'La ambigüedad de la figura del emigrante en China' (The Ambiguity of the Role of the Emigrant in China). *Revista de Estudios Asiáticos*, no. 4, pp. 161–178.

Campani, Giovanna and Maddii, Lucia (1992) 'Un monde à part: les Chinois en Toscane' (Another World: The Chinese in Toscane). *Revue européenne des migrations internationales*, vol. 8, no. 3, pp. 51–72.

Campani, Giovanna, Carchedi, Francesco and Tassinari, Alberto (1994) *L'immigrazione silenziosa: Le comunità cinesi in Italia* (Silent Migration: The Chinese Communities in Italy). Torino, Ed. della Fondazione Giovanni Agnelli.

Castells, Manuel (1998) *La era de la información: Economía, sociedad y cultura, vol. 2. El poder de la identidad* (The Age of Information: Economy, Society and Culture, vol. 2. The Power of Identity). Madrid, Alianza Editorial.

Christiansen, Flemming (1997) 'Understanding Chinese Communities in Europe: Between Primordialism and Instrumentalism'. *Leeds East Asia Papers*, no. 51, pp. 1–12.

Crissman, Lawrence (1967) 'The Segmentary Structure of Overseas Chinese Communities'. *MAN*, vol. 2, no. 2, pp. 185–205.

Dikötter, Frank (2000) 'Identidad' (Identity). In Taciana Fisac and Steve Tsang (eds) *China en transición: Sociedad, cultura, política y economía*. Barcelona, Edicions Bellaterra, pp. 165–187.

Fisac, Taciana (1998) 'Occidente y la identidad nacional china' (The West and China's National Identity). *Papeles de Cuestiones Internacionales*, no. 63, pp. 61–67.

Hutchinson, John and Smith, Anthony (eds) (1994) *Nationalism*. Oxford, Oxford University Press.

Lim, Suchen Christine (1993) *Fistful of Colours*. Singapore, EPB Publishers.

Ma, Zhuomin (1996a) 'Hua shuo Qingtianren. Zhi yi' (Talking About the Qingtianese. Part One). *Xihua zhi sheng*, no. 21, 15 March, p. 4.

—— (1996b) 'Hua shuo Qingtianren. Zhi wu' (Talking About the Qingtianese. Part Five). *Xihua zhi sheng*, no. 25, 15 July, p. 4.

—— (1996c) 'Zaoqi lü Xibanya de Qingtianren' (The first Qingtianese Migrants to Spain). *Xihua zhi sheng*, no. 27, 1 September, p. 4.

—— (1996d) 'Xibanya de huaren baozhi' (Chinese Newspapers in Spain). *Ouzhou huasheng bao*, September.

—— (1996e) 'Xibanya huaren shehui de zhongwen jiaoyu' (The Teaching of Chinese Amongst the Chinese Community in Spain). *Ouzhou huasheng bao*, September.

—— (1996f) 'Basailuona de Qingtian Fangshan ren' (Fangshan's Qingtianese in Barcelona). *Xihua zhi sheng*, no. 31, 25 December, p. 4.

Ministry of Home Affairs of Spain (1999) *Anuario Estadístico de Extranjería 1998* (Statistical Yearbook on Aliens 1998). Madrid, Ministry of Home Affairs.

Nieto, Gladys (1998) 'La enseñanza por vocación: Identidad nacional y mujeres inmigrantes chinas' (Teaching as a Vocation: National Identity and Chinese Immigrant Women). *Ofrim Suplementos* (December), pp. 143–160.

Nyíri, Pal (1998) 'Chinese Organizations in Hungary 1989–1996. A Case Study in PRC-Oriented Community Politics Overseas'. In Frank Pieke and Hein Mallee (eds) *Internal and International Migration: Chinese Perspectives*. Surrey, Curzon Press.

Pan, Lynn (1994) *Sons of the Yellow Emperor: A History of the Chinese Diaspora*. New York, Kodansha America Inc.

—— (1999) *The Encyclopedia of Chinese Overseas*. Singapore, Harvard University Press.

Qingtian Returned Overseas Chinese Association (*Zhejiang sheng Qingtian guiguo huaqiao lianhehui*) (various dates) Fieldwork Notebook.

Robinson, Vaughan (1992) 'Une minorité invisible: les chinois en Grande-Bretagne' (An Invisible Minority: Chinese in Great Britain). *Revue européenne des migrations internationales*, vol. 8, no. 3, pp. 9–31.

Townsend, John (1996a) 'Chinese Nationalism'. In Jonathan Unger (ed.), *Chinese Nationalism*. New York, M. E. Sharpe, pp. 1–30.

—— (1996b) 'Introduction'. In Jonathan Unger (ed.), *Chinese Nationalism*. New York, M. E. Sharpe, pp. xi–xviii.

Tristán, Rosa M. (1998) 'La mafia china, en Lord Windsor. Rodaje de "La fuente amarilla" de Miguel Santesmases, en un salón de bodas de la capital' (Chinese Mafia, at *Lord Windsor*. The making of 'The Yellow Fountain' by Miguel Santesmases, at a Wedding Restaurant in Madrid). *El Mundo*, 26 March.

Wang, Gungwu (1993) 'Greater China and the Chinese Overseas'. *China Quarterly*, no. 136 (December), pp. 926–948.

Wu, David Yen-Ho (1991) 'The Construction of Chinese and Non-Chinese Identities'. *Daedalus*, vol. 120, no. 2 (Spring), pp. 159–180.

Xihua zhi sheng (1996) 'Renren baodao: Xibanya Qingtian qiaobao touzi zai jiaxiang jianzao "Xihua lou"' (Charity News: Donation from Qingtianese Compatriots Living in Spain in order to Support the 'Sino-Spanish Building'). *Xihua zhi sheng*, no. 32, 25 January, p. 1.

Part IV

NATION BUILDING AND COLLECTIVE IDENTITIES

9

COLLECTIVE IDENTITY AND NATIONALISM IN EUROPE AND CHINA

Werner Meissner

Introduction

This chapter is an attempt to shed some light on the search for a national identity in the European and Chinese contexts, comparing some aspects of collective identities and nationalism in both regions.

The concept of 'identity' is extremely difficult to define: it has become a paradigm for the individual, groups and nations in their search for a safe ground in disturbed times. Since the dawn of European civilization, the notion of identity has posed a key problem of philosophy. Nevertheless, the philosophical analysis of identity does not contribute here to our understanding of collective and national identity. Identity is defined in its most general form by Erikson: 'The term identity expresses . . . a mutual relation in that it connotes both a persistent sameness within oneself (selfsameness) and a persistent sharing of some kind of essential character with others'.[1] Thus, individual identities can only be established within group identities. Each person has multiple collective identities, which can be defined through gender, kinship, space or territory (local and regional identity), social class, education, occupation, institution, religion, ethnicity, culture, and finally, nationality and supra-nationality.[2] I would like to add one more element: individuals, groups and nations always tries to redefine their identity when it is challenged, endangered or broken. This is understood as an identity crisis. The search for and redefinition of a new identity is a process of adaptation in which a new equilibrium is sought between traditional elements and new challenges. The identity crisis is solved as soon as a new equilibrium, however temporary, is attained.

The second important concept used in this chapter is nationalism. In the definition of nationalism I am still inclined to follow Kohn and his distinction between a Western, more liberal kind of nationalism, and a Central and Eastern nationalism, also called ethnic nationalism, to which German nationalism belongs. While Western nationalism was, in its origin, connected with the concepts of individual liberty and rational cosmopolitanism current in the eighteenth century, the following nationalism in Central and Eastern Europe and in Asia tended towards a different development. Dependent upon, and opposed to, influences from without, this new nationalism, not rooted in a political and social reality, lacked self-assurance: its inferiority complex was often compensated by over-emphasis and over-confidence. As Kohn rightly observed: 'all rising nationalism was influenced by the West, . . . yet this very dependence on the West often wounded the pride of the native educated class as soon as it began to develop its own nationalism, and ended in an opposition to the 'alien' example and its liberal and rational outlook'.[3]

While nationalism in Britain and France preceded the future nation-state (or in the United States it coincided with the foundation of the nation-state), in most other cases the dominating form of nationalism was a political movement that firstly developed, at least partly, in opposition to the Western nations, and aimed at the establishment of a nation-state.

The focus of this chapter is triple-edged: first, the search for a national identity in the case of Germany in the European context; second, the development of a European identity, as understood by the European Union; third, the search for a Chinese national identity since the beginning of the twentieth century, in contrast with the Western experience.

The discourse on national identity

Over the last two hundred years, the pattern of searching for a new equilibrium has dominated the intellectual discourses on national identity in Europe as well as in other civilisations. Important factors that caused identity crises in the past were the development of modern sciences, the emergence of the capitalist mode of production, and the impact of these on the individual, the society and the state.

A basic pattern of the discourses can be established in Central and Eastern European countries: the relation between a traditional self-identity on the one hand, and the challenges to it from Western thought as it has developed in the sciences and parts of philosophy since the European Renaissance on the other. The related discourses are characterized by an oscillation between rejection and acceptance. The process of rejection and convergence, attempting either to keep Western thought away or to integrate selective parts of it into the traditional world-view, or otherwise to dismiss such a world-view in the course of the reception of Western thought, can be observed in all modernizing societies up to the present. In Russia, this constituted the discourse between 'Slavophiles' and 'Westernizers' between the 1840s and the 1870s (and again today). In Germany, it was the discussion between the protagonists of a '*Sonderweg*', a special way of modernization based on the

German spirit and culture that was supposed to lead to the establishment of a strong German nation-state, and the adherents of a Western-style political liberalism. In the Islamic states it was (and still is) the struggle between clerical conservatives – or even fundamentalists – and modernists. In China, the argument was between modern Neo-Confucians and representatives of Western European and American liberalism. These two sides clashed in the philosophical controversies in 1923 on 'science and metaphysics' and in the 1930s controversy on the question of a 'complete Westernization'. In all cases, intellectuals, as well as politicians, claimed the superiority of their allegedly 'spiritual culture' (Christian faith, Islam, German spirit, Song-Ming Neo-Confucianism) over the so-called rationalist and 'material civilization' of the West, while their opponents favoured a political philosophy that was based on a utilitarian-rational world-view with the idea of a democratic representative government at its core.

The Russian case

The Slavophiles wanted Russia's future development to be based on values and institutions derived from the country's early history. They took their ideas mainly from German philosophy, especially German Idealism (Herder, Schelling, Fichte and Hegel, an interest they had in common with many Chinese scholars in the twentieth century). Nationalists such as Khomyakov and Aksakov believed that Russia should not use Western Europe as a model for its modernization but follow a course determined by its own values and history. Western Europe was morally bankrupt and Western liberalism and capitalism were outgrowths of a decaying society. The Russian people, by contrast, should adhere to the Russian Orthodox faith and unite in a 'Christian community' under an authoritarian state. Spiritual values should replace Western rationalism, materialism, individualism and liberal democracy. Dostoyevsky's novel *The Demons* was a literary expression of the Russian's perception of Western ideas as forces destructive for Russia's national identity.

The German case

Similar to their Russian counterparts, many German intellectuals rejected the ideas of the French Revolution and, further stimulated by its excesses and the subsequent Napoleonic Wars, developed the foundations of a German national identity separate from the rest of Europe. Political liberalism was weakened in Germany following the failure of the 1848 Revolution. As a corollary, political modernization and industrialization did not progress in a synchronic way. The traditional political and socio-cultural structures were not transformed during industrialization: to some extent, industrialization was stuck onto the existing state and society.[4] The Prussian landed aristocrats, the German army officer corps and the state bureaucracy clearly dodged any attempts at political reform. Political and social development, in particular the formation of a liberal, parliamentary constitutional state, therefore lagged behind technical and economic developments. What made this so dangerous was the fact that it was accompanied by the belated creation of a German nation-state (the 'delayed nation') and the search for a national identity, as Plessner has clearly shown.[5]

German Idealism, Romanticism and Historicism had always stressed the particular individuality of German intellectual life in the face of the cultures of the Western European nations. Together with the conception of the special role of German culture, these elements were merged into a defensive ideology against the ideas of Western European and American parliamentarianism and political liberalism in the field of politics, against the dominating role of empiricism, pragmatism and positivism in the field of science and philosophy, and against capitalism in the field of economics.

The German '*Sonderweg*' was an attempt to realize an alternative concept of modernization where technological and industrial development was to be carried out within traditional values and political structures or was to remain subject to these. If we collate the individual elements that its proponents tried to merge into an identity, we can draw up the following list:

1 nature: attempt to unite the spirit of the Goethe period with modern technology;
2 state: endeavour to build the modern German nation-state not through elections, but on the basis of Fichte's ideas and Hegelian state metaphysics, and not to understand it as an aggregate of autonomous individuals (Locke) but as an organism (Hegel);
3 thought: endeavour to establish the dominance of speculative philosophy (Fichte, Hegel) over the empirical sciences (Bacon, Hume) and the supremacy of intuition over the intellect;
4 spiritual life: effort to place the 'inner world' (Luther) above the 'outer world', to assert inner morality over the laws of the material world, and to shape the material world from 'within';
5 social life: attempt to place the community above society and to value the whole greater than its parts;
6 legal life: tendency to place the state higher than the rights of the individual;
7 history: emphasis of the Gothic over the Renaissance;
8 culture and civilization: the superiority of German culture (allegedly internal and spiritual) over the civilization of the West (allegedly external and material).[6]

Use was made here of the great cultural treasures of the seventeenth and eighteenth centuries. What had once been the German contribution to

European cultural identity became now a tool for developing the intellectual foundation of Germany's national identity separated from Western Europe. German culture was subsumed into German nationalism. (In this context, one could easily apply the Chinese *tiyong* concept by replacing the term *zhongxue* (Chinese learning) with 'German culture': German culture being the inward essence, and scientific thinking serving for outward application.)

The corollary of this development was the separation from Europe and its common traditions. The ideas of Fichte and Hegel, and in its dialectical negation also the philosophy of Marx, contained a breakdown from the general European tradition of political thought, in particular from the ideas of natural law, of human rights and of the liberal constitutional state. They helped to prepare the ideology of a separate German national identity and the German '*Sonderweg*', the special way of modernization.

At the end of this development stood the ideological, political and finally military conflict between the German Empire and its Western European neighbours. In the 'Ideen von 1914' ('Ideas of 1914') and the cultural-philosophical propaganda of the time, even well-known German scholars, in particular Rudolf Eucken, Paul Natorp, Johann Plenge, Werner Sombart and Ernst Troeltsch, justified the military conflict between Germany and its neighbours as a conflict between 'spiritual culture' and 'material civilization'.[7] Europe, which in the nineteenth century was a continent with powerful nation states that balanced each other out, had finally turned into two hostile blocs: Western Europe and the 'Axis powers' (*Achsenmaechte*). The First World War became the utmost expression of the European identity crisis.

After the defeat of Germany in the First World War, the political and intellectual elite did not abandon the specific German collective identity, but helped, even if unintentionally for the most part, to prepare the downfall of the Weimar Republic. Western political liberalism continued to be rigidly rejected, and the elite similarly clung on to the intellectual, historical and cultural opposition to Western Europe. German nationalism was then reinforced under National Socialism and achieved its highest level of destruction between 1933 and 1945 with the myth of a supreme German race at its core.

The issue of a European identity

As we know, Western European integration was only possible after the complete defeat of the Third Reich. After the end of the Second World War, the majority of Germany's political and social elite was ready to embrace the essential values of European political culture: a representative government, the separation of powers, human rights and democracy. The Germans ran away from their own history and towards Europe. They rediscovered their democratic traditions: the ideas of 1848 and the Weimar Constitution. With this change in their political consciousness, the intellectual precondition existed for Germany's return to Europe and subsequent European integration. The integration into the Western 'community with common values' (*Wertegemeinschaft*), economically, politically, intellectually and militarily, was the precondition for European integration.

While the end of the Second World War and the defeat of Germany paved the way for Western European integration, the end of the Cold War, and the collapse of the Soviet Union and the Eastern Communist governments opened the door for the new democratic states to join the European Union (EU) in the near future. The negative experience of totalitarian and autocratic political systems contributed to the formation of a European identity, including Western and former Eastern Europe.

National Socialism, Fascism and Stalinist Communism thus belong to modern European history and have had a terrible impact on the people of Europe. It is difficult to imagine that these movements and their underlying 'values' can ever be part of a European identity. On the contrary, the European identity stands exactly for the opposite: it partly developed out of the struggle against these political movements.

Basic elements of a European identity are also presented in official European Community (EC)/EU documents. The most important document in this respect was published by the nine foreign ministers of the European Community in Copenhagen on 14 December 1973.[8] It can still be regarded as a valid statement of European identity. Unity is described here as the basic necessity to ensure the survival of the civilization held in common by the member states. In particular, the member states wish to ensure the cherished values of their legal, political and moral order and to preserve the rich variety of their national cultures:

> Sharing as they do the same attitudes to life, based on a determination to build a society which measures up to the needs of the individual, they are determined to defend the principles of representative democracy, of the rule of law, of social justice – which is the ultimate goal of economic progress – and of respect of human rights. *All these are fundamental elements of the European identity.*[9]

Special emphasis is given to the 'diversity of cultures within the framework of a common European civilization, the attachment to common values and principles' which should give the European identity its originality and its own dynamism.[10] The issue of a European identity has also been addressed in the Treaty on the European Union. The preamble calls for a common foreign policy, security policy and defence policy, which should strengthen the 'identity and unity of Europe'. Article B states clearly that one of the EU's objectives is to maintain its identity at the international level. But of crucial importance is Article F, which states: 'The Union respects the national identity of its member states, with their political systems founded on democratic principles'. The member states thus place their national identity at the core of this concept, while at the same time underlining four common shared values: a representative democracy, the rule of law, human rights and social justice.

The foundation of the European Community and later the European Union went hand in hand with two opposed developments: on the one hand a movement towards European unification and the strengthening of a European identity, and on the other hand increasing attempts to rediscover and strengthen local and regional identities. These two developments seem to be in conflict. But actually, they are two sides of the same coin: the European identity is founded on local, regional and national identities and the EU explicitly supports the national identities of its member states. Diversity and local particularity enrich the European identity, and diversity will remain one essential principle on which the foundations of a European identity can be built.

At the same time, ethnic nationalism in its classical form has been largely overcome, if we neglect the developments in former Yugoslavia. On the one hand, the nation-state is guaranteed, on the other hand its absoluteness is reduced by the growing integration of the European Union. That has only been possible because all the member states share several essential values or have finally agreed upon the following values: representative democracies, the rule of law, the respect of human rights, market economies, social justice, and cultural diversity.

The Italian historian Frederico Chabod once wrote: 'Cultural and moral factors played the dominating role in developing the idea of Europe and European consciousness'.[11] The cultural and moral factors that Chabod mentions include the role of Christianity and Christian humanism, the philosophy of the Middle Ages; the Renaissance and the Enlightenment; the development of modern science; nationalism (liberal nationalism, ethnic/cultural nationalism); political and economic liberalism; socialism (utopian, 'scientific', and democratic); the concept of the constitutional nation state; the concept of a representative democracy; the rule of law and human rights; the concept of market economy and social justice.

All these concepts belong to the cultural and political essence of the modern European civilization, and the European identity is based on these concepts. The EU is not founded on ethnicity and language, which is virtually impossible now and in the future. The EU is based on moral and cultural values, which have been developed in European history. Some of these concepts have even found their expression in official documents like the Treaty on the European Union: Democracy, Human Rights and the Rule of Law, to which all members have to comply. These values are even part of the general admission criteria for new candidate member states wishing to join the EU. According to the declaration of Copenhagen in 1993, there are three major criteria for accession. First, the candidate states must have the capacity to fulfil the obligations of membership, that means the Constitution of the EU must be accepted and realized. The second criteria is a functioning market economy. The third one is the stability of the democratic institutions in the candidate state.[12]

Identity from below

The fragility of a European collective identity becomes even more evident if one looks at the support for the EU from EU citizens. The official description of European identity reflects the concepts and understanding of the political elite in the member states. But the idea of a European identity among the ruling elite is one thing, and the identification of the citizens with the EU seems to be another. Any concept of identity is only legitimate if supported by the affected people who have to live within or under the political structure of this identity. However, even though many Europeans still consider that the process of integration is an invaluable asset for peace and prosperity, there is evidence of public disaffection with the Union. One important question in this respect has been formulated by Reif: 'to what extent do European institutions and their representatives hold legitimacy among citizens, and to what degree and under what conditions are Europeans willing to give their allegiance to European leaders?'[13]

Analyses of public support for European integration increased between the late 1940s and 1960s. However, since 1981 when the Eurobarometer started polling regularly, it is obvious that on average only about 50 per cent of EU citizens support their country's membership in the EU. This figure went up slightly in the early 1990s, but returned to and remained quite stable at around 50 per cent in 1998.[14] The figures are similar as far as the introduction of the Euro is concerned. Similar to the German Mark, which had developed into a major symbol of German national identity, the Euro could be regarded as an important symbol of European identity.

Thus, European identity is still based on national and regional identity, and the EU explicitly supports the national identities of its member states. But at the same time, nationalism in its classical form has been overcome, if we neglect the developments in the former Yugoslavia. Not only is the nation-state guaranteed, but its absoluteness is reduced by the growing integration of the EU. This has only been possible because all the member states share several essential values or have finally agreed upon them (a representative democracy, human rights and social justice, and a national diversity – diversity is one of the key elements of a European identity).

Following the Second World War and the subsequent hegemony of the United States over Western Europe, it is obvious that nationalism is in decline in the EU member states. Furthermore, it is quite unlikely that the EU will develop into a traditional nation-state and will be able to create some kind of a European *national* identity. Important prerequisites for such a development do not exist, above all a common language. On the contrary, the EU seems to provide only an overarching structure for overcoming step by step the traditional nation-state behaviour without destroying national and regional identities. The European identity will remain, at least for a long time, a collective identity, some kind of 'Europeanness' that will be based on high regional and national attachments and common shared values.

Nationalism and collective identity in China

China's search for a new identity began in the middle of nineteenth century and ran on very different tracks and under very different conditions compared with Europe. For the discussion on Chinese nationalism and collective identities, three elements seem to be important: the dominance of ethnic/cultural nationalism; the emphasis on racism; and the nearly complete absence of liberal nationalism.

Before the twentieth century, Chinese intellectuals did not perceive China as a nation in the Western sense, although China owned more or less all the elements needed to create a national identity: a long history, a unified and highly developed culture, and a common language which has existed for several thousand years. But the concept of *tianxia,* the world under heaven, was incompatible with the idea of a nation. *Tianxia* was a *globalistic* idea of how to structure the world. And in this *tianxia*, which of course was thought to be under the leadership of China, one was Chinese because of one's language, one's culture and by descent.

Tianxia proceeds from the assumption of authority derived from cultural superiority. It is a hierarchical structure of the world order: individuals as well as other ethnic groups are not regarded as equal. In contrast to *tianxia*, the idea of nation as represented by France and the United States is based originally on the assumption of equality amongst individuals within one state and equality of all states and all nations, although Western countries frequently violated these basic principles.

The ideas of nationalism were spread into Asia by the end of the nineteenth century. Asian students who had studied in Western countries became leaders of national liberation from foreign oppression: Sun Yat-sen in China, Nehru in India, Sukarno in Indonesia. China, like many other Asian states, developed its concept of national identity out of a struggle against Western as well as Japanese imperialism. That is one of the most important differences between Chinese and Western European nationalism: Asian nationalism was a political movement that was directed against imperialism and its economic and political oppression.

The first type of Chinese nationalism was ethnic and even racist. Originally, it was a movement to get rid of the rule of the Manchus. This movement went back to the seventeenth century, when Ming Loyalists continued to fight against the newly established Qing dynasty (1644–1911). But if we look at scholars such as Gu Yanwu (1613–82), Huang Zongxi (1610–95) and Wang Fuzhi (1619–92), it is difficult to say whether the anti-Manchu movement can be regarded as a nationalist movement. This 'nationalism' in the seventeenth century was independent from Western influence. But this changed by the end of the nineteenth century. Here we can speak of anti-Manchuism as an important part of early Chinese nationalism, which was already influenced by modern Western political ideas. Manchus were regarded as an inferior alien 'race'. In general, the Manchus were held responsible for China's weakness, and also for the autocratic structure of the Chinese state. Anti-Manchuism together with anti-imperialism were expressed in the writings of Zhang Binglin (1868–1936), who already regarded China's penetration by the West as the biggest threat. In order to prevent the decline of Chinese culture, the 'yellow race' should unite against the white invaders.[15]

The second nationalist concept was *minzuzhuyi* developed by Sun Yat-sen. The Chinese characters for nationalism (*minzuzhuyi*) originally came from Japan (*minzokushugi*). But what does *minzuzhuyi* actually mean? The characters *minzu* clearly indicate a meaning of race and nation. Usually it is translated by nationalism. But this translation is very vague. *Min* means people, and *zu* can be translated by clan, which together with *zhong* (*zhongzu*) means race. *Hanzu* is translated as Han nationality.

In Sun's view, there are several elements that contribute to a nation, in particular *xuetong* (blood relationship), *shenghuo* (conditions of life), *yuyan* (language) and *zongjia* (religion). In Sun's eyes, blood relationship was the most important power that constituted the Chinese nation.[16] He also stated that Chinese culture was superior to Western civilization, but at the same time he strongly emphasized the necessity to adopt Western science. His 'nationalism' (*minzuzhuyi*) clearly belongs to the group of so-called ethnic/cultural nationalisms, comparable to the nationalism in Germany (*Volkstumsidee*) and some East European countries.

The Chinese concept of national identity and nationalism had much in common with the German concept. The fear of 'Westernization', 'materialism' and above all political liberalism can be found in both cultures. Chinese scholars also made a very clear distinction between the 'West' and Germany. Germany was not perceived as belonging to the West (the Germans themselves did not perceive themselves as belonging to the 'West' either). In their search for ideological allies against the West, the Confucians of the 1920s and 1930s therefore looked above all towards Germany (the Chinese Communists later looked towards Russia, and the liberals towards America). They hoped to be able to revive the Confucian and spiritual tradition of China by integrating German metaphysics, primarily the philosophy of Hegel and Fichte.[17] Chinese and German (mostly conservative) intellectuals even envisaged some kind of cultural cooperation in which German idealistic philosophy and Chinese philosophy would unite against Western civilization. Translation projects (German philosophical works into Chinese, and Chinese philosophical works into German) were started with exactly this purpose in mind, including amongst them of course Fichte's 'Speeches to the German nation' during Japan's occupation of Manchuria. More than 1,300 German-language books had been translated into Chinese by the beginning of the Second World War, the majority of them being works on culture and philosophy.[18]

Similar to the Slavophiles and the Germans, Chinese scholars also developed the idea of an independent way of Chinese modernization. This modernization strategy was to be based on traditional Chinese world-views and the conception of a Chinese identity that should not follow the Western models.

As an example, I will mention here Zhang Junmai (Chang Chun-mai, Carsun Chang, 1887–1969). He was an adherent of Neo-Confucianism, a strongly idealistic and mystical form of Confucianism that went back to Zhu Xi (1130–1200) and Wang Yangming (1472–1528). Zhang, who had studied in Germany, was also convinced of the superiority of the spiritual culture (*jingshen wenhua*) of China over the material culture (*wuzhi wenhua*) of the West, especially as far as the mechanistic natural sciences were concerned.[19]

In 1933–35 there was a controversy between Chinese sociologists on the issue of 'complete Westernization',[20] a term that, as we know, reappeared in the 1980s. As in the 1920s with Zhang Junmai, the well-known argument could be found here among opponents that the duty was to connect the Chinese (special) path (*dao*) with Western instruments (*qi*), to preserve the national characteristics (*guoqing*), and to shape Chinese culture on a Chinese foundation (*Zhongguo benwei wenhua*).[21]

But why were so many Chinese scholars so fascinated by the German model of modernization? The answer is very simple: Germany had proved that it was possible to build an economically and militarily strong country based on so-called 'spiritual values', with a strong authoritarian political system, without having to introduce Western principles of democracy. Germany had been defeated not because of its modernization strategy, but rather because it was too small and had too many enemies. But China was not small, China was a big country. Despite the defeat of 1918, Germany thus became a model for how China could be developed into a powerful country and how the superiority of the Chinese 'spiritual culture' (today we might perhaps speak of 'Asian values') asserted by the Neo-Confucians could be preserved.[22]

The sharpest opponents of the idea to revive Confucian tradition and to follow the German model were the group of 'Westerners', among them Hu Shi (1891–1962). They represented the influence of American liberalism, pragmatism and English empiricism in China. In contrast to the Neo-Confucians, they were convinced that only the 'scientification' of Chinese thought in all areas (i.e. not just in technology but also in the social sciences and humanities) and the 'complete Westernization' of Chinese civilization (connected with the adoption of political liberalism and a controlled capitalism) would bring about the re-establishment of China's greatness.[23] Hu Shi, under the influence of John Dewey, was also the first to recommend a federal political structure for China based on 'self-governing provinces' (*liansheng zizhi*), rather than a centralized political system.[24]

The ideas of political liberalism, parliamentarianism, the rule of law, and human rights thus achieved in the 1920s and 1930s an early, though very limited effectiveness. In contrast to the Neo-Confucians, its adherents understood the modernization of China, the adoption of the Western sciences and the dissemination of liberal ideas as a uniform, interrelated process.

The liberal concept of national identity, represented by Hu Shi, Lo Longji and other intellectuals who had been educated in the United States or in Great Britain, remained only an episode. As a result of the dictatorship of the national government and the civil war between the Communists and the Nationalists, and also as a result of the Sino-Japanese War of 1937–45, the discussion on national identity abated in the 1940s to fall almost silent after the Second World War.

Racism and nationalism

Racism is only a modern term for the biologically based dislike of other people. The traditional term 'barbarian' could easily be loaded with racial connotations, as Wang Fuzhi already did with reference to the Manchus. The list of racial stereotypes used by Chinese scholars since the nineteenth century is long.[25] Reformers from Yan Fu to Liang Qichao regarded racial identity as a key element in China's struggle for racial survival (*baozhong*) and rebirth. The 'yellow race' was engaged in a merciless struggle with the 'white race'. Darwinism combined with racism and the belief in China's cultural superiority became the main building blocks of rising Chinese nationalism. Chiang Kai-shek spoke of the 'various stocks' in China not just as one nation but as 'one race'.[26] However, one should take into consideration that this kind of language was strongly influenced by European ideas. Racism in Europe had been in vogue at the beginning of the twentieth century, and Chinese intellectuals were by no means alone in applying racial terms and theories.[27]

Racism in contemporary China seems to have become more and more important as a tool to help establish collective identity. Sautman has collected statements by high-ranking Chinese Communist cadres that reveal racial thinking, although Chinese officials claim that racism is common everywhere in the world, except China.[28] Official documents emphasize the common ancestry of the Han and the minorities. The Han and the Tibetans are regarded as parts of a common race and the early historical Tibetan and Yellow River Chinese cultures are also regarded as identical. Tibetans belong to the Chinese nation through their blood relationship. Haemoglobin studies have been conducted to prove the supposed racial kinship of the Chinese and the minorities.[29] These and other examples indicate that racism and nationalism have been on the rise in mainland China since the 1990s.[30]

Patriotism

The concept of patriotism (*aiguozhuyi*) was mentioned by Mao Zedong in his famous speech on 'The Place of the Chinese Communist Party in the National War' in 1938. In his speech, Mao said that patriotism is the realization of internationalism in the war of liberation. In the case of China, this meant the war of resistance against Japan.

During the period of Maoist patriotism the Chinese Communist leadership did not pay much attention to the national cultural heritage. Classical Chinese culture was not regarded as an important element of Chinese Communist nationalism. On the contrary, there were works of Marxism-Leninism on the damaging influence of so-called feudal culture, and as we know, during the so-called Cultural Revolution, large parts of China's cultural heritage were destroyed. The approach of the Chinese Communists to culture changed in the 1980s. In several ideological controversies, culture was regarded as an independent value, independent of its class basis. Traditional Chinese culture was reinstated as an element of Chinese nationalism, which could be used to arouse patriotic feelings as well.

Patriotism became especially important in the aftermath of the events of 1989. Then, the Chinese Communist ideology established that patriotism and socialism cannot be separated. The Party Central Committee journal *Qiushi* published a significant editorial that gave the current official view about the content of Chinese patriotism:

> Patriotism is historic-specific, having different contents under different historical circumstances. Today, if we want to be patriotic, we should love the socialist New China under the leadership of the Chinese Communist Party. As was pointed out by Comrade Deng Xiaoping in one of his speeches in 1981, 'Some people say that not loving socialism is not the same thing as not loving our motherland. Is motherland an abstract concept? If you do not love the socialist New China led by the Communist Party, what else can you love? As far as patriotic compatriots in Hong Kong, Macao, Taiwan, and other overseas areas are concerned, we should not expect them all to approve socialism. But the least they can do is not to oppose the socialist New China. Otherwise, how can they call themselves patriotic? When it comes to every citizen and every youth inside the People's Republic of China, we naturally have higher expectations'.[31]

What is the consequence of these last lines? According to what Deng said in 1990, it is not possible to criticize the Chinese Communist government without being labelled unpatriotic, and those who criticize the Chinese government are against the Chinese people.

Other authors went even further, quoting Jiang Zemin's words from 1989: 'In China today, patriotism and socialism are unified in essence'.[32] Patriotism is regarded as a premise of China's socialism, and socialism is the inevitable conclusion of genuine patriotism. However, the identity of patriotism and socialism cannot be regarded as nationalism. If a group of political leaders claim that patriotism is associated only with supporting their partisan positions, as is the case with the Chinese Communists, their behaviour can only be seen as an example of party politics and not a manifestation of true nationalism. It is understandable that politicians try to identify themselves with nationalistic sentiments, but nationalism is always more than loyalty to a party or a particular leader. In such a case we speak of partisan nationalism, which serves mainly the interests of one party.

Racism, the myth of biological origins, the evocation of China's mythical emperors, and patriotism: all these tendencies are created and/or manipulated. They are used to create new collective identities for the ossified and endangered Marxist-Leninist political structures. They are ideological tools to help prevent the disintegration of the party and the state.

Collective identity and the Chinese state

I will now turn to another aspect of identity. China has been a unitary state since ancient times. Its history has always been characterized by the struggle for a central unitary state, not a federally structured state. Creating and maintaining a strong centralized state has always been a major preoccupation of Chinese statesmen, politicians and state-oriented scholars.[33] In contrast, federal ideas have been the exception in Chinese political theory: at the beginning of the Qing dynasty, scholars such as Huang Zongxi and Gu Yanwu criticized the over-centralized and military structure of the Ming government system (the *junxian zhidu*) and advocated some kind of regional autonomy.[34] Three centuries later, in the 1920s, Hu Shi, as already mentioned, advocated 'self-governing provinces' (*liansheng zizhi*) as the foundation for a federally structured China similar to the United States. Only in the 1980s did the idea of a federal state structure reappear.

The term unitary state goes back to two state theories that were developed after the French Revolution with one common origin: Rousseau's theory of identity. The romantic republican tradition regarded the state as an expression and an instrument of the *volonté générale*, i.e. the collective will of free and equal citizens. The unitary state is indivisible. While the federal state acknowledges the existence of territorial collectives and therefore collective identities below the central level, the unitary state never tolerates any kind of regional collective entities. Therefore, the practical application of unitarianism naturally fosters authoritarian and plebiscitary political systems.

German Romanticism, while taking in Hegel's idea of unity, also developed the idea of a unitary political system, but it was merged with the idea of an authoritarian and republican nation-state. Its main feature was the idea of a nation-state detached from democratic processes based on the individual's free will. Collective identity was attached to an authoritarian and unitary state.

In China, the identification with the state went hand in hand with the 'unification of thinking' (*sixiang tongyi*), both in the past and in the present. In this respect, Zhu Xi's philosophy (1130–1200) was of special importance. Zhu Xi's thinking dominated Chinese intellectual history from the late Song to the late Qing dynasty. The main doctrine was the identity of one's mind with the 'heavenly principle' (*tianli*). *Tianli* was an all-embracing and all-penetrating category. It was everywhere: macrocosm, microcosm, state, society and the individual. At the same time, the *tianli* was embodied in the ruler's command. Knowing the *li* meant obeying the ruler's command, because he always acted in accordance with the 'heavenly principle'.

The *li* thus became a central political category, the ideological foundation of the Chinese state orthodoxy from the Ming dynasty until 1905, when the examination system was abolished. The *li* was a kind of 'spiritual putty': it held the political and social system together, binding everything through its uniformity. It also determined the different types of social connections (emperor/vassal; father/son; husband/wife). Thus, the circle of philosophy, cosmos and politics was closed: each individual was allocated his place in the social and political coordinates, which were fixed by the classical Confucian writings. By orienting their consciousness on the *li*, individuals achieved their identity within the predetermined social, political and cosmic order.

The function of *tianli* can be compared with the *lex aeterna* in Thomas Aquinas and the divination of the state in Hegel through the idea of *Weltvernunft* (world reason). *Tianli*, *lex aeterna* and *Weltvernunft* governed the macro and the microcosm. They all established a collective identity in which the individual, the society, the state and the cosmos were unified under one principle.[35] However, it was an identity established from above, by the governing elite.

Zhu Xi's doctrine of the 'heavenly *li*' was the ideological backbone of the central unitary Chinese state from the late Song dynasty until 1905.[36] If one compares this doctrine with Chinese Marxism-Leninism, then one can establish that the 'eternal' laws of dialectical and historical materialism have a similar function to the 'heavenly *li*' in Neo-Confucianism. Similar to the *tianli*, the laws of dialectic are cosmic principles, and both doctrines provide the legitimization for the ruling bureaucracy. The laws of dialectic, especially the 'law of contradiction' or the 'law of the identity of opposites' (*maodun lu* or *maodun tungyilu*), which had been formulated by Engels, are an all-embracing and all-penetrating category like the *tianli*. Macrocosm, microcosm, state, society and the individual all have to follow these fundamental laws. If following the *li* meant obeying the ruler's command, then following the laws of dialectical and historical materialism meant following the line of the party, because the party was the result of the dialectical development in history. Similar to the *li*, which was once the central political category for the Confucian bureaucracy, the 'law of contradiction' became a central political category for Chinese Marxists after 1949. It was, and still is, the ideological foundation of the Chinese state orthodoxy.[37]

After seizing power in 1949, the Chinese Communists succeeded in comprehensively repressing Western pragmatism, empiricism and liberalism as well as traditional influences in China through 'mass campaigns' and 'purges' among the intellectuals. Marxism-Leninism of Soviet origin and with Maoist characteristics finally became the general guideline for the consciousness and action of the individual, society and the state. While destroying many areas of the preceding culture, the Chinese Communists tried to determine the inner meaning of individual and group identity primarily through party ideology in order to establish a new collective identity under the control of the party.

Collective identity through 'unification of thought' and a centralist state require each other. The disintegration of the centralist political system is obviously preceded by the disintegration of collective identity. Thus the fall of the Qing dynasty was preceded by the fall of the Confucian canon and the emergence of different philosophies of life as a result of Western influence. In the light of the decay of Marxist-Leninist orthodoxy in the People's Republic of China and the emergence of new ideological currents, the question arises about the future of the centralist political system. In the Soviet Union this question has already been answered, as it has also in Yugoslavia. In China, the answer is still pending.

The development of a form of state unity founded on a world-view based on pluralistic consensus has until today only taken place in the Western democracies, and recently we have been able to observe similar developments in Taiwan and Hong Kong (see below). This development did not, however, take place in the Soviet Union, and even less so on the Chinese mainland.

In the case of China, the intellectual controversies between 1911 and 1949, and the multiplicity of ideas reflected in them, were the expression and equivalent of the inner disintegration of the country and of the absent state unity. They are in retrospect in no way comparable with the pluralistic multiplicity of ideas and competition of ideas present in the European states (with the exception of National Socialist Germany and the fascist states). The multiplicity and competition of ideas in Europe corresponds to the principle of a liberal, unified constitutional state. They are to a certain extent part of the normal everyday political life of Western democracies. But in China, at least in the past, the multiplicity and competition of ideas correspond to the country being torn apart by separation and civil wars. Here lies one crucial difference between the collective identity in China and in Europe.

Between 1949 and 1978, the prevailing ideology was of course Marxism-Leninism/Mao Zedong thought. But since the beginning of the 1980s, the policy of 'Four Modernizations' has triggered a completely unexpected new move to adopt Western thought. One can establish the following four main trends that have shaped intellectual developments since the 1980s and have emerged against the backdrop of the successive decline of the state orthodoxy: (1) the renaissance of Western non-Marxist philosophy; (2) the renaissance of political science; (3) the revival of political liberalism and the idea of 'complete Westernization' (*quanpanxihua*) (at least until 1989); and (4) the renaissance of Chinese traditional philosophy, in particular Neo-Confucianism.

Following this reception of Western thought and the renaissance of traditional thought, we have been able to observe the construction of two basic political positions, which might be the dominating political movements in the future, and both of which can to a certain extent refer to traditions in Chinese thought. Furthermore, the 1980s showed a striking renaissance of the ideological currents of the 1920s and 1930s mentioned above. There is not only an extremely disputed and officially combated tendency towards 'Westernization' in the sense of liberalism and federalism, but, as in the 1920s and 1930s, there is at the same time a counter-tendency in the form of a revival of idealistic and conservative ideologies.

What do these developments represent? Are they indicators of a desirable pluralization and democratization of Chinese society towards a new and democratic national identity? As desirable as this is, scepticism is yet called for. The Democracy Movement and its ideological foundations revealed strong deficiencies in socio-political preconditions as far as the path to a more democratically, federally and pluralistically structured state in future was concerned. The 'partial' modernization conducted at the moment by the government with the simultaneous exclusion of any political modernization might anticipate rather the opposite in the long run: it favours negative developments, and no political institutions are being created for their control. At the same time, the erection of a counter-ideology, of a 'bulwark' against the political liberalism and pluralism of the West, is being conducted, similar to the establishment of anti-Western ideologies under the influence of German philosophy in the 1920s and 1930s. In this context, it is perhaps no accident that a large number of books and articles on philosophy translated into Chinese and written in Chinese between 1987 and 1998 are on German philosophy, and here mainly on German Idealism, especially Hegel.[38]

One cannot rule out the emergence of a strong traditionalist anti-Western ideology in China, an amalgam of Confucian elements combined with set pieces of party ideology and of Western non-liberal philosophy and backed by neo-conservative intellectuals in close cooperation with the party. Under the slogan of 'patriotism' and 'Chineseness', such a nationalistic ideology could be used by the leadership to preserve its political power and privileges. The strongly anti-Western effect would perhaps enable the present or a new military leadership to legitimize itself on the basis of its own history and to maintain or to win back the control that the central state is going to lose over the regions.

One country, two identities

The case of Hong Kong

The devolution of the mainland central state and its legitimization, the collective identity defined by Marxism-Leninism, leads us to question collective identities in other regions. Here I would like to touch briefly on Hong Kong and Taiwan.[39]

With the handover of Hong Kong in 1997, Beijing achieved its first objective of national unification. Macao followed in December 1999, while unification with Taiwan seems to be very far away. However, national unification and national identity are not the same. In particular, the case of Hong Kong is an example of national unification creating problems and national 'headaches' because of the increase of different collective identities within one nation. Alongside Tibet and Xinjiang, Hong Kong has been added as another collective identity that is different from the national identity as understood by the government in Beijing.

The Beijing-selected Preparatory Committee for the handover of Hong Kong had a clear idea of Hong Kong's identity: Hong Kong residents of 'Chinese origin' were regarded as Chinese citizens, including those who had a foreign passport but held also a permanent residence card. These people would become citizens of the People's Republic of China automatically because of their blood lineage.[40] However, research on the status of collective identity in Hong Kong reveals a picture that is different from the idea of collective identity based on blood lineage. Following the different developments on the mainland and in Hong Kong, normative lifestyles and mental outlooks were heading in different directions already in the 1960s and even more in the 1980s. In 1985, about 60 per cent of Hong Kong people identified themselves not as 'Chinese' but as 'Hongkongese' (*xianggangren*) when they were asked to choose. Only 36 per cent identified themselves as Chinese, and 67.9 per cent agreed that it is difficult for them to get along with mainland Chinese.[41]

The case of Taiwan

Besides Hong Kong and Macao, the people of Taiwan have understandably developed several forms of collective identity that have changed over the past fifty years due to their different environment and are therefore different from those on the mainland.

Looking back at the Taiwan policy of the Chinese Communists, one should mention that in 1936 even Mao Zedong supported independence for

Taiwan, which was then under Japanese control.[42] The Chinese Communist Party's (CCP) documents between 1928 and 1943 also provide evidence that the party recognized the anti-Japanese resistance movement on Taiwan as a national liberation movement by a distinct Taiwanese nation (*minzu*).[43] Since the beginning of Deng Xiaoping's reform policy in 1978, the Taiwan question has become a major national issue in mainland politics: the question of national unification has become a pillar of the CCP's politics since the 1980s.[44] However, in the meantime, the former conflict between Taiwanese and mainlanders who arrived in 1948/49, the commonly perceived threat from the mainland, and the successful economic and political developments on the island, all have had an impact on the emergence of a new Taiwanese identity. Following the growing Chinese nationalism on the mainland and the missile crisis, a new type of Taiwanese identity seems to have emerged that is shared by Hakka, Minnan or second-generation mainlanders as well.[45]

On the other side, Chinese Communist cadres are using more and more racist terminology when addressing the Taiwan question. Jiang Zemin, for example, said in 1996: 'Unification is the wish of the whole body of Chinese citizens. If there is unification, then the whole people will be fortunate. If there is no unification, then there will be suffering.'[46] Jiang also spoke of the 'twenty-one million Taiwan compatriots', who, 'no matter whether from Taiwan province or other provinces, are all Chinese people, are all flesh and blood compatriots, brothers as in hands and feet'.[47]

Another example: in 1996, a Chinese scholar from Beijing University gave a lecture in Hong Kong on the Taiwan question. He was asked whether the government in Beijing would accept the outcome of a plebiscite by the people of Taiwan on the future status of the island, comparable with the plebiscite in Quebec. 'The Chinese people would never accept such a plebiscite', he replied. But as individuals the people of Taiwan should have the right to decide on their own future, somebody argued. The Beijing scholar answered: 'How can a finger decide that it wants to become independent from the body? If there was a vote on the future status of Taiwan, 1.2 billion Chinese people would have to take part in such a plebiscite, not just the people of Taiwan.'

As I have mentioned in the section on racism, there are many other statements of similar content. My conclusion is that the political leadership and scholars attached to the leadership clearly use nationalist and racist terminology in order to broaden their dwindling legitimacy and to cover up the fact that their unification policy has only limited support in these regions.

Conclusion

Hong Kong and Taiwan are Chinese regions where collective identities have been developing with a clear Western influence. Following the democratization in Taiwan, a synthesis between Western liberalism and Chinese collective identity seems to be emerging, a kind of democratic collective identity that contains elements of liberal nationalism. In view of the surge of nationalism on the other side of the Taiwan Strait, one has to ask: how will China be able to adjust to a world that needs global cooperation in all political fields in order to survive?

Compared with Europe, it has become evident that China is going a completely different way and is also at a very different point of development. However, the recent surge of nationalism and even racism in mainland China does not imply that China will necessarily turn into an expansionist country like Germany in the past, and this for two reasons: first, Beijing does not have the economic and military resources for an aggressive foreign policy; and second, nationalism is no longer the driving force of history as it was in the nineteenth century and in the struggles against imperialism.

Europe – with the exception of the Balkan crisis – has obviously achieved a point at which national identity has become integrated in a European collective identity. The many ethnic problems that still exist in Europe – the North Africans in France, the Turks in Germany, the Basque problem, Northern Ireland, etc. – cannot obscure the fact that the nations themselves as well as the individuals within them have obviously learned not only to tolerate and cooperate with each other but also to appreciate the different advantages of each other. That is last but not least also a result of the general change in daily life patterns in Europe that has taken place since the Second World War. Mass consumption, high mobility, mass media, to mention only a few, have contributed to a rising demand for cross-cultural encounters. Ethnic tensions and racist behaviour can be mainly detected among those groups that have so far had no chance to participate sufficiently in exactly these daily life patterns. Nationalism seems to be melting away, while the racism of small groups (i.e. skinheads) appears largely as a social problem.

In the case of former Yugoslavia, the reinvention of Serbian racist nationalism was not rooted in an irrational mass movement, it was rather intentionally orchestrated. The Serbian case shows in a nutshell how nationalism has been manipulated by the Belgrade political elite, 'which turned to ethnic Serbian nationalism as a deliberate post-communist strategy to keep power'.[48] A similar conclusion can be drawn for Chinese patriotism and nationalism. The nationalistic slogans and actions that have appeared in mainland China since the 1980s, and intensified after 1989, clearly have a function for domestic policies. Mobilising emotional support for national goals, in particular re-unification with Taiwan, primarily serves as a way for the leadership to justify their power following the collapse of their traditional Marxist-Leninist legitimisation.

Notes

1 Erikson (1959: 27–28).
2 Smith (1991: 3ff.); Dean (1997: 1–46). For a detailed attempt to clarify the concept with regards China, refer to Dittmer and Kim (1993).
3 Kohn (1945). Kohn's distinction has been the focus of much criticism. However, especially the German, the Russian and the Chinese cases, as well as the developments in the former Yugoslavia, seem to justify his definition. Refer to Hutchinson and Smith (1994: 160ff.).
4 Dahrendorf (1965: 55 and 59).
5 Plessner (1974). On the problems addressed here, refer to the works by Dahrendorf (1965), Faulenbach (1980), Vierhaus (1952), Holborn (1952) Kohn (1962), Klemperer (n.d.), Mosse (1964), Lübbe (1963), Stern (1986), Stromberg (1973, 1981b). From the French side, see also the essay by Groh (1983). A short but very good summary of the problems can also be found in Löwenthal (1979: 268–270).
6 Meissner (1994: 17–27).
7 Refer for example to the work by Troeltsch (1925). The small volume primarily contained speeches from 1916, compiled under chapter headings such as: 'The development of a new world of German ideas in the fight against enlightenment and natural law' (p. 3); 'German and Western European spirit in the World War' (p. 31). For more details, see Meissner (1994).
8 European Parliament. Committee on Institutional Affairs (n.d.: 57–60).
9 *Ibid.*: 58, italics by the author.
10 *Ibid.*: 59.
11 Quoted from Jacques Le Goff (1996: 78).
12 Compare with Mueller-Graff (1996: 47ff.).
13 Reif (1993: 131ff.).
14 *Eurobarometer* (1998: 18).
15 On Zhang Binglin compare with Laitinen (1990).
16 Sun (1927).
17 See Meissner (1994).
18 Lee (1975: 215–220).
19 Meissner (1994: 147–171). So far, the best biography on Zhang Junmai is Jeans (1997). The only German presentation is Hung (1980). Short presentations also exist in Tan (1972: 253–266).
20 The most important arguments of the 'Westernizers' at that time were: (1) the uniformity of a culture and the interdependence of all of its aspects (politics, philosophy, economy and social institutions); (2) the superiority of Western culture: the old Chinese culture is not suited for the modern world; (3) Westernization is a general, world-embracing trend: if China wants to have an influential place in the world, then it must Westernize itself; (4) certain parts of Chinese culture are already Westernized, but only externally (system of government, traffic system, industry), yet this Westernization is not only insufficient but dangerous, as it concentrates only on the material achievements of the West and neglects the spiritual foundations of the Western society, which are the basis of these achievements. A short but excellent overview of this whole controversy is provided by Kolonko (1983).

21 Kolonko (1983: 171).
22 In defence of Zhang Junmai, it must be added here that his political conceptions did already incorporate the ideas of the German constitutional law of the Weimar Republic, in contrast to the conceptions of many German conservatives.
23 On Hu Shi, see the still unmatched work by Grieder (1970).
24 Hu (1922). Refer also to Grieder (1970: 195).
25 Dikötter (1990).
26 Chiang (1947: 39).
27 Dikötter (1992).
28 Sautmann (1997).
29 For further details, see Sautmann (1997).
30 On the wave of nationalism in China in the 1990s, refer to Zhao (1997) and Metzger and Myers (1998).
31 Quoted after Pye (1996: 106).
32 Pye (1996: 187).
33 Hunt (1993).
34 Meissner (1994: 54ff.).
35 On the importance of Thomas Aquinas for the thought of the macrocosmic and microcosmic correspondences, see comments in Topitsch (1959: 252–255, 259). Aquinas as a political thinker is analysed by Nipperdey (1968).
36 For a detailed discussion on Zhu Xi's political thought, see Meissner (1994: 28–43).
37 Meissner (1990).
38 For more details, see Meissner (1996) and Meissner (2001).
39 On the aspects of ethnic identities, see for example Gladney (1991).
40 *Wen Wei Po*, 30 March 1996.
41 Lau and Kuan (1988: 178).
42 Snow (1978: 129).
43 Hsiao and Sullivan (1997); Hughes (1997: 12ff.).
44 Hughes (1997: 15ff.).
45 Liu (1996).
46 Refer to Jiang Zemin's speech on Chinese New Year in *Renmin ribao*, 31 January 1995.
47 *Ibid.*
48 Preston (1997: 118); Rieff (1995).

References and further reading

Bailey Jeans, Roger (1974) 'Syncretism in Defence of Confucianism: An Intellectual and Political Biography of the Early Years of Chang Chün-mai, 1887–1923'. PhD Thesis, George Washington University.

Cabestan, Jean-Pierre (1998) 'Taiwan – Mainland China: Reunification Remains More Impossible than Ever'. In Marie-Luise Naeth (ed.), *The Republic of China on Taiwan in International Politics*. Frankfurt am Main, Peter Lang, pp. 51–69.

Chiang, Kai-shek (1947) *China's Destiny*. Westport CT, Greenwood Press.

Dahrendorf, Ralph (1965) *Gesellschaft und Demokratie in Deutschland* (Society and Democracy in Germany). Munich, Deutscher Taschenbuch Verlag.

Dean, Kathryn (ed.) (1997) *Politics and the End of Identity*. Brookfield, Ashgate.
Dikötter, Frank (1990) 'Group Definition and the Idea of Race in Modern China (1793–1949)'. *Ethnic and Racial Studies*, vol. 13, no. 3 (July), pp. 420–429.
—— (1992) *The Discourse on Race in Modern China*. London, Hurst.
Dittmer, Lowell and Kim, Samuel S. (1993) 'In Search of a Theory of National Identity'. In Lowell Dittmer and Samuel S. Kim (eds) *China's Quest for National Identity*. Ithaca, Cornell University Press, pp. 1–31.
Erikson, Erik H. (1959) *Identity and the Life Cycle*. New York, Norton.
Eurobarometer (1992) no. 38 (Autumn). http://europa.eu.int/comm/dg10 .
—— (1998) no. 49 (September). http://europa.eu.int/comm/dg10 .
European Parliament Committee on Institutional Affairs (n.d.) *Selection of Texts Concerning Institutional Matters of the Community from 1950 to 1982*. Luxembourg, European Parliament.
Faulenbach, Bernd (1980) *Ideologie des deutschen Weges: Die deutsche Geschichte in der Historiographie zwischen Kaiserreich und Nationalsozialismus* (The Ideology of the German Way: The German History in the Historiography, Between Empire and National Socialism). Munich, Beck.
Gladney, Dru C. (1991) *Muslim Chinese: Ethnic Nationalism in the People's Republic*. Cambridge MA, Council on East Asian Studies, Harvard University.
Grieder, Jerome (1970) *Hu Shih and the Chinese Renaissance*. Cambridge MA, Harvard University Press.
Groh, Dieter (1983) 'Le "Sonderweg" de l'histoire allemande entre 1848 et 1945: Mythe ou réalité?' (The 'Sonderweg' of German History Between 1848 and 1945: Myth or Reality?). *Annales*, vol. 38, no. 5 (September–October), pp. 1166–1187.
Holborn, Hajo (1952) 'Deutscher Idealismus in sozialgeschichtlicher Beleuchtung' (The German Idealism in the Socio-Historical Perspective). *Historische Zeitschrift*, vol. 174, pp. 359–384.
Hsiao, Frank and Sullivan, Lawrence (1979) 'The Chinese Communist Party and the Status of Taiwan: 1928–1934'. *Pacific Affairs*, vol. 52, no. 3 (Fall), pp. 446–467.
Hu, Shih (1922) 'Liansheng zizhi yu junfageju da Chen Duxiu' (Federative Provincial Selfgovernment and Warlord Separatism). In *Hu Shi wencun II*. Shanghai, Yadong tushuguan, 1931, pp 109–119.
Hughes, Christopher (1997) *Taiwan and Chinese Nationalism: National Identity and Status in International Society*. London and New York, Routledge.
Hung, Mao-hsiung (1980) 'Carsun Chang (1887–1969). Seine Vorstellungen vom Sozialismus in China' (Carsun Chang (1887–1969): His Presentations of Socialism in China). Inaugural Dissertation. Munich, Munich University.
Hunt, Michael H. (1993) 'Chinese Identity and the Strong State: The Late Qing-Republican Crisis'. In Lowell Dittmer and Samuel S. Kim (eds), *China's Quest for National Identity*. Ithaca, Cornell University Press, pp. 62–81.
Hutchinson, John and Smith, Anthony (eds) (1994) *Nationalism*. Oxford and New York, Oxford University Press.
Jeans, Roger (1997) *Democracy and Socialism in Republican China: The Politics of Zhang Junmai (Carsun Chang), 1906–1941*. Lanham, MD, Rowman and Littlefield.
Klemperer, Klemens von (n.d.) *Konservative Bewegungen: Zwischen Kaiserreich und Nationalsozialismus* (Conservative Movements: Between Empire and National Socialism). Munich and Vienna, Oldenbourg.
Kohn, Hans (1945) *The Idea of Nationalism*. Macmillan, New York.

—— (1962) *Wege und Irrwege: Vom Geist des deutschen Bürgertums* (Ways and Wrong Ways. On the Spirit of the German Citizenship). Düsseldorf, Droste.

Kolonko, Petra (1983) 'The Challenged National Identity: When the Chinese Wanted to Become Westerners. The 'Debate on Total Westernization' in China 1934–35'. *East Asian Civilizations*, no. 2, pp. 168–174.

Laitinen, Kauko (1990) *Chinese Nationalism in the Late Qing Dynasty: Zhang Binglin as an Anti-Manchu Propagandist*. London, Curzon Press.

Lau, Hsiu-Kai and Kuan, Hsin-chi (1988) *The Ethos of the Hong Kong Chinese*. Hong Kong, Chinese University Press.

Le Goff, Jacques (1996) *Das alte Europa und die Welt der Moderne* (Ancient Europe and the World of the Moderns). Munich, Beck.

Lee, Kuo-chi (1975) 'Kultureinfluß Deutschlands auf China im 20. Jahrhundert' (German Cultural Influence in Twentieth Century China). In Joachim Hütterer et al. (eds) *Tradition und Neubeginn: Internationale Forschungen zur deutschen Geschichte im 20. Jahrhundert* (Tradition and Restart: International Research on Germany's Twentieth Century History). Köln, Berlin, Bonn and Munich, Heymann, pp. 215–220.

Liu, I-chou (1996) 'General Discrepancies in Public Attitude on Taiwan's Unification'. *Issues and Studies*, no. 9 (September), pp. 103–121.

Löwenthal, Richard (1979) *Gesellschaftswandel und Kulturkrise: Zukunftsprobleme der westlichen Demokratien* (Social Change and Culture Crisis: Western Democracies' Future Problems). Frankfurt am Main, Fischer Taschenbuch Verlag.

Lübbe, Hermann (1963) *Politische Philosophie in Deutschland* (Political Philosophy in Germany). Basel and Stuttgart, Schwabe.

Meissner, Werner (1990) *Philosophy and Politics in China: The Controversy over Dialectical Materialism in the 1930s*. Stanford and London, Hurst.

—— (1994) *China zwischen nationalem 'Sonderweg' und universaler Modernisierung: Zur Rezeption westlichen Denkens in China* (China Between National 'Sonderweg' and Universal Modernization: On the Reception of Western Thought in China). Munich, Wilhelm Fink Verlag.

—— (1996) *Die Rezeption der westlichen Politikwissenschaft in der VR China, 1987–1992: Eine Bibliographie* (The Reception of Western Political Science in the People's Republic of China, 1987–1992: A Bibliography). Münster, Lit Verlag.

—— (2001) *Western Philosophy in China, 1993–1997: A Bibliography*. Frankfurt, Berlin, Bern, New York, Paris and Vienna, Peter Lang Verlag.

Metzger, Thomas A. and Myers, Ramon H. (1998) 'The True Nature of Chinese Nationalism'. *Orbis*, vol. 42, no. 1 (Winter), pp. 21–36.

Mosse, George L. (1964) *The Crisis of German Ideology: Intellectual Origins of the Third Reich*. New York, Grosset & Dunlap.

Müller-Graff, Peter-Christian (1996) 'The European Union and Eastern European States'. *East–West Dialogue*, vol. 1, no. 1 (June), pp. 43–55.

Nipperdey, Thomas (1968) 'Thomas Morus'. In *Klassiker des politischen Denkens* (Classics of Political Thought), vol. 1, Munich, Beck, pp. 181–198.

Plessner, Helmut (1974) *Die verspaetete Nation* (The Delayed Nation). Koeln and Mainz, Suhrkamp.

Preston, Christopher (1997) *Enlargement and Integration in the European Union*. London and New York, Routledge.

Pye, Lucian (1996) 'How China's Nationalism was Shanghaied'. In Jonathan Unger (ed.) *Chinese Nationalism*. New York, M. E. Sharpe, pp. 86–112.

Reif, Karlheinz (1993) 'Cultural Convergence and Cultural Diversity as Factors in European Identity'. In Soledad García (ed.) *European Identity and the Search for Legitimacy*. London and New York, Pinter Publishers for The Eleni Nakou Foundation and The Royal Institute of International Affairs, pp. 131–153.

Rieff, David (1995) *Slaughterhouse: Bosnia and the Failure of the West*. New York, Simon & Schuster.

Sautmann, Barry (1997) 'Racial Nationalism and Chinese External Behaviour'. *World Affairs*, vol. 160, no. 2 (Fall), pp. 78–96.

Smith, Anthony D. (1991) *National Identity*. Reno, University of Nevada Press.

Snow, Edgar (1978) *Red Star Over China*. Hammondsworth & New York, Penguin.

Stern, Fritz (1986) *Kulturpessimismus als politische Gefahr: Eine Analyse nationaler Ideologie in Deutschland* (Cultural Pessimism as Political Danger: An Analysis of National Ideology in Germany). Munich, Deutscher Taschenbuchverlag.

Stromberg, Roland N. (1973) 'The Intellectuals and the Coming of the War in 1914'. *Journal of European Studies*, no. 3, pp. 109–122.

—— (1981a) *European Intellectual History Since 1789*. 3rd edition. Englewood Cliffs, Prentice-Hall.

—— (1981b) *Redemption by War. The Intellectuals and 1914*. Lawrence, Regents Press of Kansas.

Sun, Yat-sen (1927) *Sanminzhuyi* (Three Principles of the People). Shanghai, Commercial Press (reprint 1981, Taipei, China Pub. Co.).

Tan, Chester C. (1972) *Chinese Political Thought in the Twentieth Century*. Newton Abbot, David and Charles.

The Hong Kong Transition Project, Section 3 (1998) *Patriotism and Identity*. Hong Kong, Hong Kong Baptist University.

Topitsch, Ernst ([1959] 1972) *Vom Ursprung und Ende der Metaphysik* (On the Beginning and End of Metaphysics). Munich, Deutscher Taschenbuch Verlag.

Troeltsch, Ernst (1925) *Deutscher Geist und Westeuropa: Gesammelte kulturphilosophische Aufsätze und Reden* (The German Spirit and Western Europe: Compilation of Philosophical and Cultural Discourses and Essasys). Tübingen, Mohr.

Vierhaus, Rudolf (1952) 'Die Ideologie des deutschen Weges der politischen und sozialen Entwicklung' (The Ideology of Germany's Political and Social Development). In Rudolf von Thadden (ed.) (1978) *Die Krise des Liberalismus zwischen den Weltkriegen* (The Crisis of Liberalism Between the World Wars). Göttingen, Vandenhoeck und Ruprecht, pp. 96–114.

Weidenfeld, Werner (1980) *Der deutsche Weg* (The German Way). Berlin, Siedler.

Zhao, Suisheng (1997) 'Chinese Intellectuals' Quest for National Greatness and Nationalistic Writings in the 1990s'. *China Quarterly*, no. 152, December, pp. 725–745.

10

THE RISE OF A HONG KONG IDENTITY

Steve Tsang

The emergence of a Hong Kong identity as distinct from that of a Chinese identity took a long time. In the first century of British rule, from its foundation as a Crown Colony in 1843 until the Second World War in the middle of the twentieth century, Hong Kong had two distinct communities without a common or distinct identity.[1] Its Chinese residents maintained only limited contacts with the non-Chinese community and only a small number of the local Chinese elite involved themselves with the colonial government which was dominated by expatriate Britons. Indeed, the overwhelming majority of the ethnic Chinese shared much more in common with their fellow countrymen living in China proper than with their non-Chinese fellow citizens of Hong Kong. They were either sojourners or economic migrants or refugees, and were not noticeably different from other Chinese living elsewhere in China.[2] Except for a small group who had taken root locally, most intended to return to their home in China for their retirement or after making sufficient money in this British imperial outpost for a more comfortable life back home. The Chinese community of Hong Kong did not have an identity of its own before the Second World War, and the non-Chinese community was essentially an expatriate one. This situation only began to change fundamentally after 1949 when the Chinese Communist Party (CCP) came to power.

The main concerns of this chapter are to explain the historical context in which a Hong Kong identity developed in the post-war era, to examine what this identity entails, and to assess how the development of this identity has been affected by Hong Kong's demographic, cultural and political links with China. Although the Hong Kong identity which emerged is not exclusive to its citizens of Chinese extraction and many of Hong Kong's settled non-Chinese citizens shared elements of the common outlook, way of life and strong attachment to Hong Kong, the focus of this chapter remains the development of a local identity centred around its Chinese community. This is because the ethnic Chinese have not only always constituted over 95 per cent of Hong Kong's total population but have to reconcile themselves with a basic reality that their non-Chinese fellow citizens do not have to face – the concurrent identity of being Chinese as well.

Origins of an identity

The chaos of the Chinese Civil War (1945–49) which culminated in the Communist victory ushered in one of the periodic influxes into Hong Kong of people who fled from disorder, political persecution or economic hardship in China. However, on this occasion something different happened. As the Communist regime consolidated its position on the mainland of China, the prospect of many of the new immigrants returning to the mainland faded and the Hong Kong government imposed permanent immigration restrictions at the Sino-British border in 1950, to which the People's Republic of China (PRC) government responded by enforcing its own border control. Previously governments on both sides of the border had permitted Chinese persons to enter Hong Kong freely or leave for China without restrictions.[3] Until then there was in fact free and regular movement of people between the two places, which helped to account for the non-development of a sense of local identity among its Chinese residents. For thirty years after the founding of the PRC, movement of people between the two territories was reduced to a trickle (continued mainly by illegal immigration from the PRC to Hong Kong), except for short periods when a relaxation of border control by the PRC for domestic reasons led to an influx into Hong Kong, as happened in 1962 and in the latter half of the 1970s. Communist rule in China had turned the Chinese population of Hong Kong into a settled one. Those born and bred in Hong Kong since 1949 by and large had no first hand experiences of the PRC until the latter opened up in the late 1970s. This separation allowed Hong Kong to develop a political culture and an identity of its own.

After 1949, the PRC and Hong Kong followed different routes as they developed. On the Chinese mainland, the Communist experiments devised under the leadership of Mao Zedong left their marks on its residents. The land reform and its associated political campaigns of the 1950s meant the political persecution of millions of better-off people and the death of about 2 million, the Great Leap Forward of 1958 led to massive starvation that killed between 20 to 30 million, and the Great Proletarian Cultural Revolution (1966–76) brought untold sufferings to an even greater number.[4] All in all, by the admission of the CCP General Secretary in the early 1980s, Hu Yaobang, about 100 million of the PRC's citizens had suffered from some form of persecution in the first three decades of Communist rule. The same period also witnessed the most systematic and virulent attempt by any Chinese regime to destroy its Confucian heritage since Confucianism was made a kind of pre-modern state ideology in the Han dynasty (206 BC–AD 220).[5] The harshness of the early years of Communist rule and the failure of the Maoist road to socialism meant the PRC remained an under-developed country with one of the world's lowest per capita incomes before Deng Xiaoping launched his reform policy in earnest at the end of the 1970s. The outlook and the way of life of the mainland Chinese people were unavoidably affected by the earlier history of the PRC.

In Hong Kong, in sharp contrast, social, economic and political developments unfolded in an orderly and undramatic fashion. After the end of the Second World War the colonial government of Hong Kong had to respond to the twin forces of a world turning increasingly hostile to colonialism and the implied threat to its survival from the rise of the nationalistic and increasingly powerful PRC across the border.[6] It recognized that the restoration of the pre-war colonial rule, which provided for 'too much privilege, snobbery, discrimination, race prejudice, corruption and absentee exploitation' as well as 'disregard for the local people's interests' by the expatriate British elite, was untenable.[7] Slowly but steadily, the colonial government accepted the need to turn itself into an efficient, effective, fair, non-intrusive and basically honest administration which also responded to the needs and wishes of its people, though this fell short of introducing democracy. By the beginning of the 1980s, the Hong Kong government had done so well in meeting these requirements that it finally reached the standard of a good government, as practicable in the traditional expectation of the Chinese – an achievement unsurpassed in the 4,000 years of recorded history of China itself.[8] The basis on which this was built was the Anglo-Saxon concept of the rule of law. Unlike in the PRC where respect for the law fell to its nadir under Mao, who preferred *wufa wutian* (literally, no law and no heaven) or a state of lawlessness, the people of Hong Kong of all ethnic origins accepted the concept of the rule of law in their own time. This, together with the routine safeguarding of freedom in this British enclave, set the people of Hong Kong apart from the people of the PRC and gave the former a sense of a local identity based on a way of life and a world-view markedly different from that in the PRC.[9]

The life experiences of the post-war generations who grew up in Hong Kong also contributed crucially to the rise of a local identity. In the 1950s these generations were mostly too young to be a factor.[10] At that time the bulk of the adult Chinese population had experienced living in China, particularly in the Pearl River Delta. Their own life experiences often involved making a decision to leave China for Hong Kong in search of stability, good order and the prospect for a better life. They were also to a greater or lesser extent affected by or at least aware of the intensity of the struggle for power between the CCP and the Nationalist Party (KMT) in China. They often thought politics in Hong Kong would be some kind of an extension of the brutal power struggle between these two Chinese parties, which continued in the form of an unfinished civil war after the KMT retreated to its redoubt on the island of Taiwan in 1949, where it successfully prevented a Communist invasion.[11] Hence, the overwhelming majority of them preferred not to get involved in what they saw as politics. In any event, most of them were so poor and life in Hong Kong still so hard that they had to focus their attention on earning a living.[12] The 1950s thus passed without the issue of identity being raised seriously.

The emergence of a Hong Kong identity

The coming of age of the first post-war generation, which happened in the 1960s when economic conditions in Hong Kong improved greatly, changed the picture. One of the more thoughtful and articulate members of this generation reflected on his sense of identity at that time in the following terms:

> I am a Chinese born and bred here. Since I am a Chinese it would appear that I should go to the Chinese mainland or Taiwan, where I cannot only do something for my country, but can also have a good future for myself. To tell the truth I had thought of it too. However, my reflections led me to the conclusion that only by staying here can I protect my life and develop a career, for the following reasons:
>
> 1 The Chinese mainland is today under the Chinese Communists and everything there must follow the standard laid down in Mao Tse-tung [Mao Zedong] thought . . . [E]ven if I were willing to give up the freedom and dignity befitting every human being to return to the mainland to be a servant, I would still be purged and struggled against. Not only would I be unable to work for my country, even my personal safety could not be secured;
> 2 Should I go to Taiwan, I could avoid being purged and struggled against for failing to follow the ideology correctly. But that place is the preserve of those with privileges . . . Having been born in Hong Kong, the way of life and habits I have are as different from theirs as if we had come from two worlds . . .
>
> For these reasons, I feel that I had better stay in Hong Kong.
>
> The description above is all about my own affairs. But I think 90 per cent of the Chinese in Hong Kong today share a lot in common and are different only in small ways. The wealth, educational standard and social connections of individuals are mostly different, but the impossibility of returning to the mainland, unwillingness to go to Taiwan, and unsuitability to move overseas are the same for all. Since we all intend to continue to live in Hong Kong, we should change our attitude from being sojourners and visitors to considering ourselves the local people and to caring about the political affairs of Hong Kong and helping to reform them. This is the

> proper attitude when one faces reality. At the same time, if the British can see this fact clearly, they will not have to worry themselves sick unnecessarily, fearing that once the [Hong Kong] Chinese become powerful, they will want to offer Hong Kong to the Chinese Communists. Of course among the four million residents there are some Communists who would like to do so, but they are very few and far between indeed, no more than a few per cent at most. If the overwhelming majority had wanted to join the Communists, they could have returned to the mainland a long time ago rather than live the life of exiles here.[13]

As the 1960s progressed, more and more of the younger generations of locally born and educated ethnic Chinese saw Hong Kong as their home and considered themselves citizens of the territory, though the colonial nature of the government still bothered many of them. The quest for an identity among the younger and increasingly better educated generations of Hong Kong Chinese was not a straightforward linear development.

In the decade which followed, Hong Kong witnessed an intensification of a search for identity, particularly among its higher education students, who were becoming a significant element among local political activists. The strong antipathy which many Hong Kong students felt towards the Communist regime on the mainland, particularly over the spill-over of the Cultural Revolution into Hong Kong in 1967, was replaced by a new enthusiasm for 'mother China' in the early 1970s. This was caused by the PRC's taking over one of the five permanent Security Council seats at the United Nations in late 1971 and, above all, by the historic visit to the PRC by United States President Richard Nixon in early 1972. If these events ignited enormous interest in the PRC, amongst the Chinese in the United States and the Western world, they hit most Hong Kong people, especially the undergraduates, like a bombshell.[14] Suddenly they were confronted with the fact that the government in Beijing had catapulted China into the rank of a great power, which also implied the wiping away of much of China's alleged humiliation at the hands of the Western powers following the first Anglo-Chinese War (1839–42). A surge of a sense of national pride in being a Chinese person swept many off their feet. Out of this, a movement amongst higher education students was born which aimed to 'know the mother country' and embrace the regime which gave them back the pride as Chinese persons.[15] As part of their search for an identity, they also started a movement which aimed to have the Chinese language recognized as the second official language in Hong Kong, an objective which was ultimately achieved in 1974.

This phase of almost euphoric enthusiasm among Hong Kong's students did not last, however. Their understanding of the PRC was, at best superficial. They too readily took Maoist propaganda at face value in the early

1970s as they were driven by some kind of blind patriotism towards 'mother China', which many of them equated in this period with the PRC. A critical few were bewildered by various political campaigns in the PRC, such as the 'Anti-Lin Biao and Anti-Confucius campaign', which really had the widely respected Premier Zhou Enlai as the main target, while Deng Xiaoping was to fall from power in 1975. Nevertheless, most tried to put a positive gloss over such events and avoided or ignored the reality. When the vicious nature of power struggle in the PRC was unveiled and their naïveté exposed by the dramatic fall from power of the Maoist 'Gang of Four' shortly after Mao Zedong's death in 1976, their illusion could not but be shattered.[16] The young students and intellectuals of Hong Kong who were so certain of their fate only a few years earlier entered another phase of reflection and focused themselves more on trying to understand the society in which they lived.

In the meantime, several major developments happened in Hong Kong. To begin with, there was the colonial government's successful attempt to tackle bureaucratic corruption. Corruption was not a new problem in the 1970s. Like most societies, Hong Kong had suffered from corruption from its foundation, but the problem got much more serious in the 1960s.[17] An earnest attempt to tackle it was started by Governor Sir David Trench when he introduced the Prevention of Bribery Ordinance in December 1970. Armed with new power from this ordinance, the Royal Hong Kong Police started an investigation of one of its senior officers, Chief Superintendent Peter Godber, who had earlier earned a reputation for being efficient and courageous. Having previously commanded the police at the airport and still possessing a pass for the restricted area there, Godber slipped out of Hong Kong and fled to the United Kingdom with relative ease in 1973, after he realized he was about to be charged. This caused a tremendous outbreak of public indignation, which reflected on the one hand the increasing political maturity of its people, who were by then ready to take part in local political protests, and on the other hand the cynicism with which they looked at the colonial government. The Godber case had become in the public mind a test case not only of the government's determination to curb corruption but also of its integrity, honesty and responsiveness to public opinions. The colonial government, by then under Governor Sir Murray MacLehose, responded by taking the anti-corruption work out of police hands and assigning it to a brand new agency, the Independent Commission Against Corruption (ICAC), which would be answerable directly to the Governor. As the core of the administration was not corrupt, there was – contrary to the misguided public belief at the time – little resistance from within the establishment to oppose this determined anti-corruption drive. After it was established in February 1974, ICAC put special emphasis on extraditing Godber from the United Kingdom to face trial in Hong Kong. The independent judiciary duly convicted and jailed this former senior officer in due course. By doing so, this case – which for a while symbolized in the public imagination the corrupt nature of the colonial government – was turned into a show case of the government's determination and ability to tackle corruption. The success of the anti-corruption campaign became more and more visible as the 1970s drew to a close, and it gave the people of Hong Kong something to be proud of for being its citizens.

While this was happening, the Hong Kong government also wisely used its rapidly rising revenue to provide welfare for the under-privileged, before there was a strong public demand for it. Hitherto, Hong Kong's public housing scheme was mainly an emergency measure to help and resettle those who were affected or threatened by natural calamities or human disasters. Under Governor MacLehose the government launched a ten-year housing scheme boldly promising that this 'would lead to the virtual disappearance of squatter areas, eliminate overcrowding and sharing in both private and public housing (. . .) and would also keep pace with the natural expansion of the population'.[18] This new initiative was undertaken mainly because it had become affordable, since Hong Kong's economy had done spectacularly well in the preceding decade, having increased per capita GDP by 2.8 times.[19] Be that as it may, it caught the imagination of the people. This was complemented by real progress in other welfare matters, such as the introduction of universal free education for nine years and a public assistance scheme. These welfare programmes and the effects of the anti-corruption campaign changed the public perception of the government. The colonial government acquired an honest, responsive and caring image, in addition to its long-established image of being efficient, effective and non-intrusive into the life of the common people. It was only at the end of the 1970s that the Hong Kong government reached the stage of being a good government, as understood in the Confucian tradition. Thus, it became a government which the people of Hong Kong, of whatever ethnic origins, would by and large identify as their own without shame or unease.

Starting in the 1970s, Hong Kong also developed a vibrant local popular culture which increasingly mixed ideas and techniques from Western music and films with the local culture and concerns of everyday life. As the anthropologist Helen Siu aptly observed, 'the musical genres which came out of this process generally combined three elements: concern for the plight of the common folk, resonance with Chinese heroic times and their characters, and a soft touch for personal liberation and romantic love'.[20] A similar pattern developed for the locally produced films and, more importantly, television programmes. They departed from the earlier mainstream cultural productions which were dominated by the more traditional Chinese art form, and those imported from Taiwan or the PRC.[21] This indigenization of popular music, film and television programmes made visible and further reinforced the outlooks, aspirations and expressions of an increasingly distinctive culture.[22] The popular culture which emerged was based on the Cantonese language but its liveliness and vibrancy also modified the language

– by the introduction of new terms and usages – to the extent that it became recognizably different from the Cantonese then in use in Guangzhou. This new Hong Kong culture was not only embraced by the younger generations but was also accepted by the older generations generally across the classes. As a largely immigrant society in which many new fortunes were made in a generation or less, the class barrier against the spread of this new popular culture was weak. In time, this new Hong Kong popular culture would become so strong and vibrant that it would be exported to the PRC, Taiwan, Singapore and many overseas Chinese communities across the world.

The same period also saw Hong Kong's economy expand at a pace which made its previously fast growth rate look modest. Per capita GDP grew by five times between 1971 and 1981 in comparison to the 2.8 times achieved in the preceding decade.[23] It enabled a generation of hard-working and shrewd Chinese immigrants to turn themselves into self-made men and women. It also raised the profile and self-respect of the local Chinese, and created the image that Hong Kong was full of opportunities. As the 1970s drew to a close, some of the self-make billionaires had become so successful that they were in a position to challenge or even take over some of the symbols of the British establishment, the *hongs*, those business conglomerates which played a key role in the founding of Hong Kong as a Crown Colony more than a century ago. When Li Ka-shing, an immigrant from China who started his working life as an apprentice and a clerk in a clock and watch shop, purchased in 1979 John D. Hutchison, one of the sparkling gems of the original British *hongs* founded in 1828, it showed how far the Hong Kong Chinese had come from the immediate post-war years when most had to work long hours just to feed their families.[24] If the successes of Li, shipping magnate Sir Yue-kong Pao and others like them demonstrated to the Hong Kong Chinese what their most capable members could do, the swelling of the rank of the middle class, the spread of professional training and their maturing as middle managers of Hong Kong's economic successes gave them confidence and pride.[25] A Hong Kong way of life had by then become increasingly visible.

The rising affluence of Hong Kong also enabled its people to travel, not least to the PRC, which opened itself to outside visitors in the latter part of the 1970s. Those who went overseas for holidays, and thus acquired a point of reference for comparison, often came back assured in their mind of the great achievements made by Hong Kong, as well as of the idea that Hong Kong was a community with its own character.[26] For those who went to the PRC, particularly young students seeking to know 'mother China', they found themselves confronted with a harsh reality. The PRC that they saw was not quite the same as the 'mother China' they had imagined. The backwardness and the imprimatur of Maoist rule on the people and way of life in the PRC could not but make an indelible impression on them. The brutality of the Maoist rule and the destruction of the Confucian moral order could be seen in the behaviour of the ordinary people in the PRC. From first-hand experiences most, if not all, Hong Kong visitors came to realize that despite the common ethnic and cultural background, the Chinese of Hong Kong were different from the Chinese of the PRC. The two had different outlooks and ways of life.

Reinforcing the impressions that Hong Kong travellers to the PRC gained was the influx of illegal Chinese immigrants to Hong Kong from 1978 to 1980, which also led to the Hong Kong government ending what was popularly known as the 'touch base policy'. Although the border was closed in 1950, the Hong Kong government operated on a fairly liberal basis towards illegal immigrants from China for most of the following three decades. In general, an illegal immigrant from China who reached the urban areas of Hong Kong and settled there (i.e. touched base), either by being united with family members or by successfully obtaining lawful employment, would be permitted to stay, eventually gaining citizenship after seven years of residence.[27] This policy was abandoned in 1980, when the sustained nature and scale of the influx was seen to be eroding the improvement in standards that the people of Hong Kong had been working so hard to achieve.[28] The newly acquired wealth of Hong Kong and the large scale of the influx, which numbered over half a million in a period of about three years, created problems with assimilation in the short term. Since the overwhelming majority of the new immigrants were young male farmers from rural communes, who had been cut off from the world and brought up in Maoist ideology, they found Hong Kong's pace of life and multicultural energies most perplexing in the early days.[29] The difficulties they had in assimilating into Hong Kong society led to discrimination and mockery from the locally born, who created negative stereotypes of them, such as Ah Chan and Dai Huen Chai, which quickly gained public currency through the mass media, particularly the television.[30] The ending of the touch base policy and the gap existing between the locals and the new immigrants thus created a sense of us (Hong Kong people) and them (country-bumpkins from mainland China, or Ah Chan). This recognition of difference was essential for the emergence of a distinct Hong Kong identity, which became unmistakable as Hong Kong entered the 1980s.[31]

In this process the younger and mainly locally born, bred and educated generations played the primary role. However, the older generations who had arrived from China as economic migrants or refugees also shared the experiences of the younger people, watched the same television programmes, listened to the same new indigenous music, and became, though to a lesser extent, noticeably different from their mainland compatriots.

The Hong Kong identity in the 1980s

This Hong Kong identity which came about was based on a shared outlook and a common popular culture which blended traditional Chinese culture with that imported from overseas, with the influences of the United States, the United Kingdom and Japan being particularly noticeable. This shared outlook incorporated elements of the traditional Confucian moral code and the emphasis on the importance of the family, as well as modern concepts like the rule of law, freedom of speech and movement, respect for human rights, a limited government, a free economy, a go-getting attitude, and pride in the local community's collective rejection of corruption. A Hong Kong person of the early 1980s would identify with Hong Kong and at the same time feel at ease with both a Chinese heritage and, for those who claimed British nationality, travelling on a British passport issued by the Hong Kong government.[32] However, described by social anthropologist Hugh Baker as 'Hong Kong Man', he was 'not British or Western (merely Westernized)' and at the same time 'not Chinese in the same way that citizens of the People's Republic of China were Chinese'.[33] He belonged to Hong Kong and was intensely proud of it.

The rise of a Hong Kong identity among its Chinese residents at the beginning of the 1980s did not mean they no longer felt they were Chinese as well. A sense of identity is inherently a complicated and complex matter as it ultimately relies on people in a community choosing to identify with a country or a territory, and it does not need to be totally exclusive. Given the lack of any serious attempt by the British colonial administration to turn its locally born ethnic Chinese citizens into yellow Englishmen or even require them to adopt British nationality as a matter of course, most people in Hong Kong were fairly relaxed in their sense of identity. Indeed, locally born Chinese would be asked which nationality – British or Chinese – they would claim at the age of 18, at which point they were required by law to acquire an identity card. If they were born in the Colony, choosing to claim Chinese nationality would not preclude them from changing their mind in later life and registering as British subjects – the fact of being born in Hong Kong, while it was under British law, would be sufficient to entitle them to claim back their British nationality. The relaxed attitude of the colonial government allowed the Chinese in Hong Kong to have a dual sense of identity, feeling both a Hong Kong person and a Chinese person at the same time.

The Chinese identity that most Hong Kong belongers subscribed to is a complex and perhaps even convoluted one. Except for the new immigrants who had not yet been assimilated, being Chinese in Hong Kong was primarily an ethnic and cultural affiliation and generally did not mean being a Chinese citizen or national of the PRC. It often meant being a Hong Kong person of Chinese descent. The way the Hong Kong Chinese viewed this matter has been insightfully captured by David Faure:

> 'China' was to the Chinese what Christendom was to the West. 'China' was ideology and religion. He or she who is a Chinese believes in China. But that is not all. To be Chinese, he or she has also to be part of China.[34]

On how to meet the last requirement, there was no consensus among the Chinese of Hong Kong. To some, the fact that this British Colony was 'a borrowed place living in borrowed time'[35] secured from China was sufficient proof that Hong Kong was part of China. To others, their own provincial origins in China, whether it meant being Cantonese, Hunanese or something else, entitled them to claim to be part of China. A minority continued to identify with either of the two Chinese governments, in Beijing or in Taipei, both of which continued in this period to claim themselves the sole legitimate government of China. Thus, feeling Chinese and at the same time developing a Hong Kong identity, which distinguished one from a citizen of the PRC, did not produce a crisis of identity in the early 1980s.

Consequently, when a Hong Kong person referred to 'China', it was not always clear what he or she had in mind. Sometimes it meant China in a geographical or cultural sense, for which Hong Kong, Taiwan and Macao were deemed as much a part as the PRC. At other times it meant the mythical China they had in mind which did not have a clearly defined territorial confine. On yet other occasions it meant the PRC. The average Hong Kong person did not make a clear distinction between these concepts and did not refer to them consistently.

The Chinese people of Hong Kong found themselves jolted out of the complacency with which they looked at the identity issue after the governments of the United Kingdom and the PRC announced the beginning of negotiations over the future of Hong Kong in 1982. The negotiations were conducted as a bilateral affair between London and Beijing with no elected representative from Hong Kong involved. Even the unspoken assumption on the British and Hong Kong side that Governor Sir Edward Youde would represent Hong Kong was pointedly and publicly dismissed by Beijing.[36] Out of a sense of impotence and frustration in not being a party to the negotiations over their own future was born a new political activism among the people of Hong Kong. This provided impetus for a steadily rising demand for democratization and for further reflections on the question of identity.

The signing of the Sino-British Joint Declaration in December 1984 settled the future of Hong Kong – to be handed over by Britain to the PRC in 1997. This meant Hong Kong would become part of the PRC, albeit in the form of a Special Administrative Region. Except for a relatively small number who had acquired citizenship of the United Kingdom itself by residence, most Hong Kong Chinese who claimed British nationality under the British Nationality Act of 1981 saw their British connection diluted. Their status was changed from that of citizens of the United Kingdom and Colonies to that of British Dependent Territories citizens who, under this new law, specifically enjoyed no right of abode in the UK, a legal right now confined to British citizens. Even their new British Dependent Territories citizenship would end in 1997, at which point they, but not their descendants, could retain a status (British Nationals Overseas) that would allow them to use passports issued by the British government for travel but not for settlement in the United Kingdom.[37] Thus, by the time the Joint Declaration was signed, it was blatantly clear that most Hong Kong citizens of Chinese origin would become PRC nationals by 1997. As this political reality gradually sank in, more and more felt they had no choice but somehow to identify themselves with the PRC. The upshot was the gradual emergence of a new dual identity of belonging to both Hong Kong and the PRC – although in the language of the locals, the PRC was referred to, as in the old dual identity, simply as 'China'. However, there was a subtle but important change in the second identity that most Hong Kong Chinese held: the feeling of being a Chinese. Whereas a few years earlier being Chinese was an ambiguous idea meaning different things to different individuals, and being a national of the PRC only applied to very few, increasingly, being Chinese meant being a national of the PRC, albeit of a special category.[38]

Identity and crisis

This new dual identity of the Hong Kong Chinese had important implications in the realm of wider politics, which in turn impacted upon the development of a Hong Kong identity. On the one hand, as Hong Kong citizens, they wanted to preserve their own way of life under the principle of 'one country, two systems', which required non-intervention in each other's affairs by both the PRC and Hong Kong. On the other hand, feeling that they were PRC nationals too, they believed they had a right to have a say in vital matters affecting the future of the nation, which inevitably involved PRC politics. Few among the Chinese of Hong Kong could see there was in fact an inherent contradiction between asserting their right to have a say in the politics of the PRC and their demand that the PRC should not interfere into Hong Kong's domestic affairs. This dual identity made most Hong Kong Chinese over-react to a series of dramatic events in the PRC in the first half of 1989. When the students and the citizens of Beijing launched a 'democracy movement' in Tian'anmen Square, at a time when the wish of the Hong Kong Chinese for further democratic development was stalled in Hong Kong, they became emotionally involved and wanted to play a meaningful and essentially supportive role. When they supported the students by donating money, they were behaving both as citizens of Hong Kong and as proto-citizens of the PRC. Their identification with the 'democracy movement' turned them, in their minds, into instant comrades with the Beijing protesters.[39] Many had taken the view that the future for democratization in Hong Kong was linked to the development of democracy in the PRC. When tanks rolled into Tian'anmen Square and Chinese soldiers machine-gunned protesters in Beijing, many in Hong Kong watched these events on television. Their anguish and outrage were no less than that of

Beijing citizens.[40] They were frustrated about the fact that there was little they could do to help but watch in agony. However, they were also thankful to be saved from the fate of their comrades and compatriots by the Union flag which continued to fly over their heads in Hong Kong until 1997. This security and protection which they craved also gave them what one may perhaps call the survivor's guilt complex. Consequently, they attempted to do anything which might ease their conscience, such as trying to force a run on PRC-owned banks in Hong Kong by withdrawing their deposits or staging massive demonstrations.[41] None of these actions could help the hapless protesters in Beijing or save the movement from being ground to dust, but they eased to an extent the intense pain brought about by their own failure to stand by their comrades under fire. The Tian'anmen protests and massacre brought to a head the problems inherent in their new dual identity.

The immediate impact of the traumatic experiences was to reinforce their dual identity. On the one hand, the events in Beijing reminded them in the most powerful way how very different the political culture, the nature of politics and law enforcement, the way of life, the integrity of the judiciary, and the fate of human rights were north of the border, and thus highlighted the substance of their Hong Kong identity. On the other hand, the idea that what occurred in Beijing could also happen to them after the handover in less than a decade drove home the inescapable fact that they were at least PRC nationals in waiting. Torn between identification with both Hong Kong and the PRC, and at the same time, terrified of the brutal and harsh reality of PRC politics, a significant number of Hong Kong Chinese ended up choosing one of two extreme options.

At one end of the spectrum were those who had the option to emigrate choosing to leave. The number of those who emigrated from Hong Kong averaged about 20,000 each year in the early 1980s, started to rise in 1987, and shot up to 62,000 in 1990, the year when the impact of the Tian'anmen incident was felt.[42] Many of those who left did not do so because they wanted to dissociate themselves from Hong Kong. On the contrary, most kept their emotional attachment to and interest in the territory. Indeed, in the more popular destinations of Hong Kong's emigrants, such as Vancouver in Canada, these new arrivals 'carried with them many of the feelings of pride in Hong Kong's accomplishments over the course of three decades' and changed many different aspects of the overseas Chinese community there.[43] They were reluctant exiles who chose to escape for personal safety and a future in the free world for their children, but they remained emotionally identified with Hong Kong and, to a lesser extent and mainly in a negative way, with the PRC.

At the other end of the spectrum, a significant number of those who stayed in Hong Kong opted to continue the campaign to support democratization in China. This was manifested in their continued support for the Alliance in Support of the Patriotic and Democratic Movement in China, a

Hong Kong organization whose original objective, the overthrow of the lawfully constituted government of the PRC (however odious it might be) by extra-constitutional means, was justifiably deemed subversive by the PRC government.[44] Their emotional commitment to and sense of guilt about the Tian'anmen incident affected their ability to put matters in perspective. They failed to see and accept that the basis for Hong Kong to secure special treatment from the PRC government in 1997, laid down in the 'one country, two systems' principle, required Hong Kong people not to interfere in the politics of the PRC. In other words, they acted against both the best interest of Hong Kong, which needed them not to give the PRC government any excuse to intervene in Hong Kong affairs, and the cause for democracy in the PRC, which would not have been served by inviting Beijing to react to subversion by limiting the scope and pace of democratization in Hong Kong itself. Their stronger sense of identification with the PRC clouded their judgement about what action would serve the best interest of Hong Kong and its citizens, of which they were a part.

In the middle of the spectrum, where most of the general public felt, the existence of a dual sense of identity was reflected in voting behaviour. They shared with the emigrants the fear of the prospect of PRC sovereignty, and with the active supporters of the Alliance they shared antipathy towards the PRC government. Thus, in the elections for the Hong Kong Legislative Council in 1991, two years after the Tian'anmen incident, they let various candidates' stance over the Tian'anmen incident become 'the single most important variable determining their vote'.[45] Their wish 'to assert their defiance to the Chinese government with respect to the June 4th Incident' ensured the defeat for all pro-China candidates.[46] Although the same desire still affected the results of the elections of 1995, its effect was noticeably reduced. Pro-PRC candidates managed to win 16 seats out of a council of 60. The mellowing of their reactions to the Tian'anmen factor was due partly to the effect of time and partly to a recognition that the handover was less than two years away. The conflicting urges inherent in the dual identity of the Hong Kong Chinese – the Hong Kong belongers who saw the preservation of the way of life in Hong Kong as paramount, and the PRC nationals who considered it their basic right to take part in the politics of the PRC – continued to interact under the protection accorded by the continuation of British sovereignty. Nevertheless, the psychological value of this protective effect was fading.

The PRC's assumption of sovereignty over Hong Kong in July 1997 changed the context in which the conflicting urges of the Hong Kong Chinese's dual identity interacted. Now that British protection was removed, the survival instinct dictated caution. Pragmatism prevailed and the existence of the political imperative – the basic need for Hong Kong not to provoke or provide a pretext for interference from the PRC government – was accepted. There is still a dual identity among the Hong Kong Chinese, which produces conflicting urges. However, they have no choice but to try to strike a balance between these urges or try to reconcile them. They still think first and foremost of themselves as Hong Kong belongers, but they also now accept that they are PRC nationals too, though they still insist on distinguishing themselves as a special group of PRC nationals distinct from the rest of the PRC citizens.

Notes

1 Tsang (1995: 233).
2 Tsang (1990: 11).
3 British Government Colonial Office archives at Kew (1956) CO1030/383. Annex to Officer administering the government, HK to Secretary of State, savingram 1744, 10 October.
4 For the scale of execution in the early Maoist years, see Domes (1973: 51). For the scale of death by starvation as a result of the Great Leap Forward, see Becker (1996: 266–274) and Banister (1987). For a single-volume treatment of the Cultural Revolution, see Barnouin and Yu (1993).
5 For a comparative study of the fate of the Chinese culture in the PRC, Hong Kong and Taiwan after 1949, see Tsang (1997b: 30–45).
6 For a detailed and critical assessment of how the British dealt with the implied threat from the PRC, see Tsang (1997c: 294–317).
7 Tsang (1988: 27).
8 For a detailed treatment of this subject, see Tsang (1997d: 62–83).
9 *Ming bao* (1982).
10 Faure (1997a: 9).
11 The unfinished civil war only ended in the early 1990s after democratization in Taiwan had changed the political landscape there and the ruling party (by now ruled on the basis of electoral results) ceased to claim jurisdiction over all of China and accepted the *de facto* separation of Taiwan from China as a reality.
12 For an illustration of how hard life was in 1950s Hong Kong, see Faure (1997a: 254).
13 Quoted from Tsang (1995: 248–249).
14 For the impact of the Nixon visit on US opinions, see Mosher (1990: 144–159).
15 Kuo (1980: 65).
16 The 'Gang of Four' was formally headed by Jiang Qing, Mao's wife. The other members were all Maoists promoted to top positions as a result of the Cultural Revolution. They were Chang Chunqiao, Wang Hongwen and Yao Wenyuan. They were close followers of Mao.
17 For a full treatment of the corruption problem in Hong Kong, see Tsang (1995: 175–194). See also Lethbridge (1978) and Lo (1993).
18 *Hong Kong Hansard – Session 1972–3* (1973: 4).
19 Hong Kong Census and Statistics Department (1996: 13).
20 Siu (1996: 184).
21 Yao (1983: 10–20).
22 Siu (1996: 184).
23 Hong Kong Census and Statistics Department (1996: 13).

24 Chan (1996: 81).
25 For Pao's success story, see Hutcheon (1990).
26 Ye (1997: 47).
27 Tsang (1995: 286).
28 *Hong Kong Hansard 1980* (1981). Governor MacLehose's speech of 23 October 1980.
29 Siu (1996: 187).
30 Cantonese rather than *pinyin* transliteration is used for these terms as they were used in Hong Kong and gained common currency there.
31 Lau and Kuan (1988: 178).
32 Tsang (1994: 138).
33 Baker (1983: 478).
34 Faure (1997b: 105).
35 Concept borrowed from Hughes (1968).
36 *Pai shing* (1983: 7–8).
37 *A Draft Agreement between the Government of the United Kingdom of Great Britain and Northern Ireland and the Government of the People's Republic of China on the Future of Hong Kong* (1984: 31).
38 Liu (1998: 7).
39 Tsang (1997a: 156–163, particularly, 163–166).
40 There are numerous books and articles on the Tian'anmen protests and massacre. For a particularly insightful and fair account, see Wong (1997: 225–279).
41 *Dongfang ribao* (1989) and *Xin bao* (1989).
42 *Hong Kong 1991: A Review of 1990* (1991: 375).
43 Johnson (1994: 136).
44 For a collection of the Alliance's public statements, see Xianggang shimin jiyuan aiguo minzhu tundong (1998).
45 Scott (1992: 12).
46 Leung (1993: 202).

References and further reading

A Draft Agreement between the Government of the United Kingdom of Great Britain and Northern Ireland and the Government of the People's Republic of China on the Future of Hong Kong (1984). Hong Kong, Government Printers.

Baker, Hugh (1983) 'Life in the Cities: The Emergence of Hong Kong Man'. *China Quarterly*, no. 95 (September), pp. 467–479.

Banister, Judith (1987) *China's Changing Population*. Stanford, Stanford University Press.

Barnouin, Barbara and Yu, Changgen (1993) *Ten Years of Turbulence: The Chinese Cultural Revolution*. London and New York, Kegan Paul.

Becker, Jasper (1996) *Hungry Ghosts: China's Secret Famine*. London, John Murray.

British Government Colonial Office (1956) CO1030/383, Annex to OAG (Office Administering the Government), HK to Secretary of State, Savingram 1744, 10 October.

Chan, Anthony B. (1996) *Li Ka-Shing: Hong Kong's Elusive Billionaire*. Hong Kong, Oxford University Press.

Domes, Jurgen (1973) *The Internal Politics of China, 1949–1972*. London, Hurst & Company.
Dongfang ribao (1989) 5 June.
Faure, David (ed.) (1997a) *Society: A Documentary History of Hong Kong, vol. 2*. Hong Kong, Hong Kong University Press.
—— (1997b) 'Reflections on Being Chinese in Hong Kong'. In Judith Brown and Rosemary Foot (eds) *Hong Kong's Transitions, 1842–1997*. Basingstoke, Macmillan, pp. 103–120.
Hong Kong 1991: A Review of 1990 (1991). Hong Kong, Government Printers.
Hong Kong Hansard – Session 1972–3 (1973). Hong Kong, Government Printers.
Hong Kong Hansard 1980 (1981). Hong Kong, Government Printers.
Hong Kong Census and Statistics Department (1996) *Estimates of Gross Domestic Product 1961 to 1995*. Hong Kong, Census and Statistics Department.
Hughes, Richard (1968) *Borrowed Place Borrowed Time: Hong Kong and its Many Faces*. London, Andre Deutsch.
Hutcheon, Robin (1990) *First Sea Lord: The Life and Work of Sir Y. K. Pao*. Hong Kong, Chinese University of Hong Kong Press.
Johnson, Graham (1994) 'Hong Kong Immigration and the Chinese Community'. In Ronald Skeldon (ed.) *Reluctant Exiles? Migration from Hong Kong and the New Overseas Chinese*. Armonk NY, M. E. Sharpe, pp. 120–138.
Kuo, Shaotang (1980) 'Qishiniandai houqi de Xianggang xueyue' (The Student Movement in Hong Kong in the Late 1970s). *Qishi niandai*, no. 123 (April), pp. 65–66.
Lau, Siu-kai and Kuan, Hsin-chi (1988) *The Ethos of the Hong Kong Chinese*. Hong Kong, Chinese University Press.
Lethbridge, Henry (1978) *Hard Craft in Hong Kong*. Hong Kong, Oxford University Press.
Leung, Sai-wing (1993) 'The 'China Factor' in the 1991 Legislative Council Election'. In Siu-Kai Lau and Kin-Sheun Louie (eds) *Hong Kong Tried Democracy*. Hong Kong, Hong Kong Institute of Asia-Pacific Studies, pp. 187–235.
Liu, Shaojie (Siu-kai Lau) (1998) '"Xianggang ren" huo "Zhongguo ren": Xianggang huaren de shengfen, 1985–1995' (Hong Kong People or Chinese People: The Identity of the Chinese of Hong Kong, 1985–1995). In Qingfeng Liu and Xiaochun Guan (eds), *Zhuanhuazong de Xianggang* (Hong Kong in Transition). Hong Kong, Zhongwen daxue chubanshe, pp. 3–30.
Lo, T. Wing (1993) *Corruption and Politics in Hong Kong and China*. Buckingham, Open University Press.
Ming bao (1982) Editorial, 31 August.
Mosher, Stephen (1990) *China Misperceived: American Illusions and Chinese Reality*. New York, New Republic Book.
Pai shing (1983) 16 July.
Scott, Ian (1992) 'An Overview of the Hong Kong Legislative Council Elections of 1991'. In Roena Kwok, Joan Leung and Ian Scott (eds), *Votes Without Power: The Hong Kong Legislative Council Elections 1991*. Hong Kong, Hong Kong University Press, pp. 1–28.
Siu, Helen (1996) 'Remade in Hong Kong: Weaving Into the Chinese Cultural Tapestry'. In Taotao Liu and David Faure (eds), *Unity and Diversity: Local Cultures and Identities in China*. Hong Kong, Hong Kong University Press, pp. 177–196.

Tsang, Steve (1988) *Democracy Shelved: Great Britain, China, and Attempts at Constitutional Reform in Hong Kong, 1945–1952*. Hong Kong, Oxford and New York, Oxford University Press.

—— (1990) 'Identity Crisis in Hong Kong'. *Hong Kong Monitor*, September, pp. 11–12.

—— (1994) 'Political Problems Facing the Hong Kong Civil Service in Transition'. *Hong Kong Public Administration*, vol. 3, no. 1 (March), pp. 133–145.

—— (1995) *Government and Politics: A Documentary History of Hong Kong, Volume I*. Hong Kong, Hong Kong University Press.

—— (1997a) *Hong Kong: An Appointment With China*. London, I. B. Tauris.

—— (1997b) 'The Confucian Tradition and Democratization'. In Yossi Shain and Aharon Kieman (eds) *Democracy: The Challenges Ahead*. Basingstoke, Macmillan, pp. 30–47.

—— (1997c) 'Strategy for Survival: The Cold War and Hong Kong's Policy towards Kuomintang and Chinese Communist Activities in the 1950s'. *Journal of Imperial and Commonwealth History*, vol. 25, no. 2 (May), pp. 294–317.

—— (1997d) 'Government and Politics in Hong Kong: A Colonial Paradox'. In Judith Brown and Rosemary Foot (eds) *Hong Kong's Transitions, 1842–1997*. Basingstoke, Macmillan, pp. 62–83.

Wong, Jan (1997) *Red China Blues*. Toronto, Bantam.

Xianggang Shimin Jiyuan Aiguo Minzhu Yundong (ed.) (Movement of Hong Kong's Democratic and Patriotic Citizens) (1998) *Lishi xuanyan* (Historical Manifestos). Hong Kong, Ciwenhua youxian gongsi.

Xin bao (1989) 6 June.

Yao, Yao (1983) 'Xing Se Yi' (Music, Sex and Art). In Dale Lu (ed.), *Puji wenfa zai Xianggang* (Popular Culture in Hong Kong). Hong Kong, Zhuguang, pp. 10–20.

Ye, Yincong (1997) 'Bianyuan yu yunji de qiuling' (The Wandering Spirit in the Peripehry and in Confusion). In Qingqiao Chen (ed.), *Wenhua xiangxiang yu yishi xingtai: Dangdai Xianggang wenhua zhengzhi lunping* (Cultural Imaginary and Ideology: Contemporary Hong Kong Culture and Politics Review). Hong Kong, Niujin daxue chubanshe, pp. 31–52.

11

CONSOLIDATING TAIWAN'S NEW DEMOCRACY AMID COMPETING NATIONAL IDENTITIES

Yun-han Chu and Chia-lung Lin

Taiwan's transition from authoritarianism involved more than just a legitimacy crisis of the old regime. It also called into question the legitimacy of the state: its claims over sovereignty status, jurisdiction boundary, and citizenship compass. For several decades, the old regime justified its ruling legitimacy and the mainlander elite its political dominance on the basis of the 'one China principle'. Political opening has roused the long-suppressed Taiwanese consciousness, the society's quest for an independent international identity, and the conflicts between Taiwanese nationalism and Chinese nationalism over the statehood issue. As a result, struggles over democratic reform and redistribution of political power between the mainlander group and native Taiwanese become entangled with national identity disputes and issues related to Taiwan's future political relation with mainland China. Since very early on, leaders of the opposition have linked the goal of democratization directly to the issue of Taiwanese identity and the principle of self-determination.

The issue of national identity became the most unsettling factor in Taiwan's democratization as this issue, much like ethnic conflicts, revolves around the exclusive concept of legitimacy and symbol of worth. The nature of Taiwan's national identity crisis, however, differs from the secessionist-oriented interethnic struggles that have disintegrated the Soviet Union and Yugoslavia. Taiwan's internal debate tends to focus on *de jure* independence and not on *de facto* territorial separation from the state authority, considering the two sides of the Taiwan Strait have long been under separate government jurisdictions. Nonetheless, both the dangers of internal political polarization and external intervention, which are inherent in any dispute over the territorial structure of the state, are ever-present. Internally, the crisis involves a clash between two seemingly irreconcilable emotional claims about Taiwan's statehood and the national identity of the people of Taiwan. The Taiwanese nationalists advocate Taiwanese nationalism and seek permanent separation from China, while the Chinese nationalists oppose movement toward independence and favour eventual re-unification with China. In the end, the state becomes the arena in which competing forces strive to gain control of the ruling apparatus and use its power to erect a new cultural hegemony and impose its own vision of nation-building in the direction of either Taiwanization or sinicization. Externally, there is also a tug-of-war across the Taiwan Strait between two competing nation-building processes, as the People's Republic of China (PRC) also attempts to impose its vision of nation-building, i.e. the 'one country, two systems' model, on Taiwan and threatens to use military means if necessary to stop the movement toward independence.

This chapter aims to analyse the relations between Taiwan's democracy-building, state-building and nation-building. It explains why the Taiwanese identity arose, what the nature of this identity is, and how its development has interacted with the dynamics of the Cross-Strait relations. We argue that national identity is not inborn, but a socially and politically constructed sentiment that is subject to change, especially under the intensive mobilization of political elites at times of regime transition. More specifically, electoral opening has enabled the major opposition Democratic Progressive Party (DPP) to cultivate its social base in terms of ethnic and national identity. At the same time, the logic of electoral competition has compelled the incumbent Nationalist Party (KMT) to accelerate its process of Taiwanization both in terms of ideological claim and power structure. However, just as the new KMT leadership under Lee Teng-hui has registered some success in narrowing the ideological distance with the DPP, Beijing's suspicion over Taipei's hidden agenda of creeping independence grew sharply. The increasing hostility from the Chinese Communist regime has given rise to a sense of shared destiny among the people of Taiwan and fostered the growth of a new political identity that is civic in nature.

This chapter begins by clarifying some key concepts related to nationalism and analysing how the Taiwanese people's national identity and position on the statehood issue have changed over the democratization process. It then investigates how the people of Taiwan perceive the terms 'Taiwanese' and 'Chinese', whether primordially, territorially or subjectively. It will be pointed out that, for most people, Taiwanese identity is more than an ethnic identity, but a political and civic identity. Also, a significant portion of the population has multiple identities, self-identifying as both Taiwanese and Chinese. The following section examines the Taiwanese people's attitude towards solving the statehood issue via democratic procedures. Surveys found the majority of the population willing to accept a plebiscite as a means of determining Taiwan's political future, provided that the process is not rushed. We further elaborate on how Taiwan's democratization and the

Cross-Strait tension have jointly shaped Taiwan's identity politics. This chapter will conclude by bringing the issue of national security into our discussion through a two-level game perspective and by exploring the prospect of whether the new democracy can defend itself in the red shadow.

Nationhood, statehood and nation-state

Nationalism is a widely used term that has no consensual definition. Discussion on nationalism has been difficult, or even confusing at times, because three vaguely defined terms, namely, nationhood, stateness and nation-state, have frequently been used interchangeably.

For our own analytical purpose, *nationalism* is defined as a political principle that calls for the building of a nation-state or the congruence of nationhood and statehood. In other words, nationalism demands a nation to have its own political state and a state to be comprised of a homogeneous national or ethnic group. Or simply put, nationalism demands one nation, one state.[1] Nationalist movements come in many forms. For instance, some uphold *expansionism* to incorporate their fellow nationals residing in other states; some pursue *separatism*, striving to control the political destiny of their nations; and some pursue *irredentism*, where a state's minority nationals seek to unite themselves with their fellow nationals in another state.

Nationhood, or national identity, is a sense of shared identity among people who believe in their belonging to the same nation but do not necessarily demand that the nation constitutes one sovereign state. And statehood refers to a sovereign state whose people can be of different ethnic and/or national origins. Contrary to nationalism, which demands 'one nation, one state', the concepts of nationhood and statehood allow for the existence of 'one nation, multiple states' and 'one state, multiple nations', respectively.

In an ethnically divided society where people have competing visions of nationhood and statehood and different ideas about what the relations between the two should be, the institutionalization of democratic rules is naturally more complicated and difficult.[2] Since only approximately 10 per cent of the countries in the world have congruent state and ethnic borders,[3] to prevent nationalist movements from endangering democracy-building in multi-ethnic and multi-national societies, some have urged the construction of civic, liberal nationalism over ethnic nationalism, with the former defining nationhood in terms of citizenship.[4] Civic nationalism can reduce the risk of democratic breakdown in an ethnically divided society because it strives to construct a sense of political loyalty to a civic community that transcends ethnicity. As Juan Linz highlights,[5] 'democracy can be more easily consolidated in divided societies if people make efforts to build a *state-nation* rather than a *nation-state* and are able to tolerate the existence of multiple identities'.[6]

In the case of Taiwan, the issue of national identity is very complicated. First, it is important to make distinctions between the nationalist claim and the statehood claim. Taiwan's independence claim and Taiwanese identity are correlated, yet distinct. While some support Taiwan's independence primarily on nationalist grounds, others may do so out of concerns for the huge socio-economic and political disparity across the Strait. Similarly, some support Chinese unification for security reasons and economic benefits rather than out of nationalist commitment. Second, on statehood and national identity issues, many have chosen a middle-ground position, favouring the status quo over Taiwan's independence and Chinese unification, however confusing the concept of 'status quo' may be. Similarly, many have chosen to adopt dual national identities, seeing themselves as both Taiwanese and Chinese.

At the risk of over-simplification, we can construct a six-category typology to differentiate nationalists and non-nationalists based on national identity and position on the statehood issue (see Table 11.1). *Taiwanese nationalists* are those who self-identify as Taiwanese and support Taiwan's independence. *Chinese nationalists* are those who self-identify as Chinese and support Chinese unification. Those who support independence but have dual identities fall into the category of *independentists*, while those who support unification but have some degree of Taiwanese identity are classified as *unificationists*. We define those who, regardless of their national identities, prefer the status quo as *realists.* Finally, *passivists* are those who have no opinion on the stateness issue or those who find all three outcomes (Taiwan's independence, Chinese unification and status quo) equally acceptable.

In Table 11.2, we apply this six-category typology to empirical data collected in various island-wide surveys. Essentially, we rely on the respondents' answers to two questions, one on national identity and one on the statehood issue.[7] Table 11.2 exhibits the changes in people's national identity, statehood preference and attitude toward nation-state-building between 1992 and 1999. During Taiwan's democratization, those with a sense of Taiwanese identity rose sharply from 27 per cent in 1992 to 35.6 per

Table 11.1 Typology for distinguishing nationalists and non-nationalists

	Stateness preference			
National identity	*Taiwan's independence*	*Status quo*	*Chinese unification*	*No opinion*
Taiwanese	Taiwanese nationalist	Realist	Unificationist	Passivist
Taiwanese and Chinese	Independentist			
Chinese			Chinese nationalist	

Table 11.2 Changes of national identity, stateness preference and attitude on nation-state-building over time, 1992–1999

	Post-election surveys			
	1992 N=1,384	*1993 N=1,398*	*1996 N=1,376*	*1999 N=1,357*
National identity				
Taiwanese		27.1	35.6	32.9
Chinese		33.4	20.9	12.2
Taiwanese and Chinese		33.8	40.5	51.7
Statehood preference				
Taiwan independence	7.8	13.2	18.2	22.8
Chinese unification	39.5	39.3	23.0	17.4
Status quo	17.8	10.8	41.1	44.5
Attitude on nation-state-building				
Taiwanese nationalist		7.2	12.4	14.3
Independentist		6.0	5.8	8.6
Realist		10.8	41.1	44.5
Unificationist		17.0	13.4	12.2
Chinese nationalist		22.3	9.6	5.2
Passivist		36.8	17.7	15.3

Source: Data were provided by the Workshop on Political System and Change, Department of Political Science, National Taiwan University. These three face-to-face interviews were conducted after the 1991 year-end National Assembly election, the 1992 year-end legislative election, the 1995 year-end legislative election and the 1998 year-end legislative election, respectively.

Note:
Percentages in each category may not add to 100 per cent because some interviewees either gave answers that are not listed in this table or declined to answer.

cent in 1996, while Chinese identity visibly lost its popularity, dropping from 33.4 per cent in 1992 to 12.2 per cent in 1999. Meanwhile, a growing portion of the population consider themselves both Taiwanese and Chinese (33.8 per cent in 1992 and 51.7 per cent in 1999). In terms of people's statehood preference, we find a general trend of increasing support for Taiwan's independence (from 7.8 per cent in 1992 to 22.8 per cent in 1999) and a sharp drop in the support for Chinese unification (from 39.5 per cent in 1992 to 17.4 per cent in 1999). At the same time, those who prefer the status quo also rose sharply, from 17.8 per cent in 1992 to 44.5 per cent in 1999.

Based on their responses to the two questions, we can place our interviewees into the six categories in our typology. Table 11.2 shows that, between 1993 and 1999, Taiwanese nationalists rose from 7.2 per cent to 14.3 per cent, while Chinese nationalists declined significantly from 22.3 per cent to 5.2 per cent. The most dramatic change occurred in the realist category, which increased from 10.8 per cent to 44.5 per cent between 1993 and 1999. Overall, only one-fifth of the population in Taiwan falls into the two polarized categories of nationalists.

Table 11.3 further breaks down the data in Table 11.2 by the interviewees' ethnic (or 'sub-ethnic', as some may prefer) background. Not surprisingly, we find a high correlation between ethnic background and attitude towards nation-state-building. Generally speaking, when compared to mainlanders (*waishengren*), native Taiwanese (*benshengren*) tend to have a clearer sense of Taiwanese identity and are more likely to support Taiwan independence. Most Taiwanese nationalists are native Taiwanese (especially *minnan*-speaking *benshengren*) and most Chinese nationalists are mainlanders. Interestingly, the declining popularity of Chinese nationalism not only happened among the native Taiwanese but also among the mainlanders. Within the latter, self-proclaimed Chinese nationalists dropped from 59.6 per cent in 1993 to 22.5 per cent in 1996. Nonetheless, only very few of these ex-Chinese nationalists turned to Taiwan's independence cause, as it ends up being more comfortable to remain a realist and support the status quo. Amongst mainlanders, support for the status quo jumped from 5.1 per cent in 1993 to 40.1 per cent in 1996. As of 1996, only approximately 23 per cent of the mainlander population remained Chinese nationalists.

Table 11.3 Attitude on nation-state-building by ethnicity

	1996 and 1993 surveys		
	Native Taiwanese		*Mainlander*
	Minnan *N=985* *(N=989)*	*Hakka* *N=150* *(N=169)*	*N=222* *(N=198)*
Taiwanese nationalist	15.8 (9.1)	4.7 (4.7)	1.8 (0)
Independentist	7.1 (6.9)	2.7 (6.5)	2.3 (2.5)
Realist	39.6 (12.2)	52.0 (11.2)	40.1 (5.1)
Unificationist	11.3 (17.6)	15.3 (16.6)	22.1 (13.6)
Chinese nationalist	6.9 (14.9)	8.7 (21.3)	22.5 (59.6)
Passivist	19.3 (39.3)	16.7 (39.6)	11.3 (19.2)

Source: Same as Table 11.2.
Note:
Numbers in parentheses are 1993 data.

Taiwanese-versus-Chinese or Taiwanese-cum-Chinese

Based on our rough typology, the awakening of Taiwanese consciousness can be observed at three different strata: the rise in Taiwanese nationalism, the adoption of a Taiwanese identity, and the growing support for Taiwan's independence. To understand how the national identity conflict might constrain the prospect of democratic consolidation in Taiwan, we need to explore the nature of 'Taiwanese identity vs. Chinese identity' in greater detail.

Our empirical data below suggest that, while the people of Taiwan still lack a strong consensus on what the future Taiwan–mainland relationship should be, the rising Taiwanese identity is indeed more a civic identity than an ethnicity-based primordial identity. Furthermore, for those who have acquired dual identities, 'Taiwanese identity' may not necessarily be a nationalist term. They may conceive themselves as both Taiwanese citizens and ethnic Chinese at the same time. Alternatively, some may conceive themselves as ethnic Taiwanese and Chinese nationals. This means, for some people, that the two labels, Taiwanese and Chinese, do not conform perfectly to their very definition of 'national identity'. Furthermore, most nationalists, especially Taiwanese nationalists, do not reject the idea that the future of Taiwan be decided through democratic procedures.

The words 'Taiwanese' and 'Chinese' are increasingly being used by the people in Taiwan, especially politicians, as political labels for distinguishing 'us' from 'them' in the promotion of collective consciousness. Proponents of the Taiwanese identity have used phrases such as 'we are all Taiwanese', 'it's the Taiwanese people's turn', 'the misery of being a Taiwanese', 'identify with Taiwan and you are a Taiwanese' and 'let's build a new Taiwanese consciousness'. Proponents of the Chinese identity have promoted ideas such as 'we are all Chinese', 'Chinese do not attack Chinese', 'all Chinese are children of the Yellow Emperor', 'Taiwan's independence is an endeavour that betrays our Chinese Fathers' and 'the twenty-first century belongs to us Chinese'. The two terms actually mean different things to different people. Some view them as mutually exclusive, while others find them compatible or even complementary, and yet others have no trouble using the two interchangeably depending on situations. In fact, the popular connotation of the two concepts involves a variety of elements, such as ethnic origin, language, culture, residency, citizenship and identification.[8]

There is a tendency to assume that one's ethnic identity is necessarily the same as one's national identity. However, as Table 11.3 shows, although there is a high correlation between the two, one should not equate ethnic identity with national identity. In other words, not all mainlanders lack Taiwanese consciousness and not all native Taiwanese embrace Taiwanese identity. Tables 11.4 and 11.5 show how the two terms 'Taiwanese' and 'Chinese' are conceived by the people of Taiwan. A general finding is that people tend to define 'Taiwanese' using territorial/political and subjective/psychological criteria, while they identify 'Chinese' using primordial/cultural criteria.

Table 11.4 Meanings of being Taiwanese (%)

	Mass (1996) N=1,031	*Elite (1995–96) N=66*
Q. Many people in our society say 'we are Taiwanese'. What does 'Taiwanese' mean to you?		
I. Primordial–cultural criteria		
(1) those with common blood and lineage	–	3.0
(2) those who speak Taiwanese (e.g. Minnan or Hakka language)	22	6.1
(3) those with common historical or cultural background	38*	18.2
II. Territorial–political criteria		
(4) those who are born, live or work in Taiwan	55**	63.6
(5) those with Taiwan's citizenship	16***	28.8
III. Subjective–psychological criteria		
(6) those who self-identify as Taiwanese	39	31.8
(7) those with a strong sense of Taiwanese consciousness	55	16.7

Sources: The mass data are based on a telephone survey conducted by the Yuan Chien magazine in 16–18 May 1996. Data in the elite column are based on Chia-lung Lin's in-depth interviews with 66 Legislators between January 1995 and April 1996 (see Lin 1998: Appendixes 1, 2, 3).

Notes:

In the mass survey, interviewees were allowed multiple answers to this question. For the elite interviews, interviewees were asked to name and rank their answers to this question.

* In this mass survey, this choice is worded as: 'Taiwanese are those with Taiwan provincial origin'.

** In this mass survey, this question is actually divided into two parts. While 55 per cent considered those born in Taiwan as Taiwanese, 49 per cent thought that just by living in Taiwan qualifies one to be a Taiwanese.

*** In this mass survey, the choice is worded: 'Taiwanese are those who consider Taiwan as an independent country'.

For most people in Taiwan, the term 'Taiwanese' is quite loosely defined. About 55 per cent of the respondents thought that 'Taiwanese' refers to those who were born or reside in Taiwan, 55 per cent thought that having a strong sense of Taiwanese identity qualifies one to be a Taiwanese, and 39 per cent considered self-identifying as a Taiwanese as the most important criterion. However, there is also a significant portion of the population who apply a narrower, more exclusive set of criteria to the definition of Taiwanese. For instance, 38 per cent thought that being born in Taiwan

Table 11.5 Meanings of being Chinese (%)

	Elite (1995–6) N=66
Q. Many people in our society say 'we are Chinese'. What does 'Chinese' mean to you?	
I. Primordial–cultural criteria	
(1) those with common blood and lineage (i.e. the Han nation)	33.3
(2) those who speak Chinese (i.e. Mandarin)	6.1
(3) those with common historical or cultural background (i.e. the Huaren)	50.0
II. Territorial–political criteria	
(4) those who live and work in China	7.6
(5) those with the PRC (China) citizenship	40.9
III. Subjective–psychological criteria	
(6) those who self-identify as Chinese	16.7
(7) those with a strong sense of Chinese consciousness	9.1

Source: Data are based on Chia-lung Lin's in-depth interviews with 66 Legislators between January 1995 and April 1996 (see Lin 1998: Appendixes 1, 2, 3).

Note:
Interviewed political elites were asked to name and rank their answers to this question.

should be a criterion, 22 per cent thought that the ability to speak Taiwanese (whether the *Minnan* or *Hakka* dialect) is a litmus test, and 16 per cent thought that Taiwanese are those who recognize Taiwan as an independent state.

No matter how confusing a picture our empirical data might suggest, the important point is that one's national identity is, for the most part, a matter of perception. As Walker Conner points out, 'it is not *what is*, but *what people believe is* that has behavioral consequences'.[9] No matter what really constitute the differences between 'Taiwanese' and 'Chinese', it is how the differences between the two are conceptualized and whether they are considered compatible or irreconcilable that will steer the people's reactions to nationalism-related issues. One way to reconcile the differences between the two identities and to minimize their possible conflicts is for one to treat Chinese identity as a cultural expression (*huaren*) or ethnic origin (*hanren*) and to treat Taiwanese identity as a political identity shared by all those who live in the same political territory and have common citizenship. As long as those with a Chinese identity do not deny Taiwan as a sovereign political entity (whether an independent state or a geographical territory, whether under the name 'Republic of China' or 'Republic of Taiwan'), and as long as those with a Taiwanese identity do not deny the fact that the Chinese culture and the *Han* people have constituted a large portion of the Taiwanese culture and the Taiwanese people, then the surge of the Taiwanese identity would not necessarily intensify ethnic confrontation and bring about political upheavals.

National identity and statehood issues

To what extent the growth of Taiwanese identity might obstruct Taiwan's democratic development will largely depend on two factors: first, whether the people can form a basic consensus on the boundary of their state; and second, whether the people are willing to solve Taiwan's statehood disputes via democratic procedures.[10] After all, a liberal democracy is founded on the principle of majority rule and protecting minority rights. The ultimate test of whether a liberal democracy can consolidate in a divided society like Taiwan lies in whether people of different national identities can learn to trust one another and tolerate collective allegiances drastically different from their own.

Questions 1 and 2 in Table 11.6 show how people in each of our six categories define the territory and citizenship of the Republic of China (ROC). Generally speaking, there seems to be no strong consensus among the people of Taiwan on whether the territory of the ROC covers only Taiwan (and its neighbouring islands) or extends to cover the Chinese mainland as well. There is also no strong consensus on whether 'citizens of the ROC' refers only to the 21 million people of Taiwan or includes the 1.2 billion people on the mainland. From the mid-1996 survey data, we see that while 51.4 per cent of the people hold a more realistic view that the territory of the ROC does not cover the Chinese mainland, thus acknowledging the *de facto* independence of the 'Republic of China on Taiwan', 32.9 per cent of the interviewees, especially Chinese nationalists and unificationists, still regarded the Chinese mainland as part of the ROC territory. But when it comes to the question of ROC citizenship, the majority of the people (57.5 per cent) believed that it should only include the 21 million people of Taiwan, although 27.5 per cent of the people argued that the 1.2 billion people on the mainland should also be considered as ROC's citizens.

Two important points can be drawn from the response patterns to Questions 1 and 2. First, two 1996 surveys, one conducted before and one conducted after the PRC's missile intimidation around Taiwan's 1996 presidential election, show a significant shift in the people's definition of the ROC's territory and citizenship after the missile intimidation. Within the six-month period between the two surveys, those who thought that the territory of the ROC only covers Taiwan and its neighbouring islands increased from 40.7 per cent to 51.4 per cent; and those who thought the ROC citizenship refers only to the 21 million people of Taiwan also increased from 44.2 per cent to 57.5 per cent. Although we cannot make a direct inference from these data

Table 11.6 Perceived territory, citizenship and sovereignty of the ROC (%)

	Taiwanese nationalist	*Independentist*	*Realist*	*Unificationist*	*Chinese nationalist*	*Passivist*	*Total*
Mid 1996 mass survey: *(Early '96 mass survey):* *< 1993 mass survey >:*	*n=192* *(n=170)* *<n=100>*	*n=97* *(n=80)* *<n=84>*	*n=747* *(n=565)* *<n=151>*	*n=126* *(n=185)* *<n=223>*	*n=71* *(n=132)* *<n=312>*	*n=173* *(n=244)* *<n=514>*	*N=1,406* *(N=1,376)* *<N=1,398>*
Q1. Do you think the territory of the ROC only covers Taiwan and its neighbouring islands, or does it cover also the mainland?							
(1) Taiwan and its neighbouring islands	87.0 (72.4)	72.2 (65.0)	52.3 (43.4)	29.4 (28.6)	23.9 (9.1)	23.1 (30.7)	51.4 (40.7)
(2) Taiwan and the mainland	6.3 (12.4)	19.6 (23.8)	35.9 (43.9)	64.3 (61.6)	67.6 (84.4)	19.7 (23.8)	32.9 (41.6)
Q2 Do you think the citizens of the ROC refer to the 21 million people of Taiwan only, or do they include also the 1.2 billion people of the mainland?							
(1) Taiwan's 21 million people only	91.7 (77.1)	81.4 (63.8)	58.5 (47.8)	39.7 (37.3)	29.6 (11.4)	26.6 (29.5)	57.5 (44.2)
(2) Taiwan's 21 million and the mainland's 1.2 billion people	5.2 (12.9)	15.5 (25.0)	30.1 (39.1)	53.2 (53.0)	59.2 (81.8)	15.6 (27.5)	27.5 (39.0)
Q3 Who do you think has the right to determine the future of Taiwan? Only those who live in Taiwan, or also those including the 1.2 billion people of the mainland?							
(1) Only the people of Taiwan	94.3	95.9	75.4	59.5	60.6	38.7	72.7
(2) Including also the mainland people	1.6	0	15.3	27.0	32.4	4.0	12.9
Q4 Do you think it is appropriate that Taiwan's future is determined via plebiscite?							
(1) Agree	81.3 (78.8) <87.0>	77.3 (72.5) <75.0>	72.4 (56.1) <61.6>	66.7 (56.8) <59.1>	60.6 (56.1) <44.6>	35.8 (36.1) <38.7>	68.3 (56.4) <51.6>
(2) Disagree	12.5 (9.4) <8.0>	13.4 (18.8) <19.0>	17.4 (27.6) <21.9>	25.4 (28.1) <35.4>	33.8 (37.1) <49.4>	8.1 (10.2) <17.3>	16.9 (22.7) <27.5>

Source: Same as Table 11.2.

Note: Data with no parentheses are based on a general survey conducted in mid 1996 after the presidential election. Data in ( ) are based on a general survey conducted in early 1996, immediately after the 1995 year-end legislative election. Data in < > are based on a general survey conducted in the summer of 1993, after the 1992 year-end legislative election.

that the increase is a direct result of the PRC's missile test, since the two face-to-face surveys were conducted by the same research group using the same survey methods, it is logical for us to surmise that this swift and significant popular opinion change is beyond sampling errors and that the change might be related to the heated Cross-Strait tension during that period. Second, the fact that a huge portion of Taiwanese nationalists and independentists confine the sovereignty of the ROC to Taiwan and its people implies that these people have gradually come to tolerate or accept the term 'Republic of China' and treat it as a sovereign state whose sovereignty only covers Taiwan.

Question 3 asked the interviewees who they thought would have the right to determine Taiwan's future. Interestingly, there was a stronger consensus on this question. Around 72.7 per cent of the interviewees thought that only the 21 million people of Taiwan have the right to determine Taiwan's future, a view even shared by most Chinese nationalists (60.6 per cent) and unificationists (59.5 per cent). In other words, contrary to their definition of the ROC's sovereignty, most Chinese nationalists and unificationists viewed the island as the legitimate unit for making fundamental political decisions such as determining the future of Taiwan.

Question 4 explored whether the people considered it appropriate that Taiwan's future be determined via plebiscite. It turns out that most interviewees actually supported using a plebiscite to solve the statehood disputes. In fact, over the years, support for a plebiscite has climbed steadily, rising from 51.6 per cent in 1993 to 68.3 per cent in 1996. A significant discovery is that the majority of Chinese nationalists and unificationists do not reject the idea of using a plebiscite in solving critical national issues despite their fear that the majority of the people might vote for Taiwanese independence.

Given Taiwan's domestic and international situations, a gradualist approach to the statehood issue seems most acceptable to most people on Taiwan. And political reality seems to prevent both Taiwanese and Chinese nationalists from pursuing their nationalist goals with a strong sense of urgency and radical actions. To most Taiwanese nationalists and independentists, the statehood issue is not very urgent because Taiwan has long enjoyed a *de facto* independence and was never for one day ruled by the PRC. To them, what to strive for is not a separation from the PRC, but a *de jure* recognition from the international community. Therefore, as long as Taiwan retains its *de facto* sovereignty and keeps marching toward a full democracy, most Taiwanese nationalists will feel no urgency to declare independence in the immediate future. On the other hand, to most Chinese nationalists and unificationists, a speedy unification is unrealistic due to the huge socio-political disparity across the Strait. What these people identify with is the Chinese nation, not the Chinese Communist regime. Since the Chinese mainland is still under the control of the Chinese Communist Party, pursuing unification with the mainland in the near future will certainly mean surrendering a new democracy to a communist regime and sacrificing the hard-earned well-being and freedom. Since neither Taiwanese nationalists nor Chinese nationalists consider it extremely urgent to pursue their nationalist goal at all costs and to push for a final settlement in the immediate future, the status quo is likely to be prolonged for quite some time. As long as the statehood issue remains unsettled, Taiwan's political future will always be shrouded in doubt. But the waiting also buys Taiwan time to deepen its democratic reform and to prepare itself politically, socially and culturally for a peaceful settlement of the statehood issue when the situation becomes ripe.

A political explanation for the surge of a Taiwanese identity

Why did Taiwanese identity surge during Taiwan's democratization and why has it acquired a largely civic and liberal nature? First, one can argue that the seed of Taiwanese identity was deeply buried during the Japanese colonial rule and the post-war political reconstruction. Second, one should pay attention to the epic changes in the international system since the late 1970s that first precipitated the state legitimacy crisis and later aroused the aspiration for independent statehood. However, we argue that neither historical roots nor system-level changes can directly alter group identity. The effects of these historical and global forces on the people's political consciousness must be actualized through state actions, competing elites' strategies, and their mutual influences and compromises. We argue that national identities are not inborn but are socially and politically constructed sentiments that are subject to political mobilization and manipulation. While it is natural that people develop a sense of group consciousness after a long period of social integration or territorial isolation, any sudden change of group identity certainly calls for a political explanation.[11]

Throughout the post-war era, the state-directed formation of Chinese nationality continued to run into strong resistance from certain quarters of the native society, especially from victim families of the 28 February Incident, Overseas Taiwanese, and members of the Presbyterian church. The resistance had its historical roots. The development of a distinctive Taiwanese identity and its ensuing quest for independent statehood was fostered by two related historical antecedents. The first is the fifty years of Japanese colonial rule, during which the native elite was first subjected to a state-orchestrated de-sinicization campaign and later a naturalization (*huangminhua*) programme that proceeded in full gear during the last few years of the Second World War. Japan's colonial rule facilitated Taiwan's early acquisition of a semi-peripheral position relative to China through state-directed modernization programmes. And the interests of the native Taiwanese elite were incorporated into Japan's military and economic conquest of peripheral countries, including China, in the so-called Great

East Asian Co-Prosperity Zone.[12] The second historical antecedent is the 'birth defect' incurred during Taiwan's decolonization and the KMT's re-establishment of Chinese rule after the war. This birth defect, epitomized by the 28 February Incident, along with the imposed political subordination, precipitated the formation of Taiwan's independence movement among the Taiwanese in exile.[13] Despite many shared ethnic heritages between the native and the newly arrived émigré group, the 'birth defect' also attenuated the state's effort to establish the supremacy of Chinese identity over local identity through re-sinicization and mandarinization programmes.[14] As soon as the political compression was loosened, the long-suppressed Taiwanese identity re-emerged.

Taiwanese identity has surged also in part due to some epic changes in the international system. First, in the late 1970s, the KMT's claim to represent all China crumbled in a series of de-recognition crises. Next, during the late 1980s, national aspiration was encouraged by the formation of the so-called new world order which seemingly provided a window of opportunity for the admission of new states.

For an extended period following the outbreak of the Korean War, the ROC's precarious sovereign status was sustained essentially by the United States' hegemony and its post-war security arrangements. It was the United States-harboured international recognition and American security commitment that elongated the ROC's diminishing international status until the end of 1979. The PRC–US rapprochement in the early 1970s set off a series of diplomatic setbacks for Taiwan – the loss of the United Nations (UN) seat to the PRC, the expulsion from all major international organizations, and the de-recognition by major allies. These external shocks severely undermined the KMT's long-standing claim that the ROC government is the sole legitimate government of all China and weakened its entrenched one-party authoritarian regime.[15] Next came the break-up of the Eastern bloc, which was accompanied by a resurgence of ethnic and national strife. In the transition to the post-Cold War era, the political and territorial integrity of many existing states was seriously challenged. In many instances, the international community was seemingly sympathetic to the claims of certain collective entities of their rights to self-determination, autonomy or secession. At the same time, the emerging structural configuration of the Asia-Pacific security order also gave Taiwan some room for diplomatic manoeuvring, considering that the long-term goals of China, a major power aspirant, could be potentially in conflict with those of the United States, the defending hegemony, and Japan, a regional rival.[16] These developments have raised new hopes for an independent Taiwanese statehood.

However, both the growth potential of these historical seeds and the transformative potential of the so-called 'new world order' would not have brought about a fundamental shift in the people's group identity had there not been succession crisis within the KMT, electoral opening at the national level, and intensified tensions across the Taiwan Strait. In Taiwan, democratization has served as a *pulling* force, drawing people together through the process of political participation, which not only creates in them a sense of loyalty to the political system, but generates multiple issues that are of interest to different groups, thus offering them an incentive to form various cross-cutting coalitions on different issues, with no groups or interests able permanently to dominate other groups or interests. If the existence of a nation is, in the words of Ernest Renan, an everyday plebiscite,[17] then the practice of democracy in Taiwan definitely serves to nurture their sense of belonging to a civic nation. On the other hand, the PRC's hostility toward the democratizing Taiwan has served as a *pushing* force. The long-existing and ever-growing threat from the PRC has fostered a sense of common destiny that is shared by a great majority of people of Taiwan, regardless of their ethnic background. Again, drawing on Renan, having suffered together actually weighs more in the formation of a nation than sharing a triumph. After all, suffering imposes obligations and demands common efforts, which later become a collective memory that is part of each individual's life. Together, both the pulling and pushing forces have interacted and have led the people of Taiwan – who are in search of a collective identity – to gradually turn to develop a more inclusive civic identity (state-nation). Thus, it is no longer a matter of going back to the unrealized ideal of building either a unified Chinese nation-state or an independent Taiwanese nation-state.

The structuration of democratization

In order to explain better the surge of Taiwanese identity since the early 1990s, we have to turn our attention to the role played by the political elite in the construction of a new group identity and the cultivating function of democratic practices. From early on, DPP leaders have built their electoral support upon the native Taiwanese people's shared sense of suffering and deprivation. The DPP leadership played up the issue because this salient cleavage cut across socio-economic strata. It was considered an effective counter-strategy to the KMT's broadly-based socio-economic development programme and an issue that could unite DPP supporters of different social and economic interests under a common cause. However, it was the power struggle within the KMT after the passing of Chiang Ching-kuo that critically turned the tide against the prevailing official ideological claim on Chinese identity. The intra-party struggle came to a point of no return in the early 1990s, when Lee Teng-hui was challenged by his rival in the KMT's party nomination for presidential candidate. It also marks the turning point for the growth of Taiwanese identity. We will back up this claim with public opinion poll data later on.

On his way to power consolidation, Lee Teng-hui skilfully shifted the burden of defending the orthodox lines to his mainlander rival in the KMT, such as promoting the extra-constitutional arrangements amid a global wave of democratization, insisting on the 'One China principle' – when virtually all major nations had shifted their diplomatic recognition to the PRC, and upholding the Chinese identity despite the awakening of the Taiwanese identity. Instead, Lee emphasized a 'Taiwan-centred' view while managing the island's external relations and launching a series of bold policy initiatives. The redirection of foreign and mainland policies aggravated the KMT's division over the 'one China principle' and transfigured both intra-party and inter-party coalitional politics.[18] In the fierce intra-party power struggle between the mainstream and non-mainstream factions,[19] Lee characterized his rivals as a conservative group interested only in preserving its past prerogatives and identified more closely with mainland China than the 21 million people on the island. The more the non-mainstream faction questioned Lee's commitment to Chinese nationalism and objected to his effort to seek ideological accommodation with the opposition, the more popular Lee became among the native Taiwanese. Increasingly, Lee Teng-hui has been not only adored by a great majority of native Taiwanese, but also viewed as the protector of the island's autonomy from the PRC and the embodiment of the glory and honour of the Taiwanese people, especially for his dedicated efforts in accelerating the Taiwanization of the KMT's power structure, alleviating past grievances such as the 28 February Incident, restoring the pride and self-respect of the Taiwanese, and asserting a separate sovereign status for the ROC in the international community. The logic of strategic alliance compelled the DPP to side with Lee Teng-hui at all crucial junctures of the power struggle between the mainstream and non-mainstream factions. The tacit grand coalition between the DPP and the mainstream culminated in their joint effort to oust Hau Pei-tsun around the end of 1992. From then on, Lee enjoyed full control of the state apparatus, which has since then been gradually re-engineered to endorse the burgeoning Taiwanese consciousness and to cultivate a new sense of common destiny among the 21 million people. In his most revealing interview with Ryotaro Shiba, a well-known Japanese writer, in the autumn of 1994, Lee spoke of 'the misery of being a Taiwanese', implying that Taiwan has, for hundreds of years, been ruled by different foreign regimes and never got a chance to determine its own fate. This widely cited line came very close to a tacit endorsement for the principle of self-determination.

After the downfall of Hau Pei-tsun, some leading figures of the KMT's non-mainstream faction decided to break away from it and established the New Party (NP). The NP built up its electoral support initially by appealing to the besieged mentality of the mainlander voters, who were increasingly alienated by the swift Taiwanization of the KMT's power structure. In the 1994 Taipei mayoral race, the NP candidate Jaw Shao-kang boiled up the crisis mentality of voters with strong Chinese nationalist sentiments by attacking Lee Teng-hui for having a hidden agenda for Taiwan independence.

However, given the prevailing social and political conditions, both the DPP and the NP soon found out the diminishing utility of ethnic and nationalist mobilization. The first challenge nationalist elites faced in promoting ethnic nationalism was the fact that a significant portion of the population has dual identities and prefers the preservation of the status quo to anything else. To win the hearts of the median voters, the DPP and NP were induced to modify their ethnic nationalist appeals and soften their ideological stances. For the NP, an explicit ethnic and nationalist mobilization is certainly not a good approach, not only because mainlanders only account for around 16 per cent of the population, but because roughly half of NP supporters are native Taiwanese. For the DPP, intensive ethnic mobilization also has limited benefits in the late stage of the democratic transition, in part because it can no longer characterize the Lee Teng-hui led 'émigré regime'. Furthermore, after five decades of social integration, mainly through intermarriages, work and school, most native Taiwanese have relatives, friends and neighbours who are mainlanders, which makes it too costly and nearly impossible for the DPP to pursue the building of a Taiwanese state that politically excludes mainlanders. In addition, there also exists a sub-ethnic division between the *Minnan*-speaking and *Hakka*-speaking native Taiwanese, who account for about 12 to 15 per cent of the population. If the DPP overplays the ethnic card, which has been quite *Minnan*-centric, it is bound to lose favour among the *Hakka*-speaking native Taiwanese. As pointed out by Juan Linz'[20] in a heterogeneous society where people of various primordial backgrounds live together, 'building a nation-state solely on primordial ties is nearly impossible and always too costly; therefore, most nationalist elites who promote separatism are eventually induced to put more emphasis on territoriality and to shine less spotlight on primordial characteristics, albeit the importance of primordial mobilization in their initial development stage'.[21]

The third challenge for both Taiwanese and Chinese nationalists was the KMT's impressive adaptability on identity-related issues. Lee Teng-hui was able to harness the independence zeal with a call for a sense of shared destiny among the 21 million people and a gradual defection from the 'one China principle'. As an alternative to the pursuit of *de jure* independence, Lee promoted the so-called 'Republic of China on Taiwan' formula that anchors on a 'two-China model' while being ingeniously evasive, flexible and ambiguous on the issue of national unification. At the same time, the KMT's propaganda characterized the DPP's independence cause as dangerous and irresponsible and the NP's pro-unification platform as disloyal to the Taiwanese people. Lee's ingenious programme of gradually consolidating Taiwan's sovereign claim without endangering the status quo enabled the KMT to effectively reconcile the seeming contradiction between the popular aspiration for a separate identity in the international community and the prevailing concern for stability and prosperity, and to bind the two opposition parties to the two polar ends of the spectrum.

As the KMT's mainstream moved to consolidate its centrist position on this most salient issue, the DPP and NP were compelled to soften their nationalist stances. Starting in early 1995, some pragmatic leaders, notably DPP party chairmen Shih Ming-teh (1994–96) and Hsu Hsin-liang (1996–98), began to soft-paddle the Taiwan independence claim through a re-interpretation of the status quo. They argued that 'Taiwan has been an independent sovereign state for nearly half a century, thus there is no need to declare formal independence or hold plebiscite for this matter'.[22]

Parallel to the adjustments of the KMT and DPP was the NP's reformulation of its nationalist appeal, which now highlights the forming of a 'New Taiwanese' consciousness and the consolidation of the new democracy before the pursuit of unification. Since the option of an immediate unification with the mainland seems unacceptable to most people of Taiwan, the NP found it necessary to moderate its nationalist appeal and cultivate other issues for electoral survival. Immediately after the 1995 legislative election, in which the KMT barely passed the majority threshold, some NP and DPP leaders held a symbolic talk, the so-called Grand Reconciliation, to show the two parties' willingness to set aside their ethnic and ideological differences and to jointly promote reforms and the building of a coalition government. After this talk, the NP began to articulate a new set of rhetoric that emphasizes the party's sincere commitment to democracy and its willingness to cooperate with the DPP on democratic reform issues.

The above developments suggest that the democratic process has helped narrow the formerly severe polarization on the independence–unification issue. In addition, during Taiwan's regime transition, the newly installed democratic practices also served as an agent of political re-socialization. Political democratization, especially electoral opening, functioned like a whirlpool drawing common people into the political process through campaigning, voting, political discussions, participation in political parties, and social movements. The practice of democracy has made the people gradually accustomed to participating in the deliberation and decision-making of 'national' affairs and, implicitly or explicitly, has also made them accept the island as the legitimate unit of governance. Democratization not only provides a public sphere for people to communicate and understand each other, but broadens and deepens people's daily interactions by absorbing different groups and interests into the political system. Constant political participation has helped develop a sense of collective consciousness among the people, transforming the term 'Taiwan' from a geographic unit to a political society, and the term 'Taiwanese' from an ethnic term for 'native Taiwanese' to a civic term for 'citizens of Taiwan'. If the existence of a nation, as Renan stressed, can be revealed through the 'everyday plebiscite' of the people, then democratic practices in Taiwan certainly enhance the people's sense of belonging to a civic nation through their daily participation in the public sphere.

Intensified tensions across the Strait

The dynamics of Cross-Strait interactions have exerted as much influence on the island's process of state-making and nation-building as its own internal political process. Beijing's hostile unification campaign, recurring military threat, and measures of diplomatic strangulation all serve to distance the people of Taiwan from Chinese identity and strengthen their call for a separate identity. Recent years of intensified economic exchanges and cultural contacts have done little to ameliorate the Cross-Strait tension and animosity. On the contrary, Cross-Strait relations have entered a very turbulent period since the summer of 1995.[23]

The strategic interactions between Taipei and Beijing primarily operate at three levels. First, mirroring Taiwan's own internal conflict, there is a tug-of-war across the Taiwan Strait between two competing nation-building processes. On the one hand, the PRC's goal is to deter Taiwan from independence in the short run and to impose the mainland's version of nation-state-building (i.e. the one-country two-system model) on Taiwan in the long run.[24] On the other hand, Taipei's foreign and mainland policies aim to nullify Beijing's unification campaign and discredit the PRC's sovereign claim over the island in the international community.

Second, both sides attempt to gain control over the scope and speed of Cross-Strait economic exchange to serve their own political agenda. Beijing encourages the acceleration and normalization of Cross-Strait economic exchange in the hope that increased economic interdependence will bind Taipei's hands in seeking unilateral solutions to the sovereignty dispute. On the other hand, Taipei resists the possibility of Taiwan becoming another Hong Kong, reasoning that a full-scale economic integration with mainland China will eventually compromise Taiwan's political autonomy. Taipei strives to regulate the pace of Taiwan's business expansion into the mainland market in accordance with the degree of the PRC's hostility toward Taiwan.

Third, Beijing has always been both an overt and implicit party in Taiwan's internal conflict over the national identity and statehood issue. In fact, Beijing has been quite blunt about its intention to influence Taiwan's domestic politics.[25] Consequently, during Taiwan's democratic transition, the perceived need to resist the PRC's unification campaign constantly structured the domestic debate on mainland and foreign policy as well as on democracy-building and nation-building. For instance, the centrepiece of Taiwan's constitutional reform is the adoption of a semi-presidential system with direct presidential election and expanded presidential powers.[26] The semi-presidentialism was supported by both the KMT mainstream and the DPP because it was deemed imperative for safeguarding Taiwan's national interests. Both believed that a popular election for the highest executive office would not only boost Taiwan's international visibility but strengthen the government's position at Cross-Strait negotiations and/or their own domestic political bargaining. The DPP, in particular, also hoped that an island-wide popular election would help foster the development of Taiwanese nationalism.[27] In a dialectic twist, growing suspicion over the meaning and outcomes of Taiwan's democratization process provoked Beijing to step up its hostile unification campaign, which only reinforced Taiwan's popular resentment toward the PRC.

In a similar vein, Lee's decision to seek membership in the UN General Assembly was prompted not only by the expected benefits of getting Taiwan recognized by the international community as a sovereign state but also by its value in domestic political mobilization. The UN membership issue was expected to be a rallying point around which emotions of loyalty and assurance could cluster. The DPP was also actively pushing for a bid for UN membership, considering the project was deemed not only fully compatible with its independence cause, but also as a necessary foreign policy manoeuvre to counter-balance the rapid and seemingly unstoppable trend toward economic integration with mainland China. UN membership for Taiwan could provide a permanent multilateral guarantee for Taiwan's political autonomy and territorial security in the long run and sharpen the political quarrel between Taiwan and mainland China in the short run. In a way, Beijing's strong reaction to Taipei's bid for UN membership was not only expected but welcomed by the DPP, as Beijing's counter-measures would only raise the popular awareness of Taiwan's endangered sovereign status.

Lee Teng-hui tried to consolidate Taiwan's fragile new democracy on a new foundation of state legitimacy. He launched a three-prong strategy. On the international front, Lee tried to salvage Taiwan's precarious sovereign status by taking a series of new diplomatic initiatives: seeking dual recognition of the PRC and ROC, applying for membership of the General Agreement on Tariffs and Trade (GATT) and the World Trade Organization (WTO), conducting unofficial state visits, and bidding for a seat in the UN General Assembly. Next, with regard to Cross-Strait relations, Lee attempted to engage the PRC in a game of co-existence and to induce Beijing to accept a divided-nation model as exemplified by the divided Germany before 1990. On the domestic front, he tried to absorb the DPP's independence zeal by calling for the formation of 'a sense of shared destiny among the twenty-one million people' and a gradual backing-away from the so-called 'one China principle'. However, just as the KMT leadership narrowed the ideological distance with the DPP, Beijing's suspicion over Taipei's hidden agenda of creeping independence also grew sharply. Beijing was especially alarmed by Taipei's bid for UN membership, viewing it as a preparatory step for formal independence. In response, Beijing took a triple strategy of blockading Taiwan diplomatically, checking Taiwan militarily, and dragging Taiwan along economically.[28] After a futile attempt to block Lee's unofficial visit to the United States in June 1995, Beijing threatened Taipei with a week of missile tests off the northern coast of Taiwan. On the eve of the KMT Congress for presidential nomination in late August 1995, China's People's Liberation Army launched another round of missile tests near a Taiwan-controlled offshore island. The two missile tests and the ensuing shock waves caused Taiwan's stock market and the New Taiwan Dollar to plummet 30 per cent and 9 per cent, respectively, and precipitated a temporary wave of capital flight. Apparently, Chinese Comunist Party hard-liners had hoped to disrupt Lee's re-election bid and bring Taipei to its knees with these military threats. This line of reasoning led to Beijing's decision to extend the military threat well on to the election day. The strategic objectives of these threats were expanded from upsetting Lee's re-election to shaping Taiwan's domestic debate on mainland policy and foreign policy in the campaign process. However, to the disappointment of Beijing's hard-liners, the crisis in the Strait actually helped Lee's re-election as many traditional DPP supporters shifted their support out of the worry that Taiwan might lose ground to the PRC if the majority could not speak with one voice.[29]

Chen Shui-bian's electoral victory on 18 March 2000 was another frustrating turning point for the Beijing leadership. In order to avoid repeating the same mistake again, Beijing did not resort to overtly coercive measures this time. Instead, Premier Zhu Rongji issued a harshly worded warning about the dire consequence of electing pro-independence Chen Shui-bian on the eve of the election. His stern warning backfired in southern Taiwan, where Chen Shui-bian received an outpouring of support and consolidated his win over James Soong.

The dynamics of the Cross-Strait development in the last decade has made a profound impact on Taiwan's nation and state formation, as seen clearly from the growing number of people who self-identify as Taiwanese and support Taiwan's independence. The tension and animosity across the Taiwan Strait have nurtured a sense of shared destiny among the people of Taiwan. If the forming of a new group identity requires some sort of collective memory, then the PRC's military intimidation during Taiwan's first presidential election will certainly leave its mark on the memory of most Taiwanese people.

Conclusion: the security dilemma

All these developments suggest to what extent Taiwan can consolidate its new democracy and preclude the dire possibility of becoming another Hong Kong. It will depend on, among other things, the willingness of the international community to safeguard the right of self-rule and the furtherance of democracy. In this sense, democratization has created an acute security dilemma for Taiwan. On the one hand, democracy has become an essential ingredient to Taiwan's national security. It helps foster a strong sense of political solidarity, enhancing Taiwan's international legitimacy, nullifying Beijing's peaceful reunification campaign, and discrediting the PRC's sovereign claim over the island. The public's commitment to democratic values will continue to be reinforced as long as the international community is willing to reward Taiwan with a high level of recognition and support for its democratic progress.

On the other hand, Taiwan's democratization also raises the possibility of the PRC's intervention. Uncertainty about the meaning and outcomes of Taiwan's transition, in particular its potential effect on mainland China's internal political order and stability, has provoked the Communist regime to double up its hostile unification campaign. Furthermore, Taiwan's growing aspiration for a separate identity, which came with democratization, is likely to fuel an ultra-nationalistic response from the PRC. This external threat imposes an additional burden on the new democracy. The perceived need to contain Beijing's political infiltration and the so-called 'PRC's collaborators in Taiwan' is likely to clash with the respect for political pluralism, minority rights, and the due process of law. These developments suggest that as long as the PRC stands ready to infiltrate Taiwan's domestic political process and threatens to subvert any democratically elected government that allegedly promotes Taiwanese independence, with the use of force if necessary, Taiwan's new democracy may have a hard time consolidating.

In addition, Taipei also finds it difficult to reconcile the acute conflict between its political agenda and economic interests. The PRC has already become one of the island's most important trading partners, second only to the United States.[30] It is reasonable to surmise that the island's trade and investment pattern will be even more skewed after the PRC's admission into the WTO. Next, it will be a tough challenge for Taiwan to figure out how to, on the one hand, ease Beijing's deep suspicion over its 'hidden agenda' and sustain the PRC's hope for a peaceful unification; and, on the other hand, consolidate its separate identity in the international community. In a dialectic twist, the more efforts Taipei puts into upgrading its international status and modernizing its armed forces, the more suspicions Beijing will have over Taiwan's incremental and 'unofficial' approach to independence, and more counter-measures will be taken. As distrust and animosity continue to accumulate, both sides will be further away from a negotiated peace.

Notes

1 Gellner (1983: 1) suggests that nationalism is primarily a political principle, which holds that political units and national units should be congruent. According to Gellner, nationalism as a sentiment or a movement can best be defined as such: nationalist *sentiment* is the feeling of anger aroused by the violation of the

principle or feeling of satisfaction aroused by its fulfillment; and a nationalist *movement* is one actuated by a sentiment of this kind.

2 A comparison of the experiences of the former Yugoslavia and Czechoslovakia (and Spain to a certain extent) reveals how, for a country withdrawing from authoritarian rule, the way nationalism is handled can largely determine whether its transition to democracy will be smooth and successful. For analyses of how democracy-building and nation-state-building are two conflicting sets of logic in Estonia, Latvia and Russia after the disintegration of the former Soviet Union, see Linz and Stepan (1996 : 336–443) and Karklins (1994).

3 Conner (1994: 29–30).

4 For reference, see Tamir (1993), Diamond and Plattner (1994), Kupchan (1995), Miller, D. (1995), Linz and Stepan (1996), McKim and McMahan (1997), and Haas (1997).

5 Linz (1993: 2).

6 By state-nation, Juan Linz refers to a strong sense of political loyalty endowed by citizens of multi-national or multi-cultural states that proponents of homogeneous nation-states perceive only nation-states can engender.

7 The question on national identity was worded: 'In our society, some people regard themselves as Taiwanese and some view themselves as Chinese. Do you think you are Taiwanese or Chinese?' The question on the stateness preference was worded as follows: 'Some people in our society advocate that Taiwan should be an independent country and some advocate that Taiwan should unite with the Mainland. Do you support Taiwan independence or Chinese unification?'

8 There are some limited intellectual attempts to clarify the definitions of 'Taiwanese' and 'Chinese'. See Wachman (1994), Liu (1995), Rigger (1998), and Tu (1994). Hutchinson and Smith (1994: 15) conclude after an extensive review of nationalism literature that there is no agreement among scholars on 'subjective' and 'objective' factors defining a nation or on the relationship of nation/nationalism to ethnicity and to statehood.

9 Conner (1994: 75).

10 The fundamental challenge of nationalism to democratic stability comes from people's competing imaginations of the state's legitimate boundaries to which their nations should belong. If the people cannot form a consensus on what the boundary of their state should be, and hence want to join different states or create new independent states, then it will be difficult, if not impossible, to generate a justifiable 'majority rule' for democratic practices, considering that the principle of majority rule presupposes the state being a consented unit. As Sir Ivor Jennings (1956: 56) remarked decades ago, 'the people cannot decide until somebody decides who are the people'. Rustow (1970: 350–352) explicitly treated 'national unity' as a necessary background condition for democratic stability in his work on democratic transitions, highlighting that democracy is a system of rule by temporary majorities and, for rulers and policies to be changed freely, the boundaries must endure and the composition of the citizenry be continuous. According to Linz and Stepan (1996: 1), democracy requires statehood and without a sovereign state there can be no secure democracy. Simply put, *no state, no democracy*. For those who argue that a popular consensus on the boundary of the state is a necessary condition for the consolidation of any democracy, see

Rustow (1970: 350–352), Lijphart (1977), Dahl (1986: 122, 1989: 207–209), Tamir (1993: 117), and Linz and Stepan (1996: 16–37). While no democracy can be fully consolidated without a clearly defined state boundary, it is not necessary for every consolidated democracy to be a nation-state. More specifically, the minimum requirement of a consolidated democracy is a basic consensus among the people on the legitimate boundary of their state, not the necessary congruence of the imagined nation and the territorial state. In fact, the calling for the merging of national identity and political state, i.e. the building of nation-states, is exactly why democratic consolidation has been so difficult in many multi-ethnic, multiracial, or multi-national countries.

11 For the importance of political elites and their mobilization in the development of nationalism, see Brass (1991), Breuilly (1993), Thompson (1993), Brubaker (1996), Linz and Stepan (1996).

12 Cumings (1984).

13 On 28 February 1947 a single event of police brutality sparked a violent island-wide popular uprising by disaffected native Taiwanese against Nationalist rule. The Nationalists responded with a harsh military crackdown. Thousands of native Taiwanese were persecuted and purged. The tragic event had a profound and lasting effect on the Taiwanese people, reminding them of their 'common sorrow'.

14 Winckler (1992).

15 For the linkage between de-recognition crisis and regime breakdown, see Tien (1989) and Chu (1992: chapter 2).

16 Along this line of analysis, see Segal (1996).

17 See Hutchinson and Smith (1994: 17–18).

18 See Tien and Chu (1996).

19 The formation of two competing power blocs was triggered by the new foreign policy initiatives launched by Lee Teng-hui. Factionalism crystallized after Lee's nomination of Lee Yuan-tsu as his running mate, a decision opposed by many senior KMT leaders. See Tien and Chu (1994).

20 Linz (1985: 203–253).

21 Juan Linz (1985) has made this argument based on his empirical study of the nationalist movements in the Spanish and French Basque countries as well as in Catalonia and Galicia.

22 See *The China Times*, 15 September 1997.

23 Chu (1997).

24 The 'one country, two systems' formula first appeared in 1981 in a nine-point statement by Ye Jianying, Chairman of the National People's Congress Standing Committee. Deng Xiaoping reiterated this formula in a 1984 speech about China's unification.

25 In its official documents, China highlights its strategy as 'to peddle the [domestic] politics through business; to influence the [Taiwanese] government through the [Taiwanese] people'.

26 The proposal was vigorously opposed by the non-mainstream faction, which worried that a direct popular election might become a vehicle for self-determination.

27 See Lin (1993).

28 This is a direct quote from a speech by Qian Qichen, the PRC's Vice-Premier, at the 1994 annual working meeting of Taiwan affairs.

29 Most opinion polls show that traditional DPP votes accounted for at least a fifth to a quarter of the 54 per cent popular vote that went to Lee Teng-hui. This is evidenced by the aggregate election statistics as well. For instance, there is a 9 per cent gap between the overall electoral support received by the DPP presidential candidate and its National Assembly candidates of the same year.

30 For the first eleven months of 1996, Hong Kong as Taiwan's export market was already on par with the United States, accounting for 23.1 per cent and 23.2 per cent of Taiwan's total exports, respectively. See *The United Daily*, 8 January 1996, p. 19.

References and further reading

Anderson, Benedict (1991) *Imagined Communities: Reflections on the Origin and Spread of Nationalism*. London and New York, Verso.

Brass, Paul R. (1991) *Ethnicity and Nationalism: Theory and Comparison*. New Delhi, Sage.

Breuilly, John (1993) *Nationalism and the State*. Chicago, University of Chicago Press.

Brubaker, Rogers (1996) *Nationalism Reframed: Nationhood and the National Question in the New Europe*. Cambridge, Cambridge University Press.

Cheng, Tun-jen and Hsu, Yung-ming (1996) 'Issue Structure, the DPP's Factionalism and Party Realignment'. In Hung-mao Tien (ed.), *Taiwan's Electoral Politics and Democratic Transition: Riding the Third Wave*. Armonk NY, M. E. Sharpe, pp. 137–173.

Cheng, Tun-jen; Huang, Chi and Wu, Samuel S. G. (eds) (1995) *Inherited Rivalry: Conflict Across the Taiwan Straits*. Boulder, Lynne Rienner Publishers.

Chu, Yun-han (1992) *Crafting Democracy in Taiwan*. Taipei, Institute for National Policy Research.

—— (1995) 'The Security Challenge for Taiwan in the Post Cold-War Era: The Implications of Systemic Change and Domestic Transformation for the Cross-Straits Relation'. Institute report, East Asian Institute, Columbia University.

—— (1996) 'Taiwan's Unique Challenges'. *Journal of Democracy*, vol. 3, no. 7 (July), pp. 69–82.

—— (1997) 'The Political Economy of Taiwan's Mainland Policy'. *Journal of Contemporary China*, vol. 6, no. 15, pp. 229–257.

Chu, Yun-han and Lin, Tse-min (1996) 'The Process of Democratic Consolidation in Taiwan: Social Cleavage, Electoral Competition, and the Emerging Party System'. In Hung-Mao Tien (ed.), *Taiwan's Electoral Politics and Democratic Transition: Riding the Third Wave*. Armonk NY, M. E. Sharpe, pp. 79–104.

Chu, Yun-han; Hu, Fu & Moon, Chung-in (1997) 'South Korea and Taiwan: The International Context'. In Larry Diamond, MarkPlattner, Yun-han Chu and Hung-mao Tien (eds), *Consolidating the Third Wave Democracies*. Baltimore, Johns Hopkins University Press, pp. 267–294.

Conner, Walker (1994) *Ethnonationalism: The Question for Understanding*. Princeton, Princeton University Press.

Cumings, Bruce (1984) 'The Origins and Development of the Northeast Asian Political Economy'. *International Organization*, vol. 38, no. 1, pp. 1–40.

Dahl, Robert A. (1986) *Democracy, Liberty, and Equality*. London, Oxford University Press.

—— (1989) *Democracy and its Critics*. New Haven, Yale University Press.

Diamond, Larry and Plattner, Marc F. (eds) (1994) *Nationalism, Ethnic Conflict, and Democracy*. Baltimore, Johns Hopkins University Press.

Downs, Anthony (1957) *An Economic Theory of Democracy*. New York, Harper & Row.

Evans, Peter B., Jacobson, Harold K. and Putnam, Robert D. (eds) (1993) *Double-Edged Diplomacy: International Bargaining and Domestic Politics*. Berkeley, University of California Press.

Gellner, Ernest (1983) *Nations and Nationalism*. Ithaca, Cornell University Press.

Haas, Ernst (1997) *Nationalism, Liberalism and Progress*. Ithaca, Cornell University Press.

Hobsbawm, Eric J. (1990) *Nations and Nationalism Since 1780: Programme, Myth, Reality*. Cambridge, Cambridge University Press.

Hu, Fu and Chu, Yun-han. (1992) 'Electoral Competition and Political Democratization'. In Tun-jen Cheng and Stephan Haggard (eds), *Political Change in Taiwan*. Boulder CO, Lynne Rienner Publishers, pp. 177–203.

Hutchinson, John and Smith, Anthony (eds) (1994) *Nationalism*. Oxford, Oxford University Press.

Jennings, W. Ivor (1956) *The Approach to Self-Government*. Cambridge, Cambridge University Press.

Karklins, Rasma (1994) *Ethnopolitics and Transition to Democracy: The Collapse of the USSR and Latvia*. Washington DC, Woodrow Wilson Center Press (co-published by Baltimore, Johns Hopkins University Press).

Kerr, George (1965) *Formosa Betrayed.* Boston, Houghton Mifflin.

Kupchan, Charles A. (ed.) (1995) *Nationalism and Nationalities in the New Europe*. Ithaca, Cornell University.

Lijphart, Arend (1977) *Democracy in Plural Societies: A Comparative Exploration*. New Haven, Yale University Press.

Lin, Chia-lung (1998) 'Paths to Democracy: Taiwan in Comparative Perspective'. unpublished PhD dissertation, Department of Political Science, Yale University.

__ (1989) 'The Opposition Movement under an Authoritarian-Clientelist Regime: Political Explanations on the Social Base of the Democratic Progressive Party in Taiwan'. *Taiwan Research Quarterly,* vol. 2, no. 1 (Spring), pp. 117–143.

Lin, Tse-min, Chu, Yun-han and Hinich, Melvin J. (1996) 'Conflict Displacement and Regime Transition in Taiwan: A Spatial Analysis'. *World Politics*, no. 48 (July), pp. 453–481.

Lin, Tso-shui (1993) 'Popular Presidential Election and Constitutional Reconstruction'. Paper presented at a conference sponsored by the Chinese Association for Comparative Laws, 1993.

Linz, Juan J. (1985) 'From Primordialism to Nationalism'. In Edward A. Tiryakian and Ronald Rogowski (eds), *New Nationalisms of the Developed West*. Boston, Allen & Unwin, pp. 203–253.

—— (1993) 'State Building and Nation Building'. *European Review*, vol. 1, no. 4 (October), pp 355–369.

Linz, Juan J. and Stepan, Alfred (1996) *Problems of Democratic Transition and Consolidation: Southern Europe, South America and Post-Communist Europe*. Baltimore, Johns Hopkins University Press.

Lipset, Seymour M. ([1960] 1983) *Political Man: The Social Bases of Politics*. Expanded and updated edition. London, Heinemann.

Liu, I-chou (1995) 'The Conception of 'China' Among the People of Taiwan'. Paper presented at the Second Annual Conference of the Taiwanese Political Science Association, Taipei, 23–24 December.

McKim, Robert and McMahan, Jeff (eds) (1997) *The Morality of Nationalism*. Oxford, Oxford University Press.

Miller, David (1995) *On Nationality*. Oxford, Clarendon Press.

Miller, Nicholas R. (1993) 'Majority Rule and Minority Interests'. In Ian Shapiro and Russell Hardin (eds), *Political Order*. New York, New York University Press, pp. 207–250.

Nathan, Andrew J. (1992) 'The Effect of Taiwan's Political Reform on Taiwan-Mainland Relations'. In Tun-jen Cheng and Stephan Haggard (eds), *Political Change in Taiwan*. Boulder CO, Lynne Rienner Publishers, pp. 207–219.

Nathan, Andrew J. and Ross, Robert S. (1997) *The Great Wall and the Empty Fortress: China's Search for Security*. New York, W. W. Norton & Company.

Putnam, Robert D. (1988) 'Diplomacy and Domestic Politics: The Logic of Two-Level Games'. *International Organization*, vol. 2, no. 42, pp. 427–460.

Rigger, Shelley (1998) 'The National Identity Issue in Party Politics and Social Science'. Paper presented at the Workshop on Cross-Strait Relations, University of British Columbia, 21–22 August.

Riker, William H. (1982) *Liberalism against Populism: A Confrontation between the Theory of Democracy and the Theory of Social Choice*. Prospect Heights IL, Waveland Press.

Rustow, Dankwart A. (1970) 'Transitions to Democracy: A Dynamic Model'. *Comparative Politics*, vol. 2, no. 3, pp. 337–363.

Sartori, Giovanni (1987) *The Theory of Democracy Revisited*. Chatham NJ, Chatham House.

Segal, Gerald (1996) 'East Asia and the "Containment" of China'. *International Security*, no. 20 (Spring), pp. 108–112.

Shafer, Bryon E. (ed.) (1991) *The End of Realignment? Interpreting American Electoral Eras*. Madison, University of Wisconsin Press.

Shambaugh, David (1996) 'Taiwan's Security: Maintaining Deterrence amid Political Accountability'. *China Quarterly*, no. 148 (December), pp. 1284–1318.

Shiba, Ryotaro (1995) *A Taiwan Journey: A Stroll Down the Streets*. Translated by Chin-sung Lee. Taipei, Taiwan Tung Fan Publishing Co.

Tamir, Yael (1993) *Liberal Nationalism*. Princeton, Princeton University Press.

Tien, Hung-mao (1989) *The Great Transition: Political and Social Change in the Republic of China*. Stanford, Hoover Institution.

Tien, Hung-mao and Chu, Yun-han (1994) 'Taiwan's Domestic Political Reforms, Institutional Change and Power Realignment'. In Gary Klintworth (ed.), *Taiwan in the Asia-Pacific in the 1990s*. Sydney, Allen & Unwin, pp. 1–20.

—— (1996) 'Building Democratic Institutions in Taiwan'. *China Quarterly*, no. 148 (December), pp. 1103–1132.

Thompson, Mark R. (1993) 'Ethnofederalism and Democratization: The Role of Elites in Yugoslavia and the Soviet Union'. Paper presented at the American Sociological Association Meeting, Miami Beach, Florida, 13–17 August.

Truman, David B. (1951) *The Governmental Process*. New York, Knopf.

Tu, Wei-ming (ed.) (1994) *China in Transformation*. Cambridge MA, Harvard University Press.

Wachman, Alan M. (1994) *Taiwan: National Identity and Democratization*. Armonk NY, M. E. Sharpe.

Wang, Fu-chang (1996) 'Consensus Mobilization of the Political Opposition in Taiwan: Comparing Two Waves of Challenges, 1979–1989'. *Taiwanese Political Science Review*, no. 1, pp. 129–209.

Wang, Teh-yu (1996) 'Strategic Ambiguity: An Outmoded Relic of US Foreign Policy'. Working paper of American Political Science Association Conference Group on Taiwan Studies.

Wantchekon, Leonard M. and Lam, David K. (1996) 'Political Competition in a Red Shadow: The Effects of China's Military Threats on Taiwan's 1996 Presidential Election'. Working paper, Yale University.

Winckler, Edwin (1992) 'Taiwan Transition?'. In Tun-jen Cheng and Stephan Haggard (eds), *Political Change in Taiwan*. Boulder CO, Lynne Rienner, pp. 221–259.

Yahuda, Michael (1996) 'The International Standing of the Republic of China on Taiwan'. *China Quarterly*, no. 148 (December), pp. 1319–1339.

INDEX